Action
Science

Concepts, Methods, and Skills
for Research and Intervention

Chris Argyris
Robert Putnam
Diana McLain Smith

Action
Science

Jossey-Bass Publishers

San Francisco • Oxford • 1990

ACTION SCIENCE
Concepts, Methods, and Skills for Research and Intervention
by Chris Argyris, Robert Putnam, and Diana McLain Smith

Copyright © 1985 by: Jossey-Bass Inc., Publishers
350 Sansome Street
San Francisco, California 94104
&
Jossey-Bass Limited
Headington Hill Hall
Oxford OX3 0BW

Library of Congress Cataloging-in-Publication Data

Argyris, Chris (date)
    Action science.

    (The Jossey-Bass social and behavioral
science series) (The Jossey-Bass management
series)
    Bibliography: p. 451
    Includes index.
    1. Social sciences—Research. 2. Social
sciences—Methodology. 3. Action research.
I. Putnam, Robert (date). II. Smith,
Diana McLain (date). III. Title.
IV. Series. V. Series: Jossey-Bass management
series.
H62.A663   1985   300'.72   85-18054
ISBN 0-87589-665-0

Manufactured in the United States of America

The paper in this book meets the guidelines for
permanence and durability of the Committee on
Production Guidelines for Book Longevity of the
Council on Library Resources.

JACKET DESIGN BY WILLI BAUM

FIRST EDITION
    First printing: November 1985
    Second printing: April 1987
    Third printing: April 1990

Code 8528

A joint publication in
The Jossey-Bass
Social and Behavioral Science Series
and
The Jossey-Bass Management Series

Consulting Editor
Methodology of Social
and Behavioral Research

Donald W. Fiske
University of Chicago

To our students,
from whom we learn so much

Preface

Creating usable knowledge is becoming an increasingly important topic in the social sciences. Lindbloom and Cohen (1979), for example, have written about producing knowledge that can be used to formulate policies. Our focus is on knowledge that can be used to produce action, while at the same time contributing to a theory of action. The concept of usable knowledge has produced an uneasy mixture of enthusiasm and skepticism. It has generated enthusiasm because we need more usable knowledge to help manage interpersonal, community, and organizational affairs. Moreover, technological spinoffs from the physical sciences suggest that the social sciences might generate similar benefits for social practice. But there is widespread skepticism as well. Policies for dealing with poverty, discrimination, and unemployment bog down in the complexities of implementation, and in retrospect, some observers argue that these policies have made the problems worse. Programs for transforming organizations succeed each other with the seasons, leaving in their wake the weary wisdom that nothing really changes. Responsible social scientists may respond to these disappointments by turning inward to research that seems increasingly esoteric to practitioners.

In proposing an action science, we hope to articulate the features of a science that can generate knowledge that is useful, valid, descriptive of the world, and informative of how we might change it. This emphasis on advancing basic knowledge while also solving practical problems has had a long and distinguished career in science. In the natural sciences it is illustrated by the work of Louis Pasteur, who discovered much about the role of germs in illness while trying to solve problems of fermentation for French vintners. It is also illustrated by early work in operations research: scholars put aside their interest in basic research to help England solve critical practical problems during World War II. In the course of this work, they discovered exciting intellectual problems whose solution contributed to basic knowledge.

In the social sciences this emphasis on combining science and practice is usually entitled action research. We would be content to use the term *action research* if it were not for two factors. First, over the years action research has often been separated from theory building and testing. Leading social scientists distinguish action research from basic research by asserting that the intention of action research is to solve an important problem for a client and not necessarily to test features of a theory (Coleman, 1972). We believe there is value in combining the study of practical problems with research that contributes to theory building and testing.

Second, many action researchers understandably conduct their empirical work by following the current ideas about standard scientific research. The dilemma is that some of the currently accepted ideas of rigorous research may be self-limiting. To attain a certain level of rigor, the methodology may become so disconnected from the reality it is designed to understand that it is no longer useful. For example, the research that followed and built on the early studies of Lewin, Lippitt, and White (1939) on leadership styles and group climates was indeed more rigorous, yet far less usable by human beings in real-life conditions (Argyris, 1980) than the original studies.

Two of the best known exemplars of action science researchers as we understand them were Kurt Lewin and John Dewey. Both designed and executed action or demonstration experiments whose consequences they studied systematically. Both were interested in adding to fundamental knowledge while solving practical problems such as educating youngsters, influencing eating habits during World War II, or reeducating individuals about their prejudices.

Dewey and Lewin were committed to notions of better societies or to what has recently been described as liberating alternatives. In their worlds, citizens would be held responsible for becoming inquiry oriented in order to produce a society that was learning oriented and experimentally minded. This organic mix of descriptive and normative interests also characterized the great early social scientists such as Weber (Asplund, 1972).

Our view of action science builds on the ideas of these early practitioners. We maintain that social science should have an important role in generating liberating alternatives. This objective cannot be accomplished without challenging the status quo.

In social life, the status quo exists because the norms and rules learned through socialization have been internalized and are continually reinforced. Human beings learn which skills work within the status quo and which do not work. The more the skills work, the more they influence individuals' sense of competence. Individuals draw on such skills and justify their use by identifying the values embedded in them and adhering to these values. The interdependence among norms, rules, skills, and values creates a pattern called the status quo that becomes so omnipresent as to be taken for granted and to go unchallenged. Precisely because these patterns are taken for granted, precisely because these skills are automatic, precisely because values are internalized, the status quo and individuals' personal responsibility for maintaining it cannot be studied without confronting it.

In order to conduct research that includes the option of changing the status quo, one must have models of the status quo and of a different universe that can be used to create a dialectic. Thus, we are interested in research that generates and tests propositions concerning (1) the variables embedded in the status quo that keep it the status quo; (2) the variables involved in changing the status quo and moving toward liberating alternatives; (3) the variables in a science of intervention that will be required if the previous propositions are ever to be tested; and finally (4) the research methodology that will make change possible and simultaneously produce knowledge that meets rigorous tests of disconfirmability.

In our discussions with social science colleagues on how to produce valid and usable knowledge, we encounter several objections to research that attempts to alter the status quo. These objections raise valid concerns, but these concerns are often dealt with in ways that are counterproductive to science and to practice.

The first objection begins with a premise of normal science: the primary objective of science is to describe reality as accurately as possible. Hence, mainstream scientists focus on describing the world as it exists and not on changing it. The paradox is that this approach cannot describe many important features of the world as it exists. Among these features are the defensive routines that protect the status quo against change. We will probably never get a valid description of the resiliency of defensive routines by just watching and waiting. Some defenses do not even surface until the first layer of defenses has been engaged (Argyris, 1985).

A corollary to the premise that the purpose of science is to describe reality is that generating knowledge about change is a second step, one that must wait until basic descriptive knowledge has been accumulated. In action science we agree that it is important to understand the world if we are to change it. But we also believe, as Kurt Lewin said, that the opposite is true: one of the best ways to understand the world is to try to change it. In choosing not to explore ways of changing the status quo, researchers choose to perpetuate a world in which there is little knowledge about the defensive routines that maintain the status quo.

A second objection is that defensive routines may be functional and hence should not be challenged. Defenses do serve to protect individuals and organizations in important respects. But what if such defenses are functional and dysfunctional at the same time? Our data suggest that some defenses can significantly limit an individual's and an organization's capacity to learn and adapt and hence to survive and flourish. To point to the positive aspects of defensive routines as reasons for not studying how to change their negative aspects may itself be a defensive routine.

A third and related objection is that attempts to change might get out of hand and unintentionally harm participants. This is an important concern, one that researchers must constantly respond to. But what leads researchers to believe that clients will allow them to create dangerous conditions? Our experience is that social scientists are successfully denied access by subjects who do not trust the researchers or do not agree with the research. We should add that our experience is based on a model of a collaborative relationship between researcher and subjects or clients, one in which clients can make an informed choice about proceeding with the research. To the degree that the researcher has unilateral control, subjects may be less able to protect themselves.

The notion that clients have ways of protecting themselves leads to a fourth objection: the researcher could be kicked out. Confronting organizational defensive routines in a group could be dangerous. The group could unite and turn against the researcher who is trying to discuss issues that the group prefers to leave undiscussed. We agree that this is a danger, but we believe that the response need not be to withdraw from such studies. Some scientists should consider conducting research to illuminate under what conditions these dangers can be overcome.

One of the major contributions that action science makes to researchers is to help them develop the knowledge and skills needed to reduce the likelihood that they might unintentionally harm people or that participants might turn against them and to increase the clients' or subjects' commitment to research. The knowledge required is related to additional modes of inquiry, new methods of research, and the interpersonal skills to conduct this research successfully. This represents a primary thrust of our book.

Several features of normal science, including intersubjectively verifiable data, explicit inferences, disconfirmable propositions, and public testing, are also crucial to our approach. These features are designed to create challenging tests that may disconfirm our ideas. The criteria for validity must be rigorous because we are studying difficult, threatening issues that affect people's lives.

We have written this book with three purposes in mind; these correspond to the three parts of the book. The first purpose is to identify some of the primary issues in the philosophy of science that relate to action science and have been discussed through the years. In Part One we describe the major positions taken by some of the key protagonists in this dialogue. We introduce our position and conclude with a statement of our theoretical perspective. In doing so, we neither suggest that we have found the answer to these age-old questions nor do we imply that the answers we provide are complete. The reader familiar with the literature on the philosophy of science knows that these issues have a long and distinguished history. We show where we believe action science fits in this dialogue in order to set the stage for further inquiry and clarification.

The second purpose is to identify similarities and differences in the methodology of normal science and action science and to examine the implications of these for the skills that researchers may need to be action scientists. In Part Two we explore three research approaches used in contemporary social science and compare them to action science. We identify the norms and rules that guide inquiry in each of these approaches, and we discuss how each may be self-limiting. We then describe the methods of action science designed to overcome these limitations and the skills that researchers need to use such methods. These skills build on those that researchers have already learned in the methodology courses presently taught in most universities.

The third and probably most important purpose of this book is to show that a community of inquiry can be created in which the skills needed to conduct action science can be taught. Action science cannot become a science unless its skills can be made explicit and taught, so that successful action science research is more science than art. In Part Three we illustrate how we are teaching the skills of action science. Our approach is not necessarily the best, and we intend to continue our inquiry into modes of teaching action science skills. Our hope is to provide some guidelines for those researchers who may wish to learn and to teach these skills and, more importantly, who may wish to conduct empirical research on how they might teach the skills to young researchers.

Action Science is a product of genuine cooperation among the three authors. We designed and executed the book as equal partners.

We acknowledge the help of Dianne Argyris, Donald Schön, and Emily Souvaine in reading parts of the manuscript. We are greatly indebted to Marina Mihalakis, who not only typed and retyped chapters, but did so with speed, competence, and with a careful eye to what statements made or did not make sense. Marina is a great team member.

Cambridge, Massachusetts   Chris Argyris
August 1985   Robert Putnam
                                   Diana McLain Smith

Contents

The Authors

Chris Argyris is James Bryant Conant Professor of Education and Organizational Behavior at Harvard University. He was awarded the A.B. degree in psychology from Clark University (1947); the M.A. degree in economics and psychology from Kansas University (1949); and the Ph.D. degree in organizational behavior from Cornell University (1951). From 1951 to 1971, he was a faculty member at Yale University, serving as Beach Professor of Administrative Sciences and as chairperson of the Administrative Sciences department during the latter part of this period.

Argyris's early research focused on the unintended consequences for individuals of formal organizational structures, executive leadership, control systems, and management information systems—and on how individuals adapted to change those consequences (*Personality and Organization,* 1957; *Integrating the Individual and the Organization,* 1964). He then turned his attention to ways of changing organizations, especially the behavior of executives at the upper levels of organization (*Interpersonal Competence and Organizational Effectiveness,* 1962; *Organization and Innovation,* 1965).

This line of inquiry led him to focus on the role of the social scientist as a researcher and interventionist (*Intervention Theory and Method,* 1970; *Inner Contradictions of Rigorous Research,* 1980). During the past decade he has also been developing, with Donald Schön, a theory of individual and organizational learning in which human reasoning—not just behavior—becomes the basis for diagnosis and action (*Theory in Practice,* 1974; *Increasing Leadership Effectiveness,* 1976; *Organizational Learning,* 1978).

Argyris is currently working on a project that will relate the perspective presented in this book to the ideas of other researchers and practitioners. Argyris has earned honorary doctorates from the Stockholm School of Economics (1979), the University of Leuven, Belgium (1978), and McGill University (1977).

Robert Putnam is a doctoral student and an instructor in counseling and consulting psychology at Harvard University. He received the A.B. degree with honors in political science from Syracuse University (1970) and was designated a Woodrow Wilson Fellow. He studied political economy and government at Harvard University, served in the Peace Corps in Costa Rica, and worked as a counselor and training director at a human service agency in Boston. He received the Ed.M. degree in counseling and consulting psychology from Harvard University (1980).

Diana McLain Smith is a doctoral student and teaching fellow in counseling and consulting psychology at Harvard University. She received a B.A. degree with honors in political writing from Boston University (1973) and a masters degree in counseling and consulting psychology from Harvard University (1980). She has worked in the area of community mental health as an administrator and a psychotherapist and more recently as a consultant to organizations in both the private and public sectors.

Action
Science

Concepts, Methods, and Skills
for Research and Intervention

Part One

Designing a Science of Human Action

> To proceed beyond the limitations of a given level of knowledge, the researcher, as a rule, has to break down methodological taboos which condemn as "unscientific" or "illogical" the very methods or concepts which later on prove to be basic for the next major progress.
> —Kurt Lewin (1949)

The idea of an action science raises thorny philosophical and conceptual issues. Action and science are central concepts in Western thought that are more often contrasted than conjoined. We are accustomed to distinguishing between theory and practice, between thought and action, between science and common sense. Action science proposes to bridge these conceptual chasms. At this point, to be sure, our bridges are more like the slender ropes of explorers than concrete and steel cables. But we hope they help to identify the barriers to an action science and to suggest how those barriers might be overcome.

In Chapter One we place action science in the context of

1

contemporary debates in the philosophy of science. We ask what the essential features of scientific deliberation are. In our review of the mainstream account of science, we identify hard data, explicit inferences, empirically disconfirmable propositions, and systematic theory as the core features, and we emphasize the role of a community of inquirers who can rationally criticize each others' claims. These are also core features of action science. We then discuss the hermeneutic approach to the human sciences to identify the problems of interpretation that may inhibit rigorous testing. We turn to a third account of science, that associated with the work of Kuhn, for its views on the role that judgment and interpretation play in debates among scientific groups. Drawing from these three accounts of science, we suggest that the features of rational deliberation in science may also come to characterize deliberation in practical affairs. Such is the thrust of action science.

In Chapter Two we discuss the conceptual underpinnings of action science. As a science that hopes to produce knowledge that can inform action, action science requires a conception of practical knowledge that goes beyond the common conception of choosing means to achieve predetermined ends. Following Schön (1983), we emphasize the role of the agent in setting problems as well as in solving them and the importance of reflecting on action to discover the tacit knowledge embedded in it. We then describe how action science makes it possible to test competing interpretations in the action context. Just as the scientific community of inquiry is the basis of scientific rationality, so the norms and rules of inquiry in the behavioral world of a client system are the basis of deliberation in practical affairs; and action science addresses itself to those norms and rules of inquiry. We conclude the chapter by suggesting that action science is an exemplar of critical theory as formulated by the Frankfurt School. A critical theory seeks to engage human agents in public self-reflection in order to transform their world.

In Chapter Three we present the theoretical orientation that informs our work, the theory of action approach (Argyris and Schön, 1974, 1978). This is not the only conceivable approach to action science, but it is the one that has enabled us to envision an action science and to specify its features. The particulars of our approach are also a necessary preparation for our critique of other research methodologies in Part Two and our discussion of the process of learning skills with which to practice action science in Part Three.

1

Philosophical and Methodological Issues

Action science is an inquiry into how human beings design and implement action in relation to one another. Hence it is a science of practice, whether the professional practice of administrators, educators, and psychotherapists or the everyday practice of people as members of families and organizations. Action science calls for basic research and theory building that are intimately related to social intervention. Clients are participants in a process of public reflection that attempts both to comprehend the concrete details of particular cases and to discover and test propositions of a general theory.

In the following chapters we will discuss these key features of action science: (1) empirically disconfirmable propositions that are organized into a theory; (2) knowledge that human beings can implement in an action context; and (3) alternatives to the status quo that both illuminate what exists and inform fundamental change, in light of values freely chosen by social actors.

What kind of science has these concerns? The first feature, empirically disconfirmable propositions organized into a theory, is characteristic of so-called mainstream science. In it, scientific theories are seen as hypothetical-deductive systems that explain and predict regularities among events. But there is a traditional counterview that argues that the sciences of action cannot take this form, because the interpretive understanding of meanings cannot be reduced to regularities among events. Instead, human beings in everyday life create meanings and guide their actions accordingly. Clarifying the nature of action science will require that we examine this debate between the mainstream account of science and its counterview.

The second feature, knowledge that can be implemented by human beings in an action context, may suggest that we are speaking of applied science. If "applied" means no more than "intended for use," we can have no objection to this label; and indeed the tradition from which action science springs is commonly referred to as applied behavioral science. But applied science is a term that takes meaning from its contrast to basic or pure science. The dichotomy between basic science and applied science reflects a division of labor embedded in the mainstream account of science: The basic scientist generates fundamental, generalizable knowledge that is then put into practice by the applied scientist. We believe that this division of labor reinforces a pernicious separation of theory and practice. Action science attempts both to inform action in concrete situations and to test general theory. Recasting the concept of applied science will lead us to reflect on the nature of practical knowledge, a form of knowing that is traditionally contrasted to theoretical or scientific knowledge.

The third feature of action science, alternatives to the status quo that illuminate what exists and inform fundamental change in light of values freely chosen by social actors, clashes with mainstream conceptions of science. The action scientist takes a normative position. Mainstream science has sharply separated empirical theory from normative theory, and has cast doubt on the scientific legitimacy of normative theory. The split between empirical theory and normative theory is related to the split between theory and practice. Practitioners in the applied behavioral sciences have long recognized that their practice has a normative dimension. From the perspective of the mainstream account, the values of the practitioner must be sharply distinguished from those of science. Many advocates of the counterview, also, have insisted that the theorist must take a disinterested stance. We take a different view, one that we explain by drawing on the idea of critical theory as developed by scholars of the Frankfurt School, a group of German philosophers that includes Horkheimer, Adorno, and Habermas. A critical social science includes aspects of the empirical-analytic sciences (mainstream account) and the historical-hermeneutic sciences (counterview), but goes beyond them to criticize what is from the perspective of what might be. Justification of the normative stance of critical theory is based on internal criticism of the practices of the community to which it is addressed. A critical social science engages human agents in self-reflection in order to change the world.

Roots of Action Science

In proposing an action science, we take as our point of departure our own practice as researchers, educators, and interventionists working with the theory of action approach (Argyris and Schön, 1974, 1978). It is through reflecting on our practice and relating it to other literatures, including those of the philosophy of science and of social inquiry, that we hope to articulate an action science. The present book builds on previous analyses of mainstream social science (Argyris, 1980) and on reflection on the epistemology of practice (Schön, 1983).

Action science is an outgrowth of the traditions of John Dewey and Kurt Lewin. Dewey (1929, 1933) was eloquent in his criticism of the traditional separation of knowledge and action, and he articulated a theory of inquiry that was a model both for scientific method and for social practice. He hoped that the extension of experimental inquiry to social practice would lead to an integration of science and practice. He based this hope on the observation that "science in becoming experimental has itself become a mode of directed practical doing" (1929, p. 24). This observation, that experimentation in science is but a special case of human beings testing their conceptions in action, is at the core of the pragmatist epistemology. For the most part, however, the modern social sciences have appropriated the model of the natural sciences in ways that have maintained the separation of science and practice that Dewey deplored. Mainstream social science is related to social practice in much the same way that the natural sciences are related to engineering. This contrasts sharply with Dewey's vision of using scientific methods *in* social practice.

One tradition that has pursued the integration of science and practice is that exemplified by Lewin, a pioneer in group dynamics and action research. Lewin is considered the founder of the cognitive tradition within social psychology in America (Nisbett and Ross, 1980, p. 5). Citing the classic Lewinian studies of democratic and authoritarian group climates, Festinger suggests that it is because Lewin showed how complex social phenomena could be studied experimentally that many regard him as the founder of modern experimental social psychology (1980, p. viii). This is not to say, however, that each of the many research programs that can trace their core ideas to some aspect of Lewin's work are also consistent with action science. We consider Lewin himself to have been an action scientist. But since his time there has been a tendency to divorce his contributions to science from those to practice. Research in social psychology has relied on experimental methods for testing hypothesized relationships among a few variables, and it has become distant from practice. Practitioners in the applied behavioral sciences, with some exceptions, have focused on helping clients and have given little attention to testing scientific generalizations.

The Lewinian tradition of action science, in contrast, is that of scholar-practitioners in group dynamics and organizational science who have sought to integrate science and practice (for example, Argyris, 1957, 1962, 1964, 1970; Bennis and others, 1976; Bennis and others, 1973; Bradford, Gibb, and Benne, 1964; Blake and Mouton, 1964; Jaques, 1951; Likert, 1961; McGregor, 1960; Susman, 1983; Trist, 1981). Members of this tradition have emphasized the continuities between the activities of science and the activities of learning in the action context, the mutually reinforcing values of science, democracy, and education, and the benefits of combining science and social practice.

Lewin produced several conceptual maps that showed how it was possible to bridge the tensions between science and practice. As Gordon Allport noted, "Lewin's concepts are arresting because they serve equally well in depicting concrete situations, and in the task of making scientific generalizations" (Lewin, 1948b, p. viii). These conceptual maps have proven extraordinarily fruitful, both in stimulating subsequent research and in informing behavioral science intervention. They include the idea that social processes are "quasi-stationary equilibria" maintained by a balancing of driving and restraining forces, with the related heuristic that change is better accomplished by reducing restraining forces than by increasing driving forces (Lewin, 1951). The technique of force field analysis continues to be widely used by behavioral science interventionists. A second set of concepts is found in Lewin's three-step model of change as unfreezing, moving, and freezing (Lewin, 1964; Schein, 1979; Hackman and Suttle, 1977). A third set of concepts relates aspiration level and psychological success, which we will discuss in Chapter Nine. Other ideas developed by Lewin include those of "gatekeeper" and "space of free movement," which were used to explain the results of the Lewin, Lippett, and White (1939) experiments on authoritarian and democratic group climates. Such concepts may serve as exemplars for theory development in action science.

Lewin was committed to the kind of science that would improve social practice. His early concepts of action research, an activity that involves studying social systems by changing them, were the seeds of action science. Although Lewin never wrote a systematic statement of his views on action research, several themes stand out (Lewin, 1948a, 1948b, 1951; Lewin and Grabbe, 1948; Marrow, 1969; Benne, 1976; Joiner, 1983; Peters and Robinson, 1984):

1. Action research involves change experiments on real problems in social systems. It focuses on a particular problem and seeks to provide assistance to the client system.

2. Action research, like social management more generally, involves iterative cycles of identifying a problem, planning, acting, and evaluating.
3. The intended change typically involves *reeducation,* a term that refers to changing patterns of thinking and acting that are presently well established in individuals and groups. The intended change is typically at the level of norms and values expressed in action. Effective reeducation depends on participation by clients in diagnosis and fact finding and on free choice to engage in new kinds of action.
4. Action research challenges the status quo from a perspective of democratic values. This value orientation is congruent with the requirements of effective reeducation (participation and free choice).
5. Action research is intended to contribute simultaneously to basic knowledge in social science and to social action in everyday life. High standards for developing theory and empirically testing propositions organized by theory are not to be sacrificed, nor is the relation to practice to be lost.

Philosophies of Action and Science

Any claim to knowledge can be challenged by asking, "How do you know what you think you know?" Answering this question is the domain of epistemology, the theory of knowledge. It has been argued that epistemology has been the central concern of philosophy since Descartes (Rorty, 1979). And at least since the time of Newton, it has seemed that science has been the preeminent way in which human beings have generated reliable, cumulative knowledge. Hence it is not surprising that much of modern philosophy has been concerned with distinguishing science from nonscience and with specifying the conditions of scientific knowledge, an enterprise known as the philosophy of science.

There has been a second approach to the problem of epistemology, that of the analysis of ordinary or commonsense knowledge (Popper, 1959, p. 18). This approach is favored by later analytic philosophy, as practiced, for example, by the later

Wittgenstein, Strawson, Ryle, Hampshire, and Austin (Bernstein, 1971, p. 260). These philosophers have concentrated on the analysis of concepts pertaining to action. The tradition of Continental phenomenology, which has been concerned with the world of everyday life, has also preferred the second approach to epistemology.

These two approaches have collided in the philosophy of social science. According to the mainstream account of science, a view whose origins can be traced to the empiricism of Francis Bacon, Thomas Hobbes, David Hume, and John Stuart Mill, the epistemology of the social sciences is (or should be) essentially the same as that of the natural sciences. According to the traditional counterview, which arose in the nineteenth century to oppose the extension of the methods of the natural sciences to the human sciences, understanding the meanings that are the essence of social action is fundamentally different from explaining events of the natural world. The debate between these two viewpoints has continued for the past century. It is reflected, for example, in Burrell and Morgan's (1979) analysis of the more or less tacit sociological paradigms that underlie organizational theory and research. The debate has become increasingly vigorous in recent years as interpretive approaches to social inquiry press their claims against the mainstream, which they sometimes label "positivism."

In the rest of this chapter we will discuss these and other themes in the philosophy of science in order to clarify the idea of an action science. In our discussion of the mainstream account of science we will identify the core features of science that also characterize our approach. Our discussion of the counterview will identify the problems of interpretation that face the sciences of action and that are often said to render the core features of mainstream science inapplicable to the sciences of action. We believe that it is possible to implement the core features of science in the action context, and we make this argument in the following chapter.

Our argument will be that different accounts of science can be understood in terms of their construal of the relation between science and community. This approach is congruent with recent work in the philosophy and history of science. Bernstein argues that there is growing agreement that "the significant epistemological unit for coming to grips with problems of the rationality of science" is the scientific community, "an ongoing historical tradition constituted by social practices" (1983, p. 24). This view implies that the standards by which beliefs are criticized, evaluated, and justified are embedded in such social practices as forms of argument. Knowledge is community based, as it were. Indeed, all contemporary accounts of science agree that science is a social enterprise, carried on within communities of inquiry according to practices or rules for distinguishing valid from invalid claims. There is deep disagreement, however, about the characteristics of these communities and their practices.

We will discuss four construals of the relation between science and community. The mainstream view establishes, as a logical requirement for the justification of knowledge claims, a community of inquirers who can rationally criticize each other's claims. This notion, that scientific rationality is grounded in a community of inquiry, goes back at least as far as the pragmatist philosopher Charles S. Peirce, whose views on this matter are echoed in the work of Karl Popper.

The counterview of the relation between science and community rests on the observation that the sciences of action take as their domain communities of social practice. These sciences deal in "constructs of the second degree," in Schutz's phrase (1962, p. 59), because the scientist must first grasp the meanings embedded in the community being studied. Theorists of the counterview are concerned with how knowledge of the commonsense understandings of social actors is possible. In this sense the human sciences may be said to be built on an epistemology of practical knowledge.

A third view of the relation between science and community is that associated with the work of Kuhn (1962). Kuhn focuses on the scientific group as a community of practice with a distinctive language that to some degree cuts it off from other groups, and he asks what kind of rationality governs debates among different groups. This perspective can be understood as a way of seeing the mainstream view through the lens of the counterview. The epistemic principles of science are seen as embedded in the practical knowledge of groups of scientists.

The fourth view is that of action science, which seeks to enact communities of inquiry in communities of social practice. Such inquiry is a form of practical deliberation, one that is guided by norms of science as well as by norms of practice. In action science we build on the practices for coming to agreement in everyday life, in ways that make them more consistent with scientific values such as valid information and public testing.

Mainstream Account of Science

This account, corresponding to what Scheffler (1982) calls the "standard view," is widely accepted both by practicing scientists and by the informed public. While it was designed with the natural sciences in mind (especially physics), proponents argue that it characterizes all sciences insofar as they are scientific; and this has been the predominant opinion among social scientists (Bernstein, 1976). The mainstream account goes under the names of logical empiricism, critical empiricism, or critical rationalism, and is heir to the tradition of logical positivism. It has been discussed by such philosophers as Hempel (1965a, 1966), Popper (1959, 1963), Nagel (1979), and Scheffler (1981, 1982). Among the social scientists who have discussed it are Merton (1967), Campbell and Stanley (1963), and Cook and Campbell (1979).

In the mainstream account, the core features of science are "hard" data (that is, data whose validity can be checked by different observers), explicit inferences connecting data and theory, empirically disconfirmable propositions subject to public testing, and theory that organizes such propositions. Underlying these requirements is the community of inquiry that is basic to science.

Peirce was perhaps the first to argue that scientific knowledge is legitimated by the practices of a community of inquirers. He noted that no single individual should be the absolute judge of truth. No matter how strong one's inner certainty, belief might be based on prejudices that one has not realized could be questioned (Peirce, 1960, pp. 80–81). The test of truth is rather that a community of investigators, beginning with different assumptions and free to criticize any aspect of each other's work, converge on a set of beliefs. They can never be certain that their beliefs are true, but they can approach truth through a self-corrective process of rational criticism in a community of inquiry.

Scheffler has emphasized that the ideal of objectivity, which is central to the mainstream conception of science, implies independent control over assertion. Like Peirce, Scheffler links the notion of community with that of openness to possible error: "To propound one's beliefs in a scientific spirit is to acknowledge that they may turn out wrong under continued examination, that they may fail to sustain themselves critically in an enlarged experience. It is, in effect, to conceive one's self. of the here and now as linked through potential converse with a community of others, whose differences of location or opinion yet allow a common discourse and access to a shared world" (1982, p. 1).

The model of scientific explanation that is central to the mainstream conception of science has been formulated by Popper (1959) and Hempel (1965b), although the basic idea goes back to David Hume and John Stuart Mill. Popper writes, "To give a *causal explanation* of an event means to deduce a statement which describes it, using as premises of the deduction one or more *universal laws*, together with certain singular statements, the *initial conditions*" (1959, p. 59).

Scientific theories are deductive systems of universal laws. Particular events are explained by subsuming them under universal laws. The validity of proposed laws can be tested by deducing from them, in conjunction with certain initial conditions, descriptions of events that should be observed. Thus explanation and prediction are symmetrical, differing only with respect to whether the deduction is made before or after the observation of the event explained or predicted.

This model of explanation, which Hempel (1965a) calls the deductive-nomological model, may be modified by allowing the use of laws that are statistical rather than universal. In either case explanation is achieved by subsuming events under laws; hence each may be called a covering-law model. In the mainstream account, the covering-law model is the general form of explanation in all sciences, including the social sciences and history.

Two levels of scientific systematization are distinguished. The first level is that of observational laws, or statements of empirical regularities, as, for example, "water freezes at 32° F." The second level is that of theoretical laws—for example, a theory of molecular structure. Observational laws, consistent with the covering-law model, are explained by proposing theories from which they can be deduced. It is only with the development of theory from which empirical generalizations may be derived that we achieve major advances in scientific systemization.

The mainstream account distinguishes sharply between the context of discovery, which pertains to generating ideas and putting forth theories, and the context of justification (Popper, 1959, p. 31; Nagel, 1979, pp. 12–13). What is distinctive about science is not the process by which theories are proposed, but the systematic testing that they must survive if they are to be regarded as valid. It will help to understand this position if we consider the view of science that mainstream philosophers are concerned to reject. This is the view, common since the time of Francis Bacon, that science is the practice of an inductive method. In this view, the scientist carefully observes without preconceptions and then generalizes from these observations; the warrant of truth is the purity of observation and inductive inference. But, mainstream philosophers point out, for observation to be useful it must begin with some preconceptions of what is important (Popper, 1963, p. 46; Hempel, 1966, p. 11). Furthermore, they insist that there are no rules for inferring theories from observation. The scientist must invent a hypothesis, drawing on whatever sources of inspiration may be fruitful. Since this creative process cannot be systematized, the validity of scientific theories cannot depend on the context of discovery. Rather, it depends on testing what Whewell calls "happy guesses" (Hempel, 1966, p. 15) in the context of justification.

A proposed theory is tested by holding it responsible for the empirical implications that can be deduced from it. If these implications do not correspond to what is actually observed, then the theory (or some of the auxiliary hypotheses involved in the deduction) may be rejected. If a theory has no empirical implications, it cannot be tested, and it is for that reason not an acceptable scientific theory.

It has proven quite difficult to specify the appropriate logical relations between theoretical statements and observation (Hempel, 1965a, p. 101; Scheffler, 1981, p. 127). Without recounting the history of such attempts, we may note that an initial step was to conceive of observations as formulated in observation sentences. Observation sentences—or "basic statements," as Popper (1959) called them—are of the form "the cat is on the mat," or "at time t, the needle of meter m coincided with line l." The crucial characteristic of observation sentences, or of a *data-language,* is that under suitable conditions different individuals can come to a high degree of agreement that the sentence is true or false by means of direct observation. And, of course, empirical testing of scientific theories depends on the possibility of intersubjective agreement, at the level of observation, among individuals who may disagree at the level of theory.

An important contribution to the mainstream conception of empirical testing has been Popper's idea of *falsifiability.* Popper was concerned with the problem of demarcation, that is, of finding a criterion to distinguish scientific from nonscientific theories (1963, p. 40). He proposed that a scientific theory must be falsifiable, in the sense that the theory must be incompatible with certain possible results of observation (p. 36). Genuinely scientific theories must make risky predictions—predictions that might turn out to be false. On this basis Popper explained his dissatisfaction with psychoanalytic theories: They were not scientific because "there was no conceivable human behavior which could contradict them" (p. 37).

The criterion of falsifiability accords well with Popper's emphasis on rational criticism. Consistent with his distinction between the context of discovery and the context of justification, he argues that the growth of scientific knowledge occurs through conjectures that are controlled by critical testing. While we cannot hope to know that proposed theories are true, we can hope to detect and eliminate error, and thereby approach truth, by criticizing the theories and guesses of others. Hence the falsification criterion is an extension of the insight that the possibility of discovering error is central to the generating of reliable knowledge. The possibility of discovering error in proposed theories, furthermore, depends on the possibility of intersubjective agreement at the level of data and on explicit inferences that identify the theoretical implications of particular observations.

Strong tests require that hypotheses and predictions be stated prior to observation, because if observations are made and then explained, hypotheses may be selected to fit the data. We may further distinguish between passive observation and experimentation. In the first case, the researcher predicts what will occur and observes if the prediction is confirmed. In the second case the researcher brings about or prevents certain conditions that, if the hypothesis being tested is true, should lead to the occurrence or nonoccurrence of certain observable events. Experimentation is the most powerful methodology for testing theories because, by manipulating the initial conditions, the researcher can rule out alternative explanations (Campbell and Stanley, 1963; Cook and Campbell, 1979).

Accuracy is a most important criterion in choosing among competing theories. Other relevant criteria include the scope, simplicity, and fruitfulness of a given theory. When a new theory replaces an older one, the observational laws explained by the older theory are subsumed under the newer theory. Hence scientific knowledge is cumulative, as wider ranges of empirical phenomena come to be organized by deductive systems.

We can illustrate the mainstream view of scientific explanation with Merton's reformulation of Durkheim's theory of suicide (Merton, 1967, pp. 150-153). Merton's intention was to clarify the function of sociological theory and its relation to empirical research, and Bernstein (1976, pp. 11-14) takes Merton's account as exemplary of the best thinking of mainstream social scientists on this matter.

The empirical generalization that Durkheim sought to explain was the statistical uniformity that Catholics have a lower suicide rate than Protestants. Consistent with the covering-law model discussed earlier, the theorist's task is to state a set of "universal laws" and "initial conditions" from which this empirical regularity can be derived. Merton (1967, p. 151) restates Durkheim's theoretical analysis as follows:

1. Social cohesion provides psychic support to group members subjected to acute stresses and anxieties.
2. Suicide rates are functions of unrelieved anxieties and stresses to which persons are subjected.
3. Catholics have greater social cohesion than Protestants.
4. Therefore, lower suicide rates should be anticipated among Catholics than among Protestants.

Statements (1) and (2) are proposed scientific laws, while statement (3) serves as an initial condition. Given these three statements, statement (4) can be derived. As Merton notes, this example is highly simplified. We may consider it a theoretical fragment, part of a complex theoretical system that has not been fully articulated.

Merton uses this example to illustrate several functions of theory. It identifies relevant features of an empirical generalization by relating it to concepts at higher levels of abstraction, such as social cohesion. It makes it possible to connect diverse findings, such as suicide rates, divorce rates, and incidence of mental illness, all of which may be related to the degree of social cohesion. And it provides grounds for predictions that can serve to test the theory. For example, if social cohesion among Catholics declines, their suicide rate should increase. Merton also notes that theory can adequately serve these functions only if it is sufficiently precise to be testable. On the one hand, for example, it must be possible to determine if social cohesion has increased or decreased among a particular group. On the other hand, the appropriate degree of precision depends on the state of the science in question. A premature insistence on precision may inhibit progress by leading scientists to formulate their problem in ways that permit measurement but that have limited relevance to significant features of the problem.

As Merton notes, the generalization that Catholics have a lower suicide rate than Protestants "assumes that education, income, nationality, rural-urban residence, and other factors which might render this finding spurious have been held constant" (1967, p. 150n). This assumption identifies an important feature of mainstream social science, and one that is associated with much of the methodological apparatus of social research: The many variables impinging on the phenomena of interest must be held constant so that particular causal linkages can be identified. Experimental methods achieve this aim either by standardizing the experimental situation or by randomly assigning subjects to conditions. Correlational methods rely on statistical techniques for factoring out the influence of variables other than the focal variable.

Mainstream Science and Action Science

We have said that there are continuities in the core features of mainstream science and action science, including hard data, explicit inferences, public testing, and systematic theory. But there are crucial differences as well, some of which we can highlight by raising the following question of the Merton/Durkheim example: What form must scientific knowledge take in order to help us reduce the incidence of suicide? In terms of the mainstream account, to raise this question is to shift the focus of attention from basic or pure science to applied science. Merton, whose interest was in using the Durkheim example to identify features of theory in the social sciences, apparently did not consider it necessary to consider the relation of theory and practice. It is as if the theoretician need be responsible only to the criteria of pure science, leaving it to the applied scientist to tailor basic knowledge to practical ends. We will argue, in contrast, that theory that intends to contribute to practice should have features that differ from those of theory responsible only to the criteria of pure science.

Suppose that a mainstream social scientist was interested in using sociological theory to reduce the incidence of suicide. A common approach to using social science knowledge is to formulate policies intended to affect variables thought to cause social problems. Durkheim's theory suggests that greater social cohesion will lead to lower suicide rates. The question then becomes, How might we increase social cohesion? This points to one of the theoretical requirements of the applied social sciences identified by Gouldner (1961): Theory should identify variables that might be controlled by human beings to bring about change in the problem of interest. Thus the social scientist might suggest that housing policy in urban areas be aimed at fostering neighborhoods, in the belief that this will enhance social cohesion and thereby reduce crime, mental illness, and suicide.

If policies are to have an impact, they must be implemented; and their implementation has not been markedly successful, whether in the realm of urban policy (Pressman and Wildavsky, 1973), or in the realm of strategic planning in organizations (Argyris, 1985). This has rarely been a central concern of social theorists. Implementation has been seen as a problem of application, of practice, perhaps of politics, but not of theoretical science. From the perspective of action science, however, implementation is not separable from crucial theoretical issues.

One such issue concerns the mainstream strategy of "holding other variables constant." Implementation means that human beings must design action in concrete situations. Any particular situation is a complex field of multiple, interdependent, conflicting forces. Theory for practice should help the practitioner to grasp the pattern of forces operative in the situation at hand, what Lewin (1951) called the "social field as a whole." Yet human beings cannot take account of everything; we have limited cognitive capacity (Simon, 1969). This suggests

that theory should try to identify patterns that, suitably combined, will be useful in many situations. It also suggests that
theory should lend itself to testing in the action context so that
the practitioner can make corrections on-line.

A second issue is that knowledge in the service of action
cannot rest solely on the analysis of social statistics. It is necessary to get at the meanings embedded in action, at the logic of
action. Social statistics are so abstracted from the action context that they do not provide a reliable guide to action in particular situations. This criticism is explored in depth by Douglas
(1967) in a critique of Durkheim's study of suicide. Douglas,
who is a representative of the counterview that we will discuss
in the next section of this chapter, argues that "it is not possible
to study situated social meanings (for example, of suicide),
which are most important in the causation of social actions, by
any means (such as questionnaires and laboratory experiments)
that involve abstracting the communicators from concrete instances of the social action (for example, suicide) in which they
are involved" (p. 339).

We do not mean to suggest that social statistics have no
place in practical deliberation. But their informed use depends
on *interpretation* and *judgment* of their relevance in the situation at hand. These are forms of knowing that are frequently
contrasted with scientific knowing, as understood in the mainstream account of science.

A third issue is that practice involves the normative dimension. Action intended to increase social cohesion will, if
effective, have an impact on the lives of human beings. Is the
kind of increased cohesion that might be brought about a desirable objective, on balance? While reducing the suicide rate,
might it limit opportunities for differentiation? Who should decide among the probable trade-offs? Such practical, ethical
questions are typically finessed by social scientists, who leave
them to be decided in the political arena. But practical concerns
should not be regarded as tangential to theoretical social science, in our view. Rather, practice should be regarded as interdependent with the ways that knowledge is generated and with
the kinds of theory sought.

Counterview: The Logic of Action

Although social scientists have generally endorsed the mainstream account of science, there has been a traditional counterview arguing that the sciences of social action must take a different form than the natural sciences. Social phenomena are meaningful to the human beings who enact them, whereas the events of the natural world proceed quite independently of subjective meanings. In the mainstream account, this difference does not make a difference for the logic of scientific inquiry. But proponents of the counterview insist that this difference is crucial.

The counterview is not a unified movement, but rather a convergence of approaches that focus on social action and align themselves against the mainstream account of science. Wilhelm Dilthey, a German philosopher and historian with whom accounts of the counterview often begin (Dallmayr and McCarthy, 1977; Howard, 1982), directed his arguments against spokesmen of positivist empiricism such as John Stuart Mill. Whereas Mill had argued in *A System of Logic* that "the backward state of the Moral Sciences can only be remedied by applying to them the methods of Physical Science, duly extended and generalized" (cited by Putnam, 1978, p. 66), Dilthey insisted that generating reliable knowledge in the human sciences depended on understanding meanings and that the appropriate methodological model was hermeneutics, the art of textual interpretation. Contemporary advocates of hermeneutics include philosophers in the phenomenological tradition such as Gadamer and Ricoeur. The most influential offshoot of this tradition for empirical research has been Alfred Schutz's phenomenological sociology. While that is perhaps the more direct line of descent from Dilthey, philosophers in the analytic tradition inspired by the later Wittgenstein, such as von Wright (1971) and Taylor (1977), also advocate a hermeneutic approach to understanding social action. Bernstein (1976) discusses the intersection of these traditions and their critiques of mainstream social science.

The emphasis of the counterview on understanding meanings leads to a second construal of the relation between science and community, one that has been formulated by Schutz in the phenomenological tradition and by Peter Winch in the analytic tradition (Bernstein, 1976, pp. 67-68, p. 139). It may be stated as follows: Interpretations in the human sciences are second order, in the sense that they are built on (and presuppose some understanding of) the commonsense interpretations of social actors themselves. To be sure, there are procedural rules of scientific inquiry—for example, the methodological principles of sociology or anthropology. In this respect the social scientist is part of a community of inquiry, as emphasized in the mainstream account. What is distinctive to the human sciences, however, is that they must grasp the meanings embedded in another community of practice, that which they are studying. The "otherness" of the community being studied is most obvious in the case of the anthropologist doing fieldwork in an exotic culture, whereas the social scientist's commonsense understanding of his or her own culture is often taken for granted (see Geertz, 1973, pp. 14-15). But a distinction may still be made between the scientific community of inquiry and the community of practice within which the actions being studied make sense. Theorists of the counterview are concerned with how knowledge of the commonsense understandings of social actors is possible. In this sense the human sciences may be said to be built on an epistemology of practical knowledge.

Some of the differences between mainstream and counterview may be illuminated by asking, To what extent are the human sciences based on hard data, as that concept is understood by the mainstream? Recall that in the mainstream account, empirical testing of scientific theories depends on the possibility of intersubjective agreement at the level of data among observers who may differ at the level of theory. The social sciences have developed methodological procedures to ensure that data meet this test. Advocates of the counterview have argued, however, that mainstream methodologies preclude inquiry into the rich layers of meaning constructed by social actors. But the interpretive studies of the counterview seem hopelessly "soft" to mainstream social scientists. Here we will describe some arguments characteristic of the counterview. It is only when we describe our approach to action science, in the following chapter, that we will show how interpretive accounts may indeed be rigorously tested.

We will begin not with the contemporary mainstream view of what hard data should be, but with its predecessor. Recall that an important step in the development of the mainstream view was to conceive of observations as formulated in observation sentences or in a data-language. The logical positivist Rudolf Carnap, following the early Wittgenstein, proposed constructing a language of science in which all legitimate scientific statements could be expressed and that would exclude all "metaphysical" (or "cognitively meaningless") statements (Bernstein, 1971). Popper says of Carnap's proposal: "Psychology was to become radically behavioristic; every meaningful statement of psychology, whether human or animal, was to be translatable into a statement about the spatio-temporal movements of physical bodies" (1963, p. 265).

Behaviorists sought to implement this program in psychology by banishing cognitive terms from science or at least insisting that they be operationalized in terms of physical movements. This approach had the appeal of seeming to get down to the bedrock of physical movements and avoiding the indeterminacy of interpretation and meaning. This vision of the kind of data that are truly scientific has had enormous influence on the social sciences, especially in the United States. Even today, when the dominant orientations in psychology and social psychology are cognitive, it sometimes seems that the scientific ideal is to design measures that are machine readable, such as reaction times.

Later analytic philosophy, with its focus on concepts pertaining to action, can be understood as a reaction against Carnap's proposal for a physicalistic thing-language. Philosophers of action have argued that descriptions of action necessarily involve claims about the intentions of agents and the meanings of their actions (Taylor, 1964; Bernstein, 1971). They point out, for example, that the same physical movements may occur in different actions and that the same action may be carried out with different movements. They further argue that explanations of action must take into account the beliefs of actors. It is the environment as understood by the agent, the "intentional environment" in Taylor's phrase, that is associated with action, not simply the environment as a set of physical objects. Contemporary mainstream philosophers of science agree that explanations of action will normally indicate the agent's objectives and beliefs (Hempel, 1965a, p. 469).

The question now becomes, How can the meanings understood by social actors become hard data? A traditional objection to the use of cognitive terms has been that beliefs and desires are subjective rather than objective, "in the heads" of actors rather than publicly observable. Against this view Taylor has pointed out that "it is a fact that we do make and verify statements using psychological concepts in ordinary speech" (1964, p. 88). How is this possible? How is it that the meanings of action are publicly accessible?

An answer that has been associated with early versions of the counterview was that the researcher should use a method of empathic understanding, a kind of imagining of the emotions experienced by another person (Dallmayr and McCarthy, 1977). This notion was ridiculed by the positivist philosopher Otto Neurath, who compared empathic understanding to a cup of coffee that stimulates the researcher's thinking (Howard, 1982, p. 29). But this approach is also rejected by contemporary advocates of the counterview such as Geertz, who writes, "The trick is not to get yourself into some inner correspondence of spirit with your informants. . . . The trick is to figure out what the devil they think they are up to" (1983, p. 58).

The contemporary view is that understanding action is like understanding a language. It depends on intersubjective meanings and shared practices, and it is a matter of knowing rather than feelings. Meanings are not private, in this view; they are publicly accessible. An early advocate of this view was Ryle (1949), who argued that the distinction between subjective and objective (in the sense of private mental events versus public physical events), and the consequent difficulty in understanding how psychological concepts could be verified, was a legacy of the Cartesian "dogma of the Ghost in the Machine." He insisted rather that in using mental predicates, "we are describing the ways in which . . . people conduct parts of their predominantly public behavior" (p. 51). But the question remains, How is it that we can distinguish more and less accurate descriptions and that different observers can come to agreement on such matters? Ryle's answer is suggested in the following passage: "Understanding is a part of knowing *how*. The knowledge that is required for understanding intelligent performances of a specific kind is some degree of competence in performances of that kind" (1949, p. 54).

The competence required to understand action may be compared to the ability to speak a language. Von Wright, in a discussion of how we might verify attributions of intention, suggests, "Intentional behavior, one could say, resembles the use of language. It is a gesture whereby I mean something. Just as the use and the understanding of language presuppose a language community, the understanding of action presupposes a community of institutions and practices and technological equipment into which one has been introduced by learning and training" (1971, p. 114).

Like sentences in a particular language, actions make sense in a particular community of practice. The competence required to understand action is acquired with membership in the relevant community. Or, to shift to one of Ryle's examples, an observer can appreciate the stupidity or cleverness of chessplayers only if he knows the game.

Perhaps the most popular way of accounting for social action has been in terms of rules. It would seem that rules are appropriate to the description of competent performances and that they simultaneously account for the possibility of recognizing competence. We can speak of competent performance only in instances where it would be possible to recognize a mistake, and the ability to recognize mistakes depends on knowledge of the appropriate system of rules. This argument is consistent with research procedures in linguistics, anthropology, and interpretive sociology. Thus sociologists may seek to discover rules of interaction by observing how members of a community deal with deviants. Linguists probe the intuitions of native speakers and may test their understanding of rules by creating new sentences and asking if they are grammatical. Ethnographers query native informants and may seek to identify the rules of interaction that would enable one to pass for a member of the culture. These researchers explain the competent performances of members by specifying rules for generating the performances, and they rely on the tacit knowledge of members to identify rule violations (see Harré and Secord, 1972; Cicourel, 1974; Labov and Fanshel, 1977; O'Keefe, 1979; Van Maanen, 1979).

These arguments indicate that the knowledge required to understand action is embedded in the ordinary language and social practices of the community in which the action occurs. The interpretations of the human sciences are second order in the sense that they must first grasp the point of what actors do, as determined by the local context of rules and practices. But a problem remains: The interpretations even of "insiders," those with a member's grasp of the local language, often differ. This is especially true as we move from describing simple actions such as eating or combing one's hair to explaining complex patterns of action such as childrearing or supervising employees.

Even those familiar with and seemingly sympathetic to the counterview criticize its foremost theorists for not coming to grips with the problem of choosing among competing interpretations (see, for example, Bernstein, 1976). Here we will simply indicate some of the obstacles to coming to agreement on the "best" interpretation. Foremost among them is a feature of reason-explanations: It seems that it is always possible to offer further interpretations by considering more of the context of action and by citing other beliefs and desires that are logically connected with the reasons first stated (Gergen, 1982; Schafer, 1976). Hopkins comments, "We can understand a single action as issuing from a network of reasons which can be traced through in many ways" (1982, p. xiv).

Another aspect of the problem of choosing among interpretations is that actors either may conceal some of the intentions and beliefs that enter into their actions or may be simply unaware of some of these meanings. When a superior asks an employee, "How do you think you did?" he can recognize immediately that she wants him to understand that she is asking how he evaluates his performance. But he may be unsure whether she has already formed an opinion about how he did and whether she fears that he may become defensive if she states that opinion openly. Were we to interview the superior later, we might discover that she was aware only that she wanted to help the employee explore his feelings about his performance. On reflection, however, she may agree that she had doubts about his competence, and did not consider saying so because she assumed he would get upset. It is not only in psychoanalytic therapy that human beings recognize as valid descriptors of their action meanings of which they had been unaware.

Another complexity is that different actors may interpret the same action, in which they are both involved, quite differently. The superior may see herself as open, interested, and helpful; the subordinate may see her as controlling and disapproving. Interpretive sociologists such as Goffman (1959) speak of the "definition of the situation" and how it is negotiated in interaction. Participants indeed often come to define a situation similarly, but it is not unusual for their interpretations of it to diverge.

Analogues of these problems also characterize scientific explanation in the mainstream account. Complete description of the causes of any event is unattainable, multiple factors impinge on particular events, and relevant data may be inaccessible. An important difference in the two realms, however, is that people are self-interpreting beings. Their interpretations enter into their actions. Hence a proffered interpretation can be valid, in the sense of possessing causal explanatory power, only if it was a reason for the agent in question. Davidson (1980) argues that "reasons explain an action only if the reasons are efficacious in the situation" (p. 264). It makes sense for an agent to say, for example, "I can see how that might be a reason for doing what I did, but that wasn't what I was thinking." Such a response may count against the interpretation unless arguments for unawareness or unconscious motivation can be sustained. Moreover, the inaccessibility of relevant data means, in the case of action, that the best sources of relevant data (the agents involved) may be blind and biased in ways that are only partially predictable.

Hermeneutic methods for arriving at correct interpretations have been discussed by many writers. Apel speaks of "canonical methods, as for instance, grammatical interpretation, interpretation in the light of literary genre or topic, interpretation of single utterances of a work by the whole of it, and vice versa, historical interpretation, [and] psychological-biographical interpretation" (1977, p. 302). But it is a feature of all such methods that they refine interpretations by other interpretations. They do not provide ways of breaking out of what has been called the *hermeneutical circle*. For example, Taylor points out that if someone disagrees with our interpretation, we may point to other passages in the text, or other features of the context of action, that support our reading. But support for any reading can only be by means of other readings (1977, p. 103). We must always appeal to an understanding of the language involved. Taylor suggests a criterion for superior interpretations: "From the more adequate position one can understand one's own stand and that of one's opponent, but not the other way around." He adds, "It goes without saying that this argument can only have weight for those in the superior position" (p. 127).

Providing multiple perspectives, each of which is a redescription of the action, seems almost a methodological principle of the counterview. Geertz (1973), for example, appropriates Ryle's notion of "thick" description to characterize the ethnographer's task of representing multiple layers of meaning. This notion fits Taylor's criterion of adequacy, and it is a way of dealing with the circumstance that different actors may hold different interpretations of the same action. But we do not share what seems to be Taylor's pessimism about the possibility of coming to agreement on the more adequate interpretation. Open discussion among members of a community of practice can lead to agreement that one interpretation is more adequate than another, even in the opinion of those who originally held the less adequate interpretation. We will describe guidelines for such discussions when we consider action science.

Scientific Rationality as Practical Knowledge

The mainstream account, while designed with the natural sciences in mind, has been widely accepted as appropriate to the social sciences as well. The traditional counterview, while disputing this claim in respect to the social sciences, has conceded the natural sciences to the mainstream. But in recent years there have been increasing challenges to the mainstream view as an adequate account of the natural sciences. The most widely discussed of these challenges has been that of Kuhn (1962). Kuhn's argument is part of a larger movement that Bernstein (1983) calls postempiricist philosophy and history of science, a movement that includes a number of philosophers who have vociferously disagreed with Kuhn. Even this wider perspective will not enable us to take account of some lines of argument in contemporary philosophy of science—for example, the "realist" theory of science (Harré and Secord, 1972; Manicas and Secord, 1983; Outhwaite, 1983).

Our organizing device is the way in which different accounts of science construe the relation of science and community. The several lines of argument that may (rather awkwardly) be called *postempiricist* share a view of the scientific community of inquiry as a community of practice. What this means is that, in reflecting on the nature of scientific rationality, postempiricist philosophers argue that it shares the features of practical deliberation. Criteria for coming to agreement are embedded in the social practices of groups of scientists as members of particular traditions. This argument is developed in detail in Bernstein (1983). We will illustrate it here with reference to Kuhn. The discussion will serve as a bridge to action science, in which we build on the features of practical deliberation to enact norms of scientific rationality.

Kuhn (1962) has argued that the history of science does not support the image of science presented by the mainstream account. He has proposed, rather, that the growth of knowledge must be understood in terms of the community structure of science. The unit of scientific knowledge is the group of specialists who are "bound together by common elements in their education and apprenticeship, aware of each other's work, and characterized by the relative fullness of their professional communication and the relative unanimity of their professional judgment" (1970a, p. 253).

Members of such a group share a "paradigm," or a set of assumptions about what problems are important and how one might go about solving them. Members of a group who work within an accepted paradigm engage in "normal science," a puzzle-solving activity that extends the shared paradigm. When normal science leads to anomalies, or when the shared paradigm no longer supports puzzle solving, the scientific group enters a period of crisis or "revolutionary science" in which one paradigm may be replaced by another.

The controversy over Kuhn's account centers on his claim that paradigms are "incommensurable." By this he means that those who work within different paradigms do not share a set of premises on which an algorithm for theory choice may be constructed (1970b, pp. 199-200). Observation is theory laden, to the point that those who hold different theories may be said to see different worlds. This contention strikes at the heart of the mainstream conception of objectivity (Scheffler, 1982). Recall that in the mainstream account empirical testing of scientific theories depends on the possibility of intersubjective agreement at the level of observation among individuals who differ at the level of theory. Kuhn argues, in contrast, that the proponents of competing theories do not share a neutral language adequate to the comparison of observation reports (1970a, p. 266).

What is it that a group of specialists shares that enables them to engage in normal science, and the lack of which makes different paradigms incommensurable? Beyond saying that they share a "paradigm," which has become a notoriously fuzzy concept (Masterman, 1970), what are the features of the necessary disciplinary matrix? Kuhn suggests that they include shared symbolic generalizations, models, values, and exemplary problem-solutions (1970a, p. 271). We might say that members of a scientific community share a language of practice that they have learned in the course of their education and apprenticeship. Use of the language, which is to say competence in practicing science within any given community, develops through exposure to concrete problem-solutions. Practitioners learn what counts as the right kind of problem and what counts as a solution. The knowledge that is built into the language is acquired as the language is learned, by processes that are not well understood. A community of specialists is like a language community, and paradigms are incommensurable for the same reasons that translation is problematic.

Kuhn's initial (1962) account of the process of theory choice emphasized the concepts of persuasion, gestalt shifts, revolution, and conversion experiences. This led critics to complain that he portrayed theory choice as irrational (Scheffler, 1982; Lakatos and Musgrave, 1970). In his replies, Kuhn has insisted that this is a misunderstanding; rather, he is arguing that theory choice proceeds according to a different kind of rationality than that embedded in the mainstream account. Scientists do indeed debate on the basis of good reasons, including the standard list: accuracy, scope, simplicity, and fruitfulness (1970a, p. 261). But, Kuhn argues, "such reasons constitute values to be used in making choices rather than rules of choice" (p. 262). Theory choice is thus a matter of value conflict rather than of logical proof.

Kuhn seems to emphasize the negative argument that theory choice in science, involving as it does value conflict and differences in judgment, does not fit the traditional model of scientific rationality. While he insists that the process of theory choice is nevertheless rational, he has not succeeded in clarifying this new kind of rationality or in distinguishing it from irrational persuasion (Bernstein, 1976, p. 93). Paradoxically, it may be that philosophers who have sought to defend the mainstream account against Kuhn's attack have gone further toward articulating a new model of rationality. This is because, to meet Kuhn's attack, they have reinterpreted the mainstream account. For example, Scheffler (1982) agrees that observation is theory laden; but he argues that the mainstream ideal of objectivity can be preserved, because observation can still conflict with hypothesis and thereby provide independent control over assertion. Scheffler does not disagree with Kuhn's claim that criteria such as accuracy, scope, simplicity, and fruitfulness function as values rather than as rules; rather he argues that such values can serve as second-order criteria in terms of which rational debate is possible (Scheffler, 1982, p. 130). Thus Scheffler does not think that there is some algorithm for theory choice that, "properly applied, must lead each individual in the group to the same decision" (Kuhn, 1970b, p. 200); instead he provides an interpretation of scientific rationality that does not require such a procedure.

Another philosopher who has contributed to articulating a new model of rationality is Lakatos (1970), who provides a re-interpretation of Popper's falsification criterion. Lakatos is strongly critical of Kuhn's "irrationalism." In his own attempt to identify rational criteria for theory choice in science, however, he accepts several of Kuhn's points. He agrees that the history of science does not bear out the received theory of scientific rationality (p. 115). He also agrees that theories are discarded only when apparently better theories are available to take their place. And he agrees that standards of rationality are embedded in the practices of scientific communities. Extending a point made by Popper, he points out that no disconfirmed prediction "proves" that a theory is false, because the observation itself might be in error. Hence a viable "falsificationism" depends on making certain kinds of decisions—decisions based on conventions adopted by the scientific community. These include judgments that theories or conceptual schemes necessary to observation may be regarded as "unproblematic background knowledge." For example, observations in microbiology presume the validity of the optical theories embedded in microscopes. Also, theories typically predict particular events only on the assumption that other factors do not interfere. The scientific community must have standards for deciding whether this "other things being equal" clause can be regarded as unproblematic in particular cases. Lakatos writes, "The problem of 'controlled experiment' may be said to be nothing else but the problem of arranging experimental conditions in such a way as to minimize the risk involved in such decisions" (1970, p. 111n).

If it is true that the scientific community must decide whether accepted theories will be retained or new theories will be adopted, then criteria are needed to differentiate what Lakatos calls "progressive" and "degenerating" problem-shifts. A shift to a new theory (more precisely, a revised version of an older one) is progressive if it leads to the discovery of novel facts while still explaining facts explained by the older theory (1970, p. 118). It is a series of theories, not an isolated theory, that must be appraised. Thus falsification has a "historical character," and the epistemological unit is the "research program." It is because Lakatos locates criteria of rationality in the historically situated practices of the scientific community that Bernstein (1983) hears him as one of the voices of postempiricism.

Two inferences that may be drawn from the preceding discussion will be important to our later argument. First, scientific rationality can be traced to the social practices of scientific communities. This implies a continuity between science and practical deliberation. Second, there is an important distinction to be made between debate carried on in terms of prevailing standards of decision—what Kuhn calls normal science—and debate over the standards themselves. Rorty (1979, p. 320) has suggested generalizing Kuhn's concepts of normal and revolutionary science to those of normal and abnormal discourse in any area of life. Normal discourse is that which can assume common criteria for reaching agreement, and it is analogous to the idea of an algorithm for theory choice. Abnormal discourse is that in which such criteria are problematic, as is frequently the case in political debate. The deliberative process appropriate to abnormal discourse must deal with value conflict. Let us emphasize once again that such deliberation can be rational. A contribution of the postempiricist philosophy of science is the recognition that abnormal discourse, long accepted as endemic to practical affairs, is also an essential part of science. This recognition may make more palatable the notion that the features of rational deliberation in science—for example, "responsibility to the evidence, openness to argument, commitment to publication, loyalty to logic, and an admission, in principle, that one may turn out to be wrong" (Scheffler, 1982, p. 138)—may also come to characterize deliberation in practical affairs. Such is the thrust of action science, to which we now turn.

Action Science: Inquiry in Practice

In action science we create communities of inquiry in communities of social practice. To see what this entails, consider the following parallel between scientific inquiry and social practice. A scientific community enacts rules and norms of inquiry that justify its claims to knowledge. A community of social practice also has an interest in justifying such claims. To be sure, in a community of social practice the primary interest is practical, involving questions of the type, "What shall I (we) do?" In contrast, in a scientific community the primary interest is supposedly theoretical, involving questions of the type, "What is the case?" But in the pursuit of practical interests, members of a community of social practice make, challenge, and justify claims to knowledge. In so doing, they enact rules and norms of inquiry that may be more or less appropriate to generating valid information and effective action. The practice of action science involves working with a community to create conditions in which members can engage in public reflection on substantive matters of concern to them and also on the rules and norms of inquiry they customarily enact. Action science builds on the preferences of practitioners for valid information and consistency by creating conditions for public testing and potential disconfirmation of knowledge claims. In these basic respects the normative thrust of action science is the same as that of mainstream science. But the ways in which action science implements these norms frequently differ from the methodologies of mainstream science, because the key threats to validity in the action context differ from those deemed most important to research that aims at knowledge for its own sake.

Action science also enacts a community of inquiry of the kind traditional to science—a community composed of action scientists who communicate through research literature. This book is oriented toward such a community. However, what is distinctive about action science is its mode of engagement with communities of social practice. Research communications among action scientists will focus on this distinctive type of work, and much of the testing of knowledge claims will occur through engagement with client systems.

An analogy between the scientist and the human being in everyday life has been in good currency among behavioral scientists for several decades (for example, Lewin, 1951; Kelly, 1955; Heider, 1958; Schutz, 1967; Kelley, 1971; also see Argyris, 1980, p. 11n). While united in their emphasis on cognition, those who employ the analogy are of diverse theoretical perspectives. One of the distinctive features of our approach is its focus on the behavioral worlds created by human beings and their impact on generating valid information. This is the dimension of community that we have been emphasizing in our treatment of philosophies of science. Action science is oriented toward public reflection on practice in the interests of learning. A frequent focus of reflection in action science is the reconstruction and criticism of the rules and norms of inquiry customarily enacted in the community of practice, as these determine the system's capacity for learning.

Action science is not alone in advocating that communities of inquiry be enacted in communities of practice. This formulation also seems appropriate to critical theory as articulated by theorists of the Frankfurt School (Habermas, 1971; Geuss, 1981). Habermas speaks of creating conditions that approximate the "ideal speech situation," which would allow human beings to come to a rational consensus about how to conduct their affairs. To our knowledge, however, Habermas has not devoted his energies to creating such conditions in the real world.

Action science is centrally concerned with the practice of intervention. It is by reflecting on this practice that we hope to contribute to an understanding of how knowledge claims can be tested and justified in practice and of how such inquiry is similar to and different from that of mainstream science. In the following chapter we will discuss features of knowledge that can contribute to practice. This will involve discussion of an epistemology of practice for action science, empirical testing in the action context, and the relation of norms and values to knowledge in action science.

2

Action Science:
Promoting Learning
for Action and Change

In action science we seek knowledge that will serve action. The action scientist is an interventionist who seeks both to promote learning in the client system and to contribute to general knowledge. This is done by creating conditions for valid inquiry in the context of practical deliberation by members of client systems. This is what we mean when we speak of enacting communities of inquiry in communities of social practice. In this chapter we will discuss the implications of the action science orientation toward knowledge. At this point we may note three such implications:

1. Knowledge must be designed with the human mind in view. We must take account of the limited information-seeking and -processing capabilities of human beings in the action context. We must be concerned with the problem of selecting from the infinite complexity of the world that which is relevant to action.
2. Knowledge should be relevant to the forming of purposes as well as to the achieving of purposes already formed. It will not do to assume that intentions and goals are givens.

3. Knowledge must take account of the normative dimen-
    sion. Indeed, a concern with value questions is implicit in
    the injunction to attend to the forming of purposes. In an-
    swering the practical question, "What shall I do?" the actor
    forms purposes that, expressed in action, provide the best
    evidence for what that actor values. Knowledge that helps
    the actor to form purposes thereby leads to the enacting of
    values. If these values differ from the old, we have gener-
    ated knowledge that can contribute to changing the world.
    If they do not differ, we have generated knowledge that
    helps keep the world as it is. In either case, in generating
    knowledge in the service of action, we cannot avoid respon-
    sibility for its normative implications.

We may note also that action science is reflexive to an unusual degree. The action scientist is a practitioner, an interventionist seeking to help client systems. This help takes the form
of creating conditions in the behavioral world of the client system that are conducive to inquiry and learning. Lasting improvement requires that the action scientist help clients to
change themselves so that their interactions will create these
conditions for inquiry and learning. Hence the practice of action science involves teaching others the skills needed to practice action science.

The knowledge needed to practice action science is itself an appropriate domain of study for the action scientist, both
because it is itself practical knowledge and because it will be
helpful for clients to learn and to use it. An interventionist requires knowledge that can be used by human beings in the action context, including knowledge relevant to the forming of
purposes. As an agent who seeks to bring about some states of
affairs rather than others, the action scientist will be advocating
a normative position. A challenge that action science seeks to
meet is that of making these kinds of practical knowledge explicit and testable.

Pragmatic Explanation and Practical Knowledge

We can clarify the differences between knowledge in the
service of action and knowledge for its own sake by examining

what mainstream philosophers of science have to say about pragmatic explanation and the covering-law model. Pragmatic explanations are those that we offer and accept in everyday life. Several kinds of explanation may be distinguished: We may clarify the meaning of a term or obscure passage from a text; we may offer reasons that justify our behavior; we may state the rules of a game; and we may identify the antecedent factors or causes that led to an event. The covering-law model is intended to provide an ideal for the last of these kinds of explanations (Scheffler, 1981, p. 19; Hempel, 1965a, pp. 412–415). The covering-law model, as an ideal for scientific explanation, provides answers to "explanation-seeking why-questions" such as, "Why is it the case that p?" (Hempel, 1965a, pp. 334–335, 421). Hempel explicitly excludes explanations of rules and meanings from the domain of scientific explanations (pp. 412–414). This exclusion raises the issues of hermeneutics and the sciences of action that we discussed earlier and that we do not want to repeat here. Rather, we want to discuss the covering-law model on its own ground, that of causal explanation.

Mainstream philosophers of science claim that all causal explanations conform to the covering-law model (Hempel, 1965a). This should be understood as potential or ideal conformity, for everyone agrees that we accept many causal explanations in everyday life that do not appear to invoke covering laws. To illustrate, let us use Hempel's example of explaining the cracking of a car radiator on a cold night (1965b, p. 232). The covering-law explanation includes general laws pertaining to the freezing temperature of water and the increase in water pressure for a given drop in temperature, along with initial conditions such as the fact that the car was outside all night, the temperature fell from 39° F to 25° F, the radiator was full of water, and so on. All these statements are necessary so that the event to be explained, the cracking of the radiator, can be deduced by logical reasoning.

In everyday life, if someone asks, "Why did the radiator crack?" it would seem odd to reply by stating all the laws and initial conditions given in the covering-law explanation. Rather we might say, "The temperature fell into the 20s last night." In some circumstances this would be accepted as an adequate explanation. In other circumstances—for example, if the event occurred in Boston in February—the fact that the temperature fell into the 20s would not be news. In this case, an appropriate explanation might be, "I drove up from Florida yesterday, and there was no antifreeze in the radiator."

Each of these everyday explanations can be considered a sketch or an incomplete version of a covering-law explanation. In stating them, we take for granted that the other person knows that water freezes at 32° F, that water expands as it freezes, and so forth. We select only those features that we believe necessary to make the event intelligible to the other person. Such explanations are called "pragmatic" because they are tailored to achieving the purposes at hand in particular contexts. For example, in the context of Boston in February, it would probably not be sufficient to say that the temperature had dropped; the other might think, "But it's been in the 20s every night this week." Similarly, stating that there was no antifreeze in the radiator would not be sufficient, because the other would wonder why it cracked last night rather than the night before. The additional information, "I drove up from Florida yesterday," anticipates the doubts that can be expected to arise in the questioner's mind (who might yet be expected to wonder, "How could you have forgotten to add antifreeze?"). Hence the ability to give satisfactory pragmatic explanations depends on differentiating what others can be assumed to know from what will satisfy their puzzlement (see Hempel, 1965a, pp. 425–428).

We may distinguish a second aspect of pragmatic explanation, one that deals with the concept of cause. Strictly speaking, neither the drop in temperature nor the lack of antifreeze "caused" the crack in the radiator; rather, the constellation of factors stated in the full covering-law explanation, taken jointly, caused this result. This is one reason why philosophers of science speak of causal explanation rather than of cause; as John Stuart Mill argued in *A System of Logic,* there is no scientific basis for singling out one factor as the cause. We make such judgments according to the purpose at hand. Scheffler points out, "We may single out for causal status just that condition presumed subject to human control and thus capable of providing a basis for determining legal or moral responsibility" (1981, p. 24). Hence pragmatic explanations, concerned with practical issues of control and responsibility in particular contexts, select some conditions and regard them as causes according to the purposes at hand.

We now wish to extend the concept of pragmatic explanation from cases in which someone verbalizes an explanation to cases of action more generally. We conceive of action as informed by (tacit) pragmatic explanations. Any action that intends to bring about or prevent certain consequences rests on causal beliefs, assumptions, or hunches. Thus when I put antifreeze in my car, I do so to prevent a cracked radiator. In identifying causal factors that can be manipulated to bring about intended consequences, agents focus on particular factors within a constellation of circumstances. Von Wright speaks of such factors as "relative" sufficient conditions, because their sufficiency to bring about intended consequences is relative to a given constellation of background factors (1971, p. 56). We may also note that the idea that causal explanations are embedded in action fits the pragmatist conception of testing beliefs by acting on them. On the analogy with experimentation, the pragmatic explanation embedded in action is the hypothesis being tested. If the intended consequences occur, then the hypothesis is confirmed; if they do not, then it (or the auxiliary hypotheses represented by assumed background conditions) is disconfirmed.

We may now ask, What is the kind of knowledge by which actors construct pragmatic explanations (including the tacit explanations embedded in action)? At this point let us simply label it practical knowledge, and note that it is knowledge in the service of action. Covering-law explanations, by abstracting from contextually bound pragmatics, systematically omit such knowledge. For example, simply knowing the covering-law explanation for the cracked radiator would give an agent little guidance in designing explanations appropriate to a particular context. It could be claimed that knowledge of the covering-law variety is necessary to designing pragmatic explanations, in the sense that it provides a knowledge base on which to draw. But quite rudimentary knowledge of this sort, when combined with practical knowledge for constructing appropriate explanations in context and revising them as the situation develops, would be adequate for everyday affairs; whereas detailed and sophisticated covering-law knowledge in the absence of practical knowledge would leave one helpless.

We do not mean to suggest that mainstream sciences cannot construct theories of practical knowledge. On the contrary, a popular research area in contemporary social psychology has been the reasoning strategies of human beings in everyday life (Nisbett and Ross, 1980). But these explanations of practical reasoning themselves conform to the covering-law model. For example, an explanation of why a particular actor uttered the pragmatic explanation, "the temperature fell into the 20s last night," would include laws and conditions from which, ideally, that utterance (or a category of which it is an example) could be deduced. To be sure, it is unlikely that social psychologists today could state all the laws and conditions that would be necessary for the deduction. But to the degree they fell short, their explanation would be incomplete. It could be justly criticized for its incompleteness, and it would also be regarded as pointing toward the additional research that would be required to fill the gaps (Scheffler, 1981, p. 77). Thus, in the mainstream account, scientific explanations of practical reasoning are themselves to be judged by reference to the ideal of nonpragmatic explanation represented by the covering-law model.

The critical standards we are discussing are illustrative of the normative thrust of mainstream science. It holds that the better explanation specifies with greater precision the conditions that jointly determine the phenomenon being explained. Stated differently, the better explanation is that which permits the deduction of a statement that more specifically describes the phenomenon. For example, a theory that predicts an eclipse to the nearest millisecond is better or stronger than one that predicts it to the nearest second. In Popper's words: "Theories are nets cast to catch what we call 'the world': to rationalize, to explain, and to master it. We endeavour to make the mesh ever finer and finer" (1959, p. 59).

But we wish to suggest that, from the perspective of knowledge in the service of action, increasing precision is but one value among several and that, taken to an extreme, it becomes destructive of other values, hence counterproductive. Some of these other values fall under the heading of usability. Usable knowledge, in the context of social interaction, must be suited to the cognitive limits of human beings acting in real time. This means, among other things, that the actor grasp what Lewin called the "wholeness" of the problem. Yet mainstream scientists, who focus on increasing precision, have tended to isolate fragments of social reality in order to study them more closely. Another set of relevant values pertains to the kind of world created by using the knowledge being generated. If the knowledge desired is highly precise, it is generally necessary for the actor to exert a high degree of unilateral control over the setting, and that includes other people. This is because precise knowledge is generated under conditions of unilateral control, as, for example, in the experimental situation. Argyris (1980) discusses these arguments in detail.

In arguing that precision is but one of several values and that there are trade-offs among them, we are not saying that action science is never interested in increasing precision. For example, when a personnel manager says that "it is important to help people express their feelings," an action scientist might question under what conditions that advice does and does not hold. Increasingly differentiated theories are important to the extent that they help people act more competently and more justly. In using terms like *competence* and *justice,* we are, of course, raising normative issues, which we will discuss in more detail later in this chapter. At this point we wish only to note that increasing precision is also a normative consideration. If it is true, as we claim, that in the action context this goal may conflict with the goals of competence and justice, then mainstream social scientists can view issues of competence and justice as tangential to their work only by ignoring the implications of their work for action. Such ignorance is rationalized by relegating issues of use to the domain of applied science. In this model it is the responsibility of the scientist to generate the best (most precise) knowledge possible, and the applied scientist then selects the level of precision appropriate to practitioners. One consequence of this division of labor is that those responsible for generating knowledge can ignore important considerations for knowledge in the service of action. Another consequence is that those concerned with practice may not feel responsible for meeting the standards of rigor demanded in science. Indeed it is not unusual for the same individual to sharply separate his or her research activities from clinical practice or consulting activities, using high standards of rigor for research but not for practice.

In action science we propose high standards of rigor for practical knowledge. The standards appropriate to knowledge in the service of action will, however, differ in some respects from those recognized in mainstream science. As we have already noted, one such difference is that action science tempers the mainstream value of precision with values pertaining to usability and to the kind of world created by using knowledge. We may say that in action science we seek explanations that are optimally incomplete. These will be explanations that, like Lewin's early conceptual models, identify relationships among a few factors that are important for action but ignore other factors. Another feature of these explanations is that they should be capable of elaboration as necessary. In other words, knowledge in the service of action should on the one hand include explanations that have gaps, and on the other hand should include ways of filling in the gaps in accordance with the purposes at hand. We are arguing against the mainstream strategy of first developing explanations that are as precise as possible and leaving consideration of the requirements of action to applied scientists and practitioners. This approach, in our view, inhibits understanding of knowledge for action by separating science and practice.

We may note another respect, however, in which explanations in action science resemble the covering-law model: Both explain particular events by reference to recurring patterns. In the mainstream account these regularities are conceived as general laws, following Hume's analysis of lawfulness. In action science these regularities arise from the intended and unintended consequences of action by purposive agents. Philosophers of the counterview argue that regularities of human action cannot be assimilated to the covering-law model (von Wright, 1971; Harré and Secord, 1972; Manicas and Secord, 1983). Without trying to settle this issue, we simply wish to note the common reliance on recurrent patterns. The point would seem too obvious to mention were it not for the suggestions of some advocates of the counterview that social reality is so changeable that there are no dependable empirical regularities for social science to identify (for example, Gergen, 1982). However poor may be the prospects for finding "general laws of history" or laws of social behavior that remain unchanged through the ages, it is clear that agents in everyday life presume many regularities. Embedded in every action that intends to bring about or prevent certain consequences is a causal theory. These causal theories, or tacit pragmatic explanations, presume regularities of the sort, "If I do *a*, then *b* will occur." Any particular theory may, of course, be wrong. But if theories were not often correct, or correctable, which is to say if underlying regularities did not in fact exist, then practical action would be inconceivable.

An important difference between the recurring pattern explained in the sciences of action and those explained in the natural sciences is captured in the concept of the behavioral world. This is the notion that the more or less stable patterns of interaction that are the facts to be explained by the social sciences are artifacts of the actions of human agents (see Argyris and Schön, 1974; Schön, Drake, and Miller, 1984). That is, the underlying regularities that characterize human action are created and maintained by human beings as members of communities of social practice. Yet those underlying regularities are social facts, independent of the individual, that constrain and channel action. In this view human beings are seen in their dual aspect as causal agents and as "pawns" acted upon by outside forces. For example, we are socialized by the culture into which we are born, and this culture is created and recreated by human agents who might act otherwise (Berger and Luckmann, 1966; Pearce and Cronen, 1980, p. 88).

Toward an Epistemology of Practice

We have said that the goal of action science is to generate knowledge in the service of action. Such inquiry requires an epistemology of practice, that is, a theory about the kinds of knowledge relevant to action. Recall the question we posed earlier: What kind of knowledge do human beings use to construct pragmatic explanations? At that point we simply labeled it practical knowledge. Here we will begin to unpack that bundle of concepts.

Let us begin with the notion of purposiveness, which as we saw earlier is central to the concept of action. It is in light of an agent's purposes that the environment takes on meaning. For example, as Lewin noted early in his career, a battlefield has directions, a front and a back, because of the purposes of the human beings for whom it is a battlefield. We may note two ways in which purposiveness enters into the agent's selection of relevant features of the environment. First, objects may be described under many categories. As James pointed out, the skill of reasoning is in selecting as the essential quality of a thing "that one of its properties which is so important for my interests that in comparison with it I may neglect the rest" (1890, p. 335). Thus, the relevant feature of objects on a battlefield may be their capacity to give shelter. Second, the several conditions that jointly cause an event may be divided into "cause" and background conditions, as is characteristic of pragmatic explanation. Again, as noted by Mill, such discriminations are made according to the purposes at hand. Barnard's analysis of the process of decision emphasized that it is when we approach a set of circumstances with a view to accomplishing some purpose that we can distinguish "strategic factors," those which if changed would accomplish the purpose (1968, pp. 202-203).

The importance of purpose to the designing of action will be readily acknowledged. But at this point we can distinguish the mainstream epistemology of practice from that of action science. In the mainstream model, as Schön notes, practical knowledge is construed as knowledge of the relationship of means to ends (1983, p. 33). Purposes or ends are taken as givens, inputs to the decision process. Scientific knowledge is then applied to the technical problem of choosing the best means to achieve those ends. This construal is consistent with the positivist separation of fact and value, according to which rationality and knowledge pertain to the realm of facts. The choice of purposes involves value judgments, and therefore is not in the realm of scientific knowledge. This position was expressed in an early and respected text in applied psychology, which declared that "psychology may be able to tell how to sell an order of goods to a purchaser who does not want the goods, but whether this would be ethical or not psychology need not decide" (Hollingworth and Poffenberger, 1917, p. 20).

The reference to ethics should not be taken as limiting the generality of the present argument. Moral reasoning is an aspect of practical reasoning, which deals with questions about how to act. Positivist doubts about one's ability to reason in moral matters extend to all varieties of practical reasoning (Raz, 1978, p. 1). Hence the mainstream equation of practical knowledge, insofar as it is knowledge, with knowledge of the relationship of means to ends. This is taken to be the domain of applied science. It may help to note the ambiguous meaning of the term *practical.* In modern usage it commonly means useful or utilitarian, as in the sense that a table saw is a practical means of cutting wood. This is consistent with the means-ends construal of the mainstream. But a more ancient meaning of practical goes back to Aristotle's notion of *praxis,* which referred to "the disciplines and activities predominant in man's ethical and political life" (Bernstein, 1971, p. x). Practical reasoning, in this second sense of "practical," is concerned with choices about what to do. It is concerned with ends as well as means, and has a valuational or moral component. This is the sense in which Kant spoke of practical reason as distinguished from pure reason. We might add that no amount of technical knowledge, in the absence of intelligently chosen ends, is "practical" even in the first sense of the word.

Problem Setting. We can introduce our alternative to the mainstream account of practical knowledge with the help of Schön's distinction between problem solving and problem setting. Problem solving can be understood as a matter of means-ends deliberation. This is because the statement of a well-formed problem includes specification of the purposes to be achieved. But before a problem can be solved, it must be set. Real life does not present us with well-defined problems such as those at the end of the chapters of a textbook. Rather, human beings confronted with complex, ambiguous, and puzzling circumstances must pose the problems they will endeavor to solve. Schön writes: "When we set the problem, we select what we will treat as the 'things' of the situation, we set the boundaries of our attention to it, and we impose upon it a coherence which allows us to say what is wrong and in what directions the situation needs to be changed. Problem setting is a process in which, interactively, we *name* the things to which we will attend and *frame* the context in which we will attend to them" (1983, p. 40).

In accordance with this usage, we will speak of the way an actor frames a problem or a situation. The framing of a problem defines what is to count as a solution. Means-ends deliberation occurs within the context of a given frame.

It may seem that, in drawing attention to the actor's framing of the situation, we have simply pushed a reliance on a priori purposiveness back one step. For if we ask what leads the actor to frame the situation in a certain way, must we not answer that the purposes that the actor brings to the situation are key elements? It appears there is an interdependence between purposes and frames. On the one hand, an actor's purposes flow from the framing of the situation—for example, when members of a management committee frame the situation as a contest in which each tries to win for his or her department. On the other hand, we might attribute the contest frame to predispositions of members to seek to unilaterally control the task and to win, or perhaps to their career goals and their beliefs about the relation of departmental and individual success. An analytical notion that may be helpful here is that of "nested" frames and purposes. Just as means-ends analyses take on a nested quality, with the means for achieving broader purposes becoming the ends of more narrowly focused activities, so ways of framing one's work role may generate purposes that guide the framing of particular tasks.

We may also draw from what philosophers have had to say about practical reason. Practical reasoning is concerned with questions of the type, "What shall I do?" whereas theoretical reasoning is concerned with questions of the type, "What is the case?" Since Anscombe (1957), philosophers of action have re-discovered Aristotle's notion of the practical syllogism, which is to practical reasoning what the familiar demonstrative syllogism ("all men are mortal; Socrates is a man; therefore Socrates is mortal") is to theoretical reasoning. The major premise of a practical syllogism is an intention, moral imperative, or goal. The minor premise states means-ends reasoning relevant to achieving the goal, and the conclusion is an action. For example, if the major premise is "I want to get to New York today," and the minor premise is "the only way to get to New York today is by train," then the conclusion is "catch the train!"

Now, the form of the practical syllogism would seem to lend support to the notion that the intention or purpose comes first and is followed by means-ends reasoning to determine how to achieve the purpose. Certainly examples can be cited that conform to this model. But some philosophers have argued that this is far from the normal situation. Human beings must choose what to do in particular situations, and only rarely do they enter the situation with a specific intention already formed. Rather, the agent must appreciate the possibilities presented in the situation and see to what objectives these possibilities pertain. As Wiggins (1978) argues, an agent has many interests and concerns that make competing claims. The more difficult problem is not the means-ends deliberation for achieving a given interest, but rather that of seeing "what really qualifies as an adequate and practically determinate specification of that which is here to be heeded or realized or safeguarded" (p. 145). This requires a high degree of situational appreciation "to prompt the imagination to play upon the question and let it activate in reflection and thought-experiment whatever concerns and passions it should activate" (p. 144). Wiggins argues that the minor premise of a practical syllogism arises from the process of situational appreciation and that the minor premise "activates a corresponding major premise which spells out the general import of the concern which makes this feature the salient feature in the situation" (p. 147). In other words, specification of the purpose or goal to be achieved *follows* a process of "situational appreciation," which would seem to be analogous to what we have called "framing."

Tacit Knowing. We have suggested that a key step in the designing of action is that of framing the situation, because framing defines purposes in the light of which the actor can distinguish strategic factors. We must now add a set of concepts that will be familiar to cognitive psychologists and social psychologists—concepts that pertain to the knowledge by which actors frame situations and design action within frames. Like other cognitively oriented behavioral scientists, we think of human beings as having vocabularies or repertoires of theories, categories, schemas, scripts, patterns, and other forms of knowledge (see Nisbett and Ross, 1980, p. 28, for their list of "knowledge structures"). This knowledge can be thought of as in the form of rules, as is being done by researchers in artificial intelligence who are seeking to program computers to perform as experts in solving real-world problems (for example, Davis, Buchanan and Shortliffe, 1977). The notions of vocabularies, categories, and rules also point to the similarities between intentional action and language use that we have mentioned earlier. As we will discuss later in this book, mainstream research on the cognitive bases of expertise is relevant to the action science concern with competent action.

It is characteristic of action that most of the knowledge informing it remains tacit. Polanyi, the first to use the phrase *tacit knowing,* cites as an example our ability to recognize one face among thousands despite the fact that we cannot tell how we recognize the face we know (1967, p. 4). Polanyi suggests that this kind of knowledge is characteristic of our ability to recognize many kinds of "physiognomies," whether those of human beings, rock specimens, or cases of disease. We might extend the example to the ability to recognize situations, with the important difference that to recognize a situation is at the same time to frame it—an observation that points to the fact that other framings are conceivable. When we recognize Aunt Mary, we make the only correct identification; but when we recognize or frame a situation, we construct one of several possible interpretations. Typically, however, the actor is unaware of alternative possibilities.

Another common illustration of our unawareness of the knowledge that informs our actions is found in language use. Native speakers of English know that they can say, "I picked the book up," "I picked up the book," or "I picked it up." But there is no danger they might inadvertently say, "I picked up it." (The example is from Labov and Fanshel, 1977, p. 75.) Yet few native speakers would be able to state the rules that disallow the latter alternative. In an extension of this example, approaches to social inquiry that focus on rules for generating and understanding interaction recognize that human beings usually cannot state the rules they are said to follow.

The kinds of knowledge to which we refer must be inferred from skillful performances. Tacit knowing is, in effect, an hypothesis to explain the fact that human beings frequently perform skillfully. The features of skillful action are that it is effective, it appears to be effortless, and the actor need not think about how to do it. Indeed, thinking about how to perform the action may inhibit skillful performance. Classic examples of this are typewriting, driving a car, and playing tennis. We can add the examples of recognizing a face, speaking one's native tongue, and smoothing over a potentially embarrassing moment at a party. In each of these cases we may speak of skillful performance, tacit knowing, and rule following because it is possible to recognize mistakes and to distinguish more and less competent performances.

Reflecting and Acting. Schön speaks of the tacit knowledge embedded in recognitions, judgments, and skillful actions as knowing-in-action, and argues that it is the characteristic mode of ordinary practical knowledge (1983, pp. 50–54). But he also notes that people sometimes reflect on what they are doing, especially when they are puzzled or don't get the results they expect. This reflecting-in-action is a way of making explicit some of the tacit knowledge embedded in action so that the agent can figure out what to do differently.

Returning to our earlier analogy between action and experimentation, we can say that the agent is stimulated to reflect when the tacit hypotheses or pragmatic explanations embedded in action are disconfirmed. Schön suggests a more differentiated view of hypothesis testing in action by noting that the same action that tests an hypothesis is also both a probe by which the agent explores the situation and a move intended to change the situation (1983, p. 151).

Drawing on these ideas, we can now sketch a more comprehensive and dynamic model of the epistemology of practice. The agent, confronted with a complex, puzzling, and ambiguous set of circumstances, draws on tacit knowledge to frame the situation and act. The consequences of this action generate information about the situation and about the suitability of the framing and action of the agent. The agent interprets this information, again drawing on tacit knowledge. If the action-as-probe generates information inconsistent with the original framing, if the action-as-move does not achieve intended consequences or leads to unintended consequences, or if the action-as-hypothesis is disconfirmed, the agent may be led to reflect on the tacit understandings that informed the original framing and action. This reflection may or may not lead to a reframing of the situation and a new sequence of moves.

We must also keep in mind that practice is social action. When the situation that the actor frames involves other people, then the framing will include the agent's beliefs about the intentions and beliefs of other people. The consequences of action include the reactions of those others, which themselves depend on how they frame the situation and on their beliefs about the intentions and beliefs of the original actor. As we noted in our discussion of the counterview, interaction presumes intersubjective understandings in the community of practice. Action also creates shared understandings, which then enter into future action. Our account of the epistemology of practice must include the rules and norms of inquiry of the relevant community, as they are created and maintained by the actions of individuals. Thus if one actor is critical of another but withholds the criticism for fear the other will become defensive, and if the other suspects this is the case but does not say so for fear the first will become defensive, then the two of them have begun to establish the shared rule that threatening information is not discussable.

The concepts of tacit knowing and reflection suggest a different model of the relation between knowing and action than is customary. The customary model may be summed up in the statement, "Think before you act." This is what people generally mean by conscious deliberation. It is also the model that is formalized in decision theory: The actor is to anticipate the consequences of possible courses of action, assign a utility to each, and choose that course with the highest expected utility. We can agree that this model captures some aspects of reality. But our preceding discussion suggests that a more appropriate model may often be, "Act and reflect on your action." This is almost a reversal of the conventional model, and might be caricatured as, "Act before you think." The point is, of course, that intelligent action is informed by highly skillful and complex reasoning, most of which is tacit. It is necessary to act and then reflect in order to discover what reasoning informed the action. A second and more generally recognized reason for acting "first" is that action serves as a means of exploring a situation. Action produces information that can be used for the design of future action. Both of these considerations point to the importance of the dynamic aspects of the epistemology of practice. We must consider the stream of action, from acting to reflecting with a view to future action to acting again. Schön (1983, p. 163) refers to this dynamic process as "reflective conversation with the situation." The practitioner imposes a frame on the situation, and modifies it in light of the "back talk" of the situation.

We may now contrast the implications of the mainstream account and the action science account for ways of dealing with failure to achieve intended consequences. The mainstream epis-

temology of practice focuses on means-ends rationality. Failure
to achieve the intended ends leads to a reexamination of means
and a search for more effective means. The action science epistemology of practice focuses on framing or problem setting, as
well as on means-ends reasoning or problem solving. Failure to
achieve intended consequences may, given this model, lead to
reflection on the original frame and the setting of a different
problem. We will refer to the first approach as *single-loop learning* and to the second as *double-loop learning*.

     There is an instructive parallel between the notion of re-
framing and Kuhn's discussion of choice between competing
paradigms. Rorty suggests this parallel when, extending Kuhn's
ideas to philosophy, he argues his view that "new philosophical
paradigms [nudge] old problems aside, rather than [provide]
new ways of stating or solving them" (1979, p. 264). Just as
Kuhn proposes that the growth of scientific knowledge occurs
as new paradigms replace the old, so improvements in practice
may occur as new frames replace old ones. The cutting edge of
this analogy is related to Kuhn's claim that paradigms are incommensurable. Purely technical criteria (what Kuhn [1970b,
p. 200] calls an "algorithm for theory choice") apply to competing alternatives within a given paradigm or within a given
frame. If the ends are given, determination of the best means is
a technical question. This is the kind of problem that the mainstream account of science claims as its own. But if the choice is
between different frames, as it is whenever agents reflect on
their frames with a view toward possible reframing, purely technical criteria are inadequate.

     This does not mean there are no rational criteria for
choosing between frames. As Schön (1983) suggests, frame
experiments may be evaluated according to their fruitfulness in
keeping inquiry moving, in creating consequences that are favored by the "appreciation systems" of the practitioner, and so
forth. Such criteria may be compared to Kuhn's suggestion that
accuracy, scope, and simplicity function as values that guide
theory choice, but not as rules. These criteria remain vague. We
hope that future inquiry can clarify them. Our point here is that
reframing means that agents and practitioners must face the

challenge of rationally reflecting on value-laden, messy issues. The injunction to be "scientific," in the narrow sense in which science is equated with technical rationality, is equivalent to restricting attention to single-loop learning. Action science proposes a broader construal of scientific inquiry, one that asserts the possibility of rational inquiry into double-loop issues.

Empirical Testing in Action Science

In the mainstream account, as we have seen, what is distinctive about science is its critical testing of knowledge claims in the context of justification. Scientific theories must have empirical content, in the sense that the results of observation must have some bearing on the acceptance or rejection of the theory. Competent members of the scientific community should be able to agree at the level of observation, even if they disagree at the level of theory. The logic that connects theory and observation should be explicit, so that different scientists can agree whether a particular set of observations confirm or disconfirm a theory. These are the conditions of objective knowledge: falsifiable theory, intersubjective agreement on observation, explicit inferences, and a community of inquiry in which public testing occurs.

Action science shares with the mainstream an emphasis on these principles. As we will explain in this section, however, their implementation differs in action science and in mainstream science. In part this is because the domain of action science is action and interpretive understanding, with the implications identified by the counterview: The rich layers of meaning constructed by social actors, in addition to the meanings imposed by scientists, are relevant to description and explanation. Still more important is the fact that in action science, empirical testing occurs in the action context. This feature distinguishes action science from both the mainstream and the counterview. It is this feature, we suggest, that makes it possible to rigorously test interpretive knowledge and thus to bridge mainstream and counterview. At the same time, testing in the action context requires distinctive ways of implementing the mainstream principles of empirical testing.

Claims in Action Science. We will begin by describing two kinds of claims that may be tested in action science: dispositional attributions and theories of causal responsibility. These are not the only kinds of claims that may be of interest. Inquiry in action science, as in practical deliberation and science more generally, is a moving spotlight that may focus on different aspects of belief or on the rules and norms of inquiry itself. But these two kinds of claims will serve for illustrative purposes, because it should be clear that agents do sometimes make, criticize, and evaluate such claims and that this is an important practical activity.

Dispositional attributions include a broad class of statements of the form, "Agent *a* has disposition *d.*" Dispositional explanation has received much philosophical attention, and it raises many issues that we will not discuss here (Ryle, 1949; Hempel, 1965a, pp. 457–477; Davidson, 1980). Dispositions, understood as tendencies to behave in certain ways in certain situations, include desires, beliefs, attitudes, abilities, and psychological traits. Examples of dispositional attributions in ordinary speech include: "He is defensive," "she is abrasive," "he fears failure," "she thinks I am foolish," and so on. Notice that dispositions, as we use the term here, include, but are not limited to, so-called personality traits.

To assert that an actor is following a rule or tacit theory is to make a special kind of dispositional attribution. An example we will use is, "John follows the rule [or what we will later call a theory-in-use proposition], 'If I am about to deprecate someone, first deprecate myself.' "

The second kind of claims, theories of causal responsibility, are of the form: "Action (or pattern of actions) *a* will lead to (be causally responsible for) consequences *c.*" To extend our example, someone could argue, "The impact of enacting the 'deprecate self' rule will be to decrease the likelihood that the other person will challenge the validity of the actor's view." Notice that such causal hypotheses might describe either the intended consequences of the action, in which case they are the reasons for which the actor follows the rule, or the unintended consequences.

Dispositional attributions and theories of causal responsibility are complexly related. To say that someone is "insensitive," for example, seems to involve both kinds of claim: that the agent acts in certain ways and that these actions tend to create certain impacts on others. Our contribution to clarifying the relationship of dispositional and causal attributions depends on the "theory-in-use proposition," which we will discuss in the following chapter and in Part Three of this book.

Both dispositional attributions and theories of causal responsibility may be oriented to supraindividual levels of analysis. For example, a group may be said to engage in "groupthink" (Janis, 1972), with the consequence that poor decisions are made. An organization may be said to engage in defensive routines, to camouflage them, and to camouflage the camouflage, with the consequence that it becomes less able to adapt to changing conditions. As we will describe later in this book, the action scientist often creates a "map" or model of behavioral patterns in the client system that describes feedback loops that contribute both to success and to escalating error. Patterns at supraindividual levels, of course, depend on the patterned behaviors of individuals, although none of the individuals in the client system may be aware of the ways their actions serve to reinforce the actions of others. Having created such a model, the action scientist must then create conditions in which clients can test its validity for themselves. Since the model describes causal relationships, it suggests what clients could do differently that would alter the consequences described in the model. If clients choose to learn to act in these new ways, the consequences of their altered behavior provide a strong test of the causal theories embedded in the model.

Intersubjective Agreement on Data. The data of action science are the actions of individuals as members of communities of practice. The most important form of action is talk. While we by no means exclude nonverbal aspects of action, they too are like language in the sense that they are meaningful within particular communities of practice; hence talk can serve as our exemplar. Under suitable conditions, different observers can come to a high degree of agreement that a particular agent did or did not make a particular utterance. Talk can be recorded on audiotapes, and with some loss of information it can be transcribed. Thus talk is a good candidate for meeting mainstream requirements for intersubjective agreement at the level of data. At the same time, talk is meaningful. Using talk as data for the empirical testing of theory forces us to deal with the issues raised by interpretation.

The first point to note is that talk *is* action. As Austin (1962) and Searle (1969) have made clear, when people talk they are performing such actions as promising, justifying, ordering, conceding, and so forth. This relation may be obscured by commonsense expressions such as "all talk and no action." But if we think of the situations in which such a comment might be made, we can see that the talk referred to is action, namely, the action of delaying or avoiding some positive step. The separation of talk and action has also been a research strategy in linguistics, which has found it useful for some purposes to abstract language from the pragmatics of speech (Habermas, 1979, pp. 5-6). In recent decades, however, there has been much interest in the study of talk as action. This orientation has stimulated much research by social scientists who see natural conversation as "a strategic research site for studying the ways in which members of a society organize their social interactions" (Labov and Fanshel, 1977, p. 24; see also Gronn, 1983).

The problem of interpretation arises as soon as we consider that, like all action, talk is meaningful. Different hearers may interpret the same utterance differently. The possibility of interpretive ambiguity threatens the intersubjective agreement among observers so necessary to testing in the mainstream account of science. In action science we deal with this issue with the help of a conceptual device, namely, the ladder of inference. This is a schematic representation of the steps by which human beings select from and read into interaction as they make sense of everyday life. The first rung of the ladder of inference includes relatively observable data—for example, a sentence uttered by someone. This kind of data could be checked against an audiotape recording. The second rung of the ladder of inference is the cultural meaning of that utterance. This is the meaning that would be understood by anyone who was a member of the relevant language community. For example, if the utterance is "X, your performance is not up to standard" and is spoken by a superior to a subordinate, the cultural meaning is "X, the quality of your work is unacceptable." The third rung of the ladder of inference is the meaning imposed by the hearer. For example, someone might conclude that the superior's utterance was "blunt" or "insensitive."

It should be clear that the likelihood of differences in the interpretations of different observers increases the higher one goes on the ladder of inference. Hence some cardinal rules of action science are: Begin at the lowest rung of the ladder of inference, state the meanings at the next higher rung and check for agreement, and continue to the next higher rung only if there is agreement at lower rungs. These rules are meant not only for action scientists but also for agents in everyday life whenever they are dealing with important and threatening issues. Hence the criterion of intersubjective agreement is built into the rules. If cultural meanings have been checked and there is general agreement, those meanings can be treated as hard data. They become the premises for further inferences.

A second way in which ambiguities arise concerns the selection of particular utterances from a stream of conversation. For example, if we ask a member of a group, "What is going on here?" the answer might be that "the boss is chewing out Joe." Notice that this is a meaning at the third rung of the ladder of inference. It is an interpretation of the salient meaning that makes sense of a stream of conversation. If we then ask, "What has the boss said that you see as chewing out Joe?" we may be told some of the sentences that the boss has uttered. This would be data at the first rung of the ladder of inference. But we will not be told everything that the boss and Joe have said; we will be told only a few sentences, those that our respondent thinks are most important. This is characteristic of the way that human beings make sense of the situations in which they find themselves. It is related to our discussion of framing, in that the way an actor frames the situation determines what features of it are salient for him or her. Now suppose that the boss is present and she thinks we have not been told the whole story. She may say, "Yes, I did say this and that; but I also said, 'Joe, I'm concerned about how you may be feeling.' I don't see that as 'chewing out.'" This illustrates how agents' interpretations of episodes may be checked by a procedure in which an agent states both his interpretation and some utterances at the first rung of the ladder of inference on which that interpretation is based, and other agents then add other rung-one data that, in their view, confirm or disconfirm the first interpretation. The procedure may or may not lead to general agreement on a single interpretation. But it can clarify how far up the ladder of inference agreement extends and where differences arise. It both tests and displays the interpretations of agents in social settings.

Talk as a Window on Practical Reasoning. If we conceive of talk (action) as generated according to rules or tacit theories, then we can seek to infer those rules and theories from displays of talk. This is common research practice in several fields of inquiry that focus on presumed tacit knowledge, including such fields as linguistics, ethnomethodology, and sociolinguistics. In contrast to the mainstream social science objection that talk is merely "anecdotal" data, in this view talk is systematically designed according to a theory. In inferring a rule from a sample of talk, we propose a hypothesis that may be disconfirmed. This hypothesis asserts that in similar situations the actor will create similar meanings.

Agents frequently talk about what they are doing, have done, or intend to do, and they may give their reasons for so acting. This reflective talk provides another window into practical reasoning. Such accounts raise important problems, however, because we cannot assume that they are accurate. Indeed, the idea that action is informed by tacit knowledge presumes that agents cannot state many of the rules they are following. Still, agents' accounts can provide much data that is helpful in inferring rules of which they may not be aware. They may report thoughts and concerns that they did not state at the time of action, such as "I thought she was getting defensive." Such reports help clarify how the actor construes the situation. We need not assume that self-reports are accurate; they may be tested for interpretive consistency with other data. Such procedures are continuous with those we use in ordinary life to make sense of what people are doing. The difference is that in action science they become more explicit and subject to public discussion, and they are guided by rules such as those embedded in the ladder of inference (for example, "Illustrate attributions with relatively directly observable data, and ask others for their reactions").

We said earlier that agents sometimes reflect on their action, especially when unexpected results occur, and thereby discover some of the tacit reasoning that lay behind their action, as they try to figure out what they might do differently. This reflection may of course be private, and agents may report on their private reflections. But reflection may also be public—for example, when a management group discusses an organizational problem or when an individual talks with a therapist. Talk is the vehicle of public reflection. Such talk provides the best data we are likely to find for inferring the cognitive processes by which human beings reflect on action. But public reflection is also a key process by which human beings learn to act more effectively. It is by helping members of client systems to engage in public reflection that action science can both contribute to general knowledge and help clients improve their practice.

Ricoeur has argued that the human sciences depend on the "inscription" of action, the "fixing" of momentary traces so that they can be reflected upon and critically interpreted, as in the model of a text (Ricoeur, 1977). In action science we may select passages from a transcript and ask clients to reflect on them. We may ask clients to write cases that include bits of remembered or anticipated dialogue. Or the same function may be accomplished by recollecting particular sentences at the first rung of the ladder of inference and treating them as a "case" on which actors reflect. Whatever technique is used, the point is to slow down the action so that actors can reflect on the tacit understandings embedded in action.

Threats to Validity in the Action Context. The methodology of any science must be adapted to the most important threats to validity facing that science. Mainstream social science has focused on threats arising from uncontrolled variables, nonrandom assignment of subjects to conditions, learning effects from multiple testing, and so forth (Campbell and Stanley, 1963). Argyris (1980) has described how the rigorous controls used to counter such threats themselves may introduce additional threats to validity. For example, subjects may distort their responses. This is not to say that the concerns of mainstream scientists are not legitimate, but that the cure may, for some purposes, be worse than the disease.

The most important threats to validity in action science are those arising from the action context. Some of these problems may have occurred to the reader during our discussion of talk as data. For example, we described how agents' interpretations may be checked by stating the utterances on which they are based and encouraging others to cite data that may disconfirm the interpretation. Such a procedure depends on the willingness of members of social settings to discuss their disagreements. But it is common for people to withhold discordant views for fear that others will become upset or embarrassed. Similarly, we have described how agents may report thoughts that they did not state at the time of action. But people may make such disclosures strategically. They may report only what they believe will support their position or increase their status in the eyes of others. In short, the validity of inquiry in the action context is threatened by a variety of defensive routines, including self-censorship and face saving.

Our research indicates that human beings, when dealing with threatening issues, typically act in ways that inhibit the generation of valid information and that create self-sealing patterns of escalating error. For example, people automatically withhold thoughts and feelings, or state them in ways that makes it difficult for others to challenge. They speak at high levels of inference, assume that what they say is concrete and obvious, and avoid creating conditions that might disconfirm their views. They attribute defensiveness and nasty motives to others, do not state these attributions publicly, and act in ways that elicit behavior that they interpret as confirming their attributions. They are predisposed to attribute responsibility for error to others or to situational factors rather than to them-

selves. Patterns that maintain this situation are treated as undiscussable and are covered with a layer of camouflage. Many of
these features are protected by layers of genuine unawareness
and by defenses to maintain the unawareness. While this description is cast in the language of our research, its general features, and their negative implications for valid inquiry in the
action context, are congruent with the descriptions of researchers of many theoretical perspectives (Nisbett and Ross, 1980;
Goffman, 1959, 1967; Cyert and March, 1963).

In the following chapter we will describe our model of
the master program that leads individuals to design such action,
which we call Model I, and our model of the behavioral world
that is created by and reinforces Model I, which we call Model
O-I ("O" for "organizational"). These models are central to the
theory by which we explain the features described in the preceding paragraph, in that those features may be derived from
the theory. Models I and O-I may be considered a descriptive
epistemology of the action context, one that specifies the causal
factors that reduce the probability that valid knowledge will be
generated and that errors will be detected and corrected. In the
following chapter we will also describe Models II and O-II,
which constitute a normative epistemology for the action context. The action scientist seeks to deal with the threats to validity posed by Model I by creating conditions that approximate
Model II. Movement toward Model II is hypothesized to be
helpful to the client system. To act congruently with Model II,
in the face of automatic Model I action by members of the client community, requires of the action scientist a set of behavioral or clinical skills. The action scientist intends also to help
clients learn these skills, so that they may create conditions approximating Model II when the action scientist is not present.

Implicit in the forgoing discussion is the professional-
client relation that is characteristic of action science. Some
readers may wonder how the action scientist is able to create
conditions in which actors in social settings take the time to
state the data on which their interpretations are based and to
report reasoning that they usually keep private. The social psychologists Nisbett and Wilson acknowledge that such procedures

would generate useful data but regard them as "ecologically meaningless" (1977, p. 246). Gronn, an organizational ethnographer, rejects the notion of checking meanings with his subjects as "impractical and impolite" and fears that he might offend them (1981, pp. 26–27). Nisbett and Wilson represent mainstream social science, and Gronn represents the counterview. Neither combines their research with intervention.

It is because the action scientist is an interventionist seeking to help clients learn that it is possible to create the kinds of data we have been discussing. Clients are willing to reflect publicly and to discuss touchy issues because they expect to learn. It is essential, of course, that the action scientist indeed be able to help. Clients will not long tolerate an uncomfortable and time-consuming process if they do not see that it is helping them. The decision to continue the research is one that clients and action scientist must monitor in an ongoing way. If it does continue, it will be because both parties are internally committed to it and believe that important learning is at stake. Such commitment implies further research advantages. First, clients will be dealing with issues about which they feel strongly, in contrast to the typical laboratory situation in which a concept such as "learned helplessness" is operationalized as a low score on a puzzle-solving task. Second, clients will themselves be committed to monitoring the validity of the information that is generated. In mainstream research the subject may just be "doing his job." In action science the client intends to use the information generated to help make difficult changes in her life.

Yet another advantage to combining research and intervention is that causal theories are tested repeatedly as clients seek to implement them. This advantage involves a comparison of testing in action science with experimentation in mainstream science, a subject to which we turn in the next section.

Experimentation and Action Science. We have pointed out that in mainstream science there are several levels of testing, of which experimentation is the most rigorous. There are also several levels of testing in action science. In ascending order of rigor, we can ask individuals what led them to act as they did; we can observe their action in the future to see if it confirms previously developed hypotheses; and we can intervene to change previously identified patterns. Intervention is the action science analogue of experimentation. When clients involve themselves in change experiments, they engage in nontrivial learning, and they think and reflect seriously on what they are doing and what prevents them from changing. Thus in the process of intervention, better data are generated at the levels of asking and observation. Also, the kinds of learning we are interested in do not occur immediately. Many iterations are required, thus providing an action science analogue to multiple trials or replications. Each intervention, as an action intended to bring about certain consequences, is based on causal theories; and the theories are tested by seeing if the consequences that actually occur are consistent with what the theory would predict.

As we have noted in our discussion of action and causality, there is strong support for the analogy between intervention and experimentation. Experimentation is a powerful test of causal hypotheses precisely because it is an intervention into the course of nature. Still, there are important differences between the methodology of controlled experimentation and intervention in action science. We may say that experimentation is a subset or a refinement of action, one in which practical interests are bracketed for the sake of precise explanation. For example, the experimenter is frequently enjoined to control all relevant variables and to vary but one at a time. Practical action occurs in a field of multiple and interacting variables, and the agent usually does not have unilateral control over them. The methodology of experimentation allows the experimenter to determine whether situations confronting subjects are the same. In the action context, it is the interpretations of actors that are critical to determining if two situations are the same. An experiment occurs, in a sense, outside of history. But in action science, perhaps the most important consequences of any inquiry are their impact on the rules and norms that will guide future inquiry in that same community of practice.

Another important difference between intervention and experimentation is identified by Schön's observation that "the practitioner makes his hypothesis come true. He acts as though his hypothesis were in the imperative mood" (1983, p. 149). Recall Schön's notion that the action by which the practitioner tests an hypothesis is also a means of exploring the situation and a move intended to change the situation. Experimentation in mainstream science, while oriented primarily to testing, may also be oriented to probing or discovery (Hempel, 1966, pp. 20–21). But the third aspect of practice, that of action as an attempt to change the situation, is related to those pragmatic interests that are bracketed in controlled experimentation. To be sure, the scientist often does have an interest in designing experiments that confirm the hypotheses being tested, because only then (in many cases) are the results publishable. But such considerations are in a sense illegitimate, in that other scientists may justly criticize procedures that lead to confirmation at the expense of a genuine test. In practical action, in contrast, achieving the intended result is often the primary consideration.

Another way of stating this difference between action and experimentation is to say that experimentation is valid only if there is a genuine risk of disconfirmation. There is a sense, however, in which self-fulfilling prophecies are the essence of effective action. Consider, for example, the entrepreneur who is convinced that a particular location is just right for her business. The explanatory reasoning underlying this belief may be, in some objective sense, wrong; but believing it is right may lead the entrepreneur to work very hard, thus making it true. At the same time, we should note that situations are not wholly manipulable. While we may think of the explanations embedded in action as projections onto the situation that the agent seeks to make true, no one who grapples with practical action can be so solipsistic as to think that projection always makes it so. Entrepreneurs often fail, despite their positive thinking. Moves have consequences, many of which are unforeseen and unintended. The explanations embedded in action may be in error in ways that cannot be rectified by enacting self-fulfilling prophecies. We may distinguish, then, cases in which the tendency to create self-fulfilling prophecies is productive and those in which it is counterproductive. If an agent acts in ways that ensure blindness to sources of error, there is high risk of continuing ineffectiveness.

Some of the hypotheses embedded in intervention are of the kind that Schön (1983) describes, that is, moves intended to change the situation. This is the case, for example, with the hypothesis that action consistent with Model II will tend to evoke the kind of defenses that are facilitative of learning. Other hypotheses characteristic of action science, however, are of a kind that some members of the behavioral setting will wish to disconfirm. For example, the action scientist may attribute that all members of the client system are programmed with Model I theory-in-use. Clients will not like this attribution and will seek to generate data that will disconfirm it. Similarly, the action scientist may create a map of the behavioral world of the client system that, if true, calls for some wrenching changes. Clients will be motivated to look for errors in the map before acting on it. Thus an important class of the hypotheses or explanations proposed by action scientists can be expected to be subjected to critical tests by members of the relevant community of practice who have an interest in disconfirmation.

We might suggest that the principle of falsification functions in action science as a heuristic to guide criticism. While falsification is not always a prime consideration in the action context, there are many situations in which it is relevant. For example, an agent who believes that a second agent is defensive may unknowingly act in ways that evoke defensiveness, and may take the evoked defensiveness as evidence for the original attribution. This is a self-fulfilling prophecy that is also self-sealing; the result is a vicious circle. Criticism guided by the principle of falsification may then take the form, "If you act in ways that may be responsible for creating the defensiveness you see, how would you ever discover if you were wrong about the person already being defensive?" This is often a compelling criticism. Such criticism is also in order when an agent says, in effect, "The reason I know that what I say is true is that I feel it deeply." It is not that such feelings are not often right; the problem with such arguments is that there is no way for the agent or others to discover when they may be wrong. The principle of falsification thus serves to support norms of public testing by providing a way to remind agents that they might, in principle, be wrong.

Testing and Rule-Governed Interaction. Our discussion of intervention and experimentation has focused on the similarities between the logic of action and the logic of experimentation. If someone asserts that doing x will bring about y, then it should be possible to test the assertion by doing x (and refraining from doing x) and seeing if y occurs. This is the logic by which causal hypotheses are tested in the natural sciences, and we have discussed ways in which it is also relevant to practical deliberation. But there is another aspect of testing in the action context, one that pertains to actors' (mostly tacit) understandings of the rules that govern interaction.

Consider our earlier example and the assertion that "the impact of enacting the 'deprecate self' rule will be to decrease the likelihood that the other person will challenge the validity of the actor's view." How might we justify this assertion? We might reason that, if an actor deprecates himself before deprecating someone else, the impact is likely to be one of saying, "I'm no better than you, I do this too." Also, we might reason that such a move makes tacit appeal to a norm of reciprocity and equality: "I've just admitted a weakness; it would be impolite of you to now deny a weakness." Such considerations may be compelling to agents who share mastery of a system of rules for social interaction.

A related argument appeals to the agent's intentions in enacting the "deprecate self" rule. If asked to reflect on his reasoning, the agent might say, "I didn't want to make him defensive" or "I didn't want to come on as judgmental and threatening." It should be clear that these reasons logically entail the causal assertion we are discussing, that is, that the recipient will be less likely to challenge the actor's view if the latter employs the "deprecate self" rule. This argument from internal consistency with the agent's reasoning does not "prove" that the causal assertion is valid; but it does imply that, if the actor's reasoning was valid, then the causal assertion is valid.

One kind of experiment in action science is role playing, in which two or more agents talk as if they were in a particular situation. Such a procedure has more validity than simply talking about what might happen in abstract terms. The concreteness of role playing evokes the tacit understandings that constitute mastery of the system of rules of interaction. That is, human beings have tacit theories that explain and predict how other human beings are likely to react in various situations. Although far from infallible, these tacit theories have a high degree of validity when situations are enacted or are described in concrete terms. But agents can respond to abstract descriptions only by drawing on that portion of their tacit understandings that they have made explicit; and their explicit theories, or what we call their espoused theories, may be inaccurate formulations of their tacit understandings.

Discovery and Justification in Action Science. Recall that the mainstream account of science makes much of the distinction between the context of discovery and the context of justification. There are several reasons why this distinction cannot be carried through in action science. The actor in practical life has no choice but to act (even if to forebear), and actions once taken construct future constraints. This means that in the action context there is a premium on facility in creating good guesses and on the construction of fast, reliable tests. The action scientist, like the actor in everyday life, must be concerned with effective discovery lest, for example, he or she waste client time or actually harm the client system.

The importance of discovery can be clarified by reference to the cognitive limits of human beings as worked out in the pioneer work of Simon and his colleagues. March and Simon (1958) and Cyert and March (1963) explain that when individuals or organizations face situations for which routines have not been developed, they engage in search. Search is an activity that consumes resources, and it is suspended when a satisfactory alternative has been found. That is, given our cognitive limits as human beings, we do not exhaustively search out all possible alternatives; rather we search until we discover some alternative that is good enough. But this means that the order in which we generate alternatives (that is, more discoveries) is critical. The heuristics that guide the generation of alternatives will largely determine the chosen course of action. Hence practitioners who seek to improve their practice through public reflection should be interested in reflecting on how they discover problems and possible alternatives. Action science must be concerned with such issues. Indeed, to add a level of reflexivity, the action scientist must be concerned with how best to help practitioners discover problematic features in the practitioner's patterns of discovery.

It is sometimes argued, in the spirit of Kuhn, that discovery cannot be separated from justification because the paradigm (or "framing") that structures the context of discovery also determines the criteria of justification. There is some validity to this view; the way in which a problem is set identifies what is to count as a solution. But not all criteria of justification are thus determined. The very notion of discovering problematic features in practitioners' patterns of discovery implies independent criteria of justification. For example, the contrasting heuristics of discovery—"look first for the other person's responsibility" and "look first for one's own personal responsibility"—may be evaluated with respect to their consequences for creating a behavioral world conducive to generating valid information. This latter consideration, or "value," is second order with respect to the former heuristics.

The interpenetration of discovery and justification in the action context is perhaps better shown by the following argument: An actor may frame a situation in such a way that he creates self-sealing processes of escalating error. For example, if the marketing people in a corporation frame an upcoming budget meeting as a win-lose battle with research and development for scarce funds, they may act in ways that ensure that a win-lose battle will occur. Under such conditions it is unlikely they will discover if their framing was ill advised. Stated more generally, some "discoveries" may create conditions in which valid inquiry for purposes of justification cannot occur.

Action Science as Critical Theory

At several points in the preceding discussion we have mentioned the normative dimension of action science. We have noted that action has a moral aspect, as suggested by the concern of practical reasoning with questions of the type, "What shall I (we) do?" We have distinguished the epistemology of practice embedded in action science from the mainstream view by noting that practical knowledge refers not only to knowledge of the relationship of means to ends but also to the intelligent choice of ends. We have pointed out that the action scientist is an interventionist seeking to bring about some states of affairs rather than others, in our case guided by the normative theory we call Model II. And we have stated that action science seeks alternatives to the status quo that will both illuminate what exists and inform fundamental change.

The normative dimension of action science requires special comment because both the mainstream view and many versions of the counterview suggest that it is not appropriate for a scientist to advocate a normative position. The mainstream view has been heavily influenced by the positivist separation of fact and value. Only statements of fact were, on this account, held to be cognitively meaningful; value judgments were branded "emotive utterances." Accordingly scientists were to limit themselves to matters of fact. Advocates of the counterview—Schutz (1962) is one example—have rejected the positivist account, but they have thought it necessary for the social scientist to adapt a disinterested stance, a position of value neutrality.

There is, however, an influential contemporary view that argues that the theorist should adopt a normative position that offers a basis for criticism of the status quo. This position has been developed by theorists of the Frankfurt School, whose most influential member in recent years has been Jürgen Habermas. The Frankfurt School has championed "critical theory," an approach to social inquiry that seeks to unite knowledge and action, theory and practice. The critical theorist, it is said, takes a practical interest in improving human existence.

Writers of the Frankfurt School discuss two exemplars of critical theory. The first is Marxism, although the Marxism they discuss is not orthodox Marxism because their emphasis is on the critique of ideology or on the false consciousness that blinds human beings to their true interests and not on the supposed inevitability of a proletarian revolution. The second exemplar is

Freudian psychotherapy. What Marxism and Freudianism have in common is that they seek to transform the self-awareness of the subjects to whom they are addressed, in the interests of emancipation. It appears to us that action science is a third exemplar of critical theory. Action science is as unlike Marxism and psychoanalysis as they are unlike each other. But it, too, seeks to stimulate critical self-reflection among human agents so that they may more freely choose whether and how to transform their world.

In this section we will describe some features of critical theory in order to clarify the normative dimension of action science. Our discussion will rely heavily on Geuss (1981) and Bernstein (1976), each of whom has based his thoughtful treatments of critical theory largely on the writings of Habermas.

Habermas has proposed that there are three types of sciences (Bernstein, 1976, p. 191). First, the "empirical-analytic sciences" fit the description of the mainstream account. They seek hypothetical-deductive theories that describe regularities between dependent and independent variables. They serve "technical" interests in the sense that they enable human beings to extend their control over nature. Second, the "historical-hermeneutic sciences" fit the descriptions of science held by the counterview. They are concerned with communicative action, and their methodologies are those appropriate to the interpretation of texts and the understanding of meaning. They serve "practical" interests that are guided by consensual norms. And, finally, "critical social science" goes beyond the description of empirical regularities and the interpretation of meanings. It serves "emancipatory" interests by offering a critique of what is from the perspective of what might be. The methodological framework is that of self-reflection, by which human subjects can transform their self-awareness and can act to change the world. Bernstein describes the relation among the three kinds of sciences and their guiding interests: "A consistent, adequate understanding of the empirical-analytic sciences demands the existence—as Peirce and so many who have followed him have argued—of an open, self-critical community of inquirers. And the practical interest that governs the historical-hermeneutic disciplines seeks to promote such open, nondistortive communication. Implicit in the knowledge guided by the technical and practical interests is the demand for the ideal state of affairs in which nonalienating work and free interaction can be manifested" (1976, p. 198).

The three kinds of sciences should not be viewed as mutually exclusive. The natural sciences, perhaps, can be understood as purely empirical-analytic disciplines, although such an understanding does not account for the intersubjective practices of the scientific community. The sciences of social action are both empirical analytic and historical hermeneutic, although, as the polarization between mainstream and counterview indicates, the relationships between these distinctive aspects are not well understood. Critical social science includes empirical-analytic and historical-hermeneutic aspects yet goes beyond them.

Geuss (1981, p. 76) proposes that a critical theory is composed of three main constituent parts, which we summarize here:

A. A part which shows that a transition from the present state of society . . . to some proposed final state is . . . possible . . .

B. A part which shows that the transition . . . is "practically necessary," i.e. that

1. . . . the present social arrangements cause pain, suffering, and frustration . . . agents . . . only accept the present arrangements . . . because they hold a particular world-picture . . . one they acquired only because they were in conditions of coercion;

2. the proposed final state will be one which will lack the illusions and unnecessary coercion and frustration . . . which . . . will be easier for the agents to realize their true interests;

C. A part which asserts that the transition from the present state to the proposed final state can come about only if the agents adopt the

> critical theory as their "self-consciousness"
> and act on it.

This description of the features of a critical theory still appears to fit Marxism better than it does either psychoanalysis or action science. But at this point it is adequate to identify what is distinctive about critical theory. It should be clear that in order to satisfy the several claims Geuss describes, a critical theory must make many empirical assertions. On the one hand, for example, it must identify the causal links between present social arrangements and their negative consequences, and show that alternative arrangements would not create these same consequences. On the other hand, it is not clear that the claim that agents would reject their current world view if they were in a position to know better is empirical. Assuming this claim is not simply a tautology (if they had different wants, they would want different things), what is its status? And related to this, what are we to make of the reference to agents' "true interests"? Assuming agents do not now "know better" and are unaware of their "true interests," how are these to be determined? Geuss identifies the point at issue when he observes that a critical theory "doesn't merely give information about how it would be rational for agents to act *if* they had certain interests; it claims to inform them about what interests it is rational for them to have" (1981, p. 58). This claim points to the radical difference between critical theory and mainstream science.

Critical theory justifies advocacy of a normative position by adhering to the principle of internal criticism. That is, the critical theorist claims that the normative views in question are implicit in the beliefs and practices of the agents to whom the critical theory is addressed. As Geuss points out: "Human agents don't merely have and acquire beliefs, they also have ways of criticizing and evaluating their own beliefs. Every agent will have a set of epistemic principles, i.e. an at least rudimentary set of second-order beliefs about such things as what kinds of beliefs are acceptable or unacceptable, and how beliefs can be shown to be acceptable or unacceptable" (1981, p. 61).

Critical theory proceeds by making explicit the epistemic

principles that agents already use but of which they are unaware and by showing that the agents' world view is false by the
criteria of these epistemic principles. The question remains,
What are the criteria for determining if the critical theory has
validly carried through this critique? Geuss argues that it is the
agents to whom the critical theory is addressed who are the final judges of its validity. That is, the critical theory is confirmed
if those agents agree that their world view is "reflectively unacceptable" to them. "Reflective unacceptability" means that
agents will give up the belief in question when they reflect on it
in light of valid information in free discussion. This does not
mean, of course, that agents will abandon their beliefs as soon
as they are challenged. The very point of critical theory is that
agents can be wrong about these matters. Marxist theorists
speak of "false consciousness," and psychoanalytic theorists
speak of the unconscious, repression, and so on. But the ultimate criterion of validity is free assent in a discussion very like
Peirce's community of inquiry, in which the test of truth is
that investigators who begin with different views converge on
one opinion in the course of inquiry.

   The relation to Peirce is especially clear in Habermas's
version of critical theory. Habermas argues that human interaction presumes what he calls an ideal speech situation. That is,
he argues that all linguistic communication involves four kinds
of validity claims: that what is uttered is comprehensible, that
the content of what is said is true, that the speaker is being
truthful (the utterance is congruent with the speaker's intentions), and that the speech acts being performed are legitimate
(Habermas, 1979, pp. 2, 28; Bernstein, 1976, p. 211). Now, if
any of these validity claims are questioned, speakers resort to
what Habermas calls a discourse in which the claims are examined and tested. The criteria for good discourse, that is, for the
rationality of the consensus that may be achieved through discourse, are that it approximate the ideal speech situation. That
is, "What it means for a statement to be true is that it would be
the one on which all agents would agree if they were to discuss
all of human experience in absolutely free and uncoerced cir-

cumstances for an indefinite period of time" (Geuss, 1981, p. 65). This is the same definition Peirce gives of truth in scientific inquiry. Habermas argues that the ideal speech situation is the grounding for the ideas of rationality, freedom, and justice, as well as the idea of truth.

Habermas has argued that acceptability in the ideal speech situation is a "transcendental" criterion of truth, by which he means that all human beings everywhere at all times are committed to recognizing it by virtue of the nature of linguistic communication. Geuss questions this universality, pointing out that there may be some exotic cultures in which it does not hold. He agrees, however, that modern societies do accept the notion that "our real interests are the ones we would form in conditions of complete freedom of discussion" (1981, p. 67). If the criteria of the ideal speech situation are fundamental to the epistemic principles of agents in everyday life (as of course they are for scientists), then critical theory can show that a certain set of beliefs is false by showing that agents would not have adopted those beliefs had they been in ideal speech situations (that is, those beliefs could have been formed only under conditions of coercion). The setting in which such a demonstration can be recognized as valid is one that itself approximates ideal speech. Thus, on this analysis, it would be inconsistent and "false" for an advocate of critical theory to coerce (psychologically or otherwise) others to adopt the critical theory. The only form of coercion that is legitimate is the force of the better argument, as judged in free and open discussion.

As we have seen, embedded in the scientific enterprise is an ethic of responsible belief (Scheffler, 1982, p. 7). Action science extends this ethic to the realm of responsible action. In this section we describe a set of action science values that we claim are conceptually and empirically interrelated. That is, action that creates a behavioral world in which some of these values are realized tends to be guided by others of these values. We also claim that these values are embedded in the epistemic principles of client systems; and to the extent that this is not true, we would not expect the system to engage in action sci-

ence. The practice of action science, especially in the early
stages of an engagement, involves carrying through an internal
critique so that clients can become aware and can confirm or
disconfirm for themselves the degree to which they enact patterns that are inconsistent with the values they affirm.

We begin with the values of competence and justice.
When we view human beings as agents, we see designing and taking actions to achieve intended consequences as basic life activities. To say that agents seek to bring about intended consequences is to say that they seek to be competent. Justice becomes crucial as soon as we consider human agents as social
beings. The core of the concept of justice is the principle of universality, which Edgley observes is generally regarded as the
most important principle in the area of practical reason: "If a
particular person ought to do a certain thing in a particular situation, he and anyone else in a situation of the same relevant
kind ought to do the same kind of thing" (1978, p. 28).

Competence and justice are closely related, and both involve the notion of rationality. The principle of universality is a
rational principle; to assert both that "everyone should do x"
and that "I need not do x" is to be inconsistent, to act unjustly,
and to act contrary to good reasons. Agents who act in this way
can be seen as incompetent, in part because they create defensive reactions in others. Competence requires that the agent not
create counterproductive consequences, another illustration of
the principle of rationality.

Competence requires that action be informed by valid information. The popular metaphor of human agent as intuitive
scientist (Kelly, 1955; Schutz, 1967; Heider, 1958; Kelley,
1971; Nisbett and Ross, 1980) points to the importance of theories that explain the world, revised in light of evidence so that
they may be accurate. Generating valid information requires
something like a community of inquiry guided by such norms as
intersubjectively verifiable data, explicit inferences, and public
falsifiability. To assert and act on theories that are held exempt
from such criteria is unjust. That is, to assert a theory is to
make a validity claim; validity depends on susceptibility to public test; hence to claim exemption from public testing is to vio-

late the principle of universality and to say in effect that "all validity claims must be subject to test, except mine."

Creating and maintaining behavioral worlds conducive to generating valid information require conditions in which agents can make free and informed choices and feel internally committed to their choices. The requirement of free and informed choice is a necessary warrant of the validity of beliefs accepted in a community of inquiry. This is evident in Habermas's analysis of the ideal speech situation and also in the long-recognized congruence between the values of science and those of democracy. If choice is not free and informed, then we have no reason to believe that the community of inquiry will tend toward true opinions. Internal commitment is an empirical consequence of free and informed choice. In the realm of action it is also an indispensable condition for valid information over time. When human beings feel internally committed to a course of action, they more intelligently monitor its implementation. Implementation will be more competent, and it becomes more likely that information important to success will be recognized and acted upon. For example, workers who feel internally committed to producing a good product will be less likely to knowingly allow design errors to go uncorrected.

Each of the values that we have just discussed may be related to the notion of personal causal responsibility. Agents who focus on their personal responsibility are likely to act more competently and more justly than those who do not. Those who distance themselves from their personal responsibility are likely to create behavioral worlds in which valid information is not generated, choices are not recognized, and agents feel little internal commitment. While it is obvious that human beings often do blame others and do not recognize their own responsibility, they do this in the belief that they have good reasons for holding others responsible. If the action scientist, guided by the norm that people should be personally responsible, sees that people seem to be distancing themselves, and if this criticism can be made in the context of public reflection and is recognized as valid by the people involved, then it becomes possible for them to learn and to change. Action science makes this possible by creating conditions in which members of client systems can consider for themselves empirical, interpretive, and normative claims in free and open inquiry.

We can briefly summarize the aspects of action science discussed in this chapter as follows:

1. Action science intends to enact communities of inquiry in communities of social practice. Just as scientific inquiry proceeds according to rules and norms of responsible belief, so action science extends this ethic to practical deliberation.

2. Whereas mainstream science is directed primarily toward knowledge for its own sake and only secondarily toward its technical application, action science is directed toward knowledge in the service of action. It builds on an epistemology of practice that sees practical knowledge as a realm of tacit knowing that can be made explicit through reflective inquiry.

3. Whereas mainstream science emphasizes empirical claims and the counterview emphasizes interpretive claims, the domain of action science is characterized by the interpenetration of empirical, interpretive, and normative claims.

4. The covering-law model captures part of the logic of knowledge in action science. For example, the defensive routines characteristic of social systems can be derived from, and thus are explained by, the theory of Models I and O-I. But action science intends to produce knowledge that is optimally incomplete and that can be filled in as the situation requires. Theoretical constructs should be simple enough to be usable, while enabling the actor to grasp all relevant features of the situation. They should be suited to dealing with concrete situations and to making scientific generalizations. Action science focuses on the meanings and logic of action more than on regularities among contingent events.

5. The testing of knowledge claims in action science, as in mainstream science, is guided by the norms of public testing, falsifiability, intersubjective agreement on data, and explicit inferences. However, in action science these norms are used to structure and refine the practices for coming to agreement common to ordinary speech, and are extended to interpretive and normative, as well as empirical, claims. As the ground of knowl-

edge claims in mainstream science is the community of inquiry insofar as it follows appropriate rules and norms, so the ground of knowledge claims in action science is the community of practice insofar as it enacts norms for valid information, free and informed choice, and internal commitment.

6. Whereas the mainstream account of science distinguishes sharply between the context of discovery and the context of justification, in action science the two cannot be sharply distinguished.

7. Action science intends to create alternatives to the status quo and to promote learning at the level of norms and values. Inquiry focuses on double-loop learning and frame breaking, or what Rorty (1979) calls abnormal discourse. Like critical theory (Geuss, 1981), action science advocates and justifies its normative position through internal critique of the epistemic principles of the client system, which remains the ultimate judge of the validity of the critique.

3

Theories of Action

The idea of an action science that we have been describing is grounded in our practice as researchers, educators, and interventionists working within the theory of action approach (Argyris and Schön, 1974, 1978; Argyris, 1976, 1980, 1982, 1985). It may well be that other research programs and theoretical approaches can provide alternative ways of conducting action science. Our particular approach, however, provides the perspective from which we have been able to envision an action science. It is also the perspective from which we criticize and provide alternatives to examples of mainstream research in Part Two, and from which we describe the process of learning the skills necessary to conduct action science in Part Three. Hence, this chapter presents the theoretical orientation which informs our work.

The theory of action approach begins with a conception of human beings as designers of action. To see human behavior under the aspect of action is to see it as constituted by the meanings and intentions of agents. Agents design action to achieve intended consequences, and monitor themselves to learn if their actions are effective. They make sense of their environment by constructing meanings to which they attend, and these constructions in turn guide action. In monitoring the effectiveness of action, they also monitor the suitability of their construction of the environment.

The complexity of the design task far exceeds the information-processing capabilities of the human mind (Simon, 1969). Designing action requires that agents construct a simplified representation of the environment and a manageable set of causal theories that prescribe how to achieve the intended consequences. It would be very inefficient to construct such representations and theories from scratch in each situation. Rather, agents learn a repertoire of concepts, schemas, and strategies, and they learn programs for drawing from their repertoire to design representations and action for unique situations. We speak of such design programs as *theories of action*.

Theories of Action

These theories may be thought of as a very large set of complexly related propositions. The form of a proposition in a theory of action is, "In situation *s,* to achieve consequence *c,* do action *a*" (Argyris and Schön, 1974). From the perspective of the agent who holds the theory, it is a theory of control. It states what the agent should do to achieve certain results. From an observer's perspective, to attribute a theory of action to an agent is to propose a theory of explanation or prediction. In the language of the previous chapter, it is to make a dispositional attribution. The example we used is, "John follows the rule, 'If I am about to deprecate someone, first deprecate myself.' " But from John's perspective, this is a theory of control. We can see this by making explicit the intended consequence of enacting the rule, which, let us suppose, is to avoid making the other person defensive. Hence a proposition of a theory of action can be understood both as a disposition of an agent and as a theory of causal responsibility held by an agent.

Espoused Theory and Theory-in-Use. There are two kinds of theories of action. Espoused theories are those that an individual claims to follow. Theories-in-use are those that can be inferred from action. For example, when asked how he would deal with a disagreement with a client, a management consultant said that he would first state what he understood to be the substance of the disagreement, and then discuss with the client what kind of data would resolve it. This was his espoused theory. But when we examined a tape recording of what the consultant actually did in that situation, we found that he advocated his own view and dismissed that of the client.

The discrepancy between what people say and what they do is an old story. It is sometimes expressed in the saying, "Do as I say, not as I do." But the distinction between espoused theory and theory-in-use goes beyond this common conception. It is true that what people do often differs from the theories they espouse. We are saying, however, that there is a theory that is consistent with what they do; and this we call their theory-in-use. Our distinction is not between theory and action but between two different theories of action: those that people espouse, and those that they use. One reason for insisting that what people do is consistent with the theory (in-use) that they hold, even though it may be inconsistent with their espoused theories, is to emphasize that what people do is not accidental. They do not "just happen" to act in a particular way. Rather, their action is designed; and, as agents, they are responsible for the design.

Espoused theory and theory-in-use may be consistent or inconsistent, and the agent may or may not be aware of any inconsistency. The agent *is* aware of the espoused theory, by definition, since it is the theory that the agent claims to follow. Recall in this connection our previous discussion of tacit knowledge and rule-governed behavior. As many approaches to social inquiry emphasize, human beings can be understood to act according to rules that they cannot state.

Theories-in-use are the often tacit cognitive maps by which human beings design action. Theories-in-use can be made explicit by reflecting on action. But we should note that the act of reflection is itself governed by theories-in-use. Becoming an action scientist involves learning to reflect on reflection-in-action, making explicit the theories-in-use that inform it, and learning to design and produce new theories-in-use for reflection and action.

Nested Theories. Theories of action can be articulated at different levels of detail. Consider a theory-in-use description of the common interpersonal strategy that we call "easing-in": "If you are about to criticize someone who might become defensive and you want him to see the point without undue resistance, do not state the criticism openly; instead, ask questions such that if he answers them correctly, he will figure out what you are not saying." This is a relatively high-level design program. The action injunction to ask questions of a certain kind could be performed only with the help of a great many detailed propositions about the production of grammatical sentences, motor skills for speech, and so forth. Similarly, the recognition of a particular situation as one in which another person may become defensive requires the coordinated performance of complicated perceptual routines and higher-order judgments about human defensiveness.

A full specification of the theories of action held by any individual would be enormously lengthy and complex. Yet in order to understand theories of action it is necessary to make them explicit. What is required are models—simplified representations—chosen to illuminate those features of theories of action most relevant to particular fields of inquiry. Linguistics, for example, selects those features relevant to the production of grammatical sentences.

Action science concentrates on the level of abstraction at which agents in everyday life reflect on their actions. The spotlight of attention shifts depending on the concerns of agents in particular situations, but the example of the questioning strategy of easing-in illustrates a characteristic level of abstraction. Action science would probably not focus on the particular intonation patterns by which speakers of English communicate doubt, although the action scientist might indeed inquire into whether hearers attributed doubt to a speaker or into the reasoning that led an agent to communicate doubt.

The models we create in action science are shaped by our

interest in helping human beings to make more informed choices in creating the worlds in which they are embedded. Because we are interested in helping human beings design and implement action, our models should be "connectable" to concrete situations. We seek both generalizability and attention to the individual case. This is difficult to achieve, but probably no more difficult than for all human beings who must do this as agents in everyday life.

As action scientists we are concerned with the effective functioning of interventionists in behavioral systems, which range from individuals to groups, intergroups, organizations, and communities. We are therefore centrally concerned with the features of theories of action that promote or inhibit learning in behavioral systems. The models we will describe were developed in light of earlier theories about what it is in the way human beings interact that leads to escalating error and the inability to learn (Argyris, 1970). The models provide ways to test and extend the theory and, at the same time, help client systems to reflect on their theories-in-use and to learn new theories-in-use.

Modeling Theories-in-Use. Models of theories-in-use can be constructed according to the schematic frame shown in Figure 1. Governing variables are values that actors seek to satisfy.

Figure 1. Theory-in-Use Model.

Each governing variable can be thought of as a continuum with a preferred range. For example, individuals would not want anxiety to get too high; but they might not want anxiety to drop to zero, either, lest they feel bored. We commonly speak of actions as directed toward an end state, as if there were only one relevant governing variable; but in fact, human beings live in a field of many governing variables. These variables can be ignored as long as their values are within a satisfactory range; when one falls out of that range, however, the actor takes steps to bring it back to a satisfactory level. Any action can have an impact on many governing variables. Agents typically must trade off among governing variables, because actions that raise the value of one may lower the value of another.

Action strategies are sequences of moves used by actors in particular situations to satisfy governing variables. Action strategies have intended consequences, which are those that the actor believes will result from the action and will satisfy governing variables. Consequences feed back to action strategies and governing variables.

Actions have consequences for the behavioral world, for learning, and for effectiveness. Consequences may be intended or unintended, productive or counterproductive. Consequences that are unintended may nevertheless be designed, in the following sense: Action intended to achieve particular consequences may, by virtue of its design, necessarily lead to consequences that are unintended. For example, the questioning strategy of easing-in typically creates the very defensiveness that it is intended to avoid, because the recipient typically understands that the actor is easing-in. Indeed, easing-in can be successful only if the recipient understands that he is supposed to answer the questions in a particular way, and this entails the understanding that the actor is negatively evaluating the recipient and acting as if this were not the case.

The consequences of action depend on the theories-in-use of recipients as well as those of actors. One's theory-in-use includes a vast store of information about what people are like and how they will respond in various situations. We can argue that consequences are designed, whether they are intended or unintended, when they necessarily follow from the action and the actor's presuppositions about the theories-in-use of recipients.

Single-Loop and Double-Loop Learning. When the consequences of an action strategy are as the agent intends, then there is a match between intention and outcome, and the theory-in-use of the agent is confirmed. If the consequences are unintended, and especially if they are counterproductive, there is a mismatch or an error. The first response to error is typically to search for another action strategy that will satisfy the same governing variables. For example, if the agent wants to suppress conflict (governing variable) and to this end avoids saying anything that might be controversial (action strategy), but others raise threatening issues anyway (mismatch), the agent may try the strategy of talking volubly about issues on which everyone is likely to agree. In such a case, when new action strategies are used in the service of the same governing variables, we speak of *single-loop learning*. We do so because there is a change in action but not in the governing variables.

Another possibility is to change the governing variables themselves. For example, rather than suppress conflict, the agent might choose to emphasize open inquiry. The associated action strategy might be to initiate discussion of conflictual issues. In such cases we speak of *double-loop learning*. We suggested in the previous chapter that the deliberative process appropriate to double-loop learning is similar to what Rorty (1979) calls abnormal discourse. It is concerned not with choosing among competing chains of means-ends reasoning within a given set of standards, but with choosing among competing sets of standards ("frames" or "paradigms").

Having made a clear distinction between single-loop learning and double-loop learning, we must note that in fact the two kinds of learning exist on a continuum. Values and strategies may be nested, and learning that is double loop with respect to particular actions may appear single loop with respect to more encompassing governing variables. For example, both the effort to suppress conflict and the effort to discuss conflict openly might be in the interests of "getting others to do what I think best." Double-loop learning, on this account, might involve designing ways to jointly decide whether to discuss conflict. Another way of thinking of this nested quality is in terms of second-order standards by which alternative frames or paradigms may be evaluated.

There are several cues by which double-loop problems may be identified in practice. Dealing with double-loop problems requires dealing with the defenses of human beings. Thus situations in which participants give cues that they or others might feel embarrassed or threatened are likely to require double-loop learning. Problems that are undiscussable are likely to be double loop; and the undiscussability itself is most certainly a double-loop problem, as is the cover-up of the undiscussability. Problems that persist despite efforts to solve them are likely to have double-loop issues embedded in them. For example, a business might continue to lose money because it has higher costs than its competitors or because its market is shrinking. But if the business is trying the wrong solutions or if there are no solutions within its capability, why are these errors not discovered? Persistent errors in learning point to double-loop problems. These are problems that require inquiry into governing variables if they are to be solved in such a way that they remain solved.

There are instructive parallels between the theory of action approach and family systems theory. Thus, in discussing families, Watzlawick, Weakland, and Fisch (1974) distinguish between first-order change and second-order change. First-order change occurs when people decrease deviation from a set norm. This is an application of the cybernetic principle of negative feedback mechanisms (Watzlawick, Beavin, and Jackson, 1967, p. 31). For example, a thermostat turns on the furnace when the temperature falls below a certain point. In our language, the thermostat is a device for single-loop learning.

Second-order change is necessary, argue Watzlawick, Weakland, and Fisch, when the structure of the family system must undergo change. Indeed, they argue that families develop problems (and wind up in the therapist's office) when attempts at first-order change are made in situations in which the system's structure itself has to undergo change. They refer to this problem cycle as the "more of the same" syndrome. For example, Father may nag Johnny about his schoolwork, which leads the rebellious Johnny to play hookey more often, which leads Father to escalate his nagging and threats, and so forth. The therapist's role is to bring about second-order change—change that alters the structure of the system, often by interventions that reframe the meaning of what is going on.

In our approach to action science we focus on double-loop learning, the theories-in-use that inhibit it, and the ways in which theories-in-use that enhance a system's capacity for double-loop learning may be learned. We find that individuals and organizations are generally competent at single-loop learning, but are generally incompetent at double-loop learning. Family systems theorists seem to agree that human beings have little competence for double-loop learning and that the interventionist provides help by enabling double-loop learning to occur. But there is an important difference between family systems theory and our approach. We are concerned with increasing the client system's capacity for double-loop learning. The family therapist is concerned with bringing about a double-loop change, but not with increasing the family's competence to engage in double-loop learning more generally. For example, a therapist might help a family to solve a problem such as chronic bickering; but members of the family do not learn the skills to correct such situations without intervention by an outsider. Watzlawick, Weakland, and Fisch recognize this, but it does not concern them. A family might have to return to the therapist when a new problem arises; but the therapist, who is not concerned with helping the family gain insight into its problem but rather with correcting the problem, is supposed to be able to work quickly. It may in fact be more efficient to go to a therapist periodically than to learn skills for double-loop learning on one's own; and so this may be an appropriate strategy in family therapy, especially with families that are not articulate and reflective. But our practice is with organizations and with helping professionals, both counselors and consultants. These are clients for whom it is important not only to solve particular problems but to increase their capacity for double-loop learning more generally.

Model I Theory-in-Use

Argyris and Schön (1974) developed a model, or an ideal type, that describes features of theories-in-use that inhibit double-loop learning. While espoused theories vary widely, research indicates that there is almost no variance in theory-in-use (Argyris, 1976, 1982). More precisely, the theories-in-use of virtually everyone we have studied are consistent with the master program called Model I. There is considerable difference within Model I in the weightings individuals give to particular governing variables, as well as in the particular strategies individuals favor, but these lower-order variations appear to be governed by the Model I master program (see Table 1).

The four governing variables of Model I are (1) achieve the purpose as the actor defines it; (2) win, do not lose; (3) suppress negative feelings; and (4) emphasize rationality.

The primary behavioral strategies in Model I are to control the relevant environment and tasks unilaterally and to protect oneself and others unilaterally. Thus, the underlying behavioral strategy is unilateral control over others. Characteristic ways of implementing this strategy include making unillustrated attributions and evaluations, advocating courses of action in ways that discourage inquiry, treating one's own views as obviously correct, making covert attributions, evaluations, and face-saving moves such as leaving potentially embarrassing facts unstated.

The consequences of Model I strategies include defensive interpersonal and group relationships, low freedom of choice, and reduced production of valid information. There are negative consequences for learning, because there is little public testing of ideas. The hypotheses that people generate tend to become self-sealing. What learning does occur remains within the bounds of what is acceptable. Double-loop learning does not tend to occur. As a result, error escalates and effectiveness in problem solving and in execution of action tends to decrease.

In claiming that human beings are programmed with Model I theory-in-use, we are making predictions about the kinds of strategies they will and will not use, and the kinds of consequences that will and will not occur. These predictions have been tested in dozens of client groups that included thousands of individuals, and to date they have not been disconfirmed (see Argyris, 1982, chap. 3). Most people hold espoused theories inconsistent with Model I; and, when confronted with our predictions about the strategies they will use, seek to dem-

Table 1. Model I Theory-in-Use.

Governing Variables	Action Strategies	Consequences for the Behavioral World	Consequences for Learning	Effectiveness
Define goals and try to achieve them.	Design and manage the environment unilaterally (be persuasive, appeal to larger goals).	Actor seen as defensive, inconsistent, incongruent, competitive, controlling, fearful of being vulnerable, manipulative, withholding of feelings, overly concerned about self and others or underconcerned about others.	Self-sealing.	Decreased effectiveness.
Maximize winning and minimize losing.	Own and control the task (claim ownership of the task, be guardian of definition and execution of task).	Defensive interpersonal and group relationship (dependence upon actor, little additivity, little helping of others).	Single-loop learning.	

Minimize generating or expressing negative feelings.	*Unilaterally protect yourself* (speak with inferred categories accompanied by little or no directly observable behavior, be blind to impact on others and to the incongruity between rhetoric and behavior, reduce incongruity by defensive actions such as blaming, stereotyping, suppressing feelings, intellectualizing).	Defensive norms (mistrust, lack of risk taking, conformity, external commitment, emphasis on diplomacy, power-centered competition, and rivalry).	Little testing of theories publicly. Much testing of theories privately.
Be rational.	*Unilaterally protect others from being hurt* (withhold information, create rules to censor information and behavior, hold private meetings).	Little freedom of choice, internal commitment, or risk taking.	

Source: Argyris and Schön, 1974.

onstrate that our predictions are not valid. But even when Model I has been explained and people are trying to produce action that does not fit the model, they are unable to do so. This result holds whenever people are dealing with double-loop issues, which is to say whenever they are dealing with threatening issues. At best, they are able to produce strategies consistent with opposite Model I, the mirror image of Model I.

The governing variables of opposite Model I are (1) participation of everyone in defining purposes; (2) everyone wins, no one loses; (3) express feelings; and (4) suppress the cognitive intellective aspects of action. The associated behavioral strategies include emphasizing inquiry and minimizing unilateral control (Argyris, 1979).

Opposite Model I is more common as an espoused theory than as a theory-in-use. Elements from it are practiced in T-groups and nondirective therapies. Usually elements of opposite Model I are embedded in an underlying Model I theory-in-use in which unilateral protection of self and others is prominent, and competitiveness and unilateral control are present but camouflaged. It is often used in oscillation with Model I; the agent tries some elements from opposite Model I, and, if they don't seem to be working, switches to Model I. The consequences of opposite Model I for the behavioral world, for learning, and for effectiveness are similar to those of the more overt variety of Model I. In our discussion of the learning process in Part Three we will illustrate these ideas with concrete examples.

Action takes on the features represented by Model I especially in situations that agents perceive as potentially threatening or embarrassing. It is in such situations that agents are most oriented to controlling others and to protecting themselves. Self-protection frequently takes the form of attributing responsibility for error to others or to the situation rather than to oneself. The very situations that most require double-loop learning are the ones that most evoke Model I action—action that inhibits double-loop learning.

Model O-I: The Behavioral World. Individuals are embedded in a behavioral world or culture. This behavioral world has a dual nature. On the one hand, it is created by the actions of the individuals who live it. On the other hand, it has an objective existence independent of the actions of any individual. Theories-in-use, in guiding all deliberate behavior, also guide the construction of the behavioral world. At the same time, the behavioral world guides the socialization of individuals with particular theories-in-use, and creates conditions in which theories-in-use are effective or ineffective.

The consequences of Model I theory-in-use, as we have described, include defensiveness, low freedom of choice, and self-sealing processes. If it is the case that Model I identifies features of theories-in-use that are common to virtually everyone, it follows that the behavioral worlds of groups, families, and organizations will have features that correspond to Model I. The interaction of people programmed with Model I theories-in-use generates pattern-building forces (Hayek, 1967, p. 33) that create a characteristic behavioral world.

Argyris and Schön (1978) created a model of the behavioral world that is congruent with Model I theory-in-use. Model O-I ("O" signifies "organization") is a model of a *limited learning system* (Figure 2). The model states that when individuals programmed with Model I theory-in-use deal with difficult and threatening problems, they create primary inhibiting loops. That is, they create conditions of undiscussability, self-fulfilling prophecies, self-sealing processes, and escalating error, and they remain unaware of their responsibility for these conditions. Primary inhibiting loops lead to secondary inhibiting loops such as win-lose group dynamics, conformity, polarization between groups, and organizational games of deception. These secondary inhibiting loops reinforce primary inhibiting loops and together they lead people to despair of double-loop learning in organizations.

Under these conditions, organizations can correct errors that do not threaten underlying their norms, and they may also seek to correct errors that cannot be camouflaged. But they become unable to correct errors when this would require questioning and changing underlying norms. They also spin out elaborate webs of camouflage, as well as camouflage of the camouflage, and they engage in backup protective activities such as

Figure 2. Model O-I Limited Learning Systems.

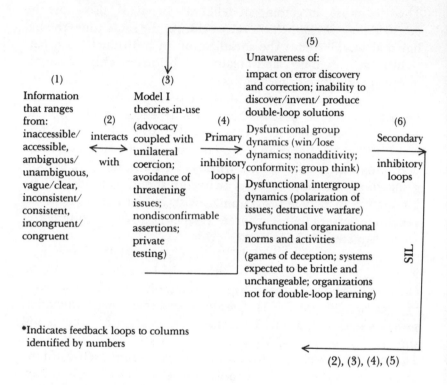

*Indicates feedback loops to columns
 identified by numbers

(2), (3), (4), (5)

Source: Argyris, 1982.

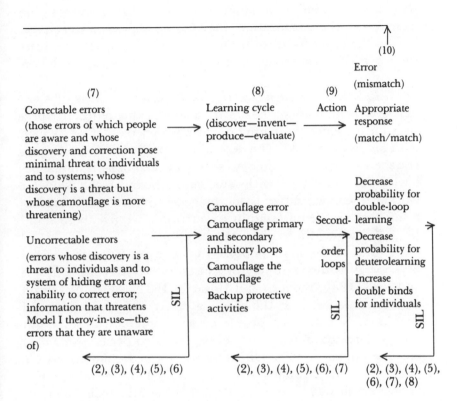

(10)

Error
(mismatch)

(7)	(8)	(9)	
Correctable errors (those errors of which people are aware and whose discovery and correction pose minimal threat to individuals and to systems; whose discovery is a threat but whose camouflage is more threatening)	Learning cycle (discover—invent—produce—evaluate) ⟶	Action ⟶	Appropriate response (match/match)

Uncorrectable errors

(errors whose discovery is a threat to individuals and to system of hiding error and inability to correct error; information that threatens Model I theroy-in-use—the errors that they are unaware of)

Camouflage error

Camouflage primary and secondary inhibitory loops

Camouflage the camouflage

Backup protective activities

Second-order loops

Decrease probability for double-loop learning

Decrease probability for deuterolearning

Increase double binds for individuals

SIL   SIL   SIL

(2), (3), (4), (5), (6)   (2), (3), (4), (5), (6), (7)   (2), (3), (4), (5), (6), (7), (8) compiling special files "just in case the boss asks." All this creates double binds for committed individuals. On the one hand they see errors and unproductive activities that, as responsible members of the organization, they feel an obligation to correct; but on the other hand, to bring these threatening issues to the surface may be perceived as disloyal and as a threat to the organization.

Relation to Other Descriptive Theories. There is substantial agreement among scholars from several theoretical perspectives on the empirical nature of the phenomena that we explain with Models I and O-I. The descriptions produced by leading researchers in social psychology, sociology, and organizational behavior are consistent with our descriptions of the Model I world. Where we differ is in the generative or causal mechanisms that we identify and in the attention we give to possibilities for changing the world as it exists.

One of the most popular topics in contemporary social psychology is the reasoning processes of everyday life (Nisbett and Ross, 1980; Einhorn and Hogarth, 1981). Much of this research has focused on the seeming errors and biases of social cognition. Not only are people prone to inferential errors, but they also reason in ways that cause errors to persist. New data are interpreted in terms of previously formed opinions, to the point that disconfirming data are ignored or misinterpreted. People act in ways that elicit data that confirm their opinions, and express great confidence in reasoning that has little validity. They are predisposed to attribute the behavior of others (but not their own) to dispositional traits.

Such findings are consistent with what we would expect from individuals programmed with Model I theory-in-use. These individuals see their own views as obvious and do not test them publicly. They make attributions about others from scanty data, act in ways that elicit data that they then interpret as confirming their attributions, and remain unaware of their responsibility for generating these data.

One of the most influential theorists of everyday interaction has proposed that people manage the presentation of self so as to establish a definition of the situation that controls how others will respond (Goffman, 1959). When events occur that disrupt the definition of the situation presented by a participant, the interaction breaks down. Participants often experience such breakdown as confusing, embarrassing, shameful, or infuriating. Hence, participants cooperate (collude?) to avoid disruption: "The person shows respect and politeness, making sure to extend to others any ceremonial treatment that might be their due. He employs discretion; he leaves unstated facts that might implicitly or explicitly contradict and embarrass the positive claims made by others. He employs circumlocutions and deceptions, phrasing his replies with careful ambiguity so that the others' face is preserved even if their welfare is not" (1967, pp. 16–17).

In our language, these are Model I strategies for the unilateral protection of self and others. The ways in which such strategies reinforce the self-sealing, error-reinforcing features of everyday reasoning should be obvious. Leaving unstated facts that might be threatening or embarrassing is a sure way to reduce the likelihood of double-loop learning.

In the field of organizational behavior, one prominent theme was first sounded by Cyert and March (1963), who pictured organizations as fields of conflict and bargaining among coalitions. Different groups have different preference orderings, and organizational goals are established through political maneuvering. The goals of an organization are frequently inconsistent, and the inconsistency is maintained by attending to the goals favored by different groups sequentially rather than simultaneously. Organizational goals are frequently nonoperational in the sense that they neither require nor preclude any particular behavior, because "nonoperational objectives are consistent with virtually any set of objectives" (p. 32). Hence by allowing organizational objectives to be inconsistent and nonoperational, it is possible to appear to satisfy more of the demands of different groups.

In our view, this is an accurate description of part of what takes place in a Model O-I world. There are inconsistencies in organizational theory-in-use, which are perceived in win-lose terms. Groups learn to protect themselves, to form coalitions with other groups to enhance their positions, and to withhold or distort information that may increase their vulnerability. These are the strategies characteristic of a limited learning system. They are rational within the constraints of an O-I world, and at the same time they inhibit the double-loop learning that might permit a better overall solution.

Model II Theory-in-Use

The action scientist is an interventionist, seeking not only to describe the world but to change it. More precisely, he or she seeks to help members of client systems reflect on the world they create and learn to change it in ways more congruent with the values and theories they espouse. The normative perspective that guides the action scientist is found in Model II (Argyris and Schön, 1974). Model II as an espoused theory is not new; indeed most people readily espouse it. But as a theory-in-use it is rare. The action scientist intends to produce action consistent with Model II, because it is by so doing that the counterproductive features of Models I and O-I can be interrupted. Just as action consistent with Models I and O-I creates threats to validity and inhibits learning, action consistent with Models II and O-II is hypothesized to enhance validity and learning. Model II provides an image of the theory-in-use that the action scientist as interventionist seeks to help clients learn.

The governing variables of Model II (Table 2) include (1) valid information, (2) free and informed choice, and (3) internal commitment. These are the features of the alternative worlds that action science seeks to create (Argyris, 1980). Creating conditions in which these values are realized is the primary task of the interventionist (Argyris, 1970).

The behavioral strategies of Model II involve sharing control with those who have competence and who participate in designing or implementing the action. Rather than unilateral advocacy (Model I) or inquiry that conceals the agent's own views (opposite Model I), in Model II the agent combines advocacy and inquiry. Attributions and evaluations are illustrated with relatively directly observable data, and the surfacing of conflict-

Table 2. Model II Theory-in-Use.

Governing Variables	Action Strategies	Consequences for the Behavioral World	Consequences for Learning	Consequences for Quality of Life	Effectiveness
Valid information.	Design situations or environments where participants can be origins and can experience high personal causation (psychological success, confirmation, essentiality).	Actor experienced as minimally defensive (facilitator, collaborator, choice creator).	Disconfirmable processes.	Quality of life will be more positive than negative (high authenticity and high freedom of choice).	Increased long-run effectiveness.
Free and informed choice.	Tasks are controlled jointly.	Minimally defensive interpersonal relations and group dynamics.	Double-loop learning.	Effectiveness of problem solving and decision making will be great, especially for difficult problems.	
Internal commitment to the choice and constant monitoring of its implementation.	Protection of self is a joint enterprise and oriented toward growth (speak in directly observable categories, seek to reduce blindness about own inconsistency and incongruity). Bilateral protection of others.		Public testing of theories.		

Source: Argyris and Schön, 1974.

Figure 3. Model O-II Learning Systems:
Facilitating Error Detection and Correction.

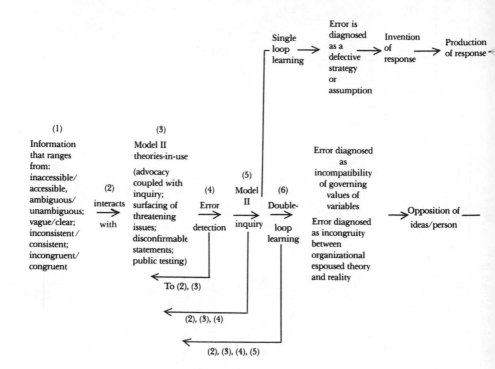

Source: Argyris, 1982.

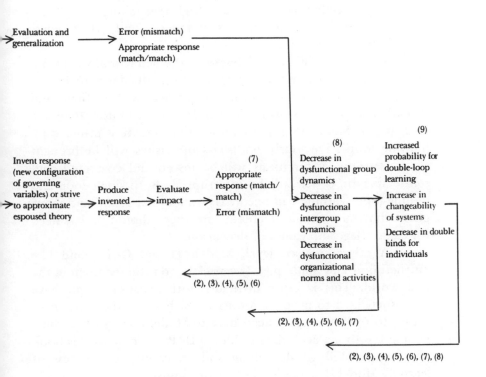

ing views is encouraged in order to facilitate public testing of them.

The consequences of Model II action strategies should include minimally defensive interpersonal and group relationships, high freedom of choice, and high risk taking. The likelihood of double-loop learning is enhanced, and effectiveness should increase over time.

Model O-II (Figure 3) describes the behavioral world created by individuals interacting on the basis of Model II theory-in-use. When members of organizations deal with difficult and threatening problems using Model II theory-in-use, they are engaging in Model II inquiry rather than creating primary inhibiting loops. Previously undiscussable issues will be brought to the surface, assumptions will be tested and corrected, and self-sealing processes will be interrupted. Both single-loop and double-loop learning can occur. Dysfunctional group and intergroup dynamics should decrease, and there should be less need for camouflage and games of deception.

At the espoused level, Models II and O-II sound like motherhood and apple pie. The trick is to produce them in the real world. This is quite difficult, both because people have been socialized to produce Model I and because the world continues to operate largely according to Model I, even when some people try to act according to Model II. Part Three of this book will be devoted to describing and analyzing the process of learning Model II at the level of theory-in-use.

Part Two

Practices, Methods, and Results of Normal Science and Action Science

Within the domain of normal science there are many different communities of inquiry, each with its own set of norms and practices. In this section, we will explore case examples from four such communities: experimental social psychology (Chapter Four); assessment research as it is used to study the fit between individual factors and organizational factors (Chapter Five); and both basic and applied ethnographic approaches as they are used to study educational contexts (Chapter Six).

In each case study we describe the researchers' approach to an important social problem: from obedience to authority, to satisfaction and productivity in the work place, to failure in the classroom. In doing so, we examine not only the methods and theoretical frameworks used but the operating assumptions that are embedded in them. We then explore the unintended consequences that result even when the researchers' thrust is implemented well, as is the case in each of these studies. Finally, we make suggestions on how some of these inner contradictions might be reduced, and we draw on case examples from action science to illustrate how these might be implemented.

After presenting the case studies, we then examine the different research approaches in light of the norms and rules that characterize the communities of inquiry in which the researchers work (Chapter Seven). We argue that researchers, like all practitioners, are bound by the rules and norms of their practice, and that these place researchers in dilemmas that cannot be resolved within their communities as they are now defined. Moreover, we try to show how the norms these researchers follow lead them to design their inquiry in such a way that the knowledge they produce is of limited use to practitioners. The basic researchers ask, "How does it happen to be?" And the applied researchers build on basic knowledge to pursue the question, "How do we achieve a given set of ends?" But both basic and applied researchers stop short of considering the practitioner's question, "How do I understand and act in real life contexts amidst all their complexity and dilemmas of value?"

In the final chapter to this section (Chapter Eight), we put forth the norms and rules that guide the practice of action science. Here we show how action science overlaps with and departs from more traditional norms of inquiry as it seeks to adapt these norms to the realm of social practice. We will show how this leads the action scientist to ask new questions, to use new methods, and to construct new solutions. We hope that these will suggest new ways of managing the dilemmas of practice—for both researcher and practitioner alike.

4

Beyond the Limitations of Normal Science: Comparing Laboratory Experiments and Action Experiments

Back in the 1960s in a couple of typical laboratory rooms at Yale, a research psychologist named Stanley Milgram conducted a series of experiments on obedience to authority (Milgram, 1974). Since then, many people have had a hard time figuring out whether we should be distressed more by what Milgram did or by what he found out. Few experiments, if any, have generated more controversy. On one side, proponents heralded it as the most important research in recent history; while on the other side, critics condemned it as the most unethical. While this debate still goes on, almost everyone agrees on one thing: Milgram's results were surprising, distressing, and important, because he found that ordinary people will obey authority even when it violates their most central values and leads them to harm others.

Milgram's experiment exemplifies social psychological inquiry into real-life dilemmas with nontrivial consequences. Experiments like Asch's (1952) on conformity, Latané and Darley's (1970) on the innocent bystander, and Zimbardo's on vandalism (1969) are all of the same genre. They look at actual moral dilemmas faced in everyday life; they uncover inconsistencies between the moral reasoning we espouse and our actual behavior; and they explore the consequences of this for both the actors and those around them. Because this research tackles such important problems, we might expect that it would yield more useful results than research that takes on issues of little social relevance or consequence. To a certain extent this is true, but even this kind of research leaves us hanging on the edge of the dilemmas it raises, not knowing how to climb beyond them.

At present, pointing to solutions is not the normative role taken by scientists, so this last statement may seem either unfair or irrelevant. One might argue that science is a two-step process. Scientists generate data and build theory first, and then let practitioners or applied social scientists figure out how to solve the problems. But this strict division between research, theory, and practice may have serious consequences for each endeavor. We may be conducting research and creating theory that would be difficult or even impossible to use to solve problems under real-life conditions. And practitioners may be acting with tacit propositions about the world that are not easily falsifiable and therefore fraught with errors that go undetected. Since the left hand doesn't know what the right one is doing, both risk making elegant but irrelevant gestures.

In this chapter we use Milgram's experiment to consider this possibility not because of its deficiencies but because of its strengths. Milgram makes explicit connections between what is studied in the laboratory and what occurs in everyday life; he devises and tests out multiple variations and hypotheses in order to understand the processes and conditions underlying obedience; and he offers an elegant and comprehensive theoretical framework in which to explain the different sources, mechanisms, and processes of obedience. We thus choose it not only because it is representative of other inquiries but because, as Milgram's obedient subjects might say, "If doing what we are supposed to do gets us into trouble, then we really do face a problem."

Obedience to Authority

In the first few pages of Milgram's study we encounter two dilemmas. First, persons who abhor hurting others will do so if ordered to by an authority. Second, while obedience is essential for social organization, it is also responsible for phenomena like the mass murder of Jews during the Second World War. One thus might be left wondering: If obedience is at once necessary *and* potentially destructive, what can we do about it? If Milgram's formulation is correct, we can do very little. But it may be that in trying to explain only what exists while not exploring what might exist, he offers an incomplete understanding of what obedience is and how we might resolve these dilemmas. To consider this possibility, let us look at how Milgram studied the problem of obedience and the theory he developed to account for it. In looking at both, we will ask two interrelated questions: What kind of learning does his methodology and knowledge generate, and what kinds of solutions are most likely to follow.

Obedience in the Laboratory. Milgram points out that it is a bit of a leap from the extermination camps in the Germany of 1940 to the Yale labs in today's United States. But in setting up his experimental situation, he tried to maintain the essential features and dilemmas of obedience to authority by constructing a situation in which a person is told by an authority to act against someone else. Using the experimental situation itself, Milgram thus devised the now famous scenario of an experimenter who ordered a naive subject to administer increasing amounts of shock to a confederate subject each time the confederate made a mistake on a learning task. Then he asked of the situation that he had contrived: How far will the subject go before refusing to carry out the experimenter's order?

Of course the confederate "learner" was not actually shocked, but the naive subjects didn't know this. Instead the subjects fully believed that they were taking part in an experiment on the effect of punishment on learning and that they were administering increasingly dangerous levels of shock to an actual learner. After all, the subjects had met the "learner"; they had seen him strapped into a chair in an adjoining room; they had watched as electrodes were attached to his wrists; they were placed behind an impressive shock generator with a range of volts from "slight shock" to "danger—severe shock"; and finally, to remove any doubts about what they were doing, they could hear the shouts and protests of the learner from the next room each time they administered a shock. Milgram thus set up a convincing scenario—so convincing that the subjects themselves were psychologically shocked to discover that it was all staged. As one subject exclaimed after being introduced to a nonplused "learner": "You're an actor, boy. You're marvelous! Oh, my God, what he [the experimenter] did to me. I'm exhausted. I didn't want to go on with it. You don't know what I went through here. A person like me hurting you, my God. I didn't want to do it to you. Forgive me, please. I can't get over this. My face is beet red. I wouldn't hurt a fly. I'm working with boys, trying to teach them, and I'm getting such marvelous results *without* punishment. I said to myself at the beginning, I don't feel you'll get anything by inflicting punishment" (Milgram, 1974, p. 82; italics his).

As this suggests, the subject was not only shocked to learn that the scenario was staged, she was also shocked to discover that while she didn't wish to hurt anyone, she had proceeded to the end of the board, where it read: "Danger—severe shock." Perhaps because of this, once the hoax was revealed, Milgram found that she and others tended to distance themselves from their responsibility for their actions. When asked why they continued, they explained that they did not believe the confederate subject was being hurt, they pointed out that an authority had required them to do so, they devalued the victim, or they cited some ideological justification for their actions. As one person put it, "In the interest of science, one goes through with it" (Milgram, 1974, p. 54).

Modifying this basic scenario, Milgram went on to examine the different mechanisms underlying obedience and to rule out alternative interpretations by varying experimental conditions. One set of variations focused on the variable of physical distance, and it was found that the more distance between the subject and the authority and the less distance between the subject and the learner, the less likely it would be that the subjects would obey. A second set of variations examined aggression as an alternative interpretation of the results. It showed that left to their own devices, subjects did not choose to shock the learner, a result that ruled out the intention to harm as a plausible explanation. A third set, which asked individuals to predict how they themselves or others would handle the situation, found that almost everyone predicted that they and others would disobey, suggesting a deep belief in their good intentions and their capacity for carrying them out in a stressful situation —a belief not borne out by how individuals actually behaved once in the situation. Finally, another variation changed who ordered the shock and who received and opposed it. For instance, in one such variation, a person with the *status* of an authority (the experimenter) was put in the *position* of a learner and strapped to the chair where he *acted* to oppose the shock. But regardless of the position or the action taken, the moment that someone with the status of authority commanded a certain action, most subjects obeyed.

But not everyone. A small percentage disobeyed, unilaterally refusing to go further and putting an end to the experiment. When told to continue, these subjects opposed the authority's commands (Milgram, 1974, p. 51):

Mr. Rensaleer: Well, I won't [continue]—not with the man screaming to get out.

Experimenter: You have no other choice.

Mr. Rensaleer: I do have a choice. (Incredulous and indignant) Why don't I have a choice? I came here on my own free will. . . .

Why Obedience? For Milgram "the fact most urgently demanding explanation" was the "extreme willingness" of most adults to act against another individual and their own values on the command of an authority (1974, p. 5). To explain this fact, Milgram concluded that while such unquestioning obedience may be "surprising and dismaying," it is nevertheless necessary for social organization. He argued that "the basic reason why [the suppression of local control] occurs is rooted not in individual needs but in organizational needs. Hierarchical structures can function only if they possess the quality of coherence, and coherence can be attained only by the suppression of control at the local level" (p. 131). Embedded in this explanation are two interrelated assumptions. The first is that there are only two ways of responding to an authority: either obey without question or unilaterally disobey, as the behavior of the subjects in his experiments in fact suggests. And the second follows from the first. If our only two options are obedience or unilateral disobedience, then it follows that social coherence would be contingent on obedience at the local level and the exertion of unilateral control at upper levels. Intuitively this makes much sense. In everyday organizational life people ordinarily do obey; and when they disobey, they usually do so unilaterally, often jeopardizing organizational coherence and survival as a result.

So herein lies the dilemma. The obedience that organizational life requires can result in anything from the little "murders" of everyday life to the mass murders in extreme situations. Hence a paradox: The very conditions deemed necessary for coherence can simultaneously create the incoherence of human suffering and slaughter. But suppose for a moment that it was possible to invent an alternative form of authority relations, one that does not yet exist but that might resolve this paradox. If this were possible, it would show that existing authority arrangements are not necessary, and it might aid us in resolving the existing dilemmas of obedience to authority. But Milgram did not submit this possibility to experimentation. In fact, the methods of the laboratory rule out such exploration. As a result, the descriptions these methods yield necessarily contain important limitations.

The Rules of the Laboratory. One rule of the laboratory is reflected in Milgram's account of his experiment. He writes that "the question arises as to whether there is any connection between what we have studied in the laboratory and the forms of obedience we so deplored in the Nazi epoch. . . . the differences ... are enormous, yet the difference may turn out to be relatively unimportant as long as certain essential features are retained. ... The question of generality, therefore, is not resolved by enumerating all the manifest differences between the psychological laboratory and other situations but by carefully constructing a situation that captures the essence of obedience" (1974, p. xii).

The logic here may be stated as follows: In order to reliably describe some phenomenon, one ought to retain its essential features and construct a situation that captures its essence. This is consistent with what Milgram actually did. The situations that he created replicated existing authority relationships, and he never called into question or tried to alter obedient responses under conditions conducive to them (closeness to authority and distance from learner). The basic assumption is that by replicating the world, we will generate a description of the phenomenon that can be generalized beyond the confines of the lab.

To a large extent we agree with this logic. But we believe that it simultaneously generates limits that most experimentalists are unaware of. One of the most important of these limits is that by not trying to alter what is, the experimentalist is unlikely to uncover the deep defensive structures that maintain existing social action and relationships. Such structures become evident only when existing social arrangements are threatened. It is at this point that our hidden defenses are mobilized and come to the surface, thereby opening up the possibility of inquiry into these structures and of transforming what is discovered. By replicating only what is, we can neither describe these defensive structures nor discover whether the social structures they maintain are in fact necessary. Only attempts at transforming what is can yield this knowledge.

But a second rule of the laboratory makes such attempts quite unlikely. As Milgram explains it: "Simplicity is the key to effective scientific inquiry. This is especially true in the case of subject matter with a psychological content. Psychological matter, by its nature, is difficult to get at and likely to have many more sides to it than appear at first glance. Complicated procedures only get in the way of clear scrutiny of the phenomenon itself. To study obedience most simply, we must create a situation in which one person orders another person to perform an observable action and we must note when obedience to the imperative occurs and when it fails to occur" (1974, p. 13).

We agree that simplicity is desirable and that complicated procedures can obscure a phenomenon. But the way simplicity is achieved in the laboratory can simultaneously confound phenomena and keep us from probing them fully. To simplify the question of obedience, Milgram focused on a limited number of variables, a priori defined and identified by him; and he had to conceal the experimental hypothesis and manipulation to avoid confounding the results. In so doing, he exerted a high degree of conceptual and situational control over the research context and the interactions that took place in it (see Cassell, 1982, for a discussion of different forms of research control). The problem is that this control, intended to minimize the effect of the experimenter and extraneous factors, can itself exert causal influence that threatens validity. Recall the subject with the beet-red face. She exclaimed, "Oh, my God, what he [the experimenter] did to me. I'm exhausted." Reactions like these suggest that the experimental hoax led subjects not only to feel distressed by their own actions but to feel that the experimenter's actions had set them up, leaving them publicly exposed and caught at violating their own values in a situation not of their own making. In short, they may have felt that someone had just pulled a fast one—which someone had—thereby influencing how the subjects accounted for their actions in the postexperimental interview. If so, then the actual experimenter may also have contributed to, and may in part have accounted for, the defensiveness and disclaimers of responsibility reflected in the subjects' self-reports.

Equally important from an action science perspective is that this form of control creates an additional limit on the kinds of inquiry possible. According to Milgram, obedience is highly learned in the course of socialization at home, at school, and at work. Over and over again we come across and internalize the axiom: "Do what the man in charge says" (1974, p. 138). Milgram continues, "Just as we internalize grammatical rules, and can thus both understand and produce new sentences, so we internalize axiomatic rules of social life which enable us to fulfill social requirements in novel situations" (p. 138).

We agree with this formulation. But suppose we now wished to discover whether these rules are alterable? First, our research suggests that altering rule-governed behavior requires commitment on the part of participants, and this in turn requires that they share control over the situation. Consequently, the variables participants identify, the meanings they impose on them, and the hypotheses they wish to test all must move to the foreground of the inquiry and can no longer be considered extraneous or be controlled unilaterally by the experimenter. Second, we have found that changing rule-governed behavior requires providing a kind of primary socialization process in which new routines for everyday life can be learned (Berger and Luckmann, 1966). This means that multiple opportunities must be provided for interrupting old rules, for experimenting with and reflecting on new ones, and for continuously reflecting on what's being learned. A few experimental manipulations would not be sufficient, and the unilateral control of the laboratory would be impossible.

Yet even if this control were possible, from our point of view it would not be desirable. Such control is more apt to foster than to alter obedient responses and diminished responsibility for one's actions. Two of the requisite conditions for obedience are the legitimacy and unilateral nature of authority relationships (Harmon, 1981; Milgram, 1974). If we wish to alter the nature and legitimacy of these relationships, we cannot do it in a context that is legitimately characterized by them. As Zuniga (1975) argued, "The epistemological strategy invariably generates the sociological one. . . . Scientists elevate the laboratory setting to the rank of ideal research paradigm. The problem is deciding whether it is the ideal representation of the power relations of a democratic society" (p. 110).

A third rule further limits our ability to alter what we describe. Theories developed in the social sciences are primarily meant to explain causal relationships, and social scientists avoid judging what is from a moral standpoint. Milgram is no exception. His intention was to understand, not to judge or to prescribe. The latter is the task of the normative realm, best pursued by practitioners or moral philosophers. Milgram adhered to this prevailing view: "The dilemma inherent in obedience to authority is ancient, as old as the story of Abraham. What the present study does is to give the dilemma contemporary form by treating it as subject matter for experimental inquiry and with the aim of understanding rather than judging it from a moral standpoint" (1974, p. xi).

This view makes good sense, given that most individuals judge the subjects in Milgram's experiment to be either sadistic or morally reprehensible. As we saw earlier, Milgram's data suggest that neither is the case. Unless commanded to do so, his subjects never chose to hurt the learner, and they were extremely distressed by their own behavior. Such judgments are thus inaccurate. But most important, they may lead individuals to underestimate their own potential to act similarly under similar circumstances. For this reason, an emphasis on understanding over moral evaluation is welcome.

Even so, we ought not to abandon moral evaluation altogether. Unless we take the stance that subjects truly had no choice, we might still evaluate the consequences of the choices they did make and the reasoning that led to their choices. In Milgram's attempt to steer clear of moral evaluation, he took a different perspective, emphasizing the causal impact of situational factors. In so doing he avoided a negative judgment, but he may have inadvertently lent credibility to the belief that we have no choice but to obey, a belief that may reinforce obedience, when we do not know if this is the case. We have not yet tested whether we might alter obedient responses in the face of situational factors that at present are conducive to obedience.

Normative theory does not require the moralizing character of Milgram's observers. One kind of normative stance may help us both describe the world and plot our course out of the dilemmas that we encounter in it. For instance, critical theory argues that it may be possible to use participants' own principles as the basis for moral critiques (Geuss, 1981). In Milgram's experiment, subjects faced competing principles or requirements, thereby generating the dilemma of obedience. They wished to simultaneously satisfy the principles of loyalty to authority and of responsibility to others—hence the stress they experienced both during and after the experiment. It therefore was not a simple case of not putting one's principles into practice but a case of conflicting principles that in the eyes of the subjects demanded a choice among polar actions: either obey or disobey. To the extent that subjects took responsibility for their actions, they evaluated their own actions negatively. Their dilemma was that they knew of no way to act that would allow them to resolve their conflict. But what if we were able to invent an alternative that would make this possible? Such an alternative would not only tell us something important about the nature of our social world (existing arrangements are not necessary), but it would also tell us how we might reconstruct that world to make it more livable.

What We Learn. Milgram's experiment yields knowledge that might be used at the levels of insight, action, and structural change. At each level the learning is important yet insufficient for resolving the core dilemma of obedience that Milgram describes.

• Insight as inoculation. Milgram's most important finding was that even well-intentioned people will harm others if ordered to do so by an authority. Yet most of us are unaware of this potential, showing that we have "little insight into the web of forces that operate in a real situation" (Milgram, 1974, p. 30). This suggests that, given the right circumstances, the best of us are capable of acting against others and our values and that we are unaware of this. Since forewarned is forearmed, we might now be on the lookout for such circumstances. And like some of Milgram's subjects, we might now try to deal more effectively with the value conflicts we encounter in these circumstances.

But such insight alone cannot solve the dilemma of obedience. Once we encounter a value conflict, we still must find some way to negotiate it more effectively. Yet if Milgram is right, this would require interrupting years of socialization to "do what the man in charge says," our predisposition to turn our sense of responsibility over to an authority, and organizational norms and structures that foster both. Moreover, it is not enough just to counter these norms and disobey; it is necessary to find actions that pose true alternatives to them, that is, actions that can resolve the dilemma rather than oscillate between its two poles.

   • Disobedience as an alternative action. In the extreme situations that Milgram had in mind, it makes good sense to unilaterally disobey. But in everyday life we encounter less extreme but nevertheless thorny dilemmas of obedience. We are asked to discipline a subordinate against our own judgment; we are told to support a policy we believe is discriminatory; we are warned that if we wish to get ahead, we have to conduct quick and dirty studies that violate our own standards. Each time we go along, we learn how to give up a little bit of ourselves, while telling ourselves: "That's how things work" or "I had no choice—it's publish or perish." There is much validity to these responses. It is indeed how things work, norms for getting ahead do exist, and individuals may not know how to manage these realities without continuing to perpetuate them. So in small increments we also learn how to give up some of our sense of personal responsibility, making larger increments more tolerable and more likely.

   These situations can serve as practice grounds for more extreme ones. Yet under these conditions, disobedience may create more problems than it solves. As Milgram suggests, if we each act unilaterally on the basis of our own discretion alone, we may do more to promote social chaos than personal responsibility. The view that obedience is necessary would soon be reaffirmed, and pleas for law and order would reassert themselves. If so, then the unilateral disobedience that is necessary in extreme situations may also be conducive to creating them. To prevent the extreme conditions might require alternatives to existing responses that normal science cannot at present discover.

   • Structural change as prevention. Milgram's results do suggest ways we might alter situations or structures, so that we might at least modify the problem of obedience. We saw earlier in Milgram's experiment that the less distance between subject and victim and the more distance from an authority, the less likely subjects were to shock the learner. Embedded in this finding is the idea of creating structures that increase our distance from authorities. Conceivably individuals at the local level could make judgments and render decisions based on information immediately available to them at that level. If adopted, this solution would transfer a good deal of authority to the local level.

Within existing hierarchical structures, it is unclear what would lead authorities to design their organizations in ways that would diminish their control. But suppose they did. To ensure coordination, individuals would still need to negotiate and resolve the conflicting judgments apt to arise from significantly different informational bases. If polarization or working at cross purposes is to be avoided, then individuals must still find some way of *acting* within these structures that would allow them to resolve conflicting views and values. Therefore, even if these structures were adopted, effective implementation would depend on initiating new actions. Structural change alone would not be sufficient.

To genuinely resolve the dilemma of obedience, it is not sufficient to simply oscillate between the two requirements that comprise it: personal responsibility and social coherence. But in studying obedience, Milgram assumed the necessity of what exists, and consequently kept his experiments within existing arrangements and responses. As a result his experiments could not yield knowledge that might help individuals break out of this oscillation between the conflicting demands that are the basis of the dilemma. We never learn of alternatives that might better manage it, and we do not discover the deep structures that maintain it. In fact, by replicating only what is, we may learn more about how to produce obedience than how to solve the dilemma it yields.

Beyond Obedience

But what if we now wished to consider the question of whether obedience is in fact necessary? As suggested previously, this would require that we create an alternative universe in two respects: a universe that departs from prevailing experimental contexts *and* that diverges from the real-life contexts in which obedience is the norm. In our view such contexts are consistent with Models I and O-I. In seminars designed to help students learn to act consistently with Models II and O-II, we seek to transform existing norms such as obedience and the unilateral control of the person in charge over subjects. Since our subjects are usually programmed with Model I competencies and therefore create O-I learning contexts, these seminars are a fertile domain for experiments designed to at once explore and transform the status quo.

What follows is a description of one such experiment that focused on obedience and how we might better understand and move beyond it. More specifically, it examined an incident in which a participant (a student) was faced with a request made by an authority (the instructor). In doing what the person in charge said, the participant went against his own view of what was right, and he came to regard himself as no longer responsible for his actions. Recall that these are the features thought by Milgram to capture the essence of obedience to authority. But in the action science experiment, the aim was to probe and to reconstruct those essential aspects of our social world that simultaneously yield desirable and undesirable effects. We therefore have an opportunity to see what an experiment with these aims looks like and to consider the knowledge it yields. The incident of obedience itself occurred within a larger action experiment designed to help participants see their actions and the risks of experimentation differently. It came to be called the *passivity experiment,* and it was set in motion by the instructor after he discovered a pattern of withdrawal that he thought was undermining the students' learning process. It took place toward the beginning of the seminar's second semester; we enter as the experiment began, so that we can set the context for our inquiry into obedience.

Passivity Experiment. At the beginning of the semester's third session, the instructor opened the class by saying that he wished to initiate an experiment. He then went on to make two inferences about the group, publicly testing to see if the group would confirm them:

> Okay, another one of my experiments. What I'd like to do is start by making two attributions about this class, which I'd like to test out, if I may.
>
> One, since our time is scarce, there is an issue of justice. Most of you believe you should not take more air time than however you measure your fair share. Is there anyone who'd disagree with that attribution? [People confirm.]
>
> And another one was that Paul, when he began, had the equivalent of what many of you might have felt was a fair share, regardless of whether you agreed with the way he began or not. [Most agreed; some said he took more than his fair share.]
>
> I then said: "Who would like to go first?" Utter silence. [Paul] looked at me; I looked at him. I looked around three or four times. Paul looked around. He finally took over.
>
> I want to know: How come? What's the dynamic here that says the guy who's already had enough air time is now asked to even use more?

The instructor opened the experiment by publicly identifying a puzzling process in the group and testing to see if the inferences that comprised it were accurate. Once others confirmed them, he then inquired into the puzzle, and a range of new data came forth about how individuals saw participation in the class. To summarize, they said the following kinds of things:

> "I feel I should say something smart or the instructor will attack me."
> "I feel I'm hiding out and easing in."
> "I'm waiting for someone to make a mistake to see what the instructor will do."
> "I'm confused about where to begin."

"I felt my intervention had to be perfect, and I had no
model of perfect."

"I don't want to appear stupid."

"I feel on the spot, like I'm breaking ice."

"I feel the need to warm up before making an intervention."

"I have a sense of impending embarrassment."

As these data suggest, individuals had been making and
holding a range of inferences about themselves, the instructor,
and what it meant to participate. In response, the instructor
tried to determine what had led to these reactions, inquiring
into what had happened and how the students had gone from
these data to their conclusions. As he did so, he checked to see
to what extent reactions were shared or differed. Through such
a process participants came to learn that the instructor had unintentionally contributed to the first person's fear of being attacked, and they saw how the class had reinforced the instructor's actions by not confronting the instructor at the time.

Later on in the experiment the instructor began to build
on these early discoveries by developing a parallel between how
participants had responded to him and how they had responded
to an authority in a case discussed the previous week. In that
case a director and her staff had become polarized over who was
responsible for the internal problems in a counseling program,
each unilateraally blaming the other and deflecting attempts to
examine his or her own responsibility. Nevertheless, of the total
responses, 65 percent of the students held the authority responsible, calling the director closed, defensive, and blind to her impact on her staff. From these data and those from the class, the
instructor began to speculate out loud that many group members might hold those in positions of authority more responsible
than they held themselves or subordinates, leading them to
react to those in power with a combination of hostility and passivity. On the one hand, they might not approve of what the authorities do, and they might privately make negative attributions about them (he'll attack me, she's controlling). On the
other hand, however, they might regard authorities as primarily

in control and responsible for these problems, thus going along and remaining unaware of how their passivity contributes to the problem.

An Individual Confronts an Authority. Throughout this inquiry the instructor played an active role in bringing to the surface and examining these issues and the dilemmas they posed for everyone's attempts to learn. But unlike an experimenter in a laboratory, the instructor made his hypotheses public and enlisted the participants' help in inquiring into them. It was the instructor's view that such moves would serve to explore participants' passivity while simultaneously helping them to break out of it. But one participant, George, took a different view. He thought these moves might inadvertently exacerbate the very passivity they were intended to remedy. He thus confronted the instructor, calling his experiment into question:

George: Can I say something about process? I'd like to tie together my reactions to what just happened to the dilemma you raised about how can you help us become less passive. It seems to me that the way you shifted gears, and even overrode what I think was going to be an objection by Donna, to continue what you call "the experiment," you were exercising unilateral control.

Instructor: Yes.

George: I feel that in a more subtle way you've been doing that throughout the entire class in that you put on the agenda the issue of our passivity, thereby displacing other things that might have been on our agenda, like the case that we prepared.

Instructor: Right.

George: My sense is that to the extent that you do that, you will continue to find us behaving in passive ways, because we then learn that the behavioral cues for what happens in here come from you.

Instructor: Let's check it out with others.

In this interchange a student confronts authority by asserting that the instructor is acting unilaterally in directing the attention of the class members to their passivity and displacing the case they had prepared. On the basis of this inference, he then goes on to predict that the instructor will foster the very passivity he wishes to eliminate. If so, the instructor would be acting contrary to his intentions, and he might inadvertently be hindering the ability of the class to learn.

To discover whether this was the case, the instructor first asked for others' reactions instead of asserting a view of his own. In this way data could be generated on how others saw his actions and the experiment, and the predisposition to fall in line with the view of an authority might be minimized. As Milgram's data also suggest, once a peer confronts an authority, it is less likely that a group will automatically continue to do what the person in charge says, and it is more likely that they will start to question the authority (1974, pp. 116-121). In an action science experiment, the instructor therefore encourages this continued confrontation by eliciting such reactions from others.

An Authority Confronts a Student. Even so, the instructor does not automatically accept the views of participants as valid. Instead, when another student, Paul, agrees with George's critique, the instructor calls Paul's view into question in the same way he has invited the students to question his:

Paul: I think [what George says] makes a lot of sense. I think it would have been preferable if you had raised the issue of our passivity as one we wanted to discuss or not discuss.

Instructor: How do you raise the issue of passivity with people you attribute to be passive?

And he then turned to George to see if he could produce such an alternative:

Instructor: Could you give a for instance, George, of how I might have done this?

George: One way [*pauses*]. I think it's a dilemma, so let me say that.

Instructor: You said that.

George: You're in a dilemma because you have knowledge to impart to us that may empower us, namely, the perception that we are passive. In order to impart that knowledge it may be necessary to exercise unilateral control. That's possible. I think the suggestion [from Paul] that you check with us whether we felt the need to discuss [it was a good one].

Instructor: Could you produce that?

In this excerpt, the instructor inquires into the alternative put forth by Paul by asking that it be produced. He thus neither accepts nor rejects the competing claim automatically, but rather asks that it be illustrated, so that he and the group might judge for themselves whether it solves the passivity dilemma. As this suggests, breaking out of passivity is not sufficient in the instructor's view. It is also necessary to submit the assertions of the students to the same scrutiny that he submits his. By taking this line, he implicitly rejects the notion that either he or his students have the right to unilaterally impose their views on the other.

An Individual Obeys. But from George's point of view, the instructor's request was problematic, since he was unaware of a way out of the dilemma and felt he could not say so. As he revealed the next week, he privately reacted by thinking, "Yikes. What do I say?" while publicly restating that it was a dilemma. So when the instructor again asked him to produce an alternative, George did as requested, role playing the following intervention:

George: I have a sense that there's an unspoken norm in here that people should take no more than their fair share of the time. Check that out, which you did. I further sense that you think that Paul took at least that amount of time last week. Check that out. For me that points out the dilemma that I think that many people had an opportunity to speak, no one did, and therefore Paul was in a sense stepping into a vacuum that was created by—I attribute—your passivity. My sense is that poses a problem for your learning, it poses a problem for this class. I think it would be worthwhile spending some time at the beginning of this class discussing that issue. Do others of you share that perception?

Instructor: [*To the class*] What's your view?

Miscellaneous voices: Sure. Yeah.

The alternative given here begins by making and testing inferences in much the same way the instructor did. But it departs at the end by explicitly asking whether the group thinks passivity is a worthy issue to pursue. As he did previously, the instructor responded to the alternative by first eliciting others' views and then stating and inviting reactions to his own. He then put forth how he saw his own actions in relation to the group:

> My view was that you didn't have a choice about Donna's case. You didn't have a choice about the short case. You didn't have a choice about the third long case. Okay?
>
> I said, "This is not set in concrete." But nobody said, "I don't want to do any of the other two." I got assent, "Go ahead, if you're doing something that's useful, we'll go along with it. If it's not, we'll tell you so." So my view is that I was staying within the assent I got from this group.

The instructor confirms that he did not give the kind of choice that George suggested he should have given, yet he implies that it was not necessary. He assumed that he continued to enjoy the assent of the group, since his agenda was not set in concrete and no one told him to stop. The instructor and the students thus have a different notion of choice and of who is responsible for generating it. From the students' point of view they ought to be explicitly asked whether or not they wish to pursue an issue. From the interventionist's perspective, however, there was a standing invitation to confront whatever was problematic, and this invitation was continuously reinforced. In his view, to add to this might have been to give the kind of choice that entraps students, because it could lead them to rely on such invitations before confronting authorities. This alternative might make the passivity dilemma even worse.

Instead of acting as he did, the interventionist might have uncritically accepted the alternative of the students because, in asserting it, they had broken out of their passivity. But to do so would be to implicitly encourage the alternative that "anything goes according to the discretion of those at local levels"; and, as Milgram argued, such a norm would undermine any possibility for coordinating conflicting views, and it would surely be unrealistic in real-life contexts. So for the instructor in this case, the experiment had just begun. In this view the moves taken by the students to overcome their passivity were insufficient for solving the dilemma. They were still based on the a priori premise that all authorities are unilaterally responsible for and in control of a process that subordinates require permission to affect. As long as this framing of the situation remained, it was unlikely that the students would be able to negotiate their conflicting views with authorities beyond the classroom. So instead of accepting their alternative, the instructor continues to ask that they put forth and illustrate their views. And as they do so, he continues to critique them, to say where his own views diverge from theirs, and to encourage others to critique his views.

An Individual and an Authority Confront Each Other. In response, George did continue to confront the instructor, at one point saying that while he recognized the validity of what the instructor had done, he thought that it put him in a dilemma:

George: My dilemma is this. It's certainly valid to do [what you did]. I think that for me this may well help to attain the goal that you espouse, to make us less passive. But I think the dilemma is one of form and content. To the extent that you define the agenda, namely, our passivity, and you essentially assert your view of it, you put yourself in the position that you did very early on in the first class, saying, "You're incompetent. I'm here telling you that, because I have a broader view, more experience, and am more competent."

Although the espoused message is, "I want you to become more competent," I think the experience for me is one of being in a situation defined by you in which you are judging me. And so although I think I intellectually get something from it which may empower me (if I'm able to practice it), the experiential learning of this class is one of continuing to be passive, and your choosing to put me in that role.

Instructor: That's helpful. If that's how others of you are experiencing it, it's important for me to know, because I don't think it is possible for me to design experiments that will reduce your passivity. I don't think that doing what you produced would have [altered the group's passivity]. . . . I don't believe that your not having control over the first three sessions means you're going to be passive, especially if part of the strategy on my part is to confront the passivity. I think you believe it will make you more passive.

George: Yes.

Instructor: One way is to test it and see what happens in the interaction as we're going.

George claims that the instructor's actions are responsible for his experience of passivity. In his view the instructor has chosen to put him in a passive role, and has unilaterally defined the agenda and asserted his view of the problem. In neither case does George illustrate or test his assertions, and in fact the data are that the instructor did publicly test his view of the problem and others confirmed it (see the initial intervention). George therefore acts in the very way he says the authority ought not to act. He "essentially asserts [his] view of it," he "puts [himself] in the position [of] saying, 'You're incompetent,' " and he puts the instructor in a "situation defined by [him] in which [he is] judging [the instructor]." This is the essence of social injustice. George requires of another what he does not require of himself under similar conditions, in this instance that they share control over the situation. Moreover, George's version of what occurred is inaccurate, and it is based on his own private experience, thereby making his view of truth nonnegotiable and rendering social justice unattainable.

In contrast, the instructor continues to confront George and to defend his own position, while keeping his views open to refutation. He states his views explicitly: "I don't think that doing what you produced would have done anything." He recognizes that there are competing views, and he suggests that they submit their different views to test: "One way is to test it and see what happens." This test is of a public nature. It asks that they search for data that everyone in the group can verify, and it consequently allows others to share control over the way the situation is defined. In so doing the instructor demonstrates an alternative to passively doing what he says or unilaterally going against his views. His actions imply the norm: Submit competing claims to public test and critique. This norm provides an alternative to the "chief axiom" cited by Milgram as "do what the man in charge says" (1974, p. 138).

Interrupting Existing Norms and Defenses. As George's assertions were critiqued in this way, existing norms and defenses began to emerge. At one point George defended his view by explaining that his intervention was designed to do what the man in charge said. As he put it:

> I tried to design an intervention of the kind
> that I think you [the instructor] wanted. I think
> my instincts about how to handle this would be a
> little different altogether.

Like Milgram's subjects, George explains that he designed his actions, not to suit his beliefs but to suit the authority's request. But unlike Milgram's experimenter, the experimenter in this case sought not only to understand such responses but to probe them in a way that would bring to the surface and work through the defenses that maintain them. So just as he called into question the students' passivity, he now questioned the tacit rules embedded in the way George acted:

> But there are two problems with your pre-
> sentation. One is that the foundation of it is what
> you feel. [And the] other is that I've said, "Would
> you produce this?" And you produced something

that you thought I wanted, not something that you would do. That says to me: If that's your psychological state and if you now put that in your generalization, then I think that people like you would in fact not learn from behavior like mine.

If you're so programmed to do for me what you think I want, even if it's not yours, then I'm not sure I'm ready to trust your feelings, unless you are ready to say, "These are the feelings of a person who when asked to produce something produces something that he thinks the professor wants, even when it's not what he wants."

The instructor suggests that there are two rules embedded in George's method of putting forth his position. The first is that he bases his views on his feelings alone, and the second is that he designs what he does to fit what the authority wants. He then builds on this by predicting that such rules will make it difficult for George to be trusted or to learn. The instructor's moves are thus aimed at extracting the tacit rules embedded in participants' actions and at showing how they necessarily lead to consequences that they themselves cannot accept. To the extent that individuals confirm this logic, they usually abandon their position and reconsider the norms or rules embedded in their actions. But ordinarily they do not confirm such logic without first defending their own, and such was the case with George. In response to the instructor's critique, George mobilized several lines of defense, each one deflecting his responsibility for the actions and outcomes that the instructor had described. Yet each time George brought forth a new line of defense, the instructor rendered his new position unacceptable by George's own standards.

To illustrate, George's assertions are followed by the instructor's moves to critique them. Notice that each time the instructor points out a gap in George's position, George switches to a new one and the instructor follows by pointing out new gaps:

George: I felt you were asking me to model Paul's suggestion. I wasn't endorsing it.

Instructor: What does it take to get you to never be put in a situation to endorse something that isn't you?

In his initial defense, George explains that he simply modeled Paul's suggestion but did not endorse it, as if this made it acceptable. But when the interventionist questions George's willingness to endorse something that is not his, George evokes a second line of defense in which he asserts that he had no choice but to do so:

George: You asked me to produce Paul's suggestion, not my own. If you had asked me to do my own, I wouldn't have acted as I did.

Instructor: You could have said, "Sorry, I'm not going to produce what he said. I'll produce what I want to produce."

Here George defends his actions by saying that he had no choice, but the instructor points out how George might have refused, thus disconfirming George's assertion. Once George sees this, he abandons this second line of defense and takes up the defense that he was only doing what is socially acceptable:

George: I think I can account for what I did as just being courteous enough to give a response, rather than a program to do what you want.

Instructor: If you know me, that's about the most discourteous thing you can do. The most courteous is to say, "You're asking me the wrong question."

By appealing to social mores, George evokes yet a third defense. But by saying that he regarded it as an insult, the instructor again makes George's defense problematic, since he shows how George's actions yielded the opposite of what he had intended.

This quick switching of defensive moves requires a good deal of fancy footwork, yet it should also suggest the consistency of George's actions. That is, even though he switches positions, a consistent logic runs through them. In each case he is in one way or another asserting either that he was not responsible for what he did or that what he did was the right thing to do. His first defensive position was that "it's not mine"; here, he simply tried to disown his intervention. When the instructor then showed how this position itself was problematic, he switched to the defensive position of "no choice," attributing responsibility to the instructor. And when the instructor disconfirmed this, he then switched to the position that he was "doing the right thing," simply being courteous, thus asserting that his actions were not as problematic as the instructor believed. But as we saw, the instructor pointed out that if that was his intention, it had backfired. With his defensive moves blocked by his own criteria, George begins to look inward for his own responsibility but only in glimmers. He reflects: "I didn't want to answer the question but somehow felt required to, perhaps because of some tacit theory of learning." But as illustrated in the dialogue that follows, it is not until his peers start to identify gaps in his position that he begins a process of actively reconsidering his actions.

Peers Confront a Peer. After much discussion, George continued to take the stance that, regardless of his alternatives, his initial critique had validity. At this point his peers began to question whether his assertion could stand up in light of what had actually happened during that class:

George: [*Summarizing*] : I had a criticism of what you did. And I think that I want to maintain that criticism regardless of the viability of any of the alternatives that I can come up with. The criticism was "people don't become less passive by your telling them that they are passive."

Tim: Maybe some people do, some people don't.

David: Yeah, I guess that's my reaction. The data for the rest of this meeting, at least the way I've seen it, is that a number of people have in fact become less passive as the meeting was worn on.

George: Not, I don't think, because of what the instructor did.

David: How could you possibly separate that out?

George: Well, by looking at when they became less passive.

Joe: What would you attribute that to, if not to the instructor?

George: Can I ask you [David] first when you think that happened?

David: It's puzzling to me, George, because my response actually when the instructor accused us of being passive was not to entrench. But was kind of, along Model I lines, "Oh, yeah? If you're going to point the finger and tell me I'm passive, I'll show you." So it would be a correct strategy for provoking someone like me to get involved.

Vince: Except that if you have to wait for the other person to provoke. The warning for you, Dave, has to be to see what happened, and say: Why did I have to wait for the instructor to provoke me, because if the next time someone has to provoke you, then you haven't learned very much.

David: Well, consider this. What was most uncomfortable was a certain recognition. He asked me to confirm something: "You wanted to cover your ass and bow out and withdraw from the group." And I had to confirm that. Once I confirmed it, I didn't like it. It wasn't something I was going to accept in myself. So, that was a challenge for me to involve myself. Once it was surfaced and discussed, it became more difficult for me to be passive.

This interchange starts out with George reiterating his claim, but this time a peer confronts him as if to say: "You might be right, you might be wrong, but we don't know yet." From here they go on to inquire into each other's views and to describe their own reactions in ways suggestive of the alternative norm put forth by the instructor: Submit competing claims to critique and test. For example, once Tim opened the possibility that George might be wrong, David came in and cited some data to suggest that this might indeed be the case: "A number of people have in fact become less passive as the meeting has worn on." Then when George asserts that this is not attributable to what the instructor did, others do not counter with an assertion of their own but ask how he arrived at that view: How could you separate out the influence of the instructor, and to what would you attribute the decrease in passivity?

When George does not answer but inquires further into David's position, David does not resist the inquiry. Rather he reports how he himself reacted to the instructor by feeling, "Oh yeah? If you're going to point the finger and tell me I'm passive, I'll show you." He thus describes at a low level of inference the way in which the instructor's actions affected how he felt, only then concluding that it was a "correct strategy" for someone like him. Once David's reactions were made public, they could be readily critiqued, and another participant, Vince, did so by pointing to their implications: David might have to wait to be provoked into action. Rather than deny this possibility or switch positions, David remains open in the sense that he stays with his position and describes it further, thus defending it in a way that provides others continued access to what it was based on, so that they might accept or reject it independently.

Thus, defensive maneuvers and the predisposition to automatically go along are not as evident in this protocol. Participants provide others access to their reactions rather than cover them up. They not only put forth their views but describe the data on which they are based. And most important, they do not prematurely accept or reject either position but critique and inquire into the competing views being considered. In so doing they follow the same norms of action science that the instructor follows. But because they are peers, they can provide data that the instructor cannot. Moreover, because of George's stance toward authority, their views may carry a weight that the instructor's do not.

An Individual Reflects on His Own Responsibility. In the week that followed, George listened to a tape recording of the session and considered what he heard in light of the questions posed in the experiment. As he did so, he began to see to what extent he had "laid a trap" for himself. He saw that, rather than acknowledge that he knew of no alternative, he had chosen to cover this up by producing one that approximated Paul's suggestion, thereby setting in motion the rest of the process. And as he listened further, he also saw ways in which the instructor had contributed to his defensiveness. He wrote down what he had discovered and returned to the class the following week to reflect publicly on his new understanding of what had occurred. First, he described the reactions that he had kept private the previous week and how this had led him to lay a trap for himself. He then identified ways in which the instructor had not fully explored his own position and how this had contributed to, rather than interrupted, his defensiveness. And, finally, when asked what the instructor should do differently, he proposed an alternative of his own. In this session, then, he focused on his own responsibility as well as the instructor's, and he made his own views confrontable as he confronted others. By doing so he broke out of the responses that had reinforced his unawareness the previous week, and he helped the instructor to do the same.

Results. But what are we to make of the outcome of this experience? The aim of an action science experiment is to describe and to transform those aspects of our social world that present us with blind spots, dilemmas, and constraints of which we are unaware. In this particular case the instructor wished to discover and to unfreeze what had caused the students' passivity, that is, what had caused them to do what the person in charge said, even when it went against their beliefs, and then to hold the authority responsible for what occurred. Implicit in such aims are the criteria by which we evaluate the results of this experiment. We thus ask: Do participants and instructor show in their actions and reflections a new way of seeing themselves and others that will enable them to transform this passivity?

The data on what happened with George and his peers suggest that the experimental hypotheses were affirmed. As a consequence of the instructor's interventions, individuals came to see themselves in a new way. David recognized his passivity for the first time, while George came to see how he had "laid a trap" for himself. Neither discovery was acceptable to them, but both ended up taking responsibility for his behavior. They confirmed the instructor's attributions, and they did not think that what they discovered was solely a product of what the instructor said or did, despite George's initial efforts to make them do so. Once they were aware of their responsibility for these results, the unacceptability of what they saw provided the impetus for new actions. David became more active, and George made his views more vulnerable to testing. We therefore see evidence of new understandings in their actions, as they not only report new insights but act consistently with them.

At the same time the experiment yields a rich description of the participants' passivity. By calling into question their passive responses, the instructor discovered that students tacitly framed authorities as significantly more in control and responsible than they themselves were. Moreover, they assumed a priori that this view was correct. With the authority's role thus framed, we could see how their own role would become that of passive recipients of the authority's actions. Later on, as the experiment unfolded further and George responded to the instructor's critique, we then uncovered some of the tacit rules that both followed from and helped to maintain a passive framing of one's role—rules such as "Do what the person in charge says" and "Base your assertions on your private experiences alone." Finally once these rules themselves were brought into the open and challenged, defenses that might otherwise have remained hidden were mobilized, as George deftly moved from one defensive position to another: "It's not mine," "I had no choice," and "I was just doing what is socially acceptable." Yet equally important from an action science point of view is the discovery that individuals can begin to enact a very different norm, one that asks them to submit competing claims to public test and inquiry. By the end of the experiment more participants had come to take an active role in critiquing and inquiring into competing views, no longer simply accepting or rejecting them.

This experiment at once brought to light the deep structures maintaining obedience and sought to enact a norm that might render obedience unnecessary for social coherence. The results of the experiment suggest that it might be possible to enact very different authority relationships from those assumed by Milgram (1974) to be necessary. If so, it means that the dilemma posed by the conflicting requirements of obedience and social cohesion might be better managed. But to explore this possibility requires not only that individuals discover their existing responses but that they try out fundamentally new ones, and this in turn requires that the researcher create conditions that go beyond the norms of mainstream science. He has to create an experimental universe that adheres to fundamentally different norms from those found either in the laboratory or in the work place.

In What Sense Was This an Experiment?

The first purpose of experiments is to induce individuals to act in a predicted manner or to choose not to do so. In this sense the episode just described was an experiment because the instructor acted in ways that he predicted would help to reduce obedience or would permit individuals to choose not to alter their behavior.

The second purpose of experiments is to produce empirical generalizations that remain valid beyond the experimental context. The strategy is to formulate hypotheses that, if not disconfirmed, become empirical generalizations. The hypotheses of this experiment may be formulated as follows: Under Model II conditions it is possible to reduce individuals' Model I automatic predispositions to unquestioned obedience in such a way that the participants will report that their sense of order and governance within the seminar are at least not harmed, and probably strengthened.

This hypothesis requires that we can establish that at least three conditions occurred. The first of these is to show that the participants (read subjects in the experiment) did act with unquestioned obedience toward the instructor when such obedience was not required by him. The transcripts do show, we suggest, that the participants did act in such a way and that many of them admitted doing so. Moreover, some not only admitted acting obediently but held the instructor at least partially responsible for their behavior.

The instructor explored the possibility that he had contributed to the students' passivity because the experimental manipulation required that he not induce obedience in the participants. And, after critical inquiry, the group came to hold themselves responsible for their obedient actions.

The second condition is to show that the instructor behaved consistently with Model II. In this particular instance this required the instructor to confront and inquire into obedient responses, while exploring the possibility that through his actions he might be unknowingly fostering such responses.

The third condition is to see whether the participants' obedient responses were reduced, while not simultaneously reducing the order and governance of the group. This task makes this experiment more complex and difficult than Milgram's. In most experiments it is assumed that subjects have the skills to produce the responses required by the experiment. For example, Milgram's experiment depended on the subjects' being able to understand orders, observe the individuals in pain, and carry out whatever decision they chose: to shock or not to shock. These skills are so obviously held by most adults that Milgram, correctly so, took them for granted. Experiments are not usually designed so that they require the subjects to use skills they do not have.

In our experiment to reduce obedience, the opposite was the case. The participants were skilled in producing, not reducing, obedience. If the experimental manipulation (creating Model II conditions) was to succeed in reducing obedience, the participants would have to acquire abilities that they did not have. These included the abilities to become aware of their automatic actions toward obedience and to learn action skills that they did not yet have, such as confronting authority in ways that ensured personal responsibility and the continued self-governance of the group.

Moreover, becoming aware of their automatic actions and their lack of skills to create the behavioral worlds they value tends to be threatening to individuals. This means that the participants in our experiment would also have to become aware of the defenses that they used when they were threatened. In other words, in our experiment we could not take for granted that the participants would have the skills to reduce obedience. They would need help to learn these skills and to create a systemic culture that reinforces them.

It is possible to assess the degree to which these requirements have been met, and we have tried to demonstrate this here in three ways. First, we can analyze the transcript to assess the degree to which the instructor acted consistently with Model II, as well as the degree to which he was willing to explore the times when he may not have been doing so.

Second, it is possible to analyze the students' initial reactions to the instructor's attempts to assess the students' unawareness of their obedient responses, as well as their defensiveness toward becoming more aware and reducing such responses.

And, third, it is possible to follow the interactions over the course of the experiment to show how some students eventually moved toward reducing their unquestioning obedience, as well as how the group norms about obedience changed.

If we wished to do so, we could continue this type of analysis in future sessions during the seminar, because there will be other opportunities to test what individuals learn. Unquestioning obedience is not likely to be reduced significantly in one episode. We could expand these studies to assess the external validity of these findings by observing the students in other sessions where they face authorities or where they themselves may take the role of an instructor who is trying to help others reduce their predisposition toward unquestioning obedience.

Another requirement embedded in this condition is to show that group norms conducive to an orderly society, self-governance, and double-loop learning have been maintained while obedience has been reduced, so that we do not have the kind of disintegration of the group's social fabric predicted by Milgram.

We could determine whether this requirement has been met in three ways. First, we could interview the participants to obtain their views on these matters. Second and more important, we could observe how the participants acted to maintain their group processes, the quality of the governance that they created, and the amount and quality of double-loop learning that occurred. It is not difficult to obtain information on all these points if tape recordings are made, as they were in this case. Observers can be added if they are available, but we have found that observers are not nearly so demanding as participants whose competence depends on the results of the experiment. A third resource to gather such data are the participants themselves. They are centrally concerned with the answers to these questions and how each contributed to them. For example, students can be broken down into smaller groups. They can listen and analyze the tapes. They can subject their own analysis to validation by others. They will probably be especially careful to develop valid data because such data are the basis for deciding how well they are learning, what they must overcome to gain the skills that they seek, and what kind of group culture is required if the group is to be a viable context for learning. In short, the data required for their learning will be consistent with the data required to answer the three questions that we asked about the internal and external validity of the experiment.

There are two other questions that may be raised regarding the internal validity of the experiment. First, might the passivity and unquestioned obedience have been an act put on by the students? This seems highly unlikely since they were trying to learn to overcome these kinds of behavior. Moreover, their initial defensive reactions suggest that they were not playing games. Also, the fact that some learned faster than others and then helped others to learn suggests that it was unlikely that they had conspired ahead of time to create the passivity experiment. The reactions in the follow-up experiment support these inferences. Second, how do we know that the changes would not have occurred without the Model II interventions (the experimental manipulation)? As shown elsewhere (Argyris, 1982), individuals are not able to produce actions consistent with Model II even though they understand the model, want to act consistently with it, have watched several groups attempt to do so, and have made several attempts themselves. Learning Model II requires supervised practice.

5

Organizational
Assessment Research:
Filling in Gaps
That Normal Science Overlooks

In this chapter we explore the relationship between our perspective and certain features of the correlational approach in research used for organizational assessment. Such studies typically inquire into the effectiveness of arrangements related to job design, the performance of organizations, the interactions among units within the organization, and the interaction between the organization and the environment (Van de Ven and Ferry, 1980, p. 9).

In most of this research literature, effectiveness is defined as producing a desired result (Van de Ven and Ferry, 1980). Our definition of effectiveness is producing a desired result in such a way that its production can continue under similar or reduced material or psychological costs. The latter condition is important as we shall see; it is possible to have a relatively effective organization slowly but covertly eating away the foundations of its effectiveness without realizing it.

Many different variables are related to organizational effectiveness. In this discussion we shall focus primarily on job design and job performance. As Hackman and Oldham (1976)

139

identify the domain, it is inquiry into what turns people on, how it is possible to improve work behavior and satisfaction and, in turn, the economic performance of the unit involved.

Basic Assumptions

The fundamental assumption of assessment research is that the fit or match between the individual and job requirements is the crucial factor. Bowditch and Buono state, for example, that "the basic premise underlying this [fit] principle is that an organization will operate more effectively and more efficiently when harmony and congruence exist between its parts. Thus, a particular set of tasks will demand a particular organizational configuration, a specific set of skills, and an appropriate decision-making subsystem. The greater the consistency between these aspects of the organization, the greater the probability of success" (1982, pp. 7, 8).

Pfeffer (1982), however, after reviewing much of the literature, has concluded that the empirical research to date has such a low predictive validity that the basic premise of the importance of fit is questionable. There are also scholars who question the assumption that fit and satisfaction necessarily correlate. For example, Landy (1978) has suggested that the satisfaction-fit perspective has its intellectual roots in theories of motivation that assume that people will expend energy to maintain or increase pleasant experiences, as well as to minimize or decrease unpleasant experiences. Given these assumptions about human motivation, the fit between the individual and the job is better to the extent that the mismatch or gap is less. Moderating this basic tenet is the empirically demonstrated phenomenon that creativity can be enhanced under conditions of optimal frustration (Barker, Dembo, and Lewin, 1941), as well as under conditions of difficult but achieveable challenge (Lewin and others, 1944).

Still another assumption is that the positive effects of a "good" fit will have their predicted effects over time. In other words, it has been assumed that the meaning of the fit to the individual is stable enough that a measure of it taken during one week will not change significantly the next week, as long as no major ability or job changes have occurred. If there are exceptions, they are random and can be controlled for by using valid sampling procedures and research instruments. But Landy (1978, p. 537) raises questions about such assumptions. He suggests a theory of job satisfaction where the very attempts at dealing with mismatch conditions may alter individuals' satisfaction. We will not be concerned with these debates here, not because they are trivial, but because we want to explore several scientific and moral gaps in the perspective of assessment research that would remain important even if the predictive validity of the research was high or if it was based on valid theories of motivation.

The scientific gap may be stated as follows: Is it possible that the research conditions and research instruments utilized in the descriptive approach have embedded in them some self-limiting conditions? Is it possible, for example, that even though a study might illustrate the Hackman-Oldham theory, the results will contain unrecognized gaps in what is reality, as long as the researchers remain descriptive? In other words, is the description of reality limited by the ideas in good currency about how to describe reality?

The moral gap is related to the issue of justice. Let us first recall that the concepts of fit, consistency, and harmony, in addition to being central to research on human performance, have been, and continue to be, key concepts in social psychology and organizational theories (for example, in dissonance theory, social comparison theory, and contingency theory). All these theories make the basic assumption that inconsistency is abhorred by human beings and that it therefore affects their performance.

Consistency is also the basis for the application of laws and for justice. Any given law is supposed to be applied equally; hence, the notion that no one is above the law. The relationships between consistency and justice have not been explored by the scholars in assessment research. Yet it seems reasonable to assume that individuals' performances could be as affected by a sense of justice or injustice as it is by a sense of satisfaction (Evan, 1976). For example, individuals could be dissatisfied with the fit but consider it just (it is a new organization or one that is in trouble). Or they could be highly satisfied, yet the fit could be unjust (men got paid more than women for equal work).

What is the impact upon an organization and society at large if the organization performs well on the basis of a fit that satisfies many employees yet is unjust? How may an awareness of injustice help to maintain performance? What is the impact of practitioners' utilizing the results from research that unknowingly couples "good" fit with injustice?

Finally, there is the assumption that mismatches can and should be reduced. This presumes that mismatches are reducible without danger to the organization or significant discomfort to the individual. In some cases this assumption is valid. Jobs have been enlarged and enriched without significant harm to most of the individuals performing them. In other cases, however, this may not be true. We are finding that many professionals who express the desire for a Model II world have great difficulty in producing such a world even when the conditions are optimal. For example, Brodtrick (personal communication, 1983), in a study of European attempts to debureaucratize organizations, discovered that those who had complained most vigorously about overregulation found that it was now "difficult to make decisions in areas where they used to be able to simply invoke a rule and hide behind it."

Later we will cite the example of a group of professionals who were very dissatisfied with the quality of feedback that they were receiving about their performance. Part of their dissatisfaction was caused by their belief that their superiors did not know how to give usable feedback. Another cause of their dissatisfaction was that they believed their superiors could, if they wished to do so, learn to give valid feedback. In either case, the superiors were judged to be at fault. The consultants were exposed to a learning experiment in which they learned that (1) they, too, did not have the skills that they insisted their superiors have; (2) they, too, were blind to their lack of skills; and (3) learning these skills was much more difficult than they had thought was the case. The gap between the feedback that they expected and what they received from their superiors remained, but now their expectations of their superiors had altered significantly. They were much more patient with, and respectful of, the gap. Their sense of dissatisfaction appeared to be reduced while their commitment to work remained high or, in the case of those individuals who were not threatened by the new learning, even increased. A few who realized how much they or others would have to learn in order to give and receive helpful feedback began to think that it would be better for them to seek other professions or jobs where they might not be as dependent on others for feedback as in their present jobs (for example, set up their own businesses).

Assessment Research in a Professional Organization

The first step in our argument is to present a study that was conducted by Argyris (1985) in three offices of a professional consulting firm. Included in the interviews were questions about the degree of fit between the needs and abilities of employees, on the one hand, and job requirements, on the other. The interviews lasted from one to two and one-half hours. All were tape recorded and most were transcribed. Since the results obtained in the three offices were almost identical, only the results in Office A will be used to illustrate the argument. Twenty-five of the thirty-five consultants in the office were interviewed and all but one of the ten managers. The findings will be organized around the Hackman and Oldham (1976) categories of skill variety, task significance, and autonomy.

One caveat before we describe the results. The research methods used in this study were not correlational in the sense that is exhibited by the rigorous research of many of the writers. The results, however, are similar. In other words, the data that were collected largely confirm the hypotheses of Hackman and Oldham. Our task is to see what gaps exist even when these hypotheses are confirmed.

One hundred percent of the consultants reported that skill variety was extremely high. The four critical skills identified by the consultants were analytical abilities (92 percent), conceptualizing ambiguous problems (84 percent), interviewing skills with clients (64 percent), and dealing with demanding, difficult clients (60 percent). The managers identified analytical and conceptual skills as being the two key skills (100 percent). They added that dealing with difficult interpersonal team relationships and managing vice-presidents were critical skills in their jobs (80 percent).

The consultants reported that task identify features were crucial. It was important that the case team, early in the client relationship, identify the issues and decompose or modularize them into whole and identifiable pieces of work (100 percent). Eighty-four percent of the consultants reported that the prime skill of a manager is to help the team achieve task identity early in the history of the relationship. One hundred percent of the managers reported the same views.

All the consultants and managers reported that their work had a high degree of task significance. The success or failure of their performance had an immediate, substantial, and clearly identifiable impact on the clients, the consulting firm, and their own careers. Both groups cited their high salaries (about which there were no negative views) as confirmation that their performance was highly significant to the clients and to the consulting firm.

Autonomy was also a crucial factor. The consultants reported that they especially liked those case assignments that provided a substantial degree of freedom and independence (92 percent). Seventy-two percent reported that these conditions did exist in most client cases. When they did not, they reported dissatisfaction and frustration. One hundred percent of the managers reported that a successful case team relationship was one in which the problem was framed early, the parts were decomposed and assigned correctly, and the major task of the manager was to provide an overall sense of direction.

Up to this point, the data would suggest, as Hackman and Oldham (1976) predict, that the consultants and managers had high internal motivations to produce work of outstanding quality. Some qualitative comments to illustrate this are:

> "Pressure on the job is self-imposed almost completely [*laughs*]. I must not only do a good job but I must be the best, or damn close to it, in whatever I do."
>
> "People around here are very bright, hard working, and highly motivated [to do an outstanding job]. They will work beyond the purple heart stage."
>
> "Most of us not only wish to succeed, but to succeed at maximum speed, *which is really what is at issue.*"

Ninety-six percent of the consultants and 70 percent of the managers reported that job pressures were high because of the very high standards; that pressures were self-imposed rather than imposed from without (80 percent and 90 percent, respectively); and that the pressures were considered legitimate or understandable when they came from the client (92 percent and 90 percent, respectively). One consultant reported that he did not feel much pressure, and then added, "But I would say I am a strong minority."

The professionals reported that receiving feedback from managers and officers was very important (96 percent). Each group reported the biggest mismatch in this area. Seventy-two percent of the professionals and 70 percent of the managers reported receiving inadequate feedback. Eighty-eight percent of the professionals and 100 percent of the managers reported that the most important obligation the firm had to individuals was "to give [them] an opportunity to do first-rate client work and to provide adequate and timely performance evaluations." The dissatisfaction with feedback appeared to influence the professionals' views about how much the firm cared for them and their careers. Those who were dissatisfied with the feedback also reported that the firm did not show very much caring.

These results are consistent with the findings reported by another consultant who had conducted a study in the same firm three years earlier. He interviewed the same number of managers and nearly 90 percent of the professionals. The consultant reported several sources of discontent, none of which were related to the job itself: One interviewee commented on the "discrepancies between the personal developmental *potential . . .*

and the extent to which those tremendous potentialities are purposefully realized." Another said that "the 'psychic costs' of working at [the firm] are unnecessarily high. 'The system' generates . . . counterproductive reactions." Examples of such reactions were: "ineffective and unsystematic performance evaluation and feedback processes," "ambiguous and sometimes conflicting signals as to 'How am I doing?' " and, "relative lack of processes and mechanisms for staff to use in resolving ambiguities about one's performance." The consultant's report also identified ineffective and at times insensitive behavior on the part of officers and managers when they did give feedback.

To conclude, the fit or match between such core job dimensions as skill variety, task identity, task significance, and autonomy were high. The consultants and the managers reported a high degree of meaningfulness in their work and a sense of responsibility for outcomes at work, as well as a high degree of internal commitment for high-quality work. But while satisfaction with the work itself was high, satisfaction with feedback and career progress was significantly lower. Some illustrative comments:

> "Feedback, I would say, is almost a joke. There are a couple of people who do a good job. But very few. Most do a very bad job; they'd be better off not doing it."
>
> "Bad, bad, bad. I haven't been able to speak to my sponsor since the first day I came here."
>
> "The trouble with feedback . . . is that it is too general. When it is specific, it is often unfair and punishing."
>
> "Feedback I get is little and when I get it, it is full of insensitivity and judgments that make little sense to me."

So far we have research results that are consistent with those obtained in studies of the fit between individual variables and organizational variables. Let us explore what gaps, if any, are embedded in these findings that may affect our description of reality. First, however, a word about the theory of action perspective on assessment research.

Action Science Approach to Assessment Studies

The notion of fit or the importance of consistency are also relevant in a theory of action approach. Where it differs from assessment research is in how fit is studied. Questionnaires and interviews provide data primarily at the espoused level. They do not provide actual behavior from which meanings could be inferred and from which theories-in-use could in turn be constructed. In our study, however, we were able to obtain such data. They shed some interesting light on the dimensions where the misfit or mismatch was most powerful, namely, the quality of feedback, interpersonal relationships, and career development.

The first set of data included cases written by nearly all the officers, managers, and consultants in the three offices. The cases used the format similar to that of the X-Y case described in Chapter Eight and in detail elsewhere (Argyris, 1982). Such cases give us a window on the range of problems organizational members consider important, the ways in which they make sense of these in their own terms or categories, and the actions they take to handle them. This form of assessment in turn allows us to see the organization as members construe it and to assess not only the problems but the way its members grapple with them. What we found in this case was that all the respondents espoused a theory of action that combined honesty with caring, concern with helpfulness, but that none of the respondents were able to produce a scenario either in oral or written form that was consistent with these features. Moreover, as is true for all our subjects to date, once having diagnosed their ineffectiveness and made a commitment to produce more consistent scenarios, they were unable to do so as judged by their fellow workshop members and themselves.

From these results we infer that all the theories-in-use were the same. The consultants did not differ from the managers or the officers. Hence, we might predict that if the consultants were in the position of having to lead others, they would do no better than the officers and managers had done. For example, if they had an opportunity to give feedback to others, they would produce feedback as ineffective as that produced by the officers.

An opportunity occurred to test this prediction in one of the offices in the firm. The officers and managers were concerned about the "morale" of the consultant group. They invited a number of consultants, selected by their peers, to conduct a study on these issues and feed the results back to them.

We now had an opportunity to see how the young consultants would behave when (1) they had the power to study and be critical; (2) they designed the research, the feedback process, and the meeting; (3) they had the backing of the officers; and (4) they had the support of an external consultant to help them. Finally, the officers and consultants invited one of us to sit in on the meeting to make sure that the officers and managers did not "pull rank" and to have a public observation of what happened as a double protection of the consultants.

In many ways the consultants were in an experimental situation where they were doing the evaluating and feeding back results under conditions that were more supportive than those available to officers or managers in everyday life. Yet, it was our prediction that the consultants would not behave differently from the way the officers or managers did when they gave feedback. The session was taped, the tape recordings were analyzed, and the relevant results were published (Argyris, 1982). As the consultants were giving feedback to the officers and managers on their performance and stewardship, they behaved precisely in the ways that they had faulted the officers and managers for behaving. They were judgmental and evaluative without illustrating their views, and they did not encourage confrontation of them. The session reached the point where the officers and managers reported that they were in a bind. On the one hand, they genuinely wanted to listen and to change. On the other hand, the feedback they were receiving was either too general or highly judgmental and insensitive. If they focused on the latter, the professionals would accuse them of "pulling rank" and being closed. If they focused on the former, there was little they could do to make constructive changes. If the officers and managers hid the fact that they were hiding their increasing sense of unjust punishment, the professionals would leave the meeting believing that they had done a good job. Since the officers and managers felt they could not change on the basis of the feedback they had received, their lack of change could be seen by the professionals as evidence of their resistance to change.

What Did We Learn?

If we focus on the objective of describing reality, we can say that through an intervention consistent with the principles of action science, we developed a much richer picture of reality than would otherwise have been available. We now know that the consultants were unable to produce more competent behavior than the officers and managers when they had a chance to do so under supportive conditions. We also know that they were blind to this fact. Blindness, from our perspective, is action, and such action is designed. That must mean that there are programs in the consultants' heads that keep them blind and programs that keep them unaware of their blindness. If this is true, it is a critical slice of reality that would have been missed by the typical assessment approach.

Finally, the assessment approach gives us no idea of the group, intergroup, and cultural defensive routines that may exist in the organization to protect and reinforce these features. Yet to decrease any mismatch would require an understanding of these features. We have found that these deep-structure, taken-for-granted features surface when we conduct training sessions to help individuals learn Model II action. As individuals strive to learn new actions and discover that they cannot, they increasingly direct their attention and energies to discovering and redesigning the barriers to these new actions at the individual, group, and organizational levels. It is thus not likely that individuals can go through the reeducative processes described in this book without examining the deep structures of their own and the organization's defensive routines.

Issues of Justice

The results of the two diagnostic interview studies indicated that the consultants were dissatisfied with the feedback activities. They believed that their superiors (and the firm) were responsible for this state of affairs. They also believed that their superiors could learn to behave more competently if they "really cared about people issues." The consultants and managers reported little or no personal responsibility for the mismatches that existed in the feedback domain.

Because of these beliefs the professionals thought it was just to ask for organizational changes and changes in the behavior of their superiors. At the organizational level they therefore sought to make feedback a right and an obligation. They recommended more attention to career development. The consultant to the study agreed with these views. He recommended that the managers and officers provide better learning and career development experiences for the young professionals. He also recommended formation of career development committees, provision of more formal training, and establishment of clearer policies on promotion. He suggested that the superiors schedule more feedback sessions and learn to conduct such sessions more competently. In order to support the justness of these recommendations, the consultant suggested that it be agreed and announced that every staff member has the right and the obligation to "seek periodic evaluation and discussion of his/her performance. . . . It should be . . . person to person . . . and thorough."

The organization confirmed the justice of these ideas by turning them into policies. Policies, of course, are espoused theories, and true reduction of the mismatches will occur only if the officers and managers behave in accordance with the intent of these policies. We suggest that, without a particular kind of reeducation and without changes in the organizational culture, the intent will not be implemented. If this is the case, then the sense of mismatch will become greater because behavior will not change even though the organization has mandated better feedback.

But the X-Y learning experiences, plus those data obtained from actual evaluation meetings, both suggest important moderating conditions. The results of the X-Y case suggest that Model I is culturally learned and that all participants acquire it in the course of socialization. Hence, individuals are not personally responsible for developing their Model I-ness. At the same time, however, the *way* they choose to behave within the framework of their Model I-ness is their choice. Individuals have master programs in their heads that define their theories-in-use. If this is so, then individuals (superiors *or* subordinates) will tend to produce conditions of insensitivity, misunderstanding, and escalating error, although they may vary widely in the behavior they select to produce these conditions. Under these conditions, how just is it to hold only superiors responsible for poor feedback? How just is it for the subordinates to assume that if the superiors wanted to behave differently, if they cared, they could do so? In our opinion, the answer is that it is not just: It requires of a superior that he or she act in ways in which the subordinates themselves do not and cannot act.

Moreover, an analysis of the tapes of actual evaluation sessions shows that the subordinates withheld their frustration and anger or expressed them toward the end in Model I ways. The former response tended to provide the superior with a false sense that "the session went well." The latter provided evidence for the primary fear of many superiors about feedback sessions, namely, that subordinates will become defensive and that not many positive results will be gained.

There are two points that we are making here. First, all concerned believed that feedback sessions should be held, that it was possible to generate rules about competent behavior, and that they themselves already followed them. Individuals may therefore believe that they are being treated unjustly when the other players do not follow the rules. But our point is that the natural, automatic responses of Model I individuals will be to violate the rules, to be unaware that they are doing so, and either not to receive feedback that may serve to penetrate their double-layered unawareness or to receive counterproductive feedback that predisposes them to blame the other person.

The second point is that, at the theory-in-use level, there is little sense of personal causal responsibility. All the individuals held the same theory-in-use, and we suggest that they learned it early in their lives. It is possible for people to alter their behavior within Model I governing variables, but the result will still be Model I actions and consequences. Moreover, any educational programs that help individuals change their actions without helping them alter their governing variables will lead to gimmicks and fads.

Although individuals have no choice in their theory-in-use and the O-I learning system, they can choose to alter their theory-in-use and, hence, the organizational learning system and culture. But such changes will not occur unless the players are committed. Thus policy recommendations—for example, everyone has a right to helpful feedback—are primarily espoused theories that provide a basis for mismatch and dissatisfaction. Nevertheless, changes in theory-in-use may lead to the view that all the players can contribute to creating conditions in which individual theories-in-use, organizational learning systems, and therefore organizational culture can be altered.

The question arises, If the players held the point of view that we are recommending, would it have altered their responses to the original questions or lessened the intensity with which they held their views? Would it have altered the degree of certainty with which they asserted that the superiors' incompetence was a sign of injustice and not caring? If the answers are yes, then the diagnostic experiences recommended by a theory of action should be added to assessment theory and practice.

If the answers are no, however, then it would be important to ask what implications this has for justice in the organization. What kind of world will be created if the desire for satisfaction becomes a more powerful motivation than the desire for justice, especially since the basis for satisfaction is competence that few may have and rules for governance that few can fulfill? For example, how can we tell when individual satisfaction becomes simply a matter of self-interest or even narcissism? Or under what conditions is it just for an organization to place a ceiling on satisfaction or on the degree of match in order to enhance organizational health?

Individuals and Double-Loop Learning

If genuine organizational change is to occur, we believe that all individuals will have to learn a theory-in-use whose utilization leads to double-loop learning. As individuals come to learn in this way, they will necessarily create new organizational learning systems and a new culture that sanctions such learning. Our candidate for the new theory-in-use for individuals is Model II; for the organizational learning system it is Model O-II.

But the further question arises, How would professionals tend to react if placed in learning environments designed to teach Model II? There are two sets of factors that influence such learning. The first set is related to the nature of the learning environment. The second set is related to the "readiness" of individuals to learn.

In the introduction to Part Three we will present a detailed description of how a group of professionals reacted to the conditions that we created. Initially, they found themselves feeling bewildered and frustrated. Bewildered that they had such difficulty in producing the action strategies that they had designed. Frustrated because their errors reoccurred even when they were sure that this would not be the case. The bewilderment and frustration, however, eventually turned to experiences of success and mastery. (Incidentally, the bewilderment and frustration were used to fuel the learning.) But what about "readiness" to learn? We can obtain some insight into this factor by reexamining the basis for the fit between the professionals and their jobs. In the left-hand column below, we present some comments that they made that illustrate their position. In the right-hand column we state the inferences we made from these comments.

Statements made by respondents	*Our inferred meanings*
Professionals are highly motivated and have plenty of initiative. The key is to provide them [with] challenging work and opportunities to learn.	The energy for work is related to the degree of challenge and learning in the work.
The people here will work beyond the purple heart stage as long as there is challenge. If there is little challenge, they become unhappy.	The energy for work is related to the degree of challenge and learning in the work.
The job we do must not only be good, it must be the best.	High but achievable level of aspiration for career success.
It would scare me to death to be here and not be a competent professional. You'd feel like shit all the time.	Deeply emotional, negative reaction to performing in a mediocre or below-average way.
There is a lot of pressure and most of it is self-imposed. For example, professionals hate to make errors. They go into a "doom-zoom" and act as if they are a bunch of fragile egos.	Reaction to error can be strongly disproportionate to the magnitude of the error.

From data such as these, it is possible to develop a model (Figure 4) of how professionals will tend to react to success and failure. The model suggests that professionals represent an intriguing combination of high aspiration for success and an equally high fear of failure. The experience of success leads to feelings of pride and exhilaration, high energy for work, strong aspirations for quality work, and the expectation of achieving a good reputation. These conditions, in turn, reinforce the aspiration for success.

Figure 4. Psychological Success-Brittleness Syndrome.

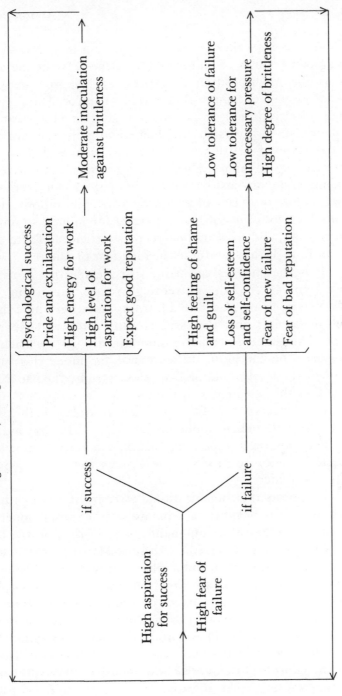

At the same time, they also provide a moderate inoculation against feelings of failure and brittleness. We define brittleness as the predisposition to express an inappropriately high sense of despair or failure when producing error. The higher the degree of susceptibility to shame and guilt and the greater the avoidance of, and fears about, shame and guilt, the greater the internal state of brittleness. Brittleness is expected to result from reactions to failure. These reactions include strong feelings of shame and guilt, loss of self-esteem and self-confidence, fear of new failure, and fear of acquiring a bad reputation. Such reactions lead to a lowering of tolerance for failure, to unnecessary pressure, and to a high degree of brittleness. These consequences in their turn reinforce the high fear of failure.

It is thus not unreasonable to conclude that professionals will tend to find the unfreezing process threatening. They are, in effect, being placed in a learning situation where there is a high probability that they will produce errors and experience failure. This indicates that closing the gap in feedback processes may be far more difficult and far more closely connected to the level of action skills possessed by the participants than either the researchers or the consultants thought would be the case. It suggests that, like the young consultants, the professionals also held beliefs about justice and satisfaction and what data were important (espoused) that helped keep them unaware of their inability to produce the actions they were requiring others to produce.

It appears that organizational assessment research has assumed that it is possible to separate satisfaction, competence, and performance, on the one hand, from justice, on the other. This assumption is consistent with such Model I governing variables as unilateral control and maximizing winning and minimizing losing. For example, assessment research that ignores justice can be used by either employees or management to strengthen their respective cases in order to win and not lose.

In a Model II world it would be difficult to separate these factors because there personal responsibility is crucial. The moment the consultants explored how they were partially responsible for "causing" their dissatisfaction, their blindness to their own incompetence, and their blindness to the difficulties that they and their superiors would have in altering their behavior, then the entire thrust of the exercise changed because the issue of justice became prominent.

Issues of justice, in turn, will probably have important implications not only for managing organizations but for creating the conditions that are necessary if researchers are to obtain valid information. And without valid information, science of any kind is in jeopardy.

6

The Ethnographic Approach to Intervention and Fundamental Change

Dianne Argyris

Ethnography, a branch of anthropology, seeks to describe the rules of social interaction in a particular setting through participant observation. The hallmarks of ethnographic methods are deep and rich descriptions of patterns of social interaction and an explication of the meanings those patterns hold for members of the culture under study. As Spradley puts it, "The central aim of ethnography is to understand another way of life from the native point of view. . . . Rather than studying people, ethnography means learning from people" (1980, p. 3).

The high percentage of children—particularly minority children—who fail to learn to read and write is a problem that has been addressed by an increasing number of researchers through the use of ethnographic methods. The majority of these studies focus on the match or mismatch between the culture of the home and the culture of the school (Philips, 1983; Heath, 1983; Scollon and Scollon, 1981; Jordan, 1981; Erickson, 1975). A smaller number have focused on how implicit class or political stratification affects school and school-related interactions (McDermott and Gospodinoff, 1981; McDermott, Goldman, Varenne, in press; Ogbu, 1982). Despite the information about school failure amassed by these researchers, however, both researchers and practitioners are questioning the degree to which this work has actually helped create the kind of change it wishes to bring about (Cazden, 1983; Kleinfeld, 1983).

This chapter joins in questioning the degree to which ethnographic study can contribute to altering the status quo of the systems under its scrutiny. We will do so by examining five widely cited and influential ethnographies. The first three of these ethnographies are from what one might call the tradition of basic or descriptive ethnographic research. They describe patterns of interaction that are linked to school failure. Of these three, two take a "cultural match" perspective (Philips, 1983; Erickson, 1975) and one a more political perspective (McDermott and Gospodinoff, 1981). Two questions will be asked of each of these three studies. First, to what degree do they meet the goals of ethnographic research, that is, completeness, accuracy, and the addition of useful knowledge? Second, do the studies contain information that will be useful for practitioners who wish to make the kinds of changes in their practice that these three ethnographers' work suggests they should make? As we shall see, these two questions are intertwined.

The remaining two studies are examples of the few ethnographic studies that have generated interventions designed to remedy the kinds of conditions described in the previously mentioned ethnographies (Jordan, 1981; Au and Jordan, 1981; Heath, 1982, 1983). These projects did much to reverse school failure. We will suggest, however, that although the changes that they recommended did address cultural conditions, the projects did not appear to establish contexts in which students and teachers could reflect on the institutional and interpersonal conditions that led to and maintained school failure in the first place. In the language of this volume, we will question whether the interventions asked practitioners to examine their theories-in-use about dealing with cultural differences.

Descriptive Ethnographic Research

Philips (1983) studied first- and sixth-grade American Indian children. She hypothesized a mismatch between the tacit

Indian cultural rules for face-to-face interaction (particularly while learning and teaching) and the tacit rules guiding face-to-face interaction in Anglo classrooms. She focused particularly on comparing cultural strategies for structuring attention and regulating turns for talking. Eye contact, pauses in conversation, gestures, and verbal turn taking are examples of the components of interaction that Philips analyzed. She hypothesized that it was the mismatch between the rules of interaction learned and practiced in the children's homes and those practiced in their classrooms that led to a high incidence of school failure of Indian children in Anglo classrooms.

McDermott and Gospodinoff (1981) studied a New York suburban first-grade class populated by children from a range of backgrounds: Italian and Jewish white children, Puerto Rican children, and black children. They hypothesized that there exist in the classroom tacit rules of interaction that, when followed, result in a paradox: a smoothly managed classroom whose very manageability is contingent on the creation of contexts that will secure the failure of minority children to learn to read. Drawing on a method of context analysis developed by Birdwhistell (1970), McDermott and Gospodinoff identified repetitive body posturings that characterized interaction in the lowest reading group, compared these with the patterns that occurred in the advanced reading group, and demonstrated how the series of positionings of the low group prevented them from staying on the task of reading, while the series of positionings of the high group supported the activity of learning to read.

Erickson (1975) studied interactions between guidance counselors and their junior college counselees. He hypothesized that the degree to which counselor and counselee perceived themselves to be alike strongly influenced the degree to which the student might receive advice, support, or special favors from the counselor. Erickson analyzed both verbal and nonverbal interaction to determine the degree to which counselors and counselees perceived themselves to be alike. He also collected data about the accuracy with which counselors and counselees read each other's implicit meanings. He found that it was not only similarity in race or ethnicity that predicted a smooth

interaction and special favors; the establishment of a "particularistic comembership," such as a shared interest in sports also
often resulted in special treatment of the counselee by the
counselor.

   School failure is an issue about which all these researchers care deeply. Therefore we assume that they want their work
to generate information that will enhance the ability of practitioners to alleviate school failure. In this, they strive to be as
complete and as accurate as possible. It is the contention of this
chapter, however, that these ethnographies share three features
that put their accuracy, completeness, and usefulness at risk. All
the ethnographers (1) make and hold inferences that are not
tested with the participants (or if they are, it is not a process
that is written about by the ethnographers); (2) they diagnose
the problem incompletely; and (3) they offer structural and
interpersonal prescriptions that are difficult to achieve.

   Before we proceed with an analysis of these features,
however, let us pause here and address the idea of usefulness.
The focus of this book is on how to produce knowledge that
can help alter the status quo. At first glance, then, this book
would seem to ask the same question of research in general that
Cazden asked of ethnographers in her 1983 presidential address to the Council on Education and Ethnography. I paraphrase here: "While we are quite proficient at adding to descriptions of how it is that educational problems such as school
failure are maintained (that is, the status quo), isn't it true that
we—the community of linguists and ethnographers—have explained educational failure without showing how it can be reversed?" (Cazden, 1983, p. 36). So far, Cazden's question and
the question of this chapter are the same. Where they differ is in
the factors that they single out as determinants of this failure to
change the status quo.

   Whereas Cazden defines the status quo as the continuing
presence of school failure, we take a different view. We define
the status quo as the set of interlocking consequences for learning and effectiveness in the world. These consequences result
from the interactions of human beings using a Model I theory-
in-use. Thus, when an action researcher sets out to diagnose a

problem such as school failure, he or she would be likely to focus on the reasoning embedded in the interactions (mostly
verbal) that the participants have and on how that reasoning
may undercut the participants' intentions, such as achieving
equal opportunity for all students in the classroom and establishing learning environments that reduce or eradicate school
failure. Thus the action scientist focuses on the individual and
group reasoning that maintains the consequence of school failure. School failure is one kind of status quo; the reasoning and
interactions that produce it and that keep the actors unaware
of it constitute another. It is this second kind of status quo that
we believe requires attention if the system is to solve the problem in such a way that it remains solved.

To illustrate: Both Philips and Erickson focus on cultural factors in their diagnosis of the causes of school failure.
What they focus less on are the ways in which teachers and
counselors reason about and handle these cultural differences.
As Kleinfeld suggests, however, "the fundamental issue is not
the existence of cultural differences in codes; these commonly
occur in transcultural learning situations, but people commonly figure out ways of dealing with them. The fundamental issue
is that some cultural groups in some circumstances decide that
they do not want to acquire the attributes of the majority culture. If this is true, educators need from anthropologists a better understanding of how and why these cultural decisions are
made, the meaning to children of what teachers ask them to do,
and whether there are possibilities for reconciliation" (1983,
p. 286).

This perspective reflects Kleinfeld's view that it is the
workings of the "cultural decisions" that need looking into. We
would, however, frame this inquiry somewhat differently, looking first not at cultural decisions so much as at the reasoning
people use about how to handle differences in the classroom
and how to handle the conflicts that result from these differences. Put another way, we would focus on the patterns of the
interacting theories-in-use of teachers and students and look at
how those patterns generated a culture for learning in the classroom. We would assert that it is only by altering this level of the

status quo that the individuals in the system can independently and permanently correct the consequence of school failure.

Limitations of Ethnographic Research

Now let us turn to an exploration of those features of ethnographic research that we believe reduces its contribution to altering the status quo. We will examine three separate research projects in three very different settings.

Ethnographers Make and Hold Untested Inferences. All ethnographers must impose meanings on their settings. The balance between discerning the meanings in the culture under study and organizing and transmitting those meanings in an attempt to describe the culture is a difficult one to maintain. If meanings are imposed on the participants' actions either too early or if the meanings are not checked with participants, then an ethnographer runs the risk of inaccurately or incompletely describing the phenomenon in which he or she is interested. Such a description also lowers the probability that it will be helpful to participants. It is the contention of this chapter that both McDermott and Gospodinoff and Erickson make and hold inferences in ways that may have these unintended consequences.

Specifically, they make inferences about the actors, guided by whatever theoretical perspective has helped them to frame their data. They do not publicly test these inferences (or the theories on which they are based) with the actors. If they do perform this kind of testing, they do not write about it and therefore presumably do not see it as an integral step in the research process. The inferences they make then become part of a causal theory that also apparently goes untested with the actors. They thus end up imposing meanings on participants that may not be accurate, and thereby reduce the probability of learning on the part of both reader and practitioner.

McDermott and Gospodinoff's analysis of one aspect of teacher behavior can serve as an example. They note that the teacher will often disrupt the low reading group (by yelling at, or getting up to discipline, someone outside the reading group) at the precise moment that the group has finally settled down to begin reading. They then make a series of inferences to explain this: "By way of inference, it can be claimed that the teacher is uncomfortable with the bottom group once it is settled and ready for instruction. In terms of the readiness of some of the children to engage in reading activities, the teacher's response to the bottom group is quite understandable. It is easier to teach children how to read when they already know how to read. The top group does not present the headaches the bottom group does" (1981, p. 22).

They then assert that the teacher often leaves the group at key times because she is uncomfortable with the task of teaching the bottom group. This attribution may be correct, but it is primarily informed by a theory that helps the researchers to interpret the teacher's actions, namely, that it is far harder to teach the low group than the high group. The teacher herself has not given any data to indicate that she believes her discomfort is the reason why she walks away from the group. As far as we know, the researchers did not test this causal inference with the teacher to see whether or not she sees it as valid. They then build on this causal inference by linking the teacher's withdrawal to the children's failure to learn to read.

The fact that this chain of reasoning goes untested may make it quite difficult for the teacher to understand and alter her behavior. This is especially true given what McDermott and Gospodinoff are careful to point out, that the teacher's behavior may be counterproductive to the students' ability to learn to read but that this is by no means her intention. They describe the teacher as "an excellent teacher who cares deeply about the children. We all know that teaching a first grade is a difficult job, and this particular teacher is excellent under the circumstances" (1981, p. 228). The perspective of this book would suggest that the teacher's actions were tacit, highly skilled, and automatic. Furthermore, we too assume that she was unaware of her actions. But the question then becomes, How might research help her to become aware of her actions and their consequences?

McDermott and Gospodinoff suggest that the conditions for her behavior are set in the larger school and societal structures. This is very likely so, but these conditions cannot be changed through one teacher's insight into them. Conditions closer to the teacher's own province of control are internal ones, namely, the reasoning that led her to act as she did. Examples of such reasoning might be found in her reaction to the low reading group; how she dealt with a possible sense of failure; and whether she attributed failure to intentional behavior on the part of the group and felt annoyed or to innate lack of ability and felt guilty or hopeless. Any of these reactions might lead to the behavior that McDermott and Gospodinoff describe, but each would contain very different prescriptions for change in the teacher's reasoning. Thus the fact that the inferences made by McDermott and Gospodinoff are not tested with the teacher makes it impossible for the reader to get a complete picture of her experience of the low reading group and may make it difficult for her to learn from the description they present.

Untested inferences also appear in Erickson's work, despite the fact that he created opportunities for the participants to comment on their own behavior, as well as on that of the actor involved. Following is an excerpt from one of the interviews in which Erickson makes attributions about each actor's meanings that are not, to our knowledge, tested with the actors. The interview takes place between a Polish-American student and a guidance counselor (Erickson, 1975, pp. 48-49):

Counselor: [*Unsmiling and formal*] What did you get in your Biology 101 last semester?

Student: Whad' I get?

Counselor: What did you get for a grade?

Student: B.

Counselor: B?

Student: Yeah.

Counselor: How about Speech 101?

Student: Speech, ah . . . ah, I th——, I think, I didn't get that one.

Counselor: [*Looks straight at the student without smiling*] What do you mean you "didn't get it"?

Student: I got some incomplete.

Counselor: Ah . . . how come?

Student: Th— . . . then I, ah, ma— I did complete them. You know, then I made up the test . . . and then they give me tha— . . .

Counselor: Did you make up the tests?

Student: The grades . . . yes, I did.

Counselor: [*Looks down at the student's transcript*] You don't know all the grades you got, though.

Student: I didn't (unintelligible) and C.

Counselor: [*Looks at student without smiling*] You didn't fail anything?

Student: No. No fail.

Erickson comments on this interchange: "When the Polish-American student indicated confusion at the beginning of the exchange by responding to a question with a question, the counselor seemed to take that to mean that the student was not intelligent or attentive. From then on he challenged the student's answers even when they were not ambiguous. The resulting tone was unfriendly and at times intimidating. Also, because the student had trouble communicating, the counselor inferred incorrectly that he was having trouble academically" (1975, p. 49).

Here Erickson begins by inferring that because the boy answered a question with a question, the counselor evaluated the boy as "not intelligent or attentive." As far as we know, this is not a meaning that the counselor assigned to his own actions, and Erickson does not connect his inference to the counselor's words or actions. Therefore it is difficult to judge the accuracy of such an inference.

Second, he says that the counselor challenged the boy's

answers in an intimidating fashion. Again, this may be so, but it may also have been that the counselor was attempting to be straightforward in a difficult situation, or that the counselor was trying to stifle his own discomfort in such a situation. No data were collected about the meanings that the counselor imposed on the situation. As in the previous study, this diminishes the completeness of the description (and possibly its accuracy), as well as the probability that an actor who might be unintentionally doing harm could begin to learn how to reason and behave differently.

Although Erickson provided the opportunity for participants to comment on their actions, as far as we know he did not share his own inferences about the meanings of their actions. Nor does the data published indicate that he asked participants to be explicit about the inferences they made about themselves. Following is another interaction between counselor and student (Erickson, 1975, p. 54):

Counselor: As far as next semester. . . . Why don't you give some thought to what you'd like to take there. . . . [*leans forward*] Do you plan on continuing along this PE major?

Student: Yeah, I guess so. I might as well keep it up . . . my PE, and [*shifts in chair*] I wanna go into counseling, too, see . . . you know, to have two way . . . like equal balance.

Counselor: I see. Ah . . . What do you know about counseling?

Student: Nothing [*smiles, averts eyes, then looks up*].

Counselor: Okay.

Student: [*Shifts in chair, smiles and averts eyes*] I know you have to take psychology courses of some sort . . . and counseling.

Counselor: [*Leans back*] Well, [*student stops smiling, looks directly at counselor, and sits almost immobile while counselor talks and shifts in chair repeatedly*] it's this is a . . . it'll vary from different places to different places. . . But essentially what you need . . . First of all you're gonna need state certification

...state teacher certification [*goes on to give more information*].

Erickson played this videotape back separately for the counselor and student and asked them both to comment. The counselor said (1975, p. 55):

> Right now we both seem to be concentrating on giving information and putting it together . . . he's got aspirations for the future, PE and uh . . . uh, counseling . . . he's a little bit ahead of himself as far as the counseling . . . as the year progressed, I guess I got the question so often that it became one of my favorite topics an' I was ready to enumerate . . . essentially what he did was that he started me off on my information.

The student had a very different experience (1975, p. 55):

> Well . . . well, I couldn't really say, but I wasn't satisfied with what he wanted to push. . . . I guess he didn't think I was qualified, you know. That's the way he sounded to me. . . . This guy here seems like he was trying to knock me down in a way, you know. Trying to say no . . . I don't think you can handle anything besides PE. You know he just said it in general terms, he didn't go up and pow! like they would in the old days, you know. This way they just try to use a little more psychology . . . they sugarcoat it this way.

The counselor describes the student's aspiration to go into counseling as suggesting that he was "a little bit ahead of himself." From this, apparently, Erickson infers that the student heard the counselor's meaning correctly. Note, however, the wide discrepancy between the view that the student was "ahead of himself" and the view that the counselor was trying to "knock [him] down." Each interpretation seems plausible, yet Erickson does not indicate how it is that he comes to see the student's imposition of meaning as the correct one. This issue is not, in Erickson's view, central to his thesis that miscommunication can occur: "Implicit messages—intended or not, read accurately or not—are important in the counseling situation" (1975, p. 55). We would agree, but would add that the intention behind these messages and the accuracy with which they are read should be of deep concern to the practitioner in the situation, particularly if he or she wishes to begin to alter the reasoning behind the behavior itself.

Erickson, like McDermott and Gospodinoff, does not attribute intentional discrimination to the counselors: "The counselors we studied were not trying to cheat their students or their schools; nor were they incompetent" (1975, p. 68). Yet if they were unaware of their behavior, the imposition of meanings rather than the discovery of them might inhibit the ability of these practitioners to learn.

Diagnoses of the Problem Are Incomplete. In this section we take a look at what ethnographers focus on when diagnosing the problem of school failure. At first glance it appears that in making a diagnosis the ethnographers considered here seek information in exactly the same domains as those that interest an action scientist. Philips, McDermott and Gospodinoff, and Erickson all seek to understand (1) action and the reasoning behind action and (2) patterns in social behavior. Moreover, they seek to understand these in a particular context.

Philips and Erickson, however, represent the majority of ethnographers of schooling in that they look at these elements in terms of cultural rules of interaction. They do not look at the reasoning that leads children and teachers to cope with cultural differences in particular ways. Recall, for instance, that Philips describes a series of actions—Indians listening and responding with certain kinds of eye contact and other metalinguistic cues. She makes inferences about the meaning of these actions. This could be put in the form of a theory-in-use proposition: "When I avert my eyes and do not directly respond, I am listening." Philips also describes the rules of paying attention in the mainstream classrooms: "When I want to show someone I am listening, I look them straight in the face and nod or respond direct-ly." Both of these propositions, when acted out in their natural contexts, are effective ways of constructing the social relation-ship of "listening to someone."

Philips's diagnosis of the dynamics that lead Indian chil-dren into trouble in school has to do with the fact that the ac-tion propositions in the school culture do not match those of the home culture. Thus, Philips describes one level of a status quo, namely, that Indian children have rules for effective learn-ing that white teachers do not share; white teachers are un-aware of these rules and therefore downgrade Indian children who, as a result, fail in school. But she fails to explore an-other, deeper status quo: What is it that (1) keeps white teach-ers from finding out about Indian children's different ways of doing things, and (2) what leads them to distance themselves from responsibility by blaming the Indian children and failing them? We would assert that both the unawareness and the dis-tancing from responsibility for error are typical Model I re-sponses. Furthermore, we would assert that Philips's prescrip-tion that cultural rules for learning should be matched with classroom rules for learning is necessary but not sufficient to alter the status quo, for this response leaves the Model I values of teachers, administrators, and even students unchanged.

Philips and others may respond that it is all well and good to espouse this kind of change as a goal but that it is a complex enough task to make children literate; why compli-cate that task by making the social dynamics of the classroom an object of change? We would agree that creating conditions that will enable children who are failing in school to succeed is no trivial accomplishment. If, however, teachers and admin-istrators can become more aware of their own responsibility for results like school failure, they may then come to act different-ly and thus reduce the problem. If teachers, administrators, and, for that matter, older children view themselves as centrally responsible for the situation, they may each become more in-ternally committed to monitoring the institution and them-selves. If teachers, administrators, and adolescent young people develop the skills to discuss threatening issues like racism, these issues will be less likely to covertly influence classroom interaction and success. Finally, an awareness of how individuals in the system unintentionally maintain conditions for school failure may contribute to the system's capacity to deal more effectively with the next threatening issue it faces, if that awareness is combined with the development of new skills.

We do not know if the kinds of changes just described in fact took place in any of the classrooms studied by the three researchers. If these changes have been made, they have not, to our knowledge, been written about. Our prediction would be that these changes in status quo would not be generated by the knowledge that Philips, Erickson, and McDermott and Gospodinoff create.

Although Philips and Erickson represent the majority of ethnographers of schooling in taking a "cultural match" approach, McDermott and Gospodinoff represent an interesting exception. In our view their diagnosis is consistent with the one that an action scientist might make, for it reveals action propositions that get at the Model I dynamics that produce such consequences as low trust, escalating error, and high defensiveness. For instance, if McDermott and Gospodinoff (1981) were to publicly confirm their attributions about the teacher's inability to deal with the low reading group, they would probably arrive at the following theory-in-use proposition: "When the teacher becomes too frustrated with the group to work effectively with them, she seeks escape and acts as if she were not doing so." If enough of these propositions could be collected, a map of the teacher's reasoning and action about coping with difficult issues could be drawn and tested with the teacher. This kind of map, as we shall see in the chapters to come, can be an effective tool not only for understanding the individual status quo (that is, the theory-in-use) but also for altering it.

Thus, we have two kinds of features embedded in these researchers' diagnoses and prescriptions that may inhibit the ability to create knowledge that can alter the fundamental status quo. One feature has to do with the domain of the diagnosis: A diagnosis of cultural mismatch fails to get at the dynamics that maintain that mismatch, namely, Model I individual and organizational theories of action. The other feature has to do with the way in which the diagnosis is used. In this case, despite giving a description of aspects of what we would call the Model I status quo, McDermott and Gospodinoff fail to generate prescriptions for change.

Prescriptions Are Difficult to Produce. All three researchers write about the implications of their work for school failure. All three have implicit and explicit prescriptions for the practitioners and the system in which they practice. They appear to be aware in varying degrees of how difficult their prescriptions are to produce. Let us begin with the implicit interpersonal prescriptions.

If teachers who are in the kinds of situations the three researchers describe care about their competence, they will, of course, want to avoid making the kinds of errors that Philips, Erickson, and McDermott and Gospodinoff suggest they unknowingly do make. They would be apt to discern in the findings of these studies implicit advice about how to interact and reason differently. Recall, for instance, that McDermott and Gospodinoff asserted that the teacher's withdrawal lessened the probability that the children would learn to read. Implicit in this analysis is advice for the teacher. If the consistent withdrawal of the teacher is counterproductive to the children's learning, then she should cease to withdraw. How useful is this advice? Note that it is not easy to stop behaving in ways that are both automatic and skillful. If McDermott and Gospodinoff's attribution about the teacher is correct (that she is frustrated by the task of teaching the lower group to read) and if she does *not* withdraw, she is faced with the task of dealing with her discomfort while trying to teach the children to read. Under these conditions, she may do more harm to the children by remaining in the group than by periodically escaping from it.

Perhaps this is not the only advice that can be inferred from this diagnosis. Assuming again that McDermott and Gospodinoff's inferences are correct, perhaps the teacher should be advised to learn new ways to teach reading so that she would not feel uncomfortable. But it may not be within the teacher's power to do so since this would involve going back to school or experimenting on her own with new methods. Thus, if McDermott and Gospodinoff's inferences are correct, acting on the implicit advice embedded in them may do little to alleviate the problem. If they are incorrect, then the advice is irrelevant.

Again, recall Erickson's set of causal inferences about the counselor and student. Erickson inferred: (1) that it was the Polish-American boy's response to the counselor's question with another question that led the counselor to judge him as unintelligent or inattentive, (2) that it was the student's trouble communicating that led the counselor to believe the boy was having academic trouble, and (3) that it was the counselor's view of the student based on these two inferences that led him not to give the student any favors.

The following advice is implicit in these causal inferences. First, don't judge another as stupid if he seems not to respond to your question immediately. Second, don't assume that if someone has trouble communicating he is in academic trouble. Finally, don't withhold special favors on the basis of possibly unfounded evaluations of a student's way of communicating. In order to follow this advice, one would have to interrupt one's learned and automatic processes of making inferences and judgments about others. How realistic is this advice? Again, its application seems problematic.

There are two ways in which a person's automatic responses can be interrupted: He can do it himself or another can do it for him. If Erickson is correct, however, people reason so automatically and at such a tacit level that they are rarely aware of either the judgments that they make or the data on which they base those judgments. Without some kind of retraining it is extremely difficult to monitor and interrupt behavior of which a person is himself unaware.

These researchers are not blind to the difficulty of bringing about the kinds of changes suggested earlier, for they also make explicit interpersonal prescriptions. They are, however, almost entirely pessimistic about the possibility of change at the individual and interpersonal level. Erickson writes, "General consciousness raising about the effects of particularism on face-to-face interaction might be useful. This would not be skill training but would make counselors, administrators, and students more aware of how they act toward and make judgments about students" (1975, p. 67). But he rejects the possibility that such training could make an appreciable difference: "The process by which particularistic attributes of social identity enter into interactions seems too complex to be performed reflectively, or stopped at will. Thus, training would probably need to be intensive and continuous (analogous to psychotherapy) and would be prohibitively expensive for a school. Training which fell short of this, in my opinion, would be just window dressing—conducting in-service training whose manifest aim is to change the status quo but whose latent function is to legitimize the organization and its standard operating procedures" (1975, p. 67).

Philips believes that the differences in attention structure she found may be physiological. She believes that the nonverbal nature of attention structures may be unchangeable because

> the nonverbal behavior involved in management of the body in social interaction is more fully learned at an earlier age than language, which may in turn be related to the earlier maturation of the parts of the brain that process nonverbal behavior. . . .
>
> Nonverbal patterns of behavior are clearly acquired through the socialization process, as evidenced by the changes in gestural patterns between one generation and another among immigrants in this country (Efron, 1941). But they are very slow to change among people who are socially segregated and do not have regular contact or identify with people who display nonverbal patterns that are different from their own [1983, p. 131].

Given this conclusion, it is not surprising that both Philips and Erickson turn to institutional and structural solutions for change. There are, however, problems with these suggestions. Philips, for instance, recommends, "Above all, it is important that all of these agents of change be structurally linked with and responsive to the minority communities' goals for their children and their knowledge of what their children need in order to grow and learn" (1983, p. 135). Without any elaboration, however, it is difficult for a change agent to know what behaviors would be "structurally linked with and responsive to minority communities' goals for their children." Most well-meaning change agents already believe that they are pursuing worthwhile goals, which is why they can in good conscience remain in their jobs.

Both Erickson and Philips suggest that schools should create conditions under which minority children can be taught by people of their own culture, who will not be automatically puzzled by nonverbal and metacommunicative cues and who will have the same communicative rules as their students. "Hire more Third-World counselors" and "get more Indian teachers in the classroom" are two such prescriptions. There is, of course, nothing inherently wrong with the idea of having Indians teach Indians, but it is problematic as a prescription when it is posed as a solution to the blindness of whites. That is, such a solution would not require the guidance counselor in Erickson's study to take a look at the unintended impact he had on the student. Nor would it require the student to consider the possibility that the counselor had not consciously meant to send the negative meanings that the student interpreted him as sending.

An additional problem with this kind of advice is that there are no data to suggest that the same ways of coping with threatening problems, that is, distancing and blaming others, don't exist between people who have the same racial or ethnic background. Indeed, research by Argyris (1982) has shown that the Model I dynamics of mistrust and defensiveness in groups will occur regardless of race.

Although they do not share their colleagues' diagnosis of cultural differences, McDermott and Gospodinoff share their pessimism about change: "Unfortunately, even if we achieve some semblance of intellectual clarity on the subject, there is considerable question as to whether we will be able to stop our

own participation in the creation of borders without considerable change in the institutional demands with which we must
deal in our everyday life. Many of our institutions certainly get
in the way of maximizing the social and psychological potential
of our children, and most of us do not have the foggiest notion
of how to proceed in rectifying the situation" (1981, pp. 229-
230).

In our view, fundamental interpersonal change is truly
difficult to achieve. The conclusion that it would be impossible
in these situations, however, remains untested. That is, neither
McDermott and Gospodinoff, Philips, nor Erickson has written
of situations in which they tested the assertion that the individual is incapable of changing. Philips, for instance, might have
attempted to retrain teachers to notice and more accurately
interpret a wider range of attention structures; McDermott and
Gospodinoff might have helped the teacher and her children to
become aware of their self-sealing patterns and to begin to alter
those patterns. Erickson might have gotten counselor and counselee together to educate both about the impact of their nonverbal behavior on each other.

In other words, McDermott and Gospodinoff, Philips,
and Erickson frame their description in the same way as Milgram
did. All these researchers accurately and rigorously describe the
world as it is, but assume that that world is unchangeable. They
do not question or test this assumption but nevertheless base
their prescriptions on it.

Here we would like to speculate upon a point Kleinfeld
makes (1983, p. 286). She points out that much of the current
ethnographic research has an unfortunate alienating effect on
majority teachers because it implicitly labels them as "bad
guys." But it is possible that the features discussed earlier—
diagnoses that focus on cultural differences, inferences that go
untested, implicit advice that is difficult to follow, and explicit
advice that addresses domains out of the teachers' control
("change policy and/or society")—also contribute to a sense of
alienation on the part of those who might most benefit from
anthropology's "special ways of knowing about the relationship

of actions to their contexts and their meanings to participants" (Cazden, 1983, p. 38).

We have looked at three ethnographers whose attempt has been to accurately and completely describe a problem so that they can add to the store of useful knowledge. The accuracy of these descriptions was questioned because the inferences the researchers made went untested (as far as we know) with the participants in their ethnographies. The completeness of these ethnographies was also questioned because they focused on an aspect of the diagnosis that does not reach deeply enough into individual reasoning about relationships to address the question of what keeps human beings unaware of how they may be contributing to a problem.

Finally, the applicability of these ethnographies to the world of the practitioner was called into question. Here the researchers themselves express doubts about their ability to contribute to direct change. We also expressed pessimism, but for different reasons—the high level of abstraction of interpersonal and structural advice was identified as problematic in that it is by the researchers' own definitions difficult or impossible for their subjects to produce.

Applied Ethnographies

The question of whether or not ethnography can contribute significantly to altering the problems it describes is one that the field has begun to take up. Considerations of the possibility of collaborative research (Florio and Walsh, 1981) are now more frequent. In her previously mentioned presidential address to the Council on Education and Ethnography, Cazden expressed concern that ethnographic research has not produced knowledge that can help provide solutions to such problems as differential treatment of ethnic minorities in school. But she also identified two important exceptions: "Of all the ethnographic/linguistic research on problems in achieving 'mutual calibration and reciprocity' of the last ten to fifteen years, I know of only two clear examples that do go beyond the status quo, two cases where ethnographers have not only described problems but stayed to collaborate with teachers in designs for change: Shirley Brice Heath's work in Appalachia and the Kamehameha Early Education Program (KEEP) in Hawaii" (1983, p. 35).

Both the examples Cazden cites would indeed appear to be exceptions to the kinds of studies we have been discussing. These are important exceptions in the sense that they created new educational contexts that in large part reversed school failure. This was done through interventions that created better matches between home and school culture. But Kleinfeld (1983, p. 286) calls for anthropologists to go beyond the "cultural conflict paradigm" and identify how decisions are made by minority children not to acquire aspects of the majority culture. She pleads for an examination of the reasoning behind these decisions and of what it is in the interactions between students and teachers that might lead to this decision—"What is the meaning to children of what teachers ask them to do" (1983, p. 286).

Our view is consistent with Kleinfeld's. We as action scientists wish to understand what kind of reasoning leads children, teachers, and administrators to interact in such a way that children fail to learn the requisite skills of schooling and the others fail to learn why this occurs. We think that one way to reverse this process is to ask actors to take a look at their individual theories-in-use about interacting, learning, and dealing with differences in a classroom. This kind of learning, whether on the individual or group level, is what we have called double-loop learning. A situation in which actors have come to learn in a double-loop way about the system they have created —its errors and successes—and have been able to alter the system as need be fulfills our definition of changing the status quo.

In what follows we will describe and examine the two ethnographically influenced interventions cited by Cazden as going beyond the status quo. We will look at the way the researchers framed or diagnosed the problem, as well as the nature of the changes implemented in the classrooms. We will look at this last aspect particularly from the point of view of whether the changes could have led to double-loop changes.

Heath's Work in Appalachia. Heath lived and worked in a rural southern community for five years. She occupied multiple roles during that time—she worked as an ethnographer, as a consutant to the local school system, and as a university professor. She was guided in all this work by two requests from the people with whom she lived: first, that she find out why it was that so many of the poor children, white and black, failed in school and, second, that she use that information to help teachers raise their level of success.

Heath began this task by conducting extensive ethnographies of communication in the communities of Roadville, the rural white community, and Trackton, the rural black one. She also gathered information—more informally and with the help of others—about the middle-class towns surrounded by these communities (Heath, 1983). She discovered systematic differences between each community in the use of print, the rules of interaction around print, and the degree to which reading and writing were bound up with community members' identities. Perhaps underlying all these differences were different ways of talking and different ways of interacting within communities. She also discovered that, although some teachers seemed to be aware that there was something different about the Roadville and especially the Trackton children, they were unable to identify the differences.

Heath disseminated this information to teachers in her role as a teacher trainer and a consultant. Her interventions had two major components. One addressed the community members' unawareness of the different styles. The second addressed the problem of how to create contexts in which children would be likely to acquire literacy. Heath addressed the first problem in her role as university professor. As a teacher of teachers, she communicated the information she gathered in her research to teachers, thereby raising their consciousness as to the different rules about print that characterized the different communities whose children they would educate. Equally important, she taught the teachers her own method for learning—that is, she taught them to be ethnographers in their own community, so that they would not have to be dependent exclusively upon Heath to function as a "translator." Thus, teachers began to study their own rules of interaction in their classrooms and in their homes.

The KEEP Intervention. The work of the researchers and educators of the KEEP program in Hawaii started as a result of the same kind of problem that initiated Heath's work: The minority children—in this case native Hawaiian children—were failing in school.

The researchers in this group began with the knowledge that the Hawaiian children were highly competent at functioning in their home culture but that, whatever competencies home life involved, they were probably significantly different from those required in school. The researchers felt that if they could identify the natural contexts in which children learn, they might be able to help educators create similar contexts in school. They called these "eliciting contexts" (Jordan, 1981, p. 16).

One of the most widely discussed contexts they created was based on an understanding of a common Hawaiian form of storytelling called *talk-story* (Watson-Gegeo and Boggs, 1977). In trying to bring this form into the classroom, teachers and researchers created a new structure for reading groups. This structure emphasized some of the features of the talk-story such as mutual participation, talking on a volunteer basis rather than in a rigid turn-taking order, and a different relationship between teacher and student, characterized by more "informality . . . overlapping speech and conarration" (Jordan, 1981, p. 18).

Double-Loop Change in Framing the Problem

The researchers in both projects detected a need for change on the level of cultural rules about communication and learning. Mismatches between intention and outcome were detected, not at an individual theory-in-use level but at a cultural theory-in-use level. In this respect their diagnoses were similar to those of Erickson and Philips. Heath framed the problem as follows:

> Trackton children's "communicative competence" in responding to questions in their own community had very little positive transfer value to these classrooms.
>
> The learning of language uses in Trackton had not prepared children to cope with three major characteristics of the many questions used in classrooms. . . . in short, school questions were unfamiliar in their frequency, purposes, and in the domains of content knowledge and skills display they assumed on the part of students [1982, p. 123].

The problem as Heath saw it was not only to teach Trackton students the rules of classroom discourse but to teach teachers the rules that the Trackton children had learned about questioning. The teachers could then incorporate them into their classroom curriculum where it seemed appropriate, thus creating a familiar and more effective environment for Trackton children.

Similarly, Jordan frames the problem of school failure in Hawaiian children as one of cultural mismatch, and prescribes the creation of a better match in the classroom:

> Children from different cultures may have been socialized to go about the learning process in different ways and in response to different contexts.
>
> One of the reasons that children of many minority groups experience difficulty in school is that they have learned to learn in ways that differ from the ways in which their teachers have learned to teach [1981, p. 16].

She prescribes the following:

> The assumption [of Keep] is that the correct course, for both practical and ethical reasons, is

not to attempt to change the children or their families to fit the schools, but rather to modify the
schools in ways that will allow them to serve minority children more effectively.

[What this position implies] is an effort to
select from the wide spectrum of available teaching practices and curricula, those that are compatible with the culture of the client population in
ways that contribute to effective education [1981,
p. 16].

We believe that the kind of inquiry outlined here is close
to double-loop inquiry. This is because it asks people to examine the tacit rules and values that guide their speech, and it does
so with an eye toward altering these rules and values. We would
argue, however, that if full-fledged double-loop learning is to
occur, the culture of the school environment must be as much
subject to reflection as is the home culture. Furthermore, we
think that an integral part of the culture of a school includes
the factors that inhibit or facilitate the ability of members of
that culture to reflect on and alter the culture. This would include questioning the reasoning of teachers and administrators
if that reasoning led them to (1) create dysfunctional conditions and/or policies in the first place; (2) to remain blind to
the fact that the conditions or policies were dysfunctional; or
to fail to effectively change the dysfunctionality if they recognized it. Put another way, the double-loop problem is not only
to get children to achieve literacy. It is to create a situation in
which failure to do so does not occur again. We believe the way
to achieve this is to give people the skills to detect, discuss, and
correct their errors at the behavioral, as well as the policy, level;
in other words, to learn in a double-loop way.

Double-Loop Change in Resolving the Problem

One way to illustrate our assertion that the KEEP program did not create a fundamental change in the status quo is
to take a look at the directly observable data of classroom and

school interaction. If we found discussion of previously undiscussable features of the school culture (such as making errors, feelings of failure, the meaning of negatively evaluating an entire group of children, and so on), or teachers confronting each other on their theories-in-use, or bilateral control of the classroom tasks—any of these would indicate that double-loop learning, or something very close to it, was going on. Unfortunately, there is not enough directly observable data on classroom interaction or teacher interaction around difficult issues for us to judge. With the data that does exist, however, we can make some inferences that lead us to believe that the kind of change in status quo addressed did not take place. How do we make such an inference?

In the KEEP program, teachers did learn to alter their behavior as well as their curriculum, but the behavioral changes that they made remained within Model I. Researchers found, for instance, that young children only felt comfortable "talking story" with adults who had a certain status. In order to successfully teach a reading lesson that incorporated talk-story, teachers had to achieve this status. This involved demonstrating "warmth and control." A teacher had to give a lot of praise and rewards, as well as openly express expectations and disapproval at slacking off: "Her clear expression of both approval and disapproval and her consistent and contingent dispensing of 'good things' in her control such as privileges, establish her in the role of a firm but friendly adult, one whose positive regard is actively sought" (Au and Jordan, 1981, p. 146).

Creating warmth and maintaining control are achieved in the KEEP classrooms partly through the use of positive behavior modification techniques. Teachers are taught to use behaviors of "praise, hugs, and the like," "positive statements to students, and so on" (Sloat, 1981b, p. 39). These behaviors may be new to teachers and the context they create for reading a more successful one, but the theory of action of behavior modification is Model I in that it leaves the teacher in unilateral control of the situation. This may be appropriate for five- to seven-year-olds. We do not expect teachers to create Model II children, but we are suggesting that teachers and administrators should attempt to create a Model II learning system with each other (we would help them to gain skills that would allow them to reflect on how they dealt with each other, how the changes of the KEEP program impacted on them, how they facilitated or inhibited learning for each other, how they monitored the success of their system, and so forth). Heath and her students identify two features of Model I behavior in the questioning strategies used by teachers in their homes: the easing-in versus directive strategy dilemma of communication and the contradiction between espoused theory and theory-in-use. Neither of these issues appears to be central to the change effort, although we would assert that both are central to double-loop learning.

Easing-in and the Directive Approach. In examining their questioning patterns at home with children, some teachers discovered that many of their questions hid directives or reprimands. An example of a question whose pragmatic function is to direct someone to do or say something is, "That's a top. You've never seen one of those before, have you?" Heath explains that, with this kind of question, "the adult was not calling for a response from the child but making a declarative statement for the child: 'No, I've never seen one of those' " (1982, p. 112).

An example of a question whose true intent is to reprimand might be, "Stop it, Jamie, why don't you behave?" Again, Heath explains that "the latter part of this utterance extends the scolding power of the imperative and calls upon the child to *think* about a response to the question, but not to respond verbally to the condemnation" (1982, p. 112).

The reasoning behind these strategies appears to be consistent with the reasoning behind the easing-in strategy identified in Chapter Three. Remember that when an actor has information that she is hiding from another but wants that other to discover it, she eases in by asking questions that, if answered correctly by the recipient, will reveal to him what the asker wants him to know. Although the teachers' questions appear similar to those of students and managers described as Model I in this book, there are also two important differences. The first is that the information to be revealed has to do with issues that

are far more concrete than those dealt with by easing-in managers and therapists. The second is that the form of the questions is more forthright: "Stop it, Jamie, why don't you behave?" sends off a clearer message than "How do you think Mr.
Y reacted to you?"

Despite these differences, however, it is our suspicion
that these questions are examples of elementary easing-in questions and that they may help children come to recognize and
use easing-in questions. This suspicion is strengthened by the
reaction that two teachers experienced when they attempted an
experiment. They decided to make the directives embedded in
the questions explicit, that is, to say what they meant. In the
framework of the theory of action, this means a shift from an
easing-in strategy to a directive one. Interestingly, both teachers
reported discomfort with this experiment: "They reported that
they felt they did not involve their children when they used
statements. They received no sense of interaction and felt they
were 'preaching' to a third party; they could not be sure they
were being heard" (Heath, 1982, p. 112).

Argyris (1982) has found that adults often express similar
views when critiquing others who use a directive strategy in their
daily interactions. Easing-in and directive strategies are two of
the poles of Model I theories of action. Model I adults will probably not be able to produce a strategy outside of these categories. Much of the training for Model II has to do with reflecting on this dilemma and designing alternative strategies that do
not produce consequences such as feeling inconsistent,
"preachy," or controlling.

Heath makes no mention of whether there was discussion
about alternatives to the questions or directives, such as the
combination of advocacy with inquiry described in Argyris
(1982). Thus, the experiment served to make teachers more
aware of elements of their theory-in-use, but not to help them
alter that theory. The focus of the change effort in the classroom is on widening the teacher's repertoire of questions, not
altering the underlying values that guide the questions. Thus,
we would predict that in the new curriculum the teachers will
still oscillate between easing-in and directive strategies, but

will do so with a significantly wider repertoire of types of questions.

Contradiction Between Espoused Theory and Theory-in-Use. Heath comments that in the course of reflecting on their practice, the teachers came to see ways in which "their own behavior exemplified patterns which were sometimes contrary to their ideals and principles, or, at the very least, unexpected" (Heath, 1982, p. 126). Achieving and reflecting on these kinds of insights are central to the practice of action science, for they are the first steps toward change. For instance, Heath found that some of the teachers had an instinct that their failure to reach the black children had to do with the possibility that the children were learning rules of interaction at home that were not congruent with classroom interaction. They felt helpless, however, to seek out information that might back up their tentative diagnosis. Heath explains that "some teachers were aware of this paradox, but felt that since they did not know how language was taught in black communities and how it was used to make children aware of the world around them, they had no basis on which to rethink their views of the language socialization of black children. The teachers could only assume these children were taught language and cognitive skills in the same ways they used to teach their own children" (1982, p. 114).

Heath's way of helping these teachers out of their dilemma was to help them learn to become observers of themselves and others. Thus, as they became competent ethnographic researchers, they could find the data they needed to support their diagnosis. However, while this is a crucial skill, it is not sufficient for changing the status quo. What is also necessary is for the teachers to ask themselves such questions as, "Why did I continue to act on what I do not believe to be the case?" (That is, that black children are socialized into language use in the same way as white children.) "What prevented me from testing with the black children and/or parents whether my attributions about the way they learn language are correct?" "Why not ask the community to help me see where I may be making mistakes?"

Had these questions been explored, they might have led to discussions of the degree to which the teachers felt able to discuss these issues among each other as well as in the black community. Thus, some data could have been generated that might have helped teachers reflect on how they deal with difficult issues like discrimination toward their students or feelings of failure in their teaching. If any such discussions took place among them, they were not written about and did not appear to be central to the intervention.

There are two other changes in the setting that might have facilitated double-loop learning had they been extended to reasoning about interpersonal relationships. The first such feature is the emphasis on the discussability of the experiments that the teachers were conducting. When they began to reflect on the different rules of language use, the teachers made much of this reflection explicit and available to the children. Thus, discussions in class of the different rules for speaking in each community became frequent: "Teachers and students came to talk openly about school being a place where people 'talked a lot about things being themselves.' Students caught onto the idea that this was a somewhat strange custom, but one which, if learned, led to success in school activities and, perhaps most important, did not threaten their ways of talking about things at home" (Heath, 1982, p. 125).

Examining the tacit rules that underlie behavior and that may affect learning and justice in organizations is a crucial step toward altering the status quo. Again, for the interventions to facilitate such a change, the reflection and discussion would have to be extended: It would be necessary to reflect on the degree to which Model I relationships, characterized by a win, don't lose mentality and unilateral control are altered or can be altered by these changes.

Teachers might also ask older students whether they were aware of the linguistic differences and, if so, what led them to remain silent about it. In this way teachers might learn what they are doing that unintentionally silences feedback from students. On their part, students might have to take a look at their assumptions about teachers' willingness to listen and to change. Thus they might have to come to examine their underlying assumptions about power and the degree to which they believe teachers (people in power) wish to change.

The second feature of Heath's intervention that is crucial

but still not sufficient is the inclusion of teachers in the data collection and change effort. In her role as a university professor, Heath was able to teach teachers how to do ethnography. The changes that were made in the classrooms were very much dependent on what each teacher found and how she decided to use her findings. Teachers were free to make whatever changes they deemed appropriate in their classrooms. Thus, Heath was able to create conditions in which teachers had a high degree of internal commitment.

The Appalachian and Hawaiian interventions helped to reverse one particular status quo that existed with Trackton children and native Hawaiian children. This was a highly complex and significant accomplishment. It served to reduce conditions of injustice in those particular settings, and, in Heath's case, for a particular period of time. (The classroom innovations ended with Heath's leaving and the advent of highly rigid state and federal education requirements.)

The changes made in the Appalachian and Hawaiian interventions are terribly important in their consequences for the children, for they learned to read, to write, and, in the case of Heath's intervention, they learned about cultural differences among their communities. But the problem of school failure represents a difficult and threatening one for educational practitioners, as well as for students, and perhaps a somewhat different challenge. The challenge for educational practitioners is to learn how to cope with threatening problems in such a way that they can establish a self-correcting, self-reflective system for the next problem they face. This is a tall order for a perhaps already overburdened group of people, whose problems may include funding cuts, unintentional or intentional racism, and vandalism. We believe, however, that action scientists, in direct collaboration with classroom practitioners, can bring about such changes. Part Three of this book outlines the complexities and challenges of learning the skills necessary for this task.

In this chapter an attempt has been made to look closely at the nature of three ethnographic descriptions of sources of school failure and how features of these descriptions may prevent them from being as useful as they might be in altering the status quo. We also looked at two applied ethnographies and asked to what extent they might have helped the educational practitioners involved in them to learn in a double-loop manner. In the next chapter we examine more closely the kinds of constraints ethnographers and other social scientists may face—particularly from their own social science communities—in attempting to produce knowledge that can contribute to altering the status quo.

7

The Social Scientist as Practitioner: Barriers to Translating Scientific Knowledge into Practical Knowledge

The social scientists in the previous three chapters all might be regarded as practitioners at work within their own distinctive communities of inquiry. Some are basic researchers, others applied; some work within the empirical-analytic tradition, others within the hermeneutic-historical tradition. But as members of a community they all follow a set of rules that tell them which problems to go after and which ones to leave alone; what kinds of solutions to seek and when to consider a problem solved; what they should do as they go about solving their problems and what they should avoid doing. As Kuhn (1970b) describes them, these rules are a part of a practitioner's stock of knowledge. Acquired during his or her apprenticeship within a particular community, they are often simply taken for granted.

But periodically practitioners take stock of such rules, and the past two decades have been such a time in the social sciences. Critics both in and outside the field have debated whether the social sciences have been studying the right problems in the right way or whether these sciences have become part of the problem rather than the solution (Mills, 1959; Zuniga, 1975; Caplan and Nelson, 1973; Ryan, 1976; Friedrichs, 1970). Out of this debate a gradual shift has taken place in the kinds of problems and methods considered legitimate for study. In the empirical-analytic tradition this has led to a move from a pure science orientation with an emphasis on laboratory methods to an approach more concerned with socially relevant problems and with developing methods that could travel beyond the confines of the laboratory (Reich, 1981; Campbell and Stanley, 1963). At the same time, those at work in the hermeneutic tradition have made a parallel move, no longer defining themselves strictly as dispassionate observers but gradually recasting their roles as helpers or advocates of those they study (Cassell, 1982; Spindler, 1982; Spradley, 1980).

Yet despite these new aspirations, researchers continue to solve their problems without taking into account what practitioners require to solve theirs. For a basic researcher, the problem is to describe and to account for some phenomenon, and for the applied researcher it is to figure out what can be done about it. The difficulty is that both consider their problems solved and their tasks complete long before considering the practitioner's problem of how to understand and act in real-life contexts amidst all the complexity and multiple dilemmas of value they pose. That problem lies beyond the borders of the communities of inquiry of the basic researcher and the applied scientist.

In this chapter we will consider an obvious point with some nonobvious implications: What you look for is what you get. Depending on the community in which he works, each researcher looks for different facts and solutions in accord with his own community's norms for inquiry. For our purposes we can distinguish four kinds of communities, representing basic and applied research within the two traditions in the social sciences (see Table 3).

What follows is a consideration of how these different community norms govern the practice of research and determine the kind of knowledge that is produced. To anticipate, we

Table 3. Communities of Inquiry.

Form of Research	Tradition	
	Empirical-Analytic	Hermeneutic-Historical
Basic	Milgram (experimental social psychologist)	Philips, Erickson, McDermott and Gospodinoff (descriptive ethnographers)
Applied	Hackman and Oldham, Lawler (assessment research/ organizational behavior)	Jordan, Heath (applied ethnographers)

Note: Many communities of inquiry exist within each of these four cells. This table focuses on generic differences among kinds of communities of inquiry.

found a paradox. By following the rules of their practice, the researchers in our case studies ended up with solutions that fell short of their own and practitioners' standards.

Figuring Out How It Happens to Be

In their practice as scientists, the basic researchers whose work we have discussed faced the theoretical problem of figuring out how some phenomenon happens to be. At the same time, the problems these researchers took on were not simply theoretical ones. Without exception they each studied a critical social problem: obedience to authority and failure to learn at school. Thus far we have a happy match between social relevance and potential usefulness, on the one hand, and theoretical requirements and interests, on the other. But now these researchers must construct some line of inquiry into these problems in order to solve their own problems, and not all lines of inquiry are equal in yielding socially useful results—even if they do lead into the most important and relevant of social problems.

First and foremost from the researchers' point of view is that an inquiry conform to the rules of their practice and then that it move along into domains most likely to yield a solution acceptable to its norms. We thus saw that Milgram constructed his inquiry to follow the rules of the laboratory context by asking: "If an experimenter tells a subject to act with increasing severity against another person, under what conditions will the subject comply and under what conditions will he disobey?" (1974, p. xii). And his search for a solution went in a direction guided by his particular community. He looked at what subjects did under conditions relevant to a social psychologist, varying situational factors such as distance and roles in order to study their psychological impact.

The descriptive ethnographers took a different but equally systematic tack in framing their inquiry. Unlike Milgram, they were not bound by the constraints of the laboratory and were not required to tailor their questions to suit such constraints. Philips (1983) could therefore ask the less precise question of whether Indian children acquired distinctive communicative codes and, if so, whether this might account for school failure, while McDermott and Gospodinoff (1981) could ask whether there might be something functional about this dysfunctionality. Once framed, their questions could also give way to a less circumscribed search. The facts these ethnographers sought were defined neither a priori nor with precision, and they were free to pursue unanticipated hunches as they arose. Nevertheless these ethnographers were as bound to the constraints of their community as Milgram was to his. They each looked for facts with an ethnographer's eye, searching for similarities and differences in communicative codes and rules of interaction and looking for what elements in their subjects' ethnic identities and early socialization processes might account for these. These are ethnographic "facts," and the ethnographic situation is thus defined, as Scholte (1974) also argues, as much by the "ethnological tradition in the head" of the ethnographer as by the nature of the culture or problem before him.

As this suggests, the questions asked and the facts sought by the experimentalist and the ethnographer are guided by different rules, and their inquiries move down different paths. Yet all the researchers were trying to solve some descriptive puzzle and to do so within the parameters of their own tradition. Milgram created situations that *limited* or *produced* obedience in order to describe and account for it, whereas the ethnographers delved into cultural factors that *led* to school failure in order to account for it.

So now the question arises: What do we get from these lines of inquiry? First of all, the "facts" they generate do not speak for themselves but must be organized into theories that can answer certain questions before they constitute a solution. Just as these researchers drew on existing conceptual tools to guide their search, they now can hang the facts they find on the conceptual structures available within their particular disciplines and traditions. Milgram therefore took his findings and formulated a solution in two steps. He first explained what led his subjects to obey by describing how certain situations resulted in psychological states that produced or limited obedient responses. Then as a basic researcher, he took a second step, asking the question "why obedience?" What does this tell us about human beings and the human condition? To answer this question, Milgram drew on what he called an evolutionary cybernetic model, "convinced" that these cybernetic principles were "very much at the root of the behavior in question" (1974, p. 125). Such models, Milgram explained, alert us to what "*must* occur" when an individual is brought into a hierarchical structure in which he no longer functions on his own but as a component of the system. And what does this model alert us to? Recall that Milgram's answer to "why obedience?" was that it was necessary for social coherence. For social organization to survive, those at the local level must cede control to those higher up. Hence over time human beings have acquired—actually have born into them—the potential for obedience. Without it social organization would be in jeopardy.

It is at this point that Milgram's problem of "why obedience?" was solved and his job was done. But notice that it is also at this point that his solution becomes our dilemma. If we foster disobedience, we may jeopardize the survival of social organization. Yet if we encourage obedience, we may jeopardize our responsibility toward other human beings.

The solutions of the ethnographers also present us with a dilemma. Once Philips (1983) and Erickson (1975) found their

facts, they too went on to put them within their tradition's as-
sumptive and theoretical frameworks. Philips explained that
teachers' inability to bridge or better handle differences was due
to conflicting communicative styles that are so highly learned
and skillful, some perhaps even neurologically based, that they
lie outside of human awareness and control. Similarly, Erickson
argued that regardless of our attempts to be fair by using universal criteria such as test scores in evaluating students, we automatically size people up by using particularistic and potentially
unfair criteria such as race, ethnicity, and so on. Moreover, he
added that these processes are so complex and highly learned
that they cannot be performed reflectively or stopped at will.

It is at this point that the ethnographers' problem of
"why failure?" was solved. But once again their solution becomes our dilemma, because what is thought necessary for competence as a teacher or counselor will necessarily lead to unfairness and failure. Framed this way, there is little we can do short
of matching teacher and student according to race or ethnicity,
a cure that may make the illness worse.

Recognizing this, McDermott and Gospodinoff attempted
to turn this solution on its head by going after an alternative explanation for what looks like interethnic miscommunication
and for what results in school failure. First, they called into
question the assumption that ethnographers like Philips and
Erickson take for granted. They pointed out that differences in
communicative codes and rules are neither "natural" nor "in
the long run irremedial," since studies such as Efron's (1941)
have shown that ethnic groups can and do bridge differences
even in their kinesic behavior. Next they cited studies and generated their own data to suggest an alternative explanation for
the existence of seemingly dysfunctional differences. They argued that it is not that such dysfunctionality is necessary but
that, paradoxically, it is functional within certain social arrangements.

Yet in the end even McDermott and Gospodinoff solved
their problem in a way that put teachers and students in a box.
"Our problem," they explained, "is that our school systems are
set up to have conscientious teachers function as racists and

bright little children function as dopes even when they are trying to do otherwise" (1981, p. 226). In other words, faced with
the present realities of school systems, teachers and students
have little choice and are destined to fail. This solution thus
gets them out of one dilemma only to plunk them down in a
new one.

But what are the implications of such solutions for the
problems these researchers study? The answer to that depends
partly on whose problem we are considering. We know already
that researchers will construct one kind of problem to suit their
purposes and practitioners another to suit theirs. How good we
consider these solutions to be depends on whose problem we
would like to solve: the researcher's problem of how to describe
causality within the requirements of their community of practice, or the practitioner's problem of how to transform causality in light of normative concerns. In what follows we will consider how adequately the researchers solved each problem.

Researcher's Theoretical Problem. In Part One we saw
that there is a divergence in what counts as a solution in the
empirical-analytic and the hermeneutic traditions. On the one
hand, accounts in the empirical-analytic tradition speak of analyzing the relationships among events and of devising causal
explanations that are abstracted from concrete situations and
thus become generalizable. These accounts are as complete and
precise as possible in order to be falsifiable. On the other hand,
accounts of the hermeneutic tradition reject the notion of
causal explanation and speak instead of understanding social action in the sense of grasping the logic of action—or more precisely, the meanings and intentions of actors embedded in the
particulars of a concrete situation. As we already saw, at stake
in what constitutes an adequate solution are different assumptions about the nature of action and human agency and how
accounts of social action can best grasp them (Chapter Two).

But in practice researchers from both traditions have
worked out an artful compromise in these domains. Most experimental psychologists now assume human agency, and with
varying success try to take into account the rules, meanings,
and intentions of their subjects, both in their methods and in

their formulations. In the same vein ethnographers often speak the language of the empirical-analytic tradition, putting the rules of actors in a causal context, considering the relationship among events, and working to rule out alternative explanations. Thus the borders distinguishing the two communities are not quite as distinct in practice as they are often thought to be. But at the same time, practitioners at work in these two communities cannot ignore their own tradition's criteria for what does and does not count as a good solution. The experimentalist must construct falsifiable explanations that have both scope and elegance, while the ethnographer must strive to accurately grasp the meanings and intentions of those she studies within the contexts in which they act. And while they can each get away with importing an occasional rule from the other's traditions, neither is permitted to move beyond the realm of explanation or understanding and into the realm of normative concerns. Researchers in the empirical-analytic tradition still aspire to keep values and facts separate and to stick to the world of facts in their solutions, whereas those in the hermeneutic tradition still try to take a disinterested stance toward their participants and to avoid imposing their own values on them.

In both traditions these norms simultaneously help and hinder the researchers' task. On the one hand, they serve to give their practice shape and meaning; while on the other hand, they put them in a double bind, because to meet one norm requires them to violate another. To illustrate what we mean, let us first consider Milgram's solution. In many respects it meets the criteria of the empirical-analytic tradition in which he worked. It disconfirmed the prevailing and erroneous view that obedience to an unjust authority is pathological or dispositional. It has a certain elegance in that it accounts for a wide range of facts with relatively few concepts. And it offers an explanation that speaks to the nature of human beings and their social institutions.

But herein lies the problem, because this explanation is not falsifiable within the norms of the empirical-analytic tradition. Recall that Milgram's solution put obedience in a hierarchical context, explaining that it is necessary for social coherence (those at the lower levels *must* cede control to superiors). To falsify this explanation would require that we construct experiments that might disconfirm it. Yet this would require going beyond the experimenter's question, "What limits or produces obedience?" to ask, "What responses and conditions might make obedience unnecessary?" And it might require looking beyond existing responses and arrangements for an answer. Yet pursuing this kind of inquiry would violate the norms of this tradition, making Milgram's explanation nonfalsifiable within it—unless of course such possibilities arose naturally over time, an unlikely event since these kinds of explanations a priori rule out such possibilities. Put more generally, any social science explanation that assumes that existing social arrangements reveal the true or necessary nature of things risks creating solutions that contain errors that this tradition cannot detect.

An alternative line of inquiry should further articulate this argument. In the domain of action theory Harmon's (1981) consideration of accountability rules ended up with a proposition that, if tested, might show that obedience is not in fact necessary for social coherence. Yet at first, Harmon's formulation of the obedience dilemma was quite similar to Milgram's. He understood obedience within the same hierarchical context of accountability rules and arrangements that mete out rewards and punishments for obeying and disobeying and that lead to social norms that are internalized and followed. His understanding of the premise underlying accountability arrangements was also similar to Milgram's: In social situations, if the action of one person affects another, he should take the other into account in the interest of consistency and fairness. Finally, like Milgram he pointed out that the accountability arrangements designed to ensure consistency separate the "doer" from the "decider," thereby fostering our propensity to perform harmful acts without feeling personally responsible. If Harmon had stopped here, we would be no further along than we were with Milgram. He would be left with the notion that what is done in the interest of consistency undermines a sense of personal responsibility for one's actions.

But Harmon neither assumed the necessity of existing accountability arrangements, nor was he bound by strictures to leave normative concerns alone. He thus went on to invent an alternative form of accountability that might better manage the obedience dilemma. It is as if he asked the question, "Given the value of the premise underlying the notion of accountability—but also given the consequences of current accountability arrangements—what form of accountability and what organizational arrangements might we create to satisfy consistency and maximize a sense of personal responsibility?" On two counts such a question falls outside the purview of the empirical-analytic tradition. It is explicitly normative in that it critically examines and puts forth what values or ends we should choose (consistency and personal responsibility), and it does not preclude inventing possibilities that exist outside of current arrangements in order to bring them about.

In answering this question, Harmon first eliminated possibilities unlikely to work on logical grounds. He ruled out unilateral discretion by those at the local level because "it runs the risk of being unchecked and arbitrary" (1981, p. 127). In so doing he rejected the only alternative to obedience in Milgram's formulation. Moreover, he did so for a reason similar to Milgram's: Fostering unilateral discretion would jeopardize consistency and coherence. He thus believed, as Milgram did, that the existing responses of ceding control or unilaterally taking it would be unlikely to manage the dilemma of conflicting requirements. Harmon therefore suggested adding an alternative to existing accountability rules, that is, a decision-rule that does not so sharply split "decider" and "doer" and that preserves consistency "without at the same time reducing a sense of personal responsibility" (p. 127). His own invention is a consensus rule under which participants must bilaterally negotiate their different views and interests, with no one person unilaterally imposing decisions on others. Under these conditions, he hypothesized that it would be less likely for one to act without feeling both personally responsible and accountable to others.

Without doubt this decision-rule is a significant departure from existing structures. Perhaps because of this Harmon speculated on what conditions might be necessary for such a rule to be implemented: the creation of mutual trust, the specification of conditions under which the rule would be best used, the belief that it can work (the success of rules may in part be a self-fulfilling prophecy), and practice and experience in such decision modes. But our point here is not so much whether or not this particular decision-rule would work. Our point is that we cannot a priori assume that it will not. It is not only a normative question, it is also an empirical one. To ignore its empirical content is to risk constructing explanations that are wrong without being able to discover that they are wrong—a violation of the norm of falsifiability. At the same time, the empirical question is inextricably tied up with normative concerns, so that pursuing this line of inquiry would violate the fact-value rule. Either way the basic researcher in the empirical-analytic tradition would be stuck.

For similar reasons the ethnographers' solutions fall short of the criteria within their tradition. Philips and Erickson both assumed that rules of interaction and meaning making are essentially unalterable: They are so automatic and complex that they cannot be brought into awareness, reflected on, or stopped at will. But how do we know they cannot? What if no data exist to suggest that they are alterable simply because these changes have not yet occurred naturally? Then the only way to discover whether we can reflect on, stop at will, or alter these rules is by trying to do so. But this kind of inquiry would violate the rules that ethnographers must follow. Their role is to leave untouched what they see. But as a result they too may miss some very basic features in how we construct and interact in the world.

Both traditions have criteria by which to judge a good solution. What this analysis suggests is that some criteria get in the way of others. In both traditions basic researchers must follow rules that in some form say, "Describe what is accurate" and "Do not delve into normative concerns." Yet this latter rule makes it likely that both traditions will generate descriptions that contain mistakes they will be unable to discover.

Practitioner's Problem. Just as a researcher's solution is expected to meet certain criteria, so is a practitioner's. As we saw in Part One, practitioners seek to understand in order to act; they try to transform, not to leave untouched, what they see; and they continuously grapple with conflicting values in the problematic situations they face. It therefore follows that their solutions should be of a certain sort. They should emphasize causal factors that are potentially within their control; they should inform practitioners how to transform what they see, even if that requires going beyond what now exists; and they should articulate some normative stance that will enable practitioners to manage conflicting values and ends. For the practitioner to be effective, he cannot ignore these requirements any more than a researcher can his. The problem is that the existing requirements for researcher and for practitioner may be quite incompatible, making the prevailing division of labor model quite questionable.

We already know that the basic premise underlying this model is that the findings of social science can contribute to the solving of social ills (see Part One). Society is to hand its problems over to the social sciences, and the social sciences are to give back theory to be applied toward their solution (Schön, 1983; Geuss, 1981). For their part basic researchers are supposed to offer explanations that can better frame social problems, thereby helping practitioners to solve them. But do they? The way a problem is framed *can* influence the solutions that are chosen (Schön, 1983; Kahnemann and Tversky, 1984). But as illustrated, the problem frames in our case studies imply solutions that fall short of the requirements a practitioner must face. These researchers gave little if any guidance on normative concerns, and they emphasized causal factors assumed to be outside a practitioner's control: historical factors (early socialization at home and at school); situational factors (inherent and necessary organizational or systemic constraints); genetic factors (membership in racial or ethnic groups); and responses thought to be automatic (nonverbal cues, reasoning processes outside our conscious awareness, and highly learned actions). At the same time they simply ruled out the possibility of gaining control over such factors. Philips and Erickson argued that our automatic responses are so far beyond our control that they cannot be altered. Milgram argued that the situational factors that foster obedience are so necessary that our potential for obedience is actually inbred. Only McDermott and Gospodinoff implied the possibility of some form of social system change, and even they said they hadn't the "foggiest notion" of how to go about achieving it. So once practitioners come face to face with these problems, there is little they can do. They have no control over the key causal factors involved. Hence the solutions of basic research become our dilemmas.

The paradox is that it may be the very efforts of these researchers to be fair and empathic that generates the practitioner's dilemma. Without exception every researcher stressed that his or her participants did not intend the consequences they described. Philips emphasized that teachers and students were not to be blamed for not comprehending one another, because this lack of comprehension resulted from early socialization processes. Erickson underscored that his counselors were neither malevolent nor "incompetent" but individuals who acted "professionally" and yet could not help but size people up in ways that might lead to unfair results (1975, p. 68). McDermott and Gospodinoff spoke of "conscientious teachers" with no choices, given the circumstances they faced (1981, p. 228). And Milgram spoke of obedience as a distressing but necessary and functional response to organizational necessities. Such stances toward participants has the positive effect of taking into consideration what practitioners are up against in the world. Actors (participants) are thus more apt to feel understood. Observers (readers) will be less apt to take a "holier than thou" perspective that can blind them to their own potential to act similarly. And we will all be less naive about the obstacles that must be faced in managing these dilemmas. The problem is that these effects are bought at the price of leaving us helpless to act differently.

But what if a researcher recognized the constraints and good intentions of actors, while also inquiring into their responsibility for acting in ways that necessarily create unintended consequences? Such a stance would require an alternative set of assumptions. The first would be that actors have and make choices—no matter how tacit they may be. The second would be that it is possible for such tacit choices to lead to consequences unintended at a fully conscious level. And the third would be that under certain conditions, it may be possible to gain access to and control over such choices. Under this set of assumptions, actors are not viewed as morally reprehensible for creating these consequences, but they can and should be held personally responsible for creating them. Later on we will describe how a researcher enacts this stance in relation to participants during the research process (see Chapter Nine). But for now, let us consider how it leads to qualitatively different solutions.

One such example can be found in Schön's (1983) study of how practitioners reflect in action. In one case study he described how a town planner found himself caught in a dilemma, in this case between obligations toward developers and obligations toward local regulatory bodies. To describe this dilemma, Schön began by inquiring into, and providing a rich description of, the contextual factors a planner faces, including a historical analysis of the conflicts inherent in the role as it has developed over time. But then he brought to the foreground other factors —most importantly, how the planner himself chose to frame his role as he interacted with the two parties and how this led him to construct a balancing act that put him in a dilemma. Notice that this account of the planner's dilemma recognizes both role and situational constraints, while highlighting what the practitioner *chose* to do to compound them, thereby generating the dilemma he faced.

At the same time, Schön regarded the town planner as well intentioned, "an individual who likes to reflect on his practice" (p. 228). He was thus faced with making sense of what prevented the planner from discovering and correcting his mistakes. Previous researchers have explained these puzzles by assuming that their participants' actions were necessary and/or outside of their control. But if Schön ascribed choice, how was he now to account for someone's choosing to act against his own intentions? Like some of the other researchers, Schön started out by assuming that the town planner was unaware of his inconsistency. But he did not then go on to assume that this unawareness was either necessary or out of the planner's control. Instead he hypothesized that the planner limited his reflection by focusing only on his strategies and ignoring how he framed his role and the situation before him. Moreover, this role itself was reinforced by theories of action that led the planner and those around him to keep private understandings that might have increased awareness and stimulated reflection had they been public.

So far Schön has formulated an explanation of the town planner's dilemma and his unawareness of the factors contributing to it. In contrast to the previous researchers, he has focused on a set of possible causes that may potentially be within the practitioner's control and therefore alterable. To pursue this possibility, Schön also pushed his inquiry past the point where the other researchers stopped. He asked the question, "What *might* have happened if, contrary to fact, the planner had become aware of his mistake? In what direction might his inquiry have gone?" (p. 230). As Schön wrote, this is a "peculiar question" because, according to his analysis, it would require the town planner to hold an alternative and rare theory of action. But as peculiar as it might be, the question was pivotal to the solution that Schön was developing, one that might help the planner work through his dilemma, while exploring whether and how this might be possible.

In the end Schön's research led to a solution that explained not only what led to the planner's dilemma but what he might do to manage it better, namely, learn an additional theory of action. To arrive at that insight, Schön had to develop a different line of inquiry. After asking the questions "what if" and "what stopped him from being aware," he had to ask questions that went "contrary to fact" and to look for different causal factors: not only the constraints inherent in the planner's role and the situation but his methods of constructing both and how he might have reconstructed them within those constraints. This inquiry itself depended on a somewhat different assumption. Schön had to assume not only that individuals construct their behavioral worlds but that they can reconstruct them if they so choose. As a result, Schön's inquiry could lead to a solution that might enable the planner to better manage the dilemma described in it.

This is not to say that the other researchers in our case studies offered no suggestions for getting out of the dilemmas they described. But they approached them from a different angle. As we saw in the case studies, most of them implied or suggested changes at the level of policy or structure alone without rigorously considering the implications of such changes or how to implement them at the level of action. For instance, Philips suggested matching teachers with students by ethnic or racial membership without addressing the possibility that this could foster further intergroup alienation at the expense of the less powerful group. And in most basic research such possibilities do go unexplored. It is not the basic researcher's job to rigorously consider the institutional and human implications of their suggestions. A brief conjecture on the "practical" implications of their results is sufficient for their purposes. Consequently, these researchers are unlikely to ever learn whether their advice generates more problems than it solves and are even less likely to take up the question of "why."

Conclusion. Each of the basic researchers in our case studies set out to solve some theoretical problem that involved a critical social problem. Although the empirical-analytic and hermeneutic traditions differed in the "facts" they sought and in the solutions they devised, both emphasized causal factors assumed to be largely outside of a practitioner's control. As a result they ended up formulating solutions that put practitioners into formidable dilemmas, and it was unclear whether their advice would get them out or generate new ones (see Table 4). But is is not only the practitioners who find themselves in a dilemma. The researchers do as well. By following the rule "Do not delve into normative concerns," they cannot fully satisfy the rule "describe the world accurately" or generate solutions that might be more helpful to practitioners.

Table 4. The Framing of Problems and Solutions (Basic Research).

Form of Research	Questions Asked	Causal Factors Found	Assumptions Made	Solution Formulated	Knowledge Produced
Ethnographers	What is it? How does it happen to be?	Emphasizes: • Differences and similarities in socialization among cultural groups • Existing rules of interaction and meaning making; communication codes; social identity. Recognizes: • Situational factors	Basic features of the world are revealed by describing the world as is Rules of interaction and meaning making are highly automatic and skilled, not apt to be altered.	Causal explanation that describes and accounts for the world as is	For science: Description of existing causal relationships that may be: • incomplete: they miss the deep structures that maintain it • inaccurate: they contain assumptions that can be difficult to falsify No descriptions of fundamental alternatives to what exists.

Experimentalists				
What is it?	Emphasizes: • Situational factors • Existing psychological and behavioral responses Recognizes: • Socialization processes	Basic features of the world are revealed by describing the world as is Existing arrangements and responses are functional and not alterable without jeopardizing organizational survival.	Causal explanation that describes and accounts for the world as is	For practitioners: • Insight into how factors outside of a practitioner's control lead to dilemmas • Little insight into what practitioners do within those constraints to maintain and reinforce them. • Little insight into how practitioners might act to transform dilemmas once face-to-face with them.
How does it happen to be?				

Figuring out How to Achieve a Given Set of Ends

Applied researchers work within the same two traditions as their basic research colleagues, but they use the tools of these traditions to figure out how to achieve some given set of ends. Hence, while they scan the solutions of basic research for clues, they then adhere to a distinctive set of rules and assumptions that allow them to use these clues to solve practical problems without violating the basic tenets of their respective traditions. This kind of building process can first be illustrated by looking at how the applied ethnographers set out to solve the problem of school failure. Like their descriptive colleagues, they subscribed to a "difference" rather than a "deficiency" model to explain failure at school. But for these researchers their problem began rather than ended here, because their task was to solve the problem of what can be done to help children to succeed at school (see Chapter Six). In Jordan's view this translated into making schools "compatible with the culture of the client population in ways that contribute to effective education" (1981, p. 16). In Heath's view it meant helping children to learn the four Rs: "to 'learn school,' meaning its rules and expectation, just as they . . . 'learn readin', writin', and 'rithmetic' " (1983, p. 281). With these different ends in mind, both researchers then went after the same question. As Heath described it, "The question was *how*?" (p. 281).

To answer this question, Heath and Jordan independently looked for ways they might use teachers' and students' existing cultural knowledge, skills, and rules in order to bridge the differences between them. Jordan emphasized that she was not looking for "radical" change in school practices (1981, p. 16), while Heath stressed that she and her teachers sought "to accommodate" group differences while teaching students mainstream rules of interaction (1983, pp. 284, 354). In taking this tack, their inquiries stayed squarely within their research traditions. They adhered to the prevailing ethnographic norm that admonishes against disrupting the rules and norms of different cultural groups, and they went after the same kinds of ethnographic "facts" sought earlier by basic researchers. At the same

time, neither accepted the solutions of their descriptive colleagues without significant modification. For instance, while
Heath drew on some of Philips' insights, she emphasized verbal
rather than nonverbal rules of interaction, and assumed a far
greater capacity to overcome differences in communicative
codes among different cultural groups. For Heath's purposes
such modifications were essential. As we saw earlier, without
them the problem of how to bridge these differences in face-to-
face interaction becomes insoluble.

A similar building process can be traced in the field of organizational behavior. Among our case studies we considered
the use of assessment models such as that of Hackman and Oldham (1975) in diagnosing and advising organizational clients
(see Chapter Five). Such models are often used in organizations
because they are designed to explain how a complex set of
interdependent variables lead to certain outcomes or goals
thought to be related to organizational effectiveness. In this
instance the researchers were interested in such outcomes as employee motivation, satisfaction, and productivity. But such
models might focus on any number of goals from a long and diverse list of possibilities—a fact of organizational life that has
rendered efforts to study and measure effectiveness problematic. How does one ever know which goals to set as appropriate
criteria? In practice, most researchers have answered this question by picking some goal of "substantial interest" to scholars
and participants and studying how organizations may reliably
be expected to achieve it (Mohr, 1982, pp. 190-191). The important question therefore is not what ends to choose but how
to achieve them.

Hackman and Lawler (1971) initially pursued this question in the field of social psychology, where they drew on the
theories of Lewin (1938) and Tolman (1959) to develop a conceptual framework for understanding job design. Several years
later Hackman and Oldham (1975) expanded on this work by
elaborating a model that could be applied by organizations interested in evaluating jobs and job redesign. The model itself
holds a strong resemblance to the causal structure found in
most theories within social psychology. Certain antecedent

conditions (mostly situational) are thought to bring about certain key psychological states, modified by individual characteristics and leading to certain behavioral consequences (compare the causal logic in Milgram's (1974) formulation of obedience in the previous section).

At this point the applied researchers had framed their problems. Because their traditions diverge, however, their frames focused on different kinds of causal factors. The ethnographers emphasized communicative codes, rules of interaction, and interactional contexts, while the assessment researchers in organizational behavior stressed situational factors such as task identity and skill variety and their effect on psychological and behavioral variables. Nevertheless each researcher pursued those causal relationships thought to be pivotal in achieving the ends they had set.

So now the question once again becomes: What kinds of solutions do these lines of inquiry yield? Just as the causal factors found by basic researchers did not in and of themselves constitute a solution, neither does the description of key causal relationships constitute a solution for applied researchers. Instead they must describe how these causal factors might be manipulated in order to produce the desired result. No matter how implicit or loosely formulated, some theory of intervention must be developed before their problem is solved.

In the case of the ethnographers we have two theories of intervention designed to meet somewhat different ends. To solve the problem she set, Heath developed strategies aimed at teaching children the four Rs—not only school subjects but rules of school interaction. She sought to do so by developing ways for teachers, parents, and children to discover and build on students' existing rules, so that they might meet existing requirements for interaction at school and later on in life. In contrast, the KEEP project described by Jordan was aimed at a somewhat different set of ends. Its policy was to adapt schools to children's culture instead of asking children to acquire the rules of the school's culture: "The assumption is that the correct course, for both practical and ethical reasons, is not to attempt to change the children or their families to fit the schools, but rather to modify the schools in ways that will allow them to serve minority children more effectively" (Jordan, 1981, p. 16).

As this suggests, Jordan and Heath may have started out with the same model to explain school failure, but they ended up stressing somewhat different ends and strategies for closing the gap between school and children. Heath's teachers, and presumably Heath, considered it only "humane" to prepare children as soon as possible for what lies ahead by adding to their repertoire of rules (1983, p. 281). In contrast Jordan thought it only "practical and ethical" to ask schools to change to fit children's rules. Yet despite these differences a sense of obviousness pervaded the legitimacy of the different ends they each set. Neither researcher indicated that she regarded them as choices to be critiqued and probed. Jordan referred to, but did not make explicit, the "practical and ethical" reasons behind KEEP's policy, as if its "correctness" was so apparent that it could go unstated.

Working within a different tradition and with a different problem, Hackman (1983) and Hackman and Oldham (1980) built on their previous work by developing a set of principles that described how to manipulate the key situational factors identified in their framing of the problem. These included redesigning structures and policies thought to affect such features of job design as task significance, autonomy, and feedback in order to engender psychological states believed to increase productivity and satisfaction at work: a sense of meaningfulness, responsibility, and knowledge. Like the ethnographers, these researchers act as if they too regarded the ends they set as somehow given in the problem. Nowhere did they question whether they were the right ends to set, nor did they suggest how they might be evaluated in light of other organizational outcomes or ends.

What, then, are the implications of these kinds of solutions? In their solutions the basic researchers did not rigorously pursue the question of how practitioners might solve the problems they had framed. It was not that they ignored or lacked concern for the question but that, within the division of labor model, the task of answering it is assigned to applied researchers and practitioners. How well we now think the applied researchers have done depends once again on whose problem we consider: the applied researcher's problem of how to achieve some given set of ends, or the practitioners' problem of how to understand and take action in a real-life context with the conflicting ends and values it poses. We will now look at the solutions of applied researchers in light of both sets of criteria.

Applied Researcher's Problem. What qualifies as a good solution for the applied researcher is a tricky question, because it involves both explicit and tacit criteria. On the one hand, the solution is supposed to tell us how to achieve the ends set in the framing of the problem; while on the other hand, it should be constructed in accord with a set of tacit rules that keep applied researchers within the norms of their particular tradition. One such rule governs the process of choosing among ends, while a second set tells researchers how to search for and choose among strategies for achieving these ends. It is assumed that, by following such rules, researchers can steer clear of normative concerns while meddling in practical affairs, thereby protecting their status as scientists. But at the same time these rules may hinder their ability to solve the problems they set without creating new ones. What follows is a consideration of these rules and their implications for problem-solving effectiveness.

• *Rule 1:* Ends should be regarded as "given" in the problem. We just saw that the question for applied researchers was not "what ends ought we to choose" but "given these ends, *how* do we achieve them?" They thus regarded the ends they set as somehow given in the problems they framed. But obviously ends do not materialize through a process of spontaneous generation. They must be set by someone somehow and without stepping into the normative realm. To do so, most applied researchers subscribe to the goal-oriented logic described earlier. If researchers or participants hold an interest in a goal, then this is a sufficient criterion for making the goal worthy of pursuit and for inquiring into efficacious ways of achieving it (Mohr, 1982).

For different reasons this criterion holds in both traditions. In the empirical-analytic tradition organizational researchers speak of pursuing ends in the service of effectiveness, and they strive to keep values separate from fact in the course of this pursuit by confining their inquiry to what they regard as the empirical question: What is the most efficacious and reliable way of achieving this set of ends? In the hermeneutic tradition we arrive at a similar destination but by way of a different rationale. The ethnographers like Hymes speak of pursuing ends in the service of communicative competence (Philips, 1983), and they strive not to impose their own or others' values or ends on participants by confining their inquiry to a similar question: How can we help participants achieve the ends they have set? This assumption has a normative bent in a dual sense. It asserts that there is value in avoiding value questions, and it assumes that it is neither necessary nor desirable to make ends the object of inquiry.

But there is a problem with this logic. Practitioners and institutions alike hold multiple and often conflicting ends that they have an interest in satisfying (Kelly, 1955; Pfeffer, 1981; Mohr, 1982; Keeley, 1984). In the pursuit of one set of ends it is thus not unlikely to violate or come up against others. Yet the applied researchers set their problems as if they were unaware of this possibility or, at the very least, regarded it as peripheral to their inquiry. But Heath's project suggests that it may not be peripheral. As her research unfolded, Heath discovered that Trackton students were unfamiliar with the rules of politeness used by teachers in giving commands and that as a result they neither understood nor followed them. In an impromptu experiment she thus asked her teachers if they would try using more directive rules for about a month. The teachers agreed, and for the following month they made explicit commands instead of hinting or making indirect requests. So rather than say something like, "Can we get ready on time?" they more often said things like, "Put your toys back where you took them from. We have to line up for lunch" (Heath, 1983, p. 283; also see Heath, 1982, p. 112, for an additional description of the experiment).

What they discovered provides important insights into the problem posed by conflicting ends. Despite the teachers' desire to adopt rules familiar to students, they were dissatisfied with what happened once they succeeded in doing so: "They reported they felt they did not involve their children when they used statements. They received no sense of interaction and felt they were 'preaching' to a third party; they could not be sure they were being heard. They viewed questions as a way to 'share talk' with children of this age" (Heath, 1982, p. 112).

This suggests that the most sincere efforts to adopt compatible rules may come up against other values or ends in which teachers also have a stake. In this case the teachers felt that the new rules ran counter to their highly valued sense of shared talk and interaction. So their wish to adopt directive rules violated their simultaneous desire to experience shared interaction. Once brought to the surface, however, this dilemma of conflicting values was never pursued. Instead, for unstated reasons some teachers simply returned to their own rules of politeness, whereas others continued to use directives while they taught students how to use hints and indirect requests (Heath, 1983, p. 283). But either way they bypassed the twofold question of whether their sense of shared talk was in fact shared and whether it was in the interest of student learning. And it may not be in their interest since shared talk is predicated on rules of indirectness that are by nature ambiguous and a source of misunderstandings; moreover, in this case the student neither shared nor followed these rules.

If we take this possibility seriously, then the question of what ends teacher and student ought to pursue itself becomes worthy of pursuit. The ends at stake are multiple, they are conflicting, and still new ones may be discovered as the inquiry unfolds further. But most important, which ends are pursued holds critical empirical and normative implications. As we saw in this case, shared talk may not in fact be shared, and its pursuit may not serve learning. Thus ends are not "given" but are a matter of continual choice, and the question is not *whether* we ought to make normative choices, but *how* we and our participants ought to make them. At present, we regard such choices as obvious. Alternatively we might regard them as choice points subject to critical inquiry, and we might make and revise our choices explicitly on the basis of mutual self-interest and in light of the empirical data that emerge as the inquiry goes forward. If we do the latter, then our task as researchers is to create conditions that would enable participants not just to achieve certain ends but to choose among them under conditions of free and informed choice (see Geuss, 1981; also see Keeley, 1984, for an interesting discussion on the conflicting criteria used to adjudicate conflicting ends).

• *Rule 2:* Scan basic research in your field of inquiry for problem-solving clues and discard those that do not fit applied purposes. This two-step rule governs the way applied problems are set by guiding the researcher's search process. The first step is characteristic of all normal science, and it specifies what facts and problems are legitimate, not by way of explicit rules but by way of exemplars and models that tacitly guide a researcher's search. As such it acts as a kind of "box." It is unlikely to "call forth new sorts of phenomena; indeed those that will not fit the box are often not seen at all" (Kuhn, 1970b, p. 24). But as Kuhn also points out, its very restrictions are what enables science to expand the scope and precision of its knowledge. It is thus a two-sided box. It at once advances existing knowledge and makes fundamentally new insights less likely.

Both sides of this building process can be seen in the applied social sciences as well. Over the course of a decade Hackman and his colleagues—Hackman and Lawler, 1971; Hackman and Oldham, 1975, 1980; and Hackman, 1983—went from the field of basic research to developing change principles that could be used in organizations. In retracing this process, we can see the implications of the search rule not only for science but also for applied researchers' ability to solve the problems they set. To review: In conceptualizing their problem, Hackman and Lawler (1971) first scanned the theories within their own research tradition for problem-solving clues, and they then drew on its instruments to pursue these clues, generating and testing propositions that built on Lewin's (1938) and Tolman's (1959) work within social psychology. Several years later Hackman and Oldham (1975) then organized these propositions into a comprehensive model characteristic of most theories within social psychology. Yet as they did so, they made sure that the model was useful. They designed it so that each major class of variables could be measured; they developed a job diagnostic survey that could be used to assess jobs and redesign programs; and finally they outlined a set of design principles that described how the situational factors identified in the model could be manipulated, primarily through policy or structural changes (Hackman, 1983).

This building process enabled Hackman and his colleagues to contribute to knowledge in their field while making it more useful to practitioners. At the same time, the case study on the consulting firm (see Chapter Five) suggests that this process might also lead practitioners to miss facts critical to solving their problem. Recall that the firm's management set forth a policy on feedback, but then found themselves unable to implement it because the managers lacked the requisite interactional rules to do so and were unaware that this was the case. Neither Hackman and Oldham's model nor their diagnostic instrument is apt to discover this gap or to give us much guidance on how to fill it. Their community of inquiry does not ask its practitioners to look for these kinds of facts (tacit rules of interaction), nor has it developed the instruments that enable us to see them. These facts, along with the instruments that allow us to see them, belong to the ethnological tradition and thus are apt to go unnoticed in this one. As a result policies that cannot be implemented are apt to get approved; and since everyone remains unaware of the gaps between them and our rules of interaction, they may create more rather than less dissatisfaction. This way the blinders we wear as researchers could end up reinforcing those of practitioners. Our own change strategies may remain insufficient for solving the problems we set. And worse yet, we may not be able to *see* what the difficulty is.

Another side to this box comes in the form of how applied researchers select clues as they scan their respective fields for them. We saw that Heath took from basic research those insights and assumptions that were useful in setting her problem, thus adopting the difference model of basic researchers like Philips. But she discarded those assumptions that would make the problem insoluble, thus rejecting the notion that these differences are either necessary or irreconcilable. This way she could use basic research to set her applied problem without letting its assumptions get in the way. But what she did not do is actively set out to disconfirm these assumptions, feeding back her results in order to revise basic theory and research. It is a rare event for applied results to ever come back to the basic realm, since it is still not regarded as a theory-building endeavor and applied researchers seldom regard their own roles in that light (see Bickman, 1981). Consequently their change efforts do not tell us when our basic assumptions about the world are unwarranted. Applied research thus overlooks one of the most critical pathways for the advance of science, if not the most critical one.

• *Rule 3:* Pick problem-solving strategies that fit within the existing constraints and norms of the practitioner's community. This is a selection rule that asks researchers to solve their problems with strategies that are compatible with existing organizational arrangements and norms of interaction. At a minimum it rules out strategies that fundamentally question or challenge what exists. The applied researchers in the case studies discussed here adhered to such a rule as they formulated each of their solutions. Jordan stressed that she was not necessarily recommending radical change in school practices but rather "an effort to select from the wide spectrum of available teaching practices and curricula, those that are compatible with the culture of the client population" (1981, p. 16). Similarly, once Heath's teachers found their new rules to be incompatible with their own values, they retreated from the change effort, dissatisfied with the results. On the one hand, then, strategies within "available" practices are sought. But on the other hand, once it becomes evident that a strategy departs from those practices, retreat is the preferred course.

There is much to be said for recognizing existing constraints and norms, since this will prevent us from underestimating what we are up against. The problem lies in a priori accepting them as nonnegotiable, thereby missing ways of solving the problems we set. In Chapter Six we showed how the oscillation between direct strategies and indirect strategies made it impossible for teachers to fully resolve the dilemma of conflicting rules that they faced. The indirect rules were ambiguous; the direct ones preachy. Either way the teachers could not be certain that they had been heard. But suppose we invented an alternative that combined directness with an inquiry into the others' reactions? We might state this rule as "Combine advocacy with inquiry," and it falls within a Model II theory-in-use. As such it is often espoused but rarely practiced (more typical is the oscillation between advocacy and inquiry described in Chapter Six). Therefore it lies outside of existing rules, and learning it would require reexamining existing norms such as those of politeness. Nevertheless it may resolve the teachers' dilemma in a way that oscillating between the two existing rules cannot. However, the point is not whether it would, because that is an empirical question that cannot be answered here. The point is that an unspoken rule stops applied researchers from considering possibilities that go beyond what exists, and yet some dilemmas may require just that, if we are to solve them. This rule thus diminishes our problem-solving effectiveness by a priori ruling out strategies that might solve the problems we set.

Practitioner's Problem. Practitioners do not evaluate outcomes by a singular set of ends given ahead of time. Some purposes practitioners may bring to the problematic situations they face; others they may discover only once they are in them. They thus evaluate outcomes in the light of multiple values and purposes, some of which may not be discovered until they act to transform situations. The teachers in Heath's project illustrated this. They achieved what they set out to do only to discover that the goal of compatible rules was incompatible with others they held, thus leaving them dissatisfied with the results. At an organizational level the consulting firm solved one mismatch by legislating the feedback that the consultants demanded, but it simultaneously created a new mismatch for the officers who lacked the skills to provide it. As these practitioners considered such results, the question they asked was not just "Did we achieve the ends we set" but "Do we like what we get?" and "Is it congruent with our fundamental values and theories?" (Schön, 1983, pp. 132–133). This suggests that effectiveness holds a special meaning for practitioners. It is not sufficient to achieve a desired end. It is necessary to do so without unknowingly creating undesired ends. So practitioners must figure out not only how to achieve a given end but how to negotiate and renegotiate the often conflictual ends they discover in problematic situations. For the practitioner, the question of "what ends" takes center stage.

Without doubt this is a messy question. No obvious criteria exist for choosing among the ends involved in setting problems and evaluating solutions. Nevertheless for practitioners it is an unavoidable task, and they receive no guidance on it from applied research as it is now defined. Problem solving for the applied researcher is confined to yielding reliable knowledge on how to achieve some end, ordinarily in the service of effectiveness. Just as Hackman and Oldham put satisfaction and production at work in the context of organizational effectiveness, so did Jordan speak of KEEP's policy in terms of educational effectiveness. At the center of applied research is the question, "how do we achieve a given end," and the question of "what ends" is relegated to the periphery. We saw already that ends are regarded as given, their correctness so obvious it can go unstated (see Jordan, 1981, p. 16) and their worthiness justified on the basis that participants hold them as a goal of interest (Mohr, 1982, pp. 190–191).

Such problem-solving logic is predicated on the assumption that it is neither necessary nor desirable to discriminate among ends. But this raises the question: not necessary or desirable for whom? As Keeley points out: "For theorists, it may be convenient to adopt a thoroughgoing relativism, but not for those who actually take part in administering complex organizations" (1984, p. 5).

To Keeley, it is not that these conflicts go unnoticed by researchers, nor is it that they are seen as unimportant for administrators. Rather he believes it is an extreme form of relativism that "permits them to say little about means of resolution and [to] feel no embarrassment about leaving such conflicts unresolved" (p. 5). But it may be that for researchers, it *is* necessary and desirable to adopt this relativist viewpoint and to leave these conflicts alone. As long as researchers can assume that ends are given by others and are not a matter of their own normative choice, Mohr writes, they can be normative in a "special sense": "The instruction is not that organizations should behave in a manner derivable from the nature of God, human beings, or the healthy society, as in much pure normative philosophy; rather the emphasis is on how an organization should behave in order to be effective and efficient. The advice is therefore based . . . on the *empirical* hypothesis that certain structures or behaviors will be functional, or efficacious, in performing a task" (1982, pp. 2-3, our italics).

Such a view permits researchers with an interest in practical affairs to take them up without giving up their status as researchers. Their question remains an empirical one; their concerns normative only in a special sense. There is much validity to this view. Whether an end can be met by one means as opposed to another *is* an empirical question. But it does not yet answer the question of how we choose among possible ends to study, and the criterion of "sufficient interest" does not allow us to circumvent the question. As Keeley points out, it is not obvious why organizational goals have more objective validity than other evaluative standards, such as those derived from individual rights (1984, p. 2) or, in light of Mohr's distinction, those derived from some notion of a healthy society. Nevertheless the applied researcher may have to veer away from this question in order to remain faithful to the norms of science. So the very question the practitioner must answer, the applied researcher must leave alone. In this sense applied research might be regarded as quite impractical despite its concern with practical affairs (see Keeley, 1984).

Conclusion. The communities in which scientists practice hold norms that tell us what questions and facts to go after, what constitutes a good solution, and what to do and avoid as we go about solving problems. Like all practice norms, they give shape, meaning and direction to our task by defining what lies within and outside its boundaries. This chapter has tried to identify these norms, the way they bind our inquiry, and the implications of this for solving the problems that researchers and practitioners face. What we found is that existing scientific norms may lead to dilemmas that cannot be resolved within them. The basic researchers formulated solutions that placed practitioners between necessary and conflicting requirements. To Milgram, the obedience that leads us to harm others is necessary for social coherence and organizational survival. To Philips and Erickson, the cultural differences that lead to school failure are based on processes that are so highly skilled and automatic, perhaps even neurologically based, that they are necessary for competence and perhaps beyond our control.

Such conclusions were derived from describing the world as is in accord with the norms of scientific communities. Yet to falsify them or to discover systematic gaps in them would require going beyond these norms. It would require that we ask whether what exists is necessary for existence, that we invent fundamental alternatives that might resolve these dilemmas, and that we submit them to experimentation. Moreover, since it would be neither practical nor ethical to design such alternatives on an arbitrary basis, we would need to construct them in light of existing empirical evidence and normative analysis, as Harmon (1981) did in developing his decision rules. Otherwise such experiments might do more harm than good or be a waste of time. But to move in this direction would be to violate the rules "Do not delve into normative concerns" and "Do not pose fundamental alternatives to what is." So just as practitioners are left in a dilemma, so are the researchers, and theirs seals shut the one they construct for practitioners.

In the applied realm the opportunity exists to break open these dilemmas. Applied researchers can intervene in practical affairs and manipulate causal variables to bring about desired outcomes. But to protect their status as scientists, they must circumvent normative questions and consequently cannot give practitioners much guidance on dilemmas of value. The ethnographers do not question the different and conflicting values held within and among cultural groups, while organizational researchers provide no suggestions on how organizations might ad-

Table 5. The Framing of Problems and Solutions (Applied Research).

Form of Research	Questions Asked	Causal Factors Found	Assumptions Made	Solution Formulated	Knowledge Produced
Applied Ethnographers	How do we achieve a given set of ends? What are the key causal factors involved?	Emphasizes: • Differences and similarities in socialization among cultural groups • Existing rules of interaction and meaning making; communication codes; social identity. Recognizes: • Situational factors	Ends can be regarded as given Conflicting ends do not need to be taken into account Solutions can be found within the existing constraints and norms of both the researchers' and the practitioners' communities	Theory of intervention designed to bridge differences in rules of interaction and cultural contexts through accommodating existing rules	For science: • Knowledge on how to achieve a given end within existing constraints • Few fundamentally new insights: —fundamental alternatives are not produced —assumptions of basic research are not revised in light of applied knowledge

| Organizational Assessment | How do we achieve a given set of ends? What are the key causal factors involved? | Emphasizes:
• Situational factors
• Existing psychological and behavioral responses

Recognizes:
• Interpersonal factors | Ends can be regarded as given

Conflicting ends do not need to be taken into account

Solutions can be found within the existing constraints and norms of both the researchers' and the practitioners' communities | Theory of intervention designed to manipulate situational factors through policy and structural changes. | For practitioner:
• Insight into how to achieve a certain end within existing constraints
• Little insight into how to negotiate conflicting ends in the problem-solving process
• Little insight into fundamentally new options or into new criteria by which to evaluate them. |

judicate conflicting interests. Instead, they take a set of ends held by some group of participants, and then inquire into how to achieve them according to the search and selection rules described previously (see Table 5). What lies outside of existing norms for inquiry and practice is considered peripheral and/or goes unnoticed. Fundamental alternatives are not invented, and conflicting values or interests are bypassed rather than engaged. Consequently, the assumptions of basic research do not get tested, and the conflicting requirements often embedded in them do not get resolved. In this way what is done to satisfy the demands of science and practice may in fact thwart the advance of both.

8

Practicing Action Science: Methods of Inquiry and Intervention

Like the social scientists discussed in the previous chapter, action scientists can be regarded as practitioners at work within their own community of inquiry. They too follow a set of norms that articulate what problems and methods are legitimate for study, that guide the setting and solving of problems, and that tell them what to do and what not to do as they go through the problem-solving process. What is most distinctive about the action science community, however, is that it enacts communities of inquiry within communities of practice. As Part One described, this means that the action scientist shares the concerns of the scientists discussed in the previous chapters, while simultaneously taking into account those of the practitioner. In generating knowledge, action scientists thus adhere to norms of falsifiability, and they aim to grasp the logic of action. But they adapt these norms to the constraints posed by the human mind and the action context, and they extend them to reach into the normative realm. Just what these norms look like in practice is what we will consider here.

So far we have traced the practice of applied and basic

researchers within the empirical-analytic and the hermeneutic-historical traditions. In so doing we have found that the practice norms of different communities within these two traditions prevent researchers from asking the kinds of questions that practitioners cannot ignore and from solving the kinds of problems that they continually face. Because action science attempts to extend its knowledge requirements to meet those of practitioners, it claims to be characterized by norms that can better negotiate these dilemmas of conflicting requirements. The present chapter will examine this assertion by reflecting back on the action science examples in the previous chapters, as we just did with the basic and applied researchers.

Transforming What Happens to Be

Like all researchers, action scientists take up the question of how some phenomenon happens to be. Yet as they do so, their search is guided by a concomitant interest in how they might eventually transform what they discover. So when Schön (1983) asked what happened in the town planner's case, he highlighted those facts assumed to be within the planner's control and therefore subject to choice, no matter how tacit (see Chapter Seven). He looked at the role that the planner had fashioned for himself in relation to other roles open to him, and he found that there were several such roles: "Like his predecessor, he could have made himself into a writer of plans, covering the walls of his office with maps and charts. Or he could have become a community organizer and advocate. He chose, instead, the intermediary role" (1983, p. 221). In a similar vein, Harmon's inquiry into existing accountability arrangements (see Chapter Seven) went after those factors that would need to be taken into account, should we choose to redesign them: the premises underlying accountability rules, our current notions of accountability and causation, and so forth (1981, pp. 117-137). In both instances, choice was assumed, and what led to those choices was pursued.

Thus far this line of inquiry is not very different from what we have seen previously (Chapter Seven). Like previous research it inquires into the causes of an important social problem, and, like applied research in particular, it goes after factors thought to be within an actor's control. Even its inquiry into underlying assumptions and values is not new, for Milgram (1974) also probed for the conflicting values and requirements at stake in obedience. But once action scientists are on their way to figuring out what happened, they then go on to ask, "What might have happened if things were fundamentally different?" For Harmon this meant asking what might happen if organizations adopted decision-rules that significantly departed from the predominant one of hierarchy. For Schön it meant asking what would have happened if the town planner had had a "very different theory of action" (1983, p. 230). It is at this juncture that their inquiry diverges from that of basic or applied research, not because they ask "what if" but because of their readiness to take the question beyond the domain of what now exists. Milgram asked "what if," but because he assumed that what exists is necessary for existence, he confined his inquiry to variations that never departed from it. In contrast, the instructor in the passivity experiment in Chapter Four actively sought and tested fundamentally different authority relations to see if what now exists might be transformed.

Nevertheless, as action scientists pursue these questions, they are guided by the norms of their community in much the same way as other researchers are guided by their norms. The facts they find and the alternatives they invent are not the result of an arbitrary search; rather they result from using a normative lens that allows these researchers to *see* them. It is the value of personal responsibility that led each of the action scientists previously discussed to find and highlight factors within an actor's control and to invent alternatives predicted to enhance it. In Harmon's case, for example, he saw the "crucial institutional task" as limiting the use of hierarchy by means of mechanisms less likely to diminish the personal responsibility of actors (1981, p. 128). A second value is that of justice, and it led Argyris to focus on how the young consultants were striving to solve their own mismatch by designing one for the officers (see Chapter Five). These are core values in action science, and as such they influence what is looked for and what is found.

This is not to say, however, that previous researchers

were unconcerned by questions of value. Jordan (1981) cited "ethical reasons" (p. 16) behind KEEP's policy to make school practices compatible with the students' culture, suggesting some notion of justice and responsibility. The difference is that these normative views are so tacit that their implications in a particular case are often unanticipated. As a result they are often fraught with inner contradictions that go unnoticed until practitioners bump into them. Such was the case with Heath's teachers when they discovered that their newly adopted rules collided with their own sense of what was right, leaving them dissatisfied with the results. It was only then that the teachers reconsidered their initial position, and they rejected its implicit notion of justice that had led them to adopt rules at the expense of their own values, while not asking others to do the same. Of course, it is impossible to anticipate all such possibilities ahead of time, and this raises an equally important difference. Once value conflict was uncovered, the action scientists actively confronted it rather than simply bypassing it. Recall that Argyris asked the consultants to consider the justice of requiring the officers to act in ways they themselves could not act, whereas in Heath's and Jordan's projects no data were provided to suggest that the question of justice was pursued. What was peripheral in previous inquiry thus becomes central in action science.

This suggests that in framing their research, action scientists move into both familiar and unfamiliar domains. As they ask the question—"How does it happen to be?"—they keep in mind and eventually take up the question, "How might we transform what we discover?" To answer this question, they use a normative lens to find the facts that will allow them both to describe and to transform what now exists.

At this point the question asked of previous research can be asked of action science: What kinds of solutions do we get from this line of inquiry? To constitute a solution, the findings must first be organized in accord with the norms of the action science community, just as the previous researchers constructed their solutions to satisfy their norms. Since in action science the aim is to understand in the service of social practice and to pose alternatives that might transform what we discover, the solutions devised by action science must be threefold, with each of the constituent parts informing the others. Action science must first offer an explanation that describes what happened in a way that implies how it might be changed. It then must formulate an alternative that transforms what was described. And finally it must develop a pathway for getting from here to there.

The threefold solution provided by Schön in his case study of the town planner illustrates these constituent parts and their relationships. To describe the planner's dilemma, Schön first brought to the foreground what he named the planner's "balancing act" —a set of strategies used to negotiate conflicting obligations toward developers, on the one hand, and the regulatory boards, on the other. Schön recounts that "the planner tries to criticize the developer's plans without discouraging him. He tries to be stringent in his review of plans and at the same time permissive. He tries to lead the developer along the right lines without reducing the developer's responsibility for his proposal. And he behaves authoritarianly while presenting himself as devoid of authority" (1983, p. 221).

Once he had described what happened, Schön began to account for what he had found. He explained, "We can see these problems, and the resulting balancing act, as a consequence of the way [the planner] has chosen to frame his role" (p. 221). At the same time, Schön ruled out the alternative explanation that it was the intermediary role itself that required these strategies. He reasoned, "It is true that his twofold objective is inherently conflictual, requiring that he negotiate with developers without infringing on the board's authority, but this is not by itself sufficient to create the conditions for the balancing act" (p. 226). In particular it did not explain why he kept these objectives private and managed the conflict between them unilaterally. To Schön it was the way in which the planner *framed* his role that required him to act thus. But what accounts for the way he chose to frame his role? Schön suggested that it was the planner's theory of action that contributed to and reinforced his role frame and at the same time made it unlikely he could discover the frame he was using. According to Schön, the planner's theory of action (Model I) consisted of a set of values and strategies that limits reflection and requires individuals to set and solve problems privately and unilaterally. Yet he added that it was a self-reinforcing system: "One could say either that he has framed his role and problems to suit his theory of action, or that he has evolved a theory of action suited to the role and problems he has framed" (p. 228).

In many respects this explanation parallels those offered in traditional research. Schön first provided a rich description of what happened, only then moving on to rule out alternative explanations. He then began to construct increasingly abstract explanations that could subsume the facts he found and account for what he described. As he did so, however, he fashioned his account so that it implied what the planner ought to change, should he so choose. It is at this point that Schön began to depart from the norms of traditional research. He implied that it was not only the planner's strategies that required change but the values by which he set his problems as well. To Schön, these were the critical variables in his account, because they were what led the planner to get stuck "between those who propose and those who dispose" (p. 234).

With this explanation set, Schön then built on it by proposing an alternative—"a very different theory of action, one conducive to the public testing of private assumptions" (p. 230) and one that might yield a very different set of facts. To describe it, he began with an abstract model (Model II) composed of a different set of values and strategies from those followed by the planner, and he then went on to spin out a series of hypothetical consequences predicted to follow from the model in this particular case. Most important among them was a greater capacity for reflection, one that extends to examining one's role and makes it less likely that errors will go undetected. In designing this kind of alternative, Schön thus built on the planner's own interest in self-reflection. As Schön described him: "The planner is an individual who likes to reflect on his practice. Indeed, his willingness to participate in our research grew out of this interest" (p. 228).

Even so, such an alternative asked the town planner to reconsider the values he held and the ends he had set in his framing of his role. And if Schön's explanation is correct, this is something that the planner cannot do, since his theory of action limits his reflection to the strategies he uses. Therefore, Argyris and Schön (1974) designed a learning process aimed at managing this paradox and at helping individuals to inquire into and redesign their theories of action.

As this suggests, Schön's solution is complete only after he has explained the planner's dilemma, while providing clues for finding ways out of that dilemma. He has posed an alternative that not only builds on what he has described but fundamentally transforms it. And he has devised a pathway for moving from here to there that is aimed at managing the paradoxes of change. In one respect such a building process resembles the way applied research builds on basic research. Both action science and applied research construct explanations in light of alternatives, and their alternatives logically follow from their explanations. For the most part this is what Heath and Jordan did in trying to solve the problem of school failure and what Hackman and his colleagues did with the problem of satisfaction and productivity at work. But Schön's solution diverges from these in two important respects. First, it reconsidered and questioned the ends pursued, as well as the means for achieving them, and it provided a learning process by which participants might inquire into and reconsider the values and ends at stake. So far we have seen that this is a domain into which neither basic nor applied research has proceeded. The second departure, made possible by the first, is that the solution put forth an alternative that fundamentally differs from what now exists. To date, the theory of action Schön proposed is rarely used. But in putting it forth, he provided the town planner with a way of better managing the conflicting requirements inherent in any practice.

So what are the implications of these kinds of solutions? Up to now, the solutions of basic and applied research have adhered to norms that require them to stop short of considering the kinds of issues practitioners are required to face. Action science claims to better manage these conflicting requirements between science and practice by adhering to key scientific requirements, while adapting them to the conditions under which practitioners must act and extending them to address questions that practitioners must ask. We turn now to consider these requirements, how action scientists satisfy them, and the implications of this for practitioners.

Action Science as a Science of Practice

As Part One outlines, action science is an inquiry into social practice, broadly defined, and it is interested in producing knowledge in the service of such practice. Thus, what counts as a solution for action science both overlaps with and diverges from prevailing scientific criteria. Like the empirical-analytic tradition, action science requires that knowledge include empirically disconfirmable propositions that can be organized into generalizable theory. But at the same time it also requires that these propositions be falsifiable in real-life contexts by the practitioners to whom they are addressed. Like applied research, action science requires knowledge to be useful. Yet in so doing it emphasizes the designing and implementation of social action, and it rejects the current dichotomy between basic research and applied research. It instead asks that its knowledge illuminate basic issues in ways that are at once generalizable and applicable in particular cases. And unlike basic or applied research in either the empirical or hermeneutic traditions, action science requires that knowledge speak to the forming of purposes, not just to the means for achieving them. As a critical theory it aims to produce knowledge that evokes critical reflection among practitioners, so that they might more freely choose whether and how to transform their practice. Let us now consider our action science cases in light of these criteria.

 • *Knowledge should include empirically disconfirmable propositions that can be organized into theory and falsified by practitioners in real-life contexts.* In the case of the consulting firm, Argyris predicted that when giving feedback, consultants would not act differently from the officers. This proposition came from an overarching theory that predicts that virtually all individuals will hold a Model I theory-in-use and will consequently make evaluations without illustrating or testing them.

In this particular case, Argyris thus anticipated that the consultants would make their evaluations in the same way as the officers had. To test this proposition, he formulated it and put it forth so that the consultants it addressed could reject it. In other words, he made it known, he stated it at a level of inference that could be easily connected to the consultants' own observations of what occurred, and he put the consultants in control of the conditions under which the test was conducted (see Chapter Five). A later part of this chapter articulates further how such tests can be undertaken in the face of threats posed by real-life contexts. For now it is sufficient to note that this requirement asks that propositions be characterized by features that allow practitioners to disconfirm them. These include making propositions public, providing the directly observable data on which they are based, making them connectable to these data, and designing conditions that are conducive to validly testing them.

In contrast, most research within the empirical-analytic tradition generates propositions that are so abstracted from what occurs that it is difficult for practitioners to reconnect them in order to independently judge whether they fit the facts of what happened. Ordinarily such data are either quantified or based on individuals' self-reports, accounts that themselves consist of conclusions quite disconnected from the data of what occurred. Conversely, ethnographers generate propositions that are easily connectable to their observations. But as the ethnographic case studies that we discussed earlier suggest, these researchers did not regard them as hypotheses that ought to be publicly tested with their participants (see Chapter Six). Either way, the practitioners to whom these propositions were addressed did not have the opportunity to reject them if they believed them to be false or to adopt them if they accepted them as valid. Since action science is at once interested in generalizable knowledge and in improving social practice through reflection on action, it fashions its propositions to fit this purpose. Thus the consultants in the consulting firm, the town planner, and the seminar participants were each given the opportunity to reject or accept the propositions made about them.

- *Knowledge must be useful in action.* In formulating his

solution, Schön (1983) developed an explanation and an alternative that could cover a wide range of facts and situations, while simultaneously addressing the particular case of the town planner. Consequently, the town planner could come to see how he had handled the particular dilemma of conflicting obligations toward developer and regulatory board. But equally important, since this knowledge was abstracted from a particular case, it also allowed him to see how he would be apt to negotiate *any* situation that poses conflicting requirements. If his theory of action is Model I, as Schön suggested, then he would be likely to manage all such situations unilaterally and to negotiate all such conflict privately, thereby limiting his capacity to uncover his mistakes and to reflect on his role. The multiple levels of inference at which this knowledge is put forth allows individuals to package a lot of complexity economically (it is abstract and generalizable knowledge), while enabling them to use it in a specific instance (it identifies what actors actually do at a concrete level so that it can be recognized in action). At the same time this feature allows action science to contribute to knowledge that is relevant to practice in general, not just to the town planner's practice in particular. If Schön's formulation is correct, then any practitioner who holds this theory of action ought to limit her reflection in the same way.

• *Knowledge should speak to the forming of purposes, not just the means by which to achieve them.* To be truly practical, a science of practice must take up the question of choice, and the question of choice necessarily involves the forming of purposes, as well as the choosing of means to realize them. Yet once we consider purposes, questions of value can no longer remain peripheral. They are part of a package that cannot be unbundled. Action science thus extends its inquiry into the normative realm; yet in so doing, it seeks to submit normative claims to rational criticism, so that practitioners can reject them as they are able to reject empirical claims. The difference lies in the criteria that determine whether a claim ought to be adopted or rejected.

As a kind of critical theory, action science justifies its own normative position on the basis of the principle of internal criticism. This means that its own normative claims are evaluated on the basis of the normative views implicit in the "epistemic principles" of the practitioners to whom they are addressed (Geuss, 1981; also see Chapter Two). But since these principles are often implicit, action scientists must first make them explicit, so that propositions can be evaluated in light of them. In the consulting firm case (see Chapter Five), Argyris illustrated how such a process might actually unfold. He began by pointing out that implicit in the consultants' demand for a policy on feedback was the principle of justice. Once the consultants confirmed this, he put forth the view that by this very principle, their own normative position was unjust. It advocated a policy that required of others what they did not require of themselves: feedback that they themselves and the two officers lacked the skills to provide. It was therefore unjust on two counts: It demanded feedback that the consultants themselves did not give, and it required the officers to solve their mismatch by imposing one on them. On this basis and in light of empirical data on the consultants' actions, Argyris then took the normative stance that they ought to reconsider their policy, recognize the gaps in their feedback skills, and work toward learning how to fill them in. This position, advocated in a context of free and open inquiry, could be evaluated by the consultants and freely adopted or rejected by them. To the extent that the consultants found their initial claim unacceptable, they abandoned it, and the researcher's claim was affirmed.

As a result of such a process, the consultants' awareness of their own principles was expanded and the inconsistencies among them illuminated. Yet equally important, the process itself provided a means by which these practitioners could inquire, in an ongoing way, into the different ends at stake in a problem and rationally critique the conflicting normative claims embedded in them. To the extent that such a process is adopted, it becomes less likely that practitioners will *unknowingly* advocate policies that would satisfy one interest while violating another. Such deliberations would become public, their guiding principles would become explicit, and their normative claims would become subject to critique on the basis of these principles and of valid information considered in free and open inquiry. In this way, the taking of a normative stance should enhance rather than constrain a practitioner's free choice.

All communities of inquiry hold norms that bind the inquiry of its practitioners, and action science is no exception. The difference we have seen here is that action science seeks to modify key scientific norms, so that the knowledge it produces might advance science and practice at one and the same time. In so doing, the action scientists in the previous chapters extended their inquiry to include the question: What might happen if things were fundamentally different? And unbound by prevailing strictures to leave questions of value alone and the world untouched, they extended their search to a consideration of ends as well as means and to the discovery of fundamental alternatives. As a result, the solutions they devised contributed to knowledge that could illuminate basic issues in science and practice.

At this point we have considered only how the action scientist frames his inquiry. We do not yet know how the action scientist actually goes about producing the knowledge that makes up his solutions. Since the methods of action science are as distinctive as the norms that frame its inquiry, the remainder of the chapter describes what these methods are.

Action Science: Rules and Methods of Inquiry

So far we have seen that action science moves into both familiar and unfamiliar domains of inquiry in the problems it sets and in the solutions it seeks. Its methods follow suit. They are designed to take on problems that are deemed important, while ensuring that the knowledge generated is at once valid and useful in action. While this requires rigor, the methods of action science are rigorous in a special sense. They emphasize the public testing of knowledge claims in accord with an explicit set of rules, but they adapt these to the action context and extend them to include all the normative, interpretive, and empirical claims that actors necessarily make as they try to understand the world in order to act. It is in this sense that we speak of action science as enacting communities of inquiry in communities of social practice. It aspires to help participants realize the norm of "responsible belief" in the realm of practical deliberation. We now turn to describing how action science methods and rules do this.

To put it most succinctly, action scientists engage with participants in a collaborative process of critical inquiry into problems of social practice in a learning context. The core feature of this context is that it is expressly designed to foster learning about one's practice and about alternative ways of constructing it. It therefore pushes back some of the constraints inherent in real-life contexts in order to enable participants to come to know their practice as they have defined it and to experiment with the new moves and competencies characteristic of a new definition. This means that the aim is in part to make known what is known so well that we no longer know it—the uncovering of tacit knowledge so that it might be critiqued. And in part the aim is to make known what is unknown—the discovery of alternatives so that they too might be critiqued. The process of critical inquiry in action science is a form of public reflection and experimentation that follows rules that can themselves be used in action contexts in order to ensure the validity and usefulness of the inquiry.

Like all methods, those of action science are designed to achieve their own particular aims in the face of the threats and obstacles most relevant to them. In the domain of action science these threats and obstacles are several. As already described, the first is that the data of action science are action, action is meaningful, and the meaning of action is ambiguous (see Chapter Two). The difficulty here is that participants will invariably select and focus on different segments from any stream of action, and they will often impose different meanings on the same segments, thereby threatening the intersubjective agreement necessary for public testing. Action science must therefore devise some process (1) that will allow participants to make explicit the data they select and the meanings they impose and (2) that will enable them to negotiate the differences in meaning that arise so that they might reach agreement. In large part the process of critical reflection is itself geared toward doing just this. It is a process by which participants can draw on the conceptual tool of the ladder of inference to make explicit the data that they select and the inferential steps that they take to reach their conclusions (see Chapter Two).

But this process itself generates a second set of threats. The process of reflection can be so threatening to participants that it evokes defensive responses that in turn threaten validity. It is not sufficient to simply reach agreement because this can be accomplished through a process of coercion and submission, as well as through a process of open and free inquiry. Like all sciences, action science aspires to enact the latter process. The problem is that, once threatened, participants will often respond to the demands of reflection in ways more characteristic of the former. To understand this more fully, consider the demands that free and open inquiry exert. Participants must be able to retrieve largely tacit inferential processes; they must be able to deal openly with challenges and conflicting views; they must reveal information that might expose their own or others' vulnerabilities; they must be able to recognize and acknowledge when they are wrong; and they must feel free to choose among competing views.

These requirements can be simultaneously experienced as both desirable and threatening to participants. They will foster learning, but they will also put participants at risk of disagreements, conflict, embarrassment, and failure, evoking defenses to minimize such risks. The dilemma is that these defenses come in forms that themselves threaten the process of inquiry. Thus, participants might conceal upsetting information, minimize or cover up conflict, go along with views they actually oppose, hesitate to submit their own views to criticism, and so on. The reflective process is therefore as laden with the potential for anxiety and defensiveness as it is with the impetus to learn. Action science must take these threats into account, building on participants' desire to learn while minimizing the threats posed by their defenses.

A third set of threats comes with the nature of the action context. Although the learning context is designed to push back some of the constraints of real-life conditions, it also attempts to follow rules that are generalizable to any action context. This means that validity must be ensured under conditions in which unilateral control of variables is neither possible nor desirable. There are too many variables involved, and efforts to unilaterally control them would either fail or, to the extent they succeeded, only confound the situation further. Thus action science must find some way of reliably choosing among competing hypotheses in the midst of high complexity and low control.

What follows in the remainder of this chapter is a description of the methods and rules that govern and sustain processes of reflection and experimentation in the face of these threats to validity. As with the methods and rules of basic and applied science, those of action science guide the processes by which data are collected, hypotheses tested, and data analyzed. What is distinctive to action science is the nature of these rules and the fact that it aims to help participants to learn them, so that they can enact them as shared norms for inquiry in a learning context.

Talk as Data: A Window onto the Logic of Action. Along with ethnography and linguistics, action science believes that action is informed by rules or tacit theories and that talk is an important form of social action (see Chapter Two; also see Gronn, 1983; Searle, 1969; Austin, 1962). According to this view, talk is not simply anecdotal data but is a window onto the logic of action. The question for the action scientist therefore is not whether talk is action but what kind of action is it? More precisely, we wish to make explicit the largely tacit propositional logic of the form "In situation *s* (as the actor constructs it), do *a* to achieve consequence *c*." This means that we must elicit data on what individuals actually say and do as they interact, as well as data on what they are thinking and feeling at the time. It is from such data that we can reconstruct the rules or propositions that must be in individuals' heads to produce the behaviors and consequences we see.

Action science has a range of methods designed to collect these data in a reliable fashion and to do so in the service of participants' learning. These include: (1) observations accompanied by audiotaping, (2) interviews, (3) action experiments, and (4) participant-written cases. Most often action scientists rely on all these methods for different purposes and as a means of cross-checking and testing what is found with each of them. But common to each method are three features characteristic of action science. The first is that data are generated in a way that makes participants feel causally responsible for them. Action scientists thus actively seek to minimize researcher control over what problems are studied, what data are selected, and the means by which they are selected or generated. At the same time they also seek to examine the impact of any control that is exerted. For instance, tape recordings are made both with and without the action scientist present, thereby providing a way to explore the possibility that the researcher's presence is responsible for previous results (the participants' actions). In addition, in choosing problems for study, participants are encouraged to pick ones that are critical to them and to their own learning. This at once serves to facilitate the learning process and minimizes the potential for knowing distortions, because participants are committed to reporting reactions or recollections as accurately as they can so that they might learn.

Nevertheless we recognize that such data still hold threats to validity. Participants might misreport what occurred or what they feel, either knowingly to prevent embarrassment or unknowingly due to forgetfulness, selective memory, and so on. There are, however, three aspects of action science that when used together minimize this risk. The first is that we ask that participants report what they and others actually did and said as best as they can recollect it, and not simply give their conclusions or perceptions of what occurred. Second, we are interested in the rules behind behavior; and we assume that given the nature of rule-learned behavior, individuals cannot consistently play at a set of rules that they do not know or have competence in. Therefore, while they might not report precisely the particulars of what was said, they are unlikely to be able to misrepresent the rules that underlie the way they reason and act. Third, we regard this assumption as an hypothesis to be tested; and since there are many methods and occasions for data collection, ample opportunities exist to detect these kinds of errors and to test this working assumption. Most important, some of these methods include direct observations that allow us to cross-check participants' reports.

One such method is the action experiment in which we have direct access to individuals' actions and can inquire what they are thinking and feeling at the moment. But this methodology contains its own threats, since the researchers risk, even seek, to "contaminate" these results by their presence and actions in an effort not only to probe individuals' actions but to help them learn a new set of skills. In a later section on hypothesis testing we will take up the question of how we contend with the researcher's impact in greater depth, but the key feature that we wish to emphasize here is true of all data-gathering procedures. Researchers actively inquire into the nature of their impact and design opportunities to probe for this, often relying on participants to gather data themselves, uninfluenced by the researchers' presence. The aim therefore is not to eliminate researcher impact altogether, but to give participants a high degree of control over the data-gathering processes and to design ways to discover the responsibility and impact that the researchers do have for the data that is collected.

A second feature of data collection is that each method is designed to elicit data on how individuals actually act and on what they are thinking and feeling at the time. Observations are thus combined with interviews or with intervention activity, so that the action scientist can get data on participants' reactions. Written cases ask that participants divide a page in half, recreate on the right side the actual dialogue of the relevant actors, and recount on the left side what they were thinking and feeling at the time but did not say. Similarly, interviews are designed to elicit from participants, not just their conclusions about situations but also what they and others actually said and did in the situation, as well as what they thought and felt at the time. And, finally, action experiments are designed to observe how participants act, while at the same time probing for and unfreezing the reasoning and reactions that keep these actions in place.

As this suggests, action scientists regard talk not only as action but as the means by which people can report what they are thinking and feeling as they act. It is from these data that we can reconstruct how actors must have constructed the situations in which they acted.

Although necessary for our purposes, this dual focus on talk-as-action and talk-as-report raises the controversial issue of self-reports: How reliable are such reports? The running controversy over this question can be described most simply by placing the different views at two polar extremes. On one side of the issue, social scientists hold that self-reports are decidedly unreliable. Individuals tell more than they know, unknowingly distort cues, and generally cannot say what led them to think or act as they did, even though they think that they can. According to this view, human beings are unaware of their reasoning processes and unaware that they are unaware. They therefore may be glad to tell you their reasons for their actions, but these may not be the reasons that in fact form the basis for their actions (Nisbett and Ross, 1980; Nisbett and Wilson, 1977; Langer, 1976). Social scientists who take the other side of the issue hold that self-reports are reliable commentaries on phenomena that are relevant and that really do exist. Individuals are the best authority regarding their thought processes, they have access to these processes, and this in fact is what defines their essence as human beings. According to this view, human beings are aware of their reasoning processes and aware that they are aware. They therefore may make mistakes, but their views can be reconciled with those of an observer's, the reasons that account for their actions can be ascertained, and it is these reasons, not mechanical causes, that are critical in explaining social behavior (Harré and Secord, 1972).

Action science believes that both views are accurate but only in certain domains. Our task is to develop theories that distinguish what processes we can report and what methods are best for exploring them (see Ericcson and Simon, 1980). The theory of action perspective attempts to do this by distinguishing between espoused theories and theories-in-use and by providing a methodology for reconstructing both. Recall that espoused theories are those theories of which actors are aware and on which they draw in order to explain their behavior. They can be elicited relatively easily by asking people why they acted as they did, but they may or may not really inform their actions. Theories-in-use, in contrast, comprise a set of mostly tacit propositions that do inform one's actual behavior, yet these may or may not be congruent with one's espoused theories. Ordinarily actors are unaware of their theories-in-use, which puts action scientists in the position of having to figure out what data will allow them to infer these theories, while not confounding them with individuals' espoused theories. Clearly it is not sufficient to ask "why" questions. We have just said that these are apt to elicit an individual's plausible yet not necessarily accurate espoused theories, simply because they are the most readily retrieved. We therefore must find some way of gaining access to internal processes that will allow us to answer "why" questions without actually asking them.

We get some helpful hints on how to proceed from an unlikely source: those who believe we are not likely to gain such access. Even though they are skeptical, Nisbett and Wilson (1977) suggest that accurate retrieval of one's reasoning might be enhanced by interrupting processes in the moment, alerting participants to their cognitive processes, and coaching them in introspective procedures. Action scientists draw on each of these tactics but have elaborated them in the form of a set of rules, described below, that tell participant and researcher what internal processes to look for and how to regard different responses.

• *Rule 1:* Interrupt interactions on-line, direct attention to internal processes, and generate the impetus to explore them. Although willing to make suggestions on enhancing retrieval, Nisbett and Wilson (1977) consider such suggestions to be "ecologically meaningless." Apparently they assume that individuals will not sit still for such probing techniques, unaware of their relevance. This may be true in ordinary social or research situations. But because the research process in action science is designed for participants' learning, such techniques become relevant, even quite meaningful. The action scientist focuses on areas of critical import to participants and relies on a range of interventions to trigger participants' interest in examining their internal processes. The passivity experiment described in Chapter Four illustrates this in that the action scientist initiated the inquiry by pointing out that participants were designing their own injustice. Since these results were unintended and the participants would not have knowingly set out to produce them, they were quite intent on retrieving the internal processes that might in part help account for the results. At the same time, we recognize that this provides no assurance that participants will in fact retrieve or report internal processes accurately, so this rule alone is not sufficient. It encourages, but alone does not ensure, reliable reports.

• *Rule 2:* Elicit the attributions and evaluations being made about self, other, or situational factors (such as tasks, time, and so forth). Since we are interested in understanding how participants understand their social world, we probe for the attributions they make about themselves, others, and situational factors. These are the data that they use to construct the problematic situations in which they act. A researcher therefore might ask for participants' reactions and in so doing uncover a range of private attributions and evaluations that were made at the time of a particular incident. The consulting students in the passivity experiment, for example, made attributions about their own "stupidity," others' "smartness," and the interventionist's "toughness." These reports are of a different status than "I withdrew because I thought that it was best to learn by observing." This latter report may reflect what the participant is thinking, but it may or may not be an accurate explanation of what led him to withdraw. The former reports, however, give us a window onto how individuals *see* the situations in which they act. This allows us to reconstruct the conditions under which they act, as they see them, so that we might then construct the proposition: "When I attribute that I'm stupid, I withdraw and cover up my stupidity." This latter proposition is not of the same type as the plausible, yet often unreliable, explanations individuals give for their own behavior. It is based on what this participant actually did, under conditions experienced and reported by him.

• *Rule 3:* Regard causal explanations as hypotheses to be tested. As unreliable as self-explanations can be, we cannot a priori assume that they are inaccurate. Instead they should be regarded as worthy of test like any other hypothesis. One such test involves searching for data that might falsify the proposition. Counselors, for instance, often say that they take an approach to their clients that will allow them to come to their own insights. But this explanation overlooks the fact that their questions often "lead" clients to insights that they already hold in their heads. Once these disconfirming data are identified, the counselor and researcher can begin to search for new hypotheses that might better account for what the counselor actually does. At this point the researcher might redirect his search toward the attributions the counselor makes about himself and his client as he asks leading questions. Researcher and counselor might discover, for instance, that the counselor was concealing negative attributions, along with predictions that these would be upsetting to the client. The counselor might report thinking, "This guy's got a real grudge going. He doesn't see his role in it at all. But if I ever said that, he'd hit the roof!" At the same time he might also be thinking about himself: "I don't know what I'd do if he got that angry here. I don't think I could handle it, but I'd better not let him know that or he'd leave." With these data we can begin to construct a very different account of the counselor's leading questions—one that gets at how he acts in the face of the inferences that he makes about his client and his own competence. We thus might arrive at the following proposition: "When at the limits of your competence, lead in and act as if you know where you are going in order to cover up that you don't."

The emphasis of this section, however, is not on the different ways of testing the causal accounts individuals give of their actions. We have addressed this previously (Chapter Two), and we will have more to say in a subsequent section about the range of ways to design tests in an action context. This section aims to explain why such accounts ought to be regarded as hypotheses to be tested and to show how they can be tested in ways that are useful to the practitioner's and the researcher's learning alike.

• *Rule 4:* Slow down and focus on the inferential steps individuals take in going from the data to their conclusions, since the very skillfulness of their inferential processes can cut individuals off from them. If we are to gain access to how individuals construct the situations in which they act, we need to find some way of getting at these processes. One way is to slow down the pace of these processes and to virtually retrace the steps that individuals take in moving from the data of what occurred to their attributions about what happened. By drawing on the ladder of inference, we can help individuals retrieve the data that they selected, the cultural meanings they imposed on the data, and the attributions and causal theories they constructed. This way we can help individuals spell out the steps involved in these tacit processes, making it easier for them to test their inferences and enabling them to discover any systematic gaps or biases embedded in them. For instance, individuals might find that they tend to focus on one kind of data while ignoring other kinds. Or alternatively, they might see that they are predisposed to take predictable kinds of inferential leaps from the data.

• *Rule 5:* Slow down and focus on individuals' emotional reactions. Individuals can also be helped to slow down and retrieve their automatic emotional responses. While it is not unusual for individuals to register a sense of distress, it is often difficult to identify what it is they are feeling and in relation to what. Yet this kind of data is also important if we are to fully understand how individuals experience and act in the situations they face. With these data we can more fully grasp what individuals feel they are up against, as well as how they manage such reactions.

The problem, however, is that these reactions are so automatic that we stop attending to them in much the same way that we lose track of our reasoning. If we are to reconnect with both our emotional and cognitive processes, we have argued, it helps to slow down, look at what happened, and retrace what was thought *and* felt at the time. But often this is not a simple task. To publicly retrace and make public these processes involves risks that themselves evoke emotional and defensive reactions that hinder the retrieval of these processes and make it difficult to report them to others. The action scientist's inquiry is thus directed at helping participants manage these reactions in a way that can sustain inquiry (see Chapters Ten and Twelve).

What we wish to emphasize here is that all action science data-gathering processes are designed to enhance and build on participants' own commitment to learning. Thus, the problems, which are selected by the participants, are ones of critical import to them. The data gathered are largely in their control, and the focus is mainly on data that can be directly observed. Participants are aided in retrieving internal processes. The interventionist strives to find inconsistencies and puzzles in participants' actions in order to engage their interest in attending to the internal processes that might in part help solve such puzzles. These rules thus serve to enlist participants' help in ensuring validity. They make participants co-investors in that norm since their own learning depends on it.

Data Analysis: Mapping out Social Action. So far we have described the way in which data are collected, and we have said that we wish to make explicit the propositional logic embedded in social action. In analyzing these data and in representing the knowledge constructed from them, action scientists must meet the criteria of their practice. This knowledge must therefore be falsifiable in an action context, usable on-line by actors, and informative of alternatives. To satisfy these criteria the action scientist draws on three analytic tools. The first includes the highly abstract explanatory and normative models that guide the direction of the analytic process. These tell the researcher what data to highlight and what data to ignore, as well as which causal sequences are important and which ones are less so. As we saw in Schön's analysis of the town planner's dilemma, Models I and II serve this function in analyses of individuals' theories of action. The second tool is the ladder of inference described in Chapter Two. It serves a triple function. First, it makes it possible to go from the data of a concrete case to more abstract models, so that these models can be falsified. Second, it makes it possible to connect generalizable knowledge to a particular case. And finally, it enables individuals to reflect on action by providing a tool that can be used to retrace and make public the inferences they draw from what happens to the conclusions they draw from events.

A third device is mapping, which is used to analyze a particular problem and to represent knowledge so that it becomes useful to those it addresses while going beyond their particular case. Ordinarily such maps are midrange representations, not as abstracted from a concrete case as are Models I and II. As such, these maps usually provide a more elaborate description of a problem—for example, the difficulties involved in implementing a matrix structure. But like the more abstract models, these maps describe the tacit logic that informs social action and the implications of this for the behavioral worlds of the actors. What a particular map looks like depends on the territory being covered. A map might describe the propositional logic embedded in one consultant's practice, the behavioral world created by a group of consultants, and so on. Nevertheless all maps represent certain aspects of the terrain, in much the same way as all topographical maps must represent in a particular way the physical configurations of different regions. The map maker knows that, regardless of the particular region, some of its aspects must be described according to certain specifications, while others can be ignored. Similarly, maps of social action vary, depending on the level of analysis and purpose at hand, but they must all capture certain aspects of social action and do so in a certain way. We will now consider what can differ and what must remain constant.

• Maps can describe different levels of analysis. At the individual level, maps can simply specify a single rule in an individual's practice. A tacit rule in one counselor's practice, for instance, went like this: "Hold the belief that clients know best except when I know better and the corollary that I know best when I know better." This rule not only served to make explicit a tacit rule in her practice, it served to explain how a counselor intent on being client centered could unknowingly act quite counselor centered. Building further, this same counselor went on to develop a more complex map of her own practice, one that described an interrelated set of propositions that told her how to act in the face of negative evaluations and a fear of evoking defensiveness (see Figure 5).

Figure 5. Map of a Counselor's Practice.

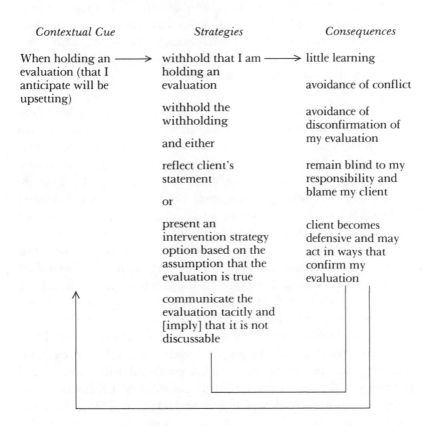

Contextual Cue	Strategies	Consequences
When holding an evaluation (that I anticipate will be upsetting)	withhold that I am holding an evaluation	little learning
		avoidance of conflict
	withhold the withholding	avoidance of disconfirmation of my evaluation
	and either	
	reflect client's statement	remain blind to my responsibility and blame my client
	or	
	present an intervention strategy option based on the assumption that the evaluation is true	client becomes defensive and may act in ways that confirm my evaluation
	communicate the evaluation tacitly and [imply] that it is not discussable	

If we decompose this map, we can see that it describes an interrelated set of rules, the conditions under which they are used, and the consequences that are apt to follow from using them. By identifying a single cue or condition and a pattern of responses, this counselor can more readily recognize those occasions or circumstances under which she is apt to violate what she intends. As a result she can begin to identify and to interrupt these responses, at first in a setting where she can learn new responses and later on with her clients. Moreover, represented as they are here, her practice rules are quite generalizable and should be useful to other counselors in training who might find themselves in the same dilemma. The map is therefore abstract enough to go beyond the circumstances of her particular case, while being concrete enough to describe with some precision what she does under the conditions specified. It is in this sense that we refer to maps as comprising midrange concepts.

At the organizational level, the interrelated factors that create, maintain, and reinforce a complex social system can also be mapped. One such map depicted the web of factors that prevented a matrix organization from implementing its structure as intended. As Figure 6 illustrates, the map began by describing the initial conditions the members faced, from work-related constraints to inconsistency to a high degree of complexity and ambiguity (column 1). Next it showed how the two prevailing sets of rules under these conditions were those of passivity and proactivity, conceptualized along a continuum that specified the individual rules that comprised these sets (column 2). At the same time it explained by way of feedback loops how the two responses combined to reinforce one another and the initial conditions. Finally, it described how this set of interrelated factors generated multiple binds that were themselves then managed by their prevailing rules. This escalated the interactional dynamics and reinforcing the initial conditions still further (columns 3, 4, and 5). In describing these factors, the map made explicit the mostly tacit processes that prevented this particular group from implementing an effective matrix team. But the literature on matrices suggests that such a map, if tested in other organizations, might be found to be quite generalizable to them as well.

• Maps can be either diagrammatic or verbal representations of action. So far the maps we have discussed have been diagrammatic, representing graphically the interrelationships among key variables. Even though they cover a great deal of complex material, such diagrams are simple enough to be managed by an actor and visually vivid enough to be recalled. They therefore allow actors to store and retrieve this knowledge while acting. But for other purposes, verbal representations can be equally retrievable and more useful. A kind of map called *scripts,* for instance, allows us to more richly describe a particular rule that, as an abstract construct, necessarily subsumes a sequence of moves and expectancies that remain implicit. One way of making them explicit is by scripting the sequence involved in a rule's enactment. To illustrate: Easing-in is a rule designed to avoid provoking defensiveness. It tells an actor to ask a series of questions in such a way that the questions lead the recipient to the insight in the actor's head. This rule is scripted here through a description of the sequence of expectancies and moves hypothesized to be in an actor's head when he produces that sequence:

The Easing-In Script

1. I know how I want you to behave and I am not going to tell you directly.
2. I will not tell you that this is the case.
3. I will ask you questions which, if you answer as I anticipate, will lead you to an understanding of my position.
4. I will expect that you will see all this without my saying it overtly.
5. I will expect that you will not discuss it.
6. I will expect that you will go along.
7. If you have questions or doubts about my intentions, I will expect that you will not raise them and will act as if you do not have any doubts.
8. If you do not behave as I expect, I will
   a. give you more time to think "constructively" by continuing my questions.
   b. eventually become more forthright about my views.
   c. attempt to argue you out of your views.
   d. conclude that your defenses are too high to permit you to learn or too difficult for me to handle.
   e. compromise and/or withdraw and act as if I am doing neither.

Figure 6. Action Map.

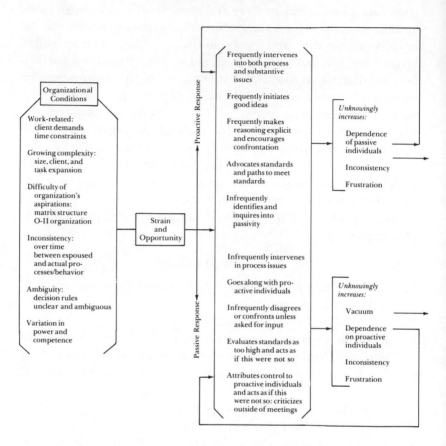

Source: Lawler and others, 1985, pp. 86–87.

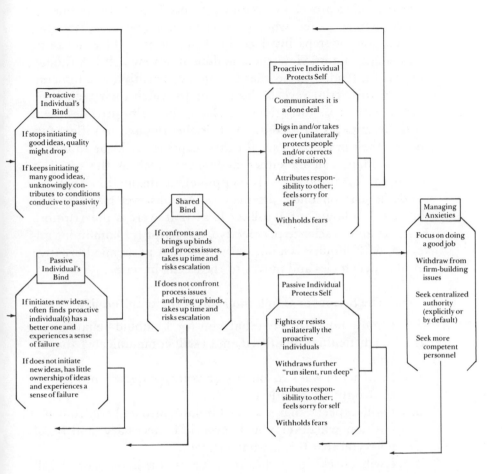

Proactive Individual's Bind

If stops initiating good ideas, quality might drop

If keeps initiating many good ideas, unknowingly contributes to conditions conducive to passivity

Passive Individual's Bind

If initiates new ideas, often finds proactive individual(s) has a better one and experiences a sense of failure

If does not initiate new ideas, has little ownership of ideas and experiences a sense of failure

Shared Bind

If confronts and brings up binds and process issues, takes up time and risks escalation

If does not confront process issues and bring up binds, takes up time and risks escalation

Proactive Individual Protects Self

Communicates it is a done deal

Digs in and/or takes over (unilaterally protects people and/or corrects the situation)

Attributes responsibility to other; feels sorry for self

Withholds fears

Passive Individual Protects Self

Fights or resists unilaterally the proactive individuals

Withdraws further "run silent, run deep"

Attributes responsibility to other; feels sorry for self

Withholds fears

Managing Anxieties

Focus on doing a good job

Withdraw from firm-building issues

Seek centralized authority (explicitly or by default)

Seek more competent personnel

Unlike the easing-in construct, this script decomposes the tacit reasoning processes necessary to produce it. In so doing it enables actors to see what they could not previously see: the discrete logical steps involved in their actions. Once aware of these steps, actors view their actions in a new light. Although they had intended to be client centered, sensitive, and noncontrolling, this script reveals the extent to which their tacit logic clashes with these intentions. As such, the script provides them with the impetus to reconsider their theories and to reflect further on their practice to see if other surprises might be found.

• Maps can be either descriptive, such as the one just discussed, or normative (prescriptive), a distinction that depends in part on one's perspective. An observer may describe the rule I follow, but I follow it as if it were a prescription. From an action science perspective, the script for combining advocacy with inquiry is a normative one that poses an alternative set of expectancies and moves to the easing-in script:

The Script for Combining Advocacy with Inquiry

1. I know how I believe that you (or I) should behave given the difficulties identified, and I will communicate* that to you.
2. I will act in ways to encourage you to inquire* into and to confront* my position.
3. I will expect* that you will inquire into and confront my position whenever you believe it is necessary, and I will tell* you that this is what I expect.
4. I will check* periodically to see if this is the case. I will hold you responsible for continual designed congruence between your actions and your thoughts.
5. If I infer incongruence between thoughts and actions, I will test* it with you openly.
6a. If I learn* that the incongruence is unintentional, then I will act to help you by going back to number one.
6b. If I learn* that the incongruence is intentional and you

*Indicates that these actions should be performed consistently with Model II rules.

are knowingly hiding this fact, then I will feel that I cannot trust you and will go back to number one.

By scripting this rule, individuals can see what it takes to produce it and how different it is from easing-in. Even though both scripts involve asking questions, the script given here reveals that the expectancies and intentions behind them are quite different.

• Maps are often nested within one another at different levels of abstraction and analysis. The organizational map described earlier contains maps of individuals' rules, organized into a more comprehensive pattern that showed their interrelationships and their impact on organizational outcomes. Similarly, individual rules themselves subsume a sequence of expectancies and moves that can be captured by scripts. We therefore find maps within maps, each with its own range of usefulness. What form the action scientists or participants choose depends in part on what is being explained and to what end. The diagrammatic form can capture with relative simplicity an enormously complex set of interrelated variables. It is thus retrievable and applicable in a way that a precise quantitative analysis or a description of everyone's moves and expectancies cannot be. It would simply contain too much information to keep in one's head while acting. Alternatively, if a particular individual wishes to produce or to alter a rule such as easing-in, a script of the sequence it informs becomes useful. The overarching decision-rule for mapping might therefore be stated as: Be as precise and complete as usefulness allows and requires for the purposes at hand.

• Maps can be falsified by those they address. Maps are a set of hypotheses to be tested, and as such they are designed to be falsifiable in an action context. The inferences embedded in them are made explicit and connected to data that are easily recognizable and observable by participants, so that the inferences can be submitted to a range of tests by them. One such test is to present the map to participants, along with the data on which it is based, actively seeking disconfirming data and alternative views. Another test is to make predictions about future events that logically follow from the map. We might predict, for instance, that the actors in a matrix will experience more and more binds and will increasingly distance themselves from their responsibility. And a third test is to design an intervention predicted to alter the interactions and the consequences depicted in the map. If the map is accurate, then we ought to be able to predict the impact of altering one aspect of it on other variables described in the map.

• Maps contain an inner logic with a predictable plot line. While themes may vary, the basic plot line of maps remains the same. Such plots ordinarily begin with the initial conditions that actors face. They then go on to describe the rules or sets of rules that individuals follow under these conditions in order to contend with them. And finally, they identify the impact of these rules and conditions on variables relevant to actors, including the initial conditions themselves. In this way maps can be said to describe the teleological and causal mechanisms involved in interactions, as well as the self-reinforcing features embedded in this causality.

• Maps take into account the constraints posed by the human mind. All maps share certain characteristics that enable individuals to store and retrieve them while acting on-line and to use them for actually producing or altering the actions represented in them. First, they are abstract and generalizable enough to cover a range of behaviors and instances, so that they can be stored economically without overwhelming actors with complex detail. Second, although abstract, maps are easily connectable to the data of what occurred, and they can be illustrated by representative examples that are vivid enough to be retrieved while acting (cf. Tversky and Kahnemann, 1973). Third, since actors lose sight of their behavior while acting but can identify internal or situational cues (Jones and Nisbett, 1972), the initial conditions specify these cues so that actors can more easily identify the situations in which they are apt to get into trouble. At the same time, by describing action rules, maps enable observers to identify and point out to unaware actors when they are in fact using them. This combination of recognizable cues and rules allows action to be interrupted for purposes of reflection. An actor can more easily retrieve what was happening at the time of the rule's use and reflect on the consequences the rule yields. If she then so chooses, she might reconsider how she constructed the situation before her (the conditions she faced), and she might invent an alternative rule, experimenting with it to see what she gets. In this way maps not only serve to describe and prescribe but to facilitate reflection on what is described and experimentation with alternatives.

Hypothesis Testing: Discovering Mistakes in Action. Action contexts are a formidable domain for ensuring the validity of tests. They are characterized by a multitude of interacting variables that cannot be isolated and manipulated one at a time. Compounding this, individuals in everyday life follow a set of rules for understanding and acting in the world that pose multiple threats to inferential accuracy and to the designing of valid tests. When individuals manage data, for example, they tend to retrieve biased samples (Tversky and Kahnemann, 1973), to see situational factors and not their own behavior (Jones and Nisbett, 1972), to lose sight of much of the data on which their inferences are based (Carlston, 1980), and to apply assymetrical standards to supporting and opposing evidence (Lord, Ross, and Lepper, 1979). In making inferences, they tend to skew them in a self-protective direction (Langer, 1976), and the more severe the consequences, the more defensive the attributions (Harvey, Harris, and Barnes, 1975). They tend to test their views privately (Argyris and Schön, 1974), and they rely primarily on confirming strategies (Mynatt, Doherty, and Tweney, 1978). Finally, when acting, they do so on the basis of private understandings that are assumed to be true, thereby creating self-fulfilling prophecies without knowing it.

Under these conditions we might easily despair of ever conducting valid tests with participants in an action context. But there is another side to this equation that works in favor of testing and that lays the foundation for rules that can ensure the validity of such tests. First of all, although it is complex, the action context is an ideal setting for repetitive and ongoing testing. We do not need to determine the status of a particular proposition once and for all in a time-limited, "one-shot" way. Instead we have multiple opportunities to construct test after test to eliminate competing hypotheses. Second, while it is true that participants follow a set of rules that jeopardize validity, it is rarely the case that they wish to do so. Quite the opposite, once they are aware of these rules, they are usually interested in acquiring those put forth by the action scientist as norms for inquiry in the learning context. Some of these were identified earlier as the rules governing processes for gathering and analyzing data, and we will now consider additional ones used to test hypotheses in an action context (see Part Three for a description of the learning process by which participants acquire them).

• *Rule 1:* Combine advocacy with inquiry. Perhaps the overarching rule of inquiry for action science is this one, because it requires that individuals regard their views as subject to critique and test, and it asks that they at once make them public and invite others to inquire into them. What form an inquiry takes depends on the view being put forth. An individual might make an attribution about someone and seek to test it with him. Or, alternatively, someone might claim that a certain strategy will yield certain outcomes and seek others' reactions. By itself this rule is not sufficient, since the way a view is put forth and reactions are offered affects whether a test is genuine. This rule must therefore be enacted in accord with those that follow.

• *Rule 2:* Illustrate your inferences with relatively directly observable data. This rule asks that when participants make a claim, they provide the data upon which it is based. If the assertion is of the form "John is acting unfairly," then they are asked to provide the data of what John said or did that led them to this view. Similarly, if someone asserts that "being supportive would make John more forthcoming in his views," they are asked to illustrate, often by means of a role play, the supportiveness hypothesized to help John be more open. In this way other participants have a means by which to judge for themselves whether the claims hold. They can see if the data about John suggest unfairness to them. They might come forth with new data or new explanations of the data that would falsify or dispute the claim. And they can determine whether the role play had the effect that was predicted by describing their responses to it and/or by seeing whether it helped John to become more open.

At first participants find it hard to retrieve the data of what occurred while acting, but since all sessions are tape recorded this does not present a significant obstacle. More important, we have found that with practice individuals can develop skill at retrieving data more accurately on-line. It may be that, as theories-in-use change and protective reasoning is reduced, retrieval is enhanced and becomes more reliable. In any event the data provided by audiotaping provides an ongoing check.

• *Rule 3:* Make your reasoning explicit and publicly test for agreement at each inferential step. Along with the previous two rules, this rule helps create conditions for public testing, this time by aiding the open probing and negotiation of different meanings. It asks that participants make explicit the inferential steps that led from the data to their conclusions, publicly seeking agreement at each step. The corollary is to return to the data in the face of conflicting meanings and retrace the steps taken to see where the meanings diverge. In making these steps public, participants can more readily detect the leaps of logic that they and others might make. They can ensure that they understand correctly the meanings others intended. They can see where they begin to disagree on what they believe is happening. And they can return and retrace their steps in an attempt to reach agreement.

• *Rule 4:* Actively seek disconfirming data and alternative explanations. One common inferential error in everyday reasoning is the strategy of seeking confirming data (Mynatt, Doherty, and Tweney, 1978). One way to counter this is to follow a rule that explicitly asks that disconfirming data and views be elicited. But often such a rule involves asking people to produce potentially negative information, since they might have to say that an individual's strategy made them defensive or that their own views are false. It is therefore not an easy rule to enact, since it must be accompanied by a willingness to take seriously these kinds of data and alternative explanations. By "take seriously," we mean that the actor must actively inquire into the new data or explanations and design ways of understanding the discrepancies by either designing tests of the competing views or reexamining the different inferences being made from the data. It would not be sufficient, however, to leave it at "you have your view or data and I have mine."

• *Rule 5:* Affirm the making of mistakes in the service of learning. This rule in part is designed to create conditions conducive to enacting the previous rules. Illustrating views, making one's inferences explicit, and seeking disconfirming data all put participants at risk of discovering they are wrong. Of course this is the purpose of experimentation, but the problem is that it evokes our defenses against failure. One way to counter these defenses is to regard mistakes as the raw material of learning, worthy of consideration and exploration. The difficulty here, however, is that participants are predisposed to take a different view of errors, one that involves regarding them more as crimes worthy of punishment. Not surprisingly, such a frame can act as a formidable obstacle to enacting these rules. We will see later that the learning of them is largely contingent on reframing what it means to make mistakes and what it takes to learn.

• *Rule 6:* Actively inquire into your impact on the learning context. Unlike most social scientists, the action scientist wishes to influence the inquiry at hand. For instance, she wishes to enact as norms the rules under discussion, thus helping participants to learn them. In a different vein, the action scientist can also make mistakes that affect participants, at times hindering their learning. In the passivity experiment in Chapter Four, for instance, George thought the interventionist's actions might inadvertently be doing more to reinforce his and his fellow students' responses than to alter them. This rule asks that action scientist and participants alike inquire into such possibilities and understand the nature of the impact that they do have: Is it what they intended? Do they like the results that their interventions yield? This rule recognizes that the interventionist cannot eliminate the possibility of influence altogether and that he does not wish to do so. The aim of action science is to serve participants' learning and to enable them to change by virtue of the researchers' influence. The task therefore is not to diminish the interventionist's influence but to inquire into whether the influence is intended and whether it is the right influence to exert. This inquiry, of course, is pursued in accord with the other rules presented here.

• *Rule 7:* Design ongoing experiments to test competing views. Often individuals will disagree in their assertions about what is happening and what ought to happen. In the passivity experiment George asserted that the interventionist was reinforcing passivity, thus giving his view of what would happen if the interventionist continued to act in the same way. At the same time he thought another approach would be better and put forth his idea of what should happen. In both instances the interventionist had a different view, yet rather than impose his own view or regard the differences as nonnegotiable, he designed ways to test them. In the first instance, he suggested that they see what would happen as a result of his moves: "One way is to test it and see what happens in the interaction as we're going." In the second instance he asked George to role play his alternative to test whether it had the impact he predicted and whether it yielded results that might foster the learning he sought.

Similarly, some social scientists have questioned the validity of a protocol that action scientists use to test the claim that individuals hold Model I theories-in-use. Since this view raises an important issue, we will describe the protocol here, examine the questions it raised, and look at the test designed to see if the negative view of the protocol was confirmed. The protocol in question was the X and Y case, a learning instrument developed to test whether participants hold a Model I theory-in-use. (For a more detailed discussion, see Argyris, 1982). The case offers examples of what a superior, Mr. Y, said to a subordinate, Mr. X:

1. "X, your performance is not up to standard."
2. "You seem to be carrying a chip on your shoulder."
3. "It appears to me that this has affected your performance in a number of ways. I have heard words like *lethargy, un-*

committed, and *disinterested* used by others in describing
your recent performance."
4. "Our senior professionals cannot have those characteristics."
5. "Let's discuss your feelings about your performance."
6. "X, I know you want to talk about the injustices that you
    believe have been perpetrated on you in the past. The problem is that I am not familiar with the specifics of those
    problems. I do not want to spend a lot of time discussing
    something that happened several years ago. Nothing constructive will come from it. It's behind us."
7. "I want to talk about you today and about your future in
    our system."

Once participants have read the case, the interventionist
asks them to evaluate how well Mr. Y performed his task of
helping X to "shape up or ship out." Participants uniformly
evaluate Y as ineffective; and, as they do so, the interventionist
creates a collage of their diagnoses and modifies it until all participants agree that it represents their views. At this point the
interventionist then infers the causal theory embedded in their
diagnosis: "If someone is blunt, insensitive, and so on, then the
recipient will feel misunderstood and defensive, and little learning will occur," and he tests for agreement among participants
to see if this represents their view. Once they confirm that it
does, the interventionist then identifies a puzzle: If participants
told Y their diagnosis, they would be enacting the very causal
theory that they criticize Y for enacting with X. Telling someone he is blunt and insensitive is itself blunt and insensitive,
and by this microcausal theory it would be expected to cause
defensiveness and inhibit learning.

Typically, participants react by defending their actions
and reasoning processes, and the interventionist treats each objection as an hypothesis to be tested, encouraging participants
to role play what they would actually say to Y. When they do
so, they discover that they use either a forthright or an easing-
in strategy, but in each case they find that they communicate
what was in the diagnosis and create the very conditions that it

predicted and that they wished to avoid. Even when the interventionist predicts this will occur and the participants know
these predictions, believe they are false, and strive to disconfirm them, they still discover that other participants evaluate
them as having acted in ways consistent with them.

The X-Y case has now been used with thousands of individuals in scores of groups (see Argyris, 1982). In each case participants have acted in the ways predicted by Model I, indicating that little to no variance exists at the level of theory-in-use.
Social scientists are understandably skeptical of this result, and
it is this lack of variance that raised the question of whether it
might be an artifact of the X-Y case. According to this view, it
is not that everyone is programmed with a Model I theory-in-use
but that the X-Y case elicits responses that confirm the theory.
To summarize, this critique is composed of the following kinds
of assertions: The protocol extracts a few sentences from different points in a conversation, and each sentence is thus isolated from its context. The protocol gives only Y's side of the
conversation, and this may induce people to react negatively to
Y. And, finally, Y acts in ways that have the cultural meanings
of "authoritarian, controlling, and disapproving," putting the
respondents in a state of apprehension as to how they should
feel in X's place. Because of this, respondents feel indignation
with Y, and their responses are more a consequence of this
emotional state than of an underlying Model I theory-in-use.
One way we might respond to these possibilities is to point to
the other kinds of evidence that support the theory. For example, when individuals write out cases of situations in which they
have been involved, they reveal the same theory-in-use. Similarly, tape recordings or observations of spontaneous interactions in organizations show the same features. It is difficult to
see how researchers could be held responsible for data that are
produced by individuals who are working alone and who may
never have been in an action science project.

Nevertheless, to test the possibility that the X-Y case elicits confirming data, we developed another protocol, the A-B
case (see Exhibit 1). Unlike the X-Y case, this one presents a
single episode rather than excerpts from several points in a con-

Exhibit 1. A-B Case.

Context: B is a supervisor at a community center. B is concerned about A, who is a volunteer counselor. A used to be a client of the center, and lately she has again been coming in for help. B is concerned that A's personal difficulties may be interfering with her performance as a counselor. B decides to talk to A in the hope that A will agree to limit her counseling work.

B: It seems like it might be time to start thinking about whether your roles—whether both counseling here and being a client, is kind of becoming a problem.

A: Why is it a problem?

B: I'm not saying it is. I guess I'm just curious to hear your thoughts on it. Is it confusing to you? I imagine it might be.

A: No. Why should it be? It's not confusing.

B: I'm not trying to attack you in any way whatsoever. I'm merely just asking a question. We haven't talked about any of this stuff for a really long time.

A: Fine. That's fine, and my answer is no, it's not a problem.

B: Well, I've heard from C that sometimes you say that you come here needing help, and you're frustrated because nobody is free to see you. And then you decide, "Maybe I should be working now." Do you really feel like at those times you are at your best to be a counselor, that you're able to put your stuff aside?

versation, and it provides both sides of the conversation rather than only one. Unlike Y, the supervisor B appears to make an attempt to be caring and supportive and to reduce the risk that A will perceive her as authoritarian, controlling, and disapproving. At the same time, B is still an authority, she disapproves of what she believes A is doing, and she does not drop the issue when A says there is no problem. Some social scientists have argued that this in itself creates an inherently Model I situation. In our view it may create an inherently threatening situation, but it does not need to be handled in a Model I fashion. Individuals in positions of authority must find some way to evaluate and handle the possible incompetence of subordinates. The question is how they fulfill this responsibility, and what choices they make as they do so.

Despite the contextual differences in the case and B's easing-in strategy, the results were the same as in the X-Y case. Participants evaluated B negatively, they used a micro-causal theory of defense to diagnose the case, and they violated that theory once they acted, whether they eased in or were forthright. All the data suggested that their theories-in-use were Model I, and the same inconsistencies found in the X-Y experiment were found here. It therefore does not appear that the X-Y case is responsible for eliciting confirming data.

This chapter describes action science as an inquiry into social practice. The questions it asks, the facts it goes after, and the solutions it devises are designed to generate knowledge in the interest of such practice. At the same time we have said that action science aims to enact communities of inquiry in communities of practice by helping participants to realize the norm of responsible belief. But to do so requires that the action scientist enact the rules of inquiry just described in real-life contexts, and this in turn means that practitioners must use those rules. At present, practitioners adhere to everyday rules of inquiry that clash with those of action science and they are unaware this is the case. Thus the action scientist must help practitioners become aware of the rules they now use and teach an alternative set, so that practitioners might skillfully enact them on their own. How the action scientist does so is the question that the remainder of this book addresses.

Part Three

Developing Skills for Useful Research and Effective Intervention

One criticism of action science is that it is more an art than a science. According to this view, it requires skills only a handful have mastered, and since these cannot be made explicit or taught to others, the mystery of this mastery can never be solved. If this is so, then at best action science is a form only a few can produce; at worst it is an idea that will remain just that: an idea. We take such a possibility seriously. By itself its premise is compelling. There *is* a good deal of artistry in the practice of action science, a kind of tacit expertise that tells its practitioners what to look for, how to view a situation, and how to transform what they see. But we believe this is true of competence or expertise in many areas. Certainly, the practice of any science involves the skillful enactment of both explicit and tacit rules in a way that might similarly be considered a form of artistry. At the same time, we do not want to dismiss too quickly the possibility that the acquisition of action science skills is so uniquely difficult that, unlike competencies in other methods, it will necessarily remain rare.

To consider this possibility, we have taken the process of

acquiring these skills as an object of inquiry, asking the dual question: What are the requisite skills of action science, and what does it take to learn and to teach them? We can answer the first part of this question here by extrapolating from the rules described in the previous chapter. One necessary set of skills is quite familiar, since it comprises those required to carry out other scientific methods. For instance, just as experimentalists should be well versed in the logic of experimentation, so should action scientists display a grasp of what it takes to construct falsifiable hypotheses and to design valid ways of ruling out alternative explanations. And just as ethnographers should be adept at observational techniques, so should action scientists evidence an ability to manage very large amounts of data without becoming overwhelmed by them and to systematically draw inferences from these data.

But another set of skills is unique to action science, stemming from the way action scientists engage with participants in the research process. In an action science project, the logic behind the researcher's methods, the actions used to produce them, and the methods themselves all become as much an object of inquiry as the interactions of particpants. In the passivity experiment, for instance, the participants turned the experiment itself into the focus of inquiry by pursuing the possibility that the logic the interventionist used to design it was inconsistent and that the actions he used to produce it might create a self-fulfilling prophecy (see Chapter Four). As noted then, the interventionist encouraged this inquiry. He asked for views from other participants, made his reasoning explicit, and invited the group to critique it as he did their reasoning. As this suggests, the participants exerted considerable control over the design and direction of the inquiry and over the inferences drawn from the data. But most important the interventionist designed the experiment to directly contribute to participants' learning, and he held himself accountable to them for doing so, seeking to know when he was not carrying out his intention and turning to participants to learn about this.

Taken together, these features add up to a fundamentally different role relationship between participant and researcher, one that demands a new set of skills. Researchers must be willing to make themselves vulnerable and to put their own reasoning and actions on the line, subjecting them to the same scrutiny to which they subject the reasoning and actions of participants. They must be able to contend with their own defensive reactions and remain open when their views and actions are called into question, often without much compassion or skill. And they must do all this while simultaneously negotiating a dilemma faced by researcher and participant alike. On the one hand, the process is intended to be jointly controlled, with participants taking responsibility for their own learning; while on the other hand, the process necessarily starts out under conditions of inequity. At the outset participants are largely unaware of their theories-in-use and only vaguely aware or able to envision the alternatives posed by the action scientist.

Participants therefore enter the process in a position of dependence on the interventionist. They discover in an explicit sense that they know their own theories-in-use less well than the interventionist does, and they have scarcely any idea about how to remedy the gaps they uncover in them. Understandably this discovery triggers experiences of distress and anxiety that themselves evoke reactions that can get in the way of working through the dilemma that triggers them. Participants may conceal, even from themselves, the inconsistencies of their actions. They may resist the help of the interventionist in discovering these inconsistencies or the alternatives that might reduce them. Or they may grow hostile toward the interventionist for what they construe as his unnecessary exertion of power. The action scientist must be able to contend with such reactions, not by becoming defensive, but by inquiring into what leads to these reactions in order to move beyond them.

So the question now becomes: What does it take to learn and to teach these skills, given what participant and interventionist are up against? In a nine-month seminar that spanned two semesters, we had the opportunity to study this question by researching the process involved in teaching action science skills to graduate students at a professional school who were interested in research and consulting. In the following chapters we will describe this research project because in so doing we can serve a dual purpose. First, the project will help us see what is involved in learning and teaching the skills necessary to conduct an action science project. But second and equally important, it will permit us to describe the process by which action science seeks to enact a community of inquiry in a community of practice. Since this process is a complex one, involving the continual unfolding of new actions on the part of participant and instructor alike, we present an overview of the project in this introduction. In subsequent chapters we will dig more deeply into what this process of learning requires and involves.

Unfreezing

During the fall semester approximately sixty participants attended a weekly lecture class, and in the first three weeks they all went through what we call the initial unfreezing process. This process, typically initiated at the start of an action science project, interrupts participants' unawareness of their theory-in-use while testing the hypothesis that this theory-in-use is Model I. The notion of unfreezing was itself first developed by Lewin (1964), and it is predicated on the idea that existing theories or skills must be brought to awareness and unlearned before new ones can be learned. To achieve this, the interventionist first generates data that participants recognize as a valid sample of their behavior. This is accomplished by using the X-Y case described in the previous chapter. Participants are asked to make a diagnosis of Y and then to role play how they would help him. Once these data are generated, the interventionist then makes and publicly tests a series of low-level inferences about the nature of participants' theories-in-use, inquiring into his responsibility for the results (see Argyris, 1982, for a full description of this phase).

As participants engaged in the unfreezing process, they became aware of their theories-in-use for the first time, and this triggered a range of reactions. In previous research a model was developed to describe this initial process and the reactions it elicits. Since it continues to represent well the earliest phase of the project, we include it here as Figure 7.

Figure 7. Unfreezing Process.

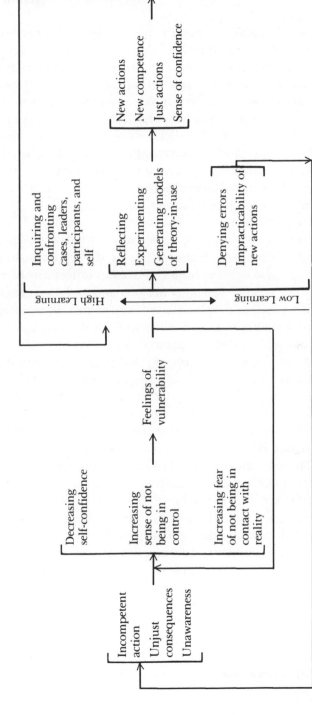

Source: Argyris, 1982.

As the model indicates, participants first become aware through their own evaluations that they are acting inconsistently and unfairly, but they remain unaware of what leads them to do so (column 1). As the process continues, their self-confidence begins to decrease, and they start to feel less in control of themselves and less in touch with reality (column 2), evoking feelings of vulnerability (column 3). Efforts to manage this vulnerability vary, depending on the individual and the actions of the interventionist (column 4). Some participants may act defensively but remain open to learning—for example, by confronting the interventionist while examining their own actions. Alternatively, other participants may act in ways that inhibit learning, rejecting efforts to examine their own errors or holding others responsible for them. Notice that, as the feedback loops indicate, those who actively inquire into and reflect on their actions tend to get glimmers of new actions and to feel increased competence, as well as a new sense of confidence. In contrast, those who avoid such moves and resist looking at their errors tend to reinforce their present actions and their unawareness.

After these first three weeks of the unfreezing process, participants joined smaller discussion sections with ten to fifteen students in addition to attending the larger lecture class. At this point the focus shifted somewhat. Once aware that they had been unaware of their theories-in-use, participants now became intent on discovering and mapping out these tacit theories. The remainder of the fall seminar was thus devoted mainly, but not exclusively, to helping participants develop skills of reflection, so that they might become increasingly aware of their existing theories-in-use. For the most part the media used for this purpose were participant-generated cases and transcripts of seminar interactions. The cases were usually what we called "button-pushing" cases, that is, descriptions of actual dialogue and unspoken reactions in situations that were difficult or threatening and that thus triggered the case writer's most automatic responses. These then became the subject of inquiry in both discussion sections and lecture classes, and participants tried to help the case writer to reflect on the problems in the case and to generate alternatives. While the group did this, the interventionist consulted to the group on how well it was doing, and the group consulted to the interventionist on how well he or she was doing. The sources of reflection were thus multiple: the written case, participants' efforts to help the case writer, the interventionist's efforts to help the participants, and their efforts to help the interventionist be of help. It should not be difficult to imagine how complex and at times confusing this reflective hall of mirrors became.

Learning a New Theory-in-Use

A smaller group of participants enrolled for the spring semester. The selection process for this seminar was twofold. First, participants interested in continuing stated their interest. Following that, the top twenty students from this group, judged by grades received during the previous semester, were accepted. Of the twenty students selected, eighteen chose to attend and stayed for the entire semester. While this second semester built on and continued the previous semester's learning, in several respects the transition between semesters was not continuous. The senior interventionist, who had conducted the lecture class but not a smaller section, was now the senior instructor of the smaller seminar. Participants did not know the senior instructor as well as they had known their previous section leaders and were therefore confronted with forming a new relationship with a new small-group leader. In addition, participants from the different small groups came together to form what in many respects was a new group composed of individuals who did not all know one another. But the use of cases and transcripts and the process of reflective experimentation remained the staples of learning.

Only now the stakes were higher. Increasingly, participants took as their goals the learning of a new theory-in-use and the competence to manage the learning process on their own. While participants held these goals from the outset, the interventionists initially tried to calibrate such aspirations, since participants had to first develop an awareness of their existing theories and a competence in reflecting on them. But by this second semester, it became more realistic for participants to work toward consistently enacting new rules and eventually stringing them together in sequences that could yield new consequences. As aspirations were raised, new impediments to them were also uncovered. Basic assumptions or frames about what it meant and took to learn new skills and manage the learning process became more evident, and a process of reframing the learning process gradually began to emerge.

As the year unfolded, most participants evidenced a greater ability to use these new rules and to manage their own learning, both by their own evaluation and that of the instructors. More and more often the puzzles that their actions generated became a source of curiosity rather than anxiety; they evidenced a greater willingness to explore their own and others' defenses; and they began to take a stance toward those they helped that allowed them to critique the others' actions while maintaining a sense of empathy for the dilemmas they experienced. Along with this and reinforcing it, participants also developed a greater conceptual and tacit understanding of the rules and values embedded in a Model II theory-in-use. They could now enact a wider range of rules; they had a better grasp of the conditions under which certain rules should be applied; and they could more readily identify and interrupt on-line the use of problematic rules.

What follows in the subsequent chapters is a description of this year-long seminar and the learning that occurred in the course of it. Because action science skills are required to teach these skills, the seminar provides the opportunity to see such skills in action and to consider what it takes to learn them. Most important, it gives a window onto the process by which action science seeks to enact a community of inquiry in a community of practice, the obstacles that must be negotiated, and the ways in which instructor and participant alike try to do this. We therefore begin our discussion of the seminar as the action scientist and the participant emerge from the unfreezing process, and we describe the dilemmas they both must contend with if learning is to go forward (Chapter Nine). We then describe the way in which the interventionist seeks to establish a context conducive to reflective experimentation in light of the dilemmas described in the previous chapter (Chapter Ten). We then describe the process by which individuals learn the rules for action science as they redesign their theories-in-use (Chapter Eleven). Finally, we show how the interventionist seeks to break the frames that inhibit experimentation in action and how he helps participants to experiment with new frames (Chapter Twelve).

9

Engaging
the Learning Process

Learning any new skill is necessarily fraught with dilemmas. It depends on practice, but the learner cannot practice what she does not yet know. The intent is to develop competence, but initially the learner faces repeated failure. The goal is to add to one's present skills, but at times these may get in the way of learning new ones and may need to be interrupted. So while the aim is to become more skillful, at first the learner becomes less so: She must slow down what was quick, pay attention to what was automatic, and make awkward what was smooth.

Learning to skillfully enact the rules of action science is no exception, yet it is complicated still further by participants' unawareness. As they enter the unfreezing process, they assume they hold one set of skills when they actually hold another; they are unaware of this gap; and, once aware, they still do not recognize what it will take to fill it in or that the skills that they are now using are inadequate. As one student reflected (Higgins, 1985): "I had entered the class with this theory of learning: If I read the required books and listen to all lectures and section discussions, I will learn the skills that will make me a better practitioner. Put more succinctly, by reading and listening, I'll learn. This theory informed my behavior which was to read and listen, but not participate. I felt comfortable with this learning strategy, as it had worked well in past learning situations—or so I thought." To learn the skills of action science, it is not sufficient to just read and listen. It is necessary to act and to reflect publicly on that action in order to discover existing theories-in-use and to experiment with new ones. Yet this entails risk and discomfort. It requires that participants design learning experiments that will yield unexpected failures. As this becomes more and more evident, a bind arises. As the same student again reflected, "I felt very uncomfortable and reluctant to carry out the behaviors designed to expand and deepen learning. It meant moving out of my silent comfortable niche and plunging into vulnerability, insecurity, and self-doubt. [But] I could see that without risks, I wouldn't learn much." If participants are to learn the rules of action science, they must learn how to work through such learning dilemmas. This chapter describes the nature of these dilemmas, what leads to them, and how they can be either reinforced or renegotiated in the service of learning.

Orientations Toward Learning

Throughout the learning process, participants want to simultaneously move in two different directions. On the one hand, they want to discover their theories-in-use so they can learn; while on the other hand, they want to cover them up so they can protect themselves from the pain and vulnerability that learning involves. This finding is not unique to our work. Such ambivalence seems to be generic to all growth and learning that is central to one's sense of self (Diamond, 1983; Sullivan, 1953). But we have found that *how* individuals manage this ambivalence is critical. Some participants take a protective stance. They approach the learning process afraid to make mistakes for fear of appearing foolish or stupid; they shy away from experimentation and withdraw in the face of reflection; and they resent those who appear to be learning and blame them for their own experience of failure. Others take a different stance. They approach learning with some of the same fears but also with the confidence that the way through these fears is to jump in, to make mistakes, and to reflect on them; they embrace experimentation and grow excited over the possibilities for reflection; and they appreciate their peers' contributions and mistakes, seeking to learn from them.

What follows is a map that describes these two orientations and their implications for working through dilemmas of learning. As the map shows (see Figure 8), these orientations are conceptualized along a continuum to emphasize that individuals actually draw from aspects of both orientations. At the same time, we have found that early in the seminar individuals tend to draw most heavily on the understandings and rules embedded in a more protective orientation. It is not until they become aware of its limits that they begin to experiment with those characteristic of a more reflective orientation. As this suggests, in the course of learning individuals can and do renegotiate how they engage in the learning process, traveling up the continuum from a protective to a reflective orientation. Subsequent chapters describe what the instructors do to stimulate this movement, while this chapter maps out the understandings and strategies that make up the two orientations.

This map begins where participants begin: with the conditions they all must face as they engage in the learning process (column 1). It then goes on to distinguish between the ways in which individuals with each orientation frame and experience this process (columns 2 and 3), the learning strategies and dilemmas that the two orientations evoke (columns 4, 5, and 6), and the consequences that they each yield for the learning context (column 7).

Initial Conditions (Column 1). The tasks that individuals face in life are a key source of uncertainty and anxiety, since they place requirements on us that we fear we cannot meet (Hirschhorn, 1982). The more complex, novel, and ambiguous the task, the higher the demands and the greater our uncertainty over whether or not we can accomplish it. Each of these features characterizes the task of learning a new theory-in-use.

First, the task is complex in several respects. The theories-in-use that individuals wish to learn include a multitude of rules, some nested within others and each with its own range of usefulness. Some of these rules may conflict, and all of them are aimed at satisfying a different set of purposes that those participants follow. Moreover, processes of reflection are themselves the object of reflection, which in turn can become the object of reflection and so on, making the layers of reflective discussion multiple, complicated, and at times even circuitous. Finally, the web of reasoning that gets unraveled in action and examined in reflection is characterized by intricate and elaborate strands of logic, difficult to trace or to distinguish from one another.

Second, the task is at once novel and ambiguous. No clear criteria exist to specify what constitutes a mistake, and no definitive end point exists. Instead we speak of approximating new values, when these are themselves novel and ambiguous. Few individuals evidence them in action, and they cannot be observed directly but must be inferred from action, a process that is itself ambiguous. What's more, no single or explicit way of acquiring these new values or skills exists. There are multiple paths, and much of the knowledge about how to discover and negotiate them remains tacit.

These task-related features reinforce one another and multiply the risks of failure, posing clear and present dangers to individuals' self-esteem and bringing into play such defenses as withdrawal from the task, distortion of how well one is doing, the blaming of others, and so forth. Participants thus find that they must simultaneously contend with a threatening task and their own predisposition to undermine it. Compounding this, they have just emerged from the initial unfreezing process with a hybrid state of awareness. On the one hand, they are now aware of the outcomes that their actions yield, and they are committed to redesigning them. On the other hand, they remain unaware of what leads them to act as they do, and they are uncertain about whether or not they want to find out. This particular mixture of awareness of outcomes and unawareness of causes can raise the level of threat further: Individuals are no longer uncertain only about the task but are now uncertain

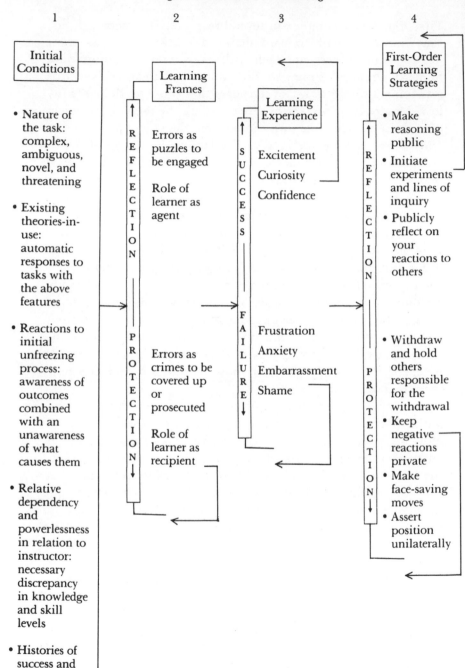

Figure 8. Dilemmas of Learning.

5

Learning Binds

If I participate and take risks, I may be seen by peers as competitive and unfair and/or I might make mistakes or hurt others.

Yet if I hold back and withdraw, I'm unfair to myself, I will not be of help to others and I might not learn.

* * *

If I'm quiet and withdrawn, others may see me as weak and dependent.

Yet if I reveal my feelings, others may still see me as weak and dependent

* * *

If I raise these dilemmas, I may be seen as making errors and as being weak and dependent

Yet if I don't raise them, they may immobilize me and I will not learn

6

REFLECTION

Second-Order Learning Strategies

- Publicly identify and inquire into dilemmas and apparent inconsistencies

- Reflect on errors and redesign actions

- Publicly examine one's own, as well as others', responsibility

PROTECTION

- Couch attributions as feelings and claim a right to them
- Use fancy footwork: Switch to whatever view will defend your position and act as if you are not switching
- Cover up the cover-up
- Seek and offer protective support

7

Impact on Learning Context

REFLECTION

Culture of reflective experimentation: Strategies contribute to norms of interaction that expand and deepen learning

PROTECTION

Culture of protectionism: Strategies contribute to norms of interaction that inhibit learning about themselves as well. Because of this, they place themselves in a position of dependency on the interventionist, relying on what they perceive to be his or her ability to accurately predict outcomes, to offer compelling accounts of action, and to effortlessly enact alternative actions and consequences. But at the outset such mastery is a mystery, the mystery is a tough one to solve, and the participants' deductive powers are now suspect in their own minds.

Historically this particular group of participants had not experienced such threats of failure nor the need to depend to such a degree on another person. The majority of them had succeeded academically, and many had already begun successful professional careers. They were unaccustomed to discovering gaps in their skills that they could not fill in on their own. For some this provided a source of confidence in the face of failure, but for others the novelty made the hurdles only seem higher with little time to learn how to scale them, since the seminar would last only nine months. Participants knew that after this nine months, they would have to continue to develop their new expertise by themselves.

Early on these conditions are unavoidable. Everyone encounters them as they begin to engage in the learning process. They act as an interrelated set of factors that reinforce one another and that cannot be ignored. They are the "givens" in the problem of learning, and all participants must come to terms with them in some way.

Framing the Problem of Learning (Column 2). Even so, the way that participants come to terms with these conditions is not given. It involves choice, as tacit as such choice may be, and it begins with choosing how to frame the situation before them: what to pay attention to and what to ignore, how to name the facts they see, and how to organize these into a meaningful pattern (Schön, 1983). In this instance, participants must figure out what it means and takes to learn. In other words, they must frame the problem of learning. But in so doing, they do not start from scratch. Instead, as Schön (1983) writes, they begin to see the familiar in the unfamiliar: "When a practitioner makes sense of a situation he perceives to be unique, he *sees* it *as* something already present in his repertoire. . . . The familiar situation functions as a precedent, or a metaphor, or—in Thomas Kuhn's phrase—an exemplar for the unfamiliar one" (p. 138).

Once in use, frames act as templets that we attempt to "fit over" situations in order to make sense of them (see Kelly, 1955, pp. 8-9). They serve to bracket off what is relevant, they give meaning to what we see, and they figure into our calculus of how to act. As Schön (1983) notes, "Seeing *this* situation as *that* one, one may also *do* in this situation *as* in that one" (p. 139). Schön (1979) uses the problem of urban slums to illustrate how this occurs. Urban slums might be framed either as blighted areas or as natural communities. But each frame implies different actions. "Blight" is a disease metaphor, and it suggests pockets of infection that should be cleaned out lest they infest healthy ones. In contrast, "natural communities" is a wildlife metaphor, and it suggests that urban slums should be preserved, protected, or helped.

Ordinarily such frames go unnoticed, so tacit and obvious is the reasoning behind them. But we have found that it is possible to bring them into awareness by interrupting interactions as they occur and directing individuals' attention to what they are doing, thinking, and feeling at the time (see Chapter Eight). From these data we can begin to reconstruct how individuals must have constructed the situations in which they acted.

As participants in the seminar reflected on how they engaged in the learning process, we began to gain access to how they were framing the problem of learning: both what it meant to make mistakes and how they were constructing their roles as learners. While these frames varied somewhat from person to person and from situation to situation, a gradual trend could be discerned over time, that is, participants tended to move from a protective framing to one more conducive to reflection and experimentation (see column 2).

• Role Frames. We already know that every participant encounters the same initial givens described in column 1: a complex and ambiguous task, existing theories-in-use that can hinder learning, dependence on instructors, and so on. But the way participants frame their roles as learners leads them to regard and consequently manage these same givens quite differently. As the map illustrates, we conceptualize this variance along a reflection/protection continuum, depending on the frame's capacity to sustain the reflective inquiry necessary for learning. While these are continuous rather than discrete categories, persons who frame their role more as agents tend to regard the initial givens as formidable but alterable and to see themselves and their peers as responsible for working through them. Conversely, those who frame their role more as recipients tend to see these initial givens as outside their control and to assign responsibility for working through them to others.

We can see this distinction in the case of two participants whom we will call Lee and Carol. The two of them construct qualitatively different problems and solutions out of the same initial givens. The first excerpt describes Lee's anger toward Carol, a reaction she expresses just after Carol has expressed anxiety about making errors:

Actual Dialogue	*Inferred Meaning*
Lee: I'd like to give you feedback, Carol. I have been angry at things you've said in previous weeks, because you	I've been angry at you.
were so involved in the process others didn't seem to matter. You were so eager to learn that it was blocking out other people. And I felt	You were so eager and involved that it prevents others from learning.
blocked out, angry, and jealous. I didn't say anything but I thought about it for two weeks.	I thought about this, but I chose to say nothing.

Shortly afterward Lee goes on to describe her reactions to the whole group:

Lee: I do resent the aggressiveness. I felt that at the be-	I resent the aggressiveness.

ginning of this course, people
were competing and people
were not hearing what people   It prevents me from speak-
were saying and they were   ing.
jumping in, and I didn't like
that. So I agree and it would
prevent one from speaking.

Lee's reactions serve as clues to how she constructs her
role and the situation before her. She starts out by saying that
she sees her peers as competitive and aggressive: They are
"jumping in" and "not hearing what people were saying." She
then acts as if she assumes her perceptions to be true, and she
builds on this assumption to take a third step: She attributes
that her peers' aggressiveness prevents her from participating
and presumably from learning. With the situation framed this
way, she then chooses to keep silent for two weeks, she holds
others responsible for her lack of participation, and she increasingly resents them for it. Finally when one of the more "aggressive" participants reveals her own vulnerabilities, Lee regards
this as an opportunity to express her own reactions and does so.

The way Lee constructs this scenario—both how she
understood it and how she acted in it—allows us to make out
the role she frames for herself and the resulting problems she set
out to solve. When Lee first saw her peers as competitive and
aggressive, she faced a choice point; she might have understood
and dealt with what she saw in any number of ways. She might
have considered their actions mistakes and intervened in order
to be of help. Alternatively, she might have focused on how
their actions could hinder her learning, designing a move to prevent them from doing so. But the role that Lee framed for herself precluded her from acting in either of these ways. Such
moves would require that she see herself as responsible for her
learning, and Lee's actions and reactions suggest someone who
regards herself as a passive recipient, someone who is "being
blocked out" by others. With this role set, Lee is most apt to
do what she in fact does do: withdraw at first and then, at a
relatively safe moment, intervene to get others to create the

conditions that she believes she requires if she is to learn. The paradox is that this makes it more difficult for both her and others to learn. If her private attributions about her peers are right, they will not learn from them as long as they remain private; and if they are wrong, she is unlikely to discover it. Yet Lee acts as if she is unaware of these possibilities. It is as if while acting, her role leads her to focus only on what others are doing to constrain her, preventing her from seeing to what extent she may be designing her own constraints.

This is not to say that the conditions Lee and others are up against do not act as constraints. She and her peers do have only a limited amount of time, and they do compete for their fair share of air time, jumping in and jockeying for the floor. But during this same two-week period Carol regarded and managed these same conditions in ways that expanded and deepened her learning. Faced with the choice of whether or not to risk a role play, Carol spent a good deal of time privately designing an intervention but then decided to jump in and to test out her idea. Later on when a peer interrupted her as she was reflecting on her intervention, she said that she had not finished and defended her request for a "fair share" of time. At a still later point, she became mystified by the differences in how her peers and the interventionist handled a particular case, and she expressed her puzzlement, initiating a series of questions aimed at decoding the tacit logic that informed the interventionist's actions.

This sequence of moves suggests that Carol framed a very different problem and role for herself in face of the same constraints. As with Lee, Carol had a series of choice points: whether or not to role play, whether or not to concede the floor, and whether or not to leave it up to the instructor to demystify the knowledge embedded in his actions. Although we do not have direct access to how Carol understands the situation before her, as we did with Lee, we might infer from her actions that she understood herself to be facing the following problems: how she might reduce the risks of a role play (she takes great care in designing it); how she might maintain the floor (she explains she's not finished); and how she might get at the differences between the instructor's theories and the participants' theories

(she goes after the instructor's reasoning in an attempt to understand how their actions ended up with different results). The
overall problem that these questions suggest is, How can *I* create
the conditions necessary for learning, a problem set that implies
that Carol regarded herself as the agent of her own learning and
personally responsible for it.

It is not unusual for participants to assume this role early
on, but it poses a conflictual situation. On the one hand, it
puts them in a better position to learn: Carol discovered new
mistakes and helped to bring to the surface the logic in the
interventionist's actions. On the other hand, however, the discovery of mistakes can generate embarrassment and anxiety.
Initially participants manage this conflict by oscillating between
the two role frames, sustaining the role of agent for longer and
longer periods of time and in the face of greater risks. But one
of the key impediments to sustaining this role is a frame about
errors that, to differing degrees, all participants bring to the
learning process.

• Framing of errors. Errors are the raw material for any
learning process. Curiously, this is a proposition that participants understand conceptually and advise others to follow but
that virtually all of them discard in action. When participants
discover errors, they act as if they believe that they are not only
wrong but wrong for being wrong. We can see this in the following dialogue as a participant hesitates to role play and, when
asked what stopped him, explains:

Actual Dialogue	*Inferred Meaning*
Participant: I know I won't be able to follow through, to make a complete interven-tion. And while I know that it's okay to just go part way, somehow I don't want to role play when I know I'll get stuck.	I recognize I will not be able to complete the inter-vention without making an error.
	I know this is okay.
	But when I know I am apt to make an error, I somehow do not want to act.

And in reflecting on her withdrawal in a different class, Carol communicates similar meanings:

Carol: It was just that the intervention had to be perfect. During the break I worked on it and talked to [one of the instructors] because I wanted it to be perfect enough that I wouldn't be totally embarrassed. Basically, I just didn't want to appear stupid.

I wanted the intervention to contain no errors.

If it has too many errors, I will be totally embarrassed.

If I made errors, I thought I would look stupid.

Such responses are typical. There is essentially no variance at the outset in how individuals frame mistakes; they simply regard them as wrong to make. We see this frame in use in the preceding dialogue as participants try to make sense of their own errors or potential errors. Errors are considered taboo, and the possibility of making one is sufficient to stop them in their tracks. Elsewhere this same frame operates as individuals react to others' mistakes, either growing angry at them for making the mistakes or rescuing them from owning up to them. This frame thus acts as the premise to the conclusion that errors should be either covered up or punished.

An alternative frame regards mistakes as puzzles to be engaged and solved, thereby making them opportunities for learning. A seminar graduate illustrates the reasoning that constitutes this frame, as he reflects on the errors he made during a meeting with colleagues:

Actual Dialogue

Graduate: It was pretty depressing, but then I realized it is also a superb opportunity for learning, because this incident is almost an exact replay of an incident I never really resolved.

Inferred Meaning

It was depressing at first, but then I realized it was an opportunity to learn.

In the same piece he then goes on to unravel what led to this pattern, and afterward he described that he was left with the following reaction:

Graduate: Ironically, I find all of this hopeful . . . because I know sooner or later, I will find myself in a similar situation and will not have to frame it in the same way. There is a way out of the dilemma.

What I have learned from error gives me hope.

In reframing the situation, I have discovered a way out of the dilemma.

Seeing his errors as a kind of puzzle enabled this participant to dig into the pattern he had discovered, to pursue the question of what led him to "replay" such patterns, and to experiment on paper with different ways out of the dilemma he saw. What he learned ended up transforming his initial feelings of depression into hope, as he came to experience a sense of success in diagnosing the source of his dilemma and to discover new ways of framing the situation.

Early in the seminar such frames are rarely evidenced in action, no matter how frequently they might be espoused. One reason for this may be that our earliest exemplars for learning predispose us to look at errors in a protective light. As Sullivan (1953) suggested, we learn to learn as children in ways that are associated with disapproval and anxiety, and we develop strategies of avoidance to protect ourselves from these reactions so that we can develop and grow (Diamond, 1983). In adulthood this early learning returns to roost, as the learning frames and strategies we developed in childhood begin to jeopardize the very growth and learning they were initially designed to ensure.

In our seminars participants start out afraid to make mistakes, and they draw back from the risks of experimentation and reflection in order to avoid a sense of failure. As a result, they end up reinforcing the very conditions they face: Dependence on the instructors is increased rather than diminished, the complexity of learning a new theory goes unmanaged, and the failure they wish to avoid becomes more likely. If learning is to go forward, it is necessary for participants to reframe what it means to make mistakes and what it takes to learn.

Psychological Success and Failure (Column 3). In early work on aspiration levels, Lewin and others (1944) studied the process by which individuals set goals and the implications of this process for experiences of success and failure. As summarized by Argyris (1970), they found that an individual experiences a sense of success when:

- he is able to define his own goals;
- the goals are related to his central needs, abilities, and values;
- he defines the paths to these goals; and
- the achievement of the goals represents a realistic level of aspiration for him. A goal is realistic to the extent that its achievement represents a challenge or a risk that requires hitherto unused, untested abilities.

In addition, they found that a sense of success led individuals to stay at tasks and to incrementally raise the levels of the goals they set, while a sense of failure led individuals to lower their goals. Repeated failure led to diminished confidence, defensive attributions, and eventual withdrawal from the task (Hoppe, 1976; Lewin and others, 1944). Similarly, in our research we have found that a repeated sense of failure tends to trigger fears of more failure, to reinforce a protective framing of errors and one's role, and to increase self-doubt, embarrassment, and dependence on others. Conversely we have also found that a sense of success tends to spark interest and curiosity, feelings of mastery, and a sense of excitement over the possibilities for learning. These experiences thus act like a kind of motor that can either supply or cut off the impetus for inquiry.

If this is so, the question of what governs these experiences of success and failure becomes critical. According to Lewin and others (1944) and Hoppe (1976), success depends on individuals' setting their aspiration levels high but not outside the "boundary of their ability": If the level is too low, they will experience little mastery or success in surpassing it; if it is too high, they will experience repeated failure. But how do individuals determine this boundary? Ordinarily they look to past performance. Yet this is precisely where participants run into difficulty. Their perception of their performance is likely to be quite different from their actual performance. They have been unaware of their theories, the outcomes they produce, and the actions they inform. They are thus apt to believe that they already have the new skills or that these skills will be relatively easy to learn. As a result, each time they discover that this is not the case, they experience a sense of failure, and they continue to do so until they set more realistic goals.

If this is so, how can participants discover what more realistic levels are? Usually the way to do this is to act, to receive feedback about how well one is doing, and to readjust levels in light of this feedback. Yet here too participants can get into difficulty. When they experience failure, these are often the very actions that are the most difficult to produce, since a sense of failure triggers fears of more failure, feelings of humiliation, and defensive attributions. Under these conditions, it is less likely that one will elicit the feedback necessary to readjust one's level of aspiration to a more realistic level.

So participants face a dilemma. To experience a sense of success, they need to set realistic levels of aspirations, yet they cannot do so as long as they automatically refuse to lower their sights in order to defend against feelings of failure. One way to manage this dilemma takes us back to how participants frame errors. To the extent that individuals consider it wrong to be wrong, they will aspire to avoid errors. As one participant put it, she wanted her intervention to be perfect. From her vantage point errors were evidence of failure and were to be avoided and covered up, thereby making a realistic assessment of abilities unlikely. But what if discovering errors was regarded as evidence of success? This reformulation transforms notions of success and failure in a way that enables participants to reflect on their errors.

What this analysis suggests is that the way individuals frame and experience the task before them is highly interactive. A protective framing of errors tends to make it difficult to set realistic levels of aspiration, which in turn results in experiences of failure, which then reinforce a protective framing of errors, and so on. Similarly, the way individuals frame their roles in order to avoid failure makes it impossible to create conditions for psychological success: As recipients, they do not define their own goals or the paths to those goals but leave it up to others. So, paradoxically, the very ways in which participants seek to protect themselves from failure create failure and keep a sense of success out of reach. Alternatively, more reflective frames enable individuals to more accurately reflect on and assess their abilities, thereby increasing experiences of success. Using these frames, they can make their aspirations more realistic and acquire an increasing ability to see themselves more accurately.

First-Order Learning Strategies (Column 4). It is through acting that we can probe, understand, and change existing theories, yet some actions can sustain this inquiry better than others. It is on this basis that we distinguish between protective action strategies and reflective action strategies in the map. A second distinction is between first-order strategies and second-order strategies, a distinction meant to recognize that, once we act, we draw on backup strategies to manage the new situation that our initial actions created. The actions that constitute these first- and second-order strategies may overlap or vary from person to person or from situation to situation. One person's second-order strategy may become another's first-order strategy. What is important is not the particular action but the function of the strategy, with second-order strategies providing the opportunity either to reinforce or to reflect on our first-order strategies and the situations they yield.

Protective strategies flow from a protective framing of errors and the role of learner as recipient, each of them decreasing the vulnerability of the actor and thereby impeding the path of inquiry. Here we focus on four of the most prevalent strategies: (1) withdraw and hold others responsible for withdrawing, (2) keep reactions private, (3) make face-saving moves, and (4) assert reactions unilaterally.

1. Withdraw and hold others responsible for withdraw-

ing. This strategy is often evoked to avoid mistakes and the embarrassment that they generate. The participant who backed off from role playing in this chapter and those in the passivity experiment who drew back from participating (Chapter Four) illustrate how individuals either withdraw and say little or wait until others make mistakes before risking mistakes of their own. The logic behind this strategy is that by withdrawing, one avoids errors. But because this strategy renders experimentation and practice impossible, it is itself a kind of error. It prevents individuals from discovering the success that can be experienced in detecting errors and makes it easier to distort what one can and cannot do. Actors can privately hang on to the belief that if they only had the chance to participate, they would not make the same errors as their peers. As a result, aspiration levels remain unrealistically high, which in turn increases the potential for a sense of failure. At the same time, the strategy cannot create a sense of success. Instead, it increasingly generates feelings of guilt, as actors grow angry at themselves for violating their own principles of openness and their own wish to learn. To defend against these feelings, actors soon begin to blame others for their withdrawal, as we saw Lee do earlier. It is at this point that the strategy seals itself, and eventually its logic paints the actor into a corner. With their own standards unattainable and errors taboo, individuals come to feel and act as if they were immobilized, unable to take a step without experiencing a sense of failure or humiliation.

2. Keep negative reactions private. Ordinarily reactions that are kept private consist of negative feelings and defensive attributions that serve to legitimate one's actions and take on an assumed-to-be-true nature that in turn lays the basis for further reasoning and action. Recall Lee's feelings of resentment and her attribution that others' competitiveness prevented her from participating. Such reactions appealed to an ideology of noncompetitiveness and served to legitimate her remaining quiet in a way that made it bearable. Secure in her perceptions, she then acted on them as if they were true without testing them or raising them as a subject for inquiry.

Predictably, those who withdraw use Lee's strategy, but

more verbal participants use it as well, systematically censoring any negative emotional reactions or attributions made about themselves and others. In the passivity experiment in Chapter Four we discovered that both quiet and verbal participants had censored their reactions the previous week. As a result the group lost access to how its members saw and experienced the learning process, and they could no longer learn about the difficulties people faced.

3. Make face-saving moves. Since participants regard errors as taboo, they usually anticipate that they may embarrass or upset someone should they point out his mistakes. They thus try to mitigate the impact of doing so by making different face-saving moves (Goffman, 1967; Brown and Levinson, 1978). One such move is to criticize themselves while simultaneously criticizing someone else. This way they communicate that while they see problems in what the other is doing, they themselves are no better, thereby avoiding the possibility of also one-upping the other. The problem is that this approach can lead the recipient to think, "So why is he talking? He's got the same problem" —a thought recipients then keep to themselves in order to save the actor's face.

A second face-saving move is to couch criticisms in a shroud of ambiguity or to ease out of them altogether. An actor might say, "I'm just curious, but I think you and I may be sort of missing each other slightly—but then it may just be me." The actor in this excerpt is disagreeing with the other's view, but there are so many qualifiers that it becomes quite ambiguous: "I'm just curious," "sort of missing each other," and "it may just be me." As Goffman described the actor using such strategies: "He employs circumlocutions and deceptions, phrasing his replies with careful ambiguity so that other's face is preserved even if their welfare is not" (1967, pp. 16-17).

As these examples suggest, face-saving moves carry with them multiple messages. Because they are informed by rules of polite discourse, because such rules are shared, and because we know that they are shared and that everyone else knows it too, it communicates that we wish the other would not get upset, that he would follow the same rules of politeness, and that he would be a good sport and help out in averting an embarrassing moment. This multiple message serves to put the recipient in a bind. On the one hand, he may want to be a good sport; while on the other hand, he may be perplexed by the critique or even see it as inaccurate and unfair, but feel he will violate the rules in saying so. To manage this bind, he may begin to draw on the same face-saving strategies himself, making it even harder to get at what has led to the critique in the first place. A second message is embedded in the rule's purpose. Because face saving is designed to mitigate the impact of a criticism and we all know that that is the intention, it may communicate that the error is so bad or the recipient so brittle that the criticism must be served up carefully. Although enacted to support the recipient, the rule can therefore end up adding insult to anticipated injury and make it difficult to learn of one's mistakes.

4. Assert your position unilaterally. This strategy involves making views public but doing so in a way that minimizes one's vulnerability, often by stating them at high levels of inference while acting as if they are concrete and obvious. To illustrate, we give a collage of statements made by one participant, Paul, to a consultant who had just brought a case to class for help:

> "I found myself frustrated by your approach."
> "I felt it was demeaning of her."
> "You communicated she needed to be made okay."
> "You elicited her first statement from her" [quotes statement].
> "I have a very strong reaction to her statement."
> "You let it evolve."
> "You guided it."

Unlike the views described so far, Paul's are public and direct. But he keeps them at a high level of inference, making attributions such as "it was demeaning" and "you guided it." At no point does he include the data of what the consultant did so that she might offer an alternative explanation for her actions or point out gaps in his reasoning. Moreover, he does not put his views forth as if they are inferences, but as if they are obvious and concrete. He acts as if he assumes them to be true. He invites no inquiry into them, and he uses them as the basis for both his intervention and his feelings, saying that he is "frustrated" and had a "very strong reaction." It is in this sense that we think of the strategy as protective. By regarding his views as facts and not inviting inquiry into them, he makes himself less vulnerable. Nevertheless it is also true that Paul's strategy makes him more vulnerable than the strategies of withdrawal and self-censorship would. At least we know his reaction; that is a start. From here we might ask that he illustrate his views, we might point out that others could see the situation differently, and we might inquire into what leads him to be frustrated with another's mistake. With more passive variants of protection, it is more difficult to initiate such processes.

To summarize, protective strategies, particularly the more passive variants, feed back to reinforce the initial conditions participants face: First, the less vulnerable they make their reasoning, the less likely it is that participants can become aware of and redesign their existing theories-in-use; and, second, the longer this is the case, the longer it will take to close the gap in competence and control between instructor and participant. Similarly, the strategies serve to reinforce a protective framing of errors and the role of learner: First, the less experimentation and experience with errors, the less likely it is that one will reframe what it means to make them; and, second, the less one takes responsibility and initiative, the less responsibility and commitment one will feel for the learning process. Finally, the strategies make it unlikely that aspiration levels can be revised or a sense of success experienced, so that avoidance of failure is bought at the price of experiencing no success. Over time the pressures to perform mount, errors remain untenable, goals stay unattainable, and time becomes scarcer. Eventually, efforts to avoid a sense of failure escalate these very feelings and people come to feel immobilized and hopeless.

In contrast, reflective strategies stem from the role of learner as agent. They involve greater risk taking than protective strategies in that they are characterized by a high degree of initiative coupled with a greater degree of vulnerability. Here we look at three such strategies: (1) make reasoning public, (2) initiate experiments and lines of inquiry, and (3) publicly reflect on reactions to others.

1. Make reasoning public. This strategy involves bringing one's views to the surface, while recognizing and trying to make explicit the inferential steps that led to them. Although this reasoning may contain gaps and inconsistencies, this strategy puts participants in a better position to discover and probe them. For instance, when one participant, Vince, thought that the interventionist had interrupted someone, he intervened, first describing what had occurred and then saying that this led him to "infer" that the interventionist had "stopped" her from finishing. Unlike more protective strategies, these moves made Vince vulnerable. By providing the data on which his inferences were based, he not only made his view public but also made it easier to disconfirm. And by admitting that his conclusion was an inference, not a fact, he recognized and communicated that he might be wrong, that other views might better account for the data, or that the data themselves might be incomplete. As it turned out, the interventionist cited data that Vince had missed, offering an alternative interpretation to account for these new data. But it was because he illustrated his view that the group was able to discover that Vince had overlooked data when framing the situation. And once having discovered this, the group was then able to explore whether Vince's omission was systematic, hypothesizing for the first time that Vince and others might be predisposed to frame the actions of people in positions of power in a particular light and to then selectively attend to those data that fit that frame.

This strategy of making one's reasoning public is often adopted by participants as they emerge from the unfreezing process. At that time they recognize that their theories-in-use lead them to make inferences at high levels of abstraction, to disconnect these from the data of what occurred, and to be so skillful at both that they lose sight of the inferential nature of the process, regarding their views as facts on which to act or to build further inferences. Once aware of all this, many try to slow the process down, begin to differentiate between fact and inference, and start to provide the data that led to their views. But such a process is not a purely cognitive one. It is not just a matter of slowing down, retracing steps, and retrieving data. At a conceptual level most participants recognize the importance of making their reasoning public right away, but it usually takes a longer period of time to skillfully and consistently produce it. One reason for this is that it is difficult to interrupt and slow down what is highly automatic behavior. But another reason is that this strategy brings to awareness important gaps in how participants understand and take action in the world. While such discoveries offer opportunities for learning, they can disrupt participants' confidence in their ability to make their way in the world. Vince's strategy put him in a position where he not only discovered an error in this particular instance but a frame about persons in positions of power that predisposed him to make such errors. The strategy thus requires more than the cognitive skills of retracing one's inferential steps and of retrieving data. It requires being able to risk being wrong.

2. Initiate experiments and lines of inquiry. Earlier when we considered the two role frames constructed by participants, we described how one role frame emphasized taking responsibility for designing and creating opportunities for learning (column 2). Here we take a look at one of the action strategies that logically follows from such a frame: the initiating of experiments and lines of inquiry. To illustrate, consider an impromptu experiment initiated by several participants in order to figure out how to help their peers take more responsibility. It began when a few participants held others responsible for the physical and psychological space they experienced in the seminar. As one person put it, she felt the group was "keeping them out." In response to this problem, four approaches or strategies were put forth as a way to solve it, and each one was tried out and became the object of reflection.

The first approach was suggested by Paul. He said that he could see how people might feel cut out but that he wanted to trust that they could take care of themselves. He ended by "inviting" them to jump in. We might call such a strategy: "Affirm the other's reactions but invite them to take responsibility for them.'' This strategy thus asks participants to act differently (to take more responsibility), but it empathizes with rather than confronts their passivity.

One participant, Lee, responded to this by repeating the assertion she had made previously: It was the competitiveness of her peers that prevented her from participating. The instructor then put forth a second strategy that differed from Paul's: "Confront the student's passivity by pointing out its consequences for her." In enacting this strategy, the instructor first noted that Lee's assertions were untested and that others might not confirm them. He then added that as long as she left it up to others to provide the space she required, she would have trouble in life. With some flair, he then ended by saying: "If I went into every meeting wondering how they felt about me, I think I could be as immobilized as Lee is." In response, several people winced; Lee said she felt nailed.

Building on these reactions, another participant, George, predicted that the instructor's approach could backfire. He thought it might make people withdraw more for fear of ridicule. He thus suggested yet a third strategy: "Confront passive actions without singling out any one individual." He then tested out his suggestion by roleplaying, "If I worried about what everyone said, I'd be immobilized." This new approach then led the instructor to reflect back on the reasoning that had led him to intervene as he had. Afterward Paul came back in to suggest yet a fourth approach: If the instructor had stated in his intervention the reasoning he had just made public, would that have been more useful?

We now have four competing approaches on the table. Or put as the students might frame it, we have three approaches put forth as alternatives to what the group ended up calling the instructor's "zap" approach with Lee. The inquiry from here led to some paradoxical findings. On the one hand, several people winced and felt a "sinking feeling" in response to this approach; yet on the other hand, these same people said that they immediately wanted to go back and listen to the tape and that they would think about it for a while—that what the instructor said would stay with them. The other approaches, while warmer and in some sense even more accurate, did not stimulate the same defensiveness nor the same impetus for further inquiry.

Without doubt such experimentation does not approximate the control and precision of the laboratory. But what it does do is sustain a process by which people can dig into different possibilities and consider their consequences, breaking new ground by asking—"What if we did this?" and "What about that?"—and then stepping back to see what they've got and where it may lead. In this experiment the group asked: "What did we get?" "Is it what we intended?" "Do we like what we got?" As Schön (1983) explains and as we have noted previously, such experiments involve the testing of different moves and either affirming or negating them depending on the results they produce. Equally important, this experimentation was designed by participants to take the inquiry in directions that were important to them. Without their initiative in designing such tests, learning would have been limited to an examination of one alternative on the terms of the one advocating it. Strategies that initiate these kinds of experiments thus expand the domain of inquiry and keep it moving in directions determined by instructor and participants alike.

A second variant of this strategy involves initiating lines of inquiry into different actions to tease out the web of reasoning embedded in them. We described earlier how Carol did this by asking a series of questions that helped to uncover the tacit reasoning informing the instructor's moves. Elsewhere participants probed one another's actions, trying to solve the same mystery on the basis of the same clues, namely, the actions they observed. In either case this strategy helped them to get at the way actors made sense of the situations before them, at the rules they followed, and at the purposes they pursued.

3. Publicly reflect on your reactions to others. Previously we saw how protective strategies involve either withholding one's reactions or asserting them unilaterally, while a more reflective strategy involved making one's reasoning public by retrieving the data that led to a particular view. However, while this latter strategy is one that people grasp early, they

may not be able to consistently produce it, particularly when they are upset. Participants may thus decide to simply remain quiet. An alternative to withdrawal, however, is to make one's reactions public but to regard them as a source of one's own learning, thereby making them the object of inquiry and inviting others to help solve the puzzle of what triggered them in the first place.

One participant, George, did this after he found himself getting angry when his role play with a participant-as-client (Mary) came to a halt and two of his peers intervened. Perplexed by his anger, he waded in:

Actual Dialogue	*Inferred Meaning*
George: I want to explore my angry reaction to feeling manipulated by my client, to see if others felt manipulated, and if so, if they felt angry.	I want to explore my reactions: Did others see the situation as I did? And if so, did they feel the same about it?
(And soon after): First, I was angry at Mary and then Dave and Paul came in. But why angry at Mary?	I found myself also getting angry at others. How come?

At this point his peers came in to help. As they went over what had happened, they found that others had also seen his "client" as manipulative but that not everyone had felt angry toward her, as George had. It was this observation in part that led the group to hypothesize that it may not have been his client's defenses, but perhaps his own inability to deal with them, that triggered his reactions. If he had been able to deal more effectively with her defenses, perhaps he would not have responded as angrily. It may be that her defenses served to reveal upsetting gaps in his skills, thus triggering his own defenses.

George's attempt to reflect on his own reactions put him in the role of a client, and his reactions became the data to be explained. This is quite different from what we saw in the case of the more protective strategies used by Paul and Lee, who simply assumed that their reactions told us more about others than about themselves. This is not to say that George's reactions tell us nothing of use about his client. His client could learn from them that others might react to her defenses by either becoming angry and frustrated or by distancing themselves and withdrawing. But here George is the client, and he does not want to react this way toward others' defenses because he recognizes that such reactions could limit his ability to deal with his clients' defenses. As George came to see this, his learning became an exemplar for others. Other participants learned from his particular case and discovered a generalizable heuristic that they too could use: One's anger may say at least as much about one's own incompetence as about anyone else's, so examine the reasons for it first.

To summarize, reflective strategies make the actor vulnerable, emphasize his own responsibility for events, require him to take initiative, and contribute to and sustain learning in the group. While they do not require fundamentally new theories-in-use, they do put participants in a better position to learn them by reinforcing conditions conducive to learning and by eliminating those that thwart it. The more participants experimented and made their reasoning public, the more they became aware of the causal factors that led to the unexpected and often bewildering outcomes discovered during the unfreezing process. In the same vein, complexity became easier to manage, as these strategies provided a way to incrementally unravel it by reflecting on action and inferring the rules that inform it. And, finally, as the group mapped out more domains and tried out more alternatives, it began to develop what we call *hybrids*: skills that incrementally depart from existing theories and move toward new ones by combining features from both, thereby narrowing the gap in competence between instructor and participant.

These same strategies also helped the group to break out of the frames that can cut off the impetus for learning, while reinforcing those that fuel it. By making errors public, the strategies provided tests of the two competing frames about errors. To the extent that these experiments generated more learning than feelings of humiliation, they began to break the frame of errors that says it is wrong to be wrong and to affirm the frame that regards errors as the basis for further inquiry. And by influ-

encing the direction of inquiry, these strategies reinforced feelings of commitment, control, and responsibility toward the
learning process in participants, thereby creating conditions
conducive to a sense of success.

   Learning Dilemmas (Column 5). As soon as participants
begin to engage in the learning process through their actions, dilemmas come to life. Picture for a moment the well-intentioned
learner. Right from the start his actions are confronted and explored as he is asked: What led you to do this? Can you say
what prevented you from doing that? What is it that you were
feeling or thinking? From the beginning, his actions yield puzzles and surprises as he discovers that what he intended is not
what he produced, that what he wanted to avoid he created,
and that what he believed others should not do, he himself did.
And, finally, just when he is trying his best to be helpful, a peer
with the same theory-in-use becomes defensive, attributes nasty
motives to him, and says he is not only being unhelpful but unfair and hurtful. Through acting and reflecting on his actions,
he soon comes to learn just how tenuous his previous grasp of
reality was.

   It is at this point that numerous dilemmas come to life. A
more talkative and forthright participant experiences the following dilemma:

> "If I'm active and forthright, my more quiet peers see me
>   as competitive and unfair."
> "Yet if I hold back, I begin to act passively, I'm unfair to
>   myself, and I may not learn."

A quieter participant experiences a different but equally difficult dilemma:

> "If I'm quiet and withdrawn, others may see me as weak
>   and dependent."
> "Yet if I reveal my feelings, they may still see me as weak
>   and dependent."

And at one time or another, everyone felt caught in the dilemma of:

"If I participate, I may not contribute anything, I'm apt to make errors, and I might even hurt others, since I'm not yet skillful."

"Yet if I remain or become quiet, I still won't contribute anything, this itself is a kind of error, I won't help my peers, and I will never become skillful."

Compounding them all, each participant saw himself or herself in the bind of:

"If I raise these dilemmas, I trigger the ones noted earlier: It may not contribute anything, it may be seen as an error, and it will take up precious time."

"Yet if I don't raise them, they will immobilize me, so again I won't contribute anything and I won't learn."

These dilemmas are framed in the light of participants' existing theories-in-use and the frames embedded in them. It is their automatic response to errors and vulnerabilities that lead them to frame the dilemma as if they are damned if they do and damned if they don't. Even those who frame their roles as agents and thus take a more active stance may fear the results of taking risks. Since they are bound to make mistakes and since they look upon mistakes as taboo, they are stuck. If these dilemmas remain private and go unresolved, they can become immobilizing, as the last statement suggests. Yet as it also suggests, such dilemmas are as difficult to live with as they are to raise, leaving participants with the problem of how to manage them. And it is to strategies for managing them that we turn next.

Second-Order Action Strategies (Column 6). As noted earlier, second-order strategies help us to manage the situations our initial actions create. This means that any of the strategies described as first-order strategies may be used as second-order strategies, and vice versa. Once confronted, someone who has previously made her reasoning public may feel, "I tried being direct and got clobbered. I might as well withdraw." Conversely, someone who has been quiet may begin to see this as an error and decide to publicly reflect on her withdrawal. In plotting these second-order strategies, the map continues to distinguish between protective strategies and reflective strategies. Whereas the former reinforce first-order actions and impede the learning process, the latter reexamine first-order actions and keep the process of reflection moving (compare defense type A and B in Argyris, 1982).

Second-order protective strategies decrease the vulnerability of actors, thereby reducing the possibility for reflection on action. The four most typical strategies are to (1) couch attributions as feelings and claim a right to them; (2) use fancy footwork, that is, switch to whatever view will defend your position and act as if you are not switching; (3) cover up the cover-up; and (4) seek and offer rescuing moves.

1. Couch attributions as feelings and claim a right to them. In our culture, feelings are like sacred cows. It is as though it were against some eternal law to call them into question. Of course, when the sacred cow wanders into our own backyard, we may regret that this is so. Consider the following interchange as a case in point. It occurred as a group of counselors gave feedback to Mary:

Karen: I feel like you [Mary] haven't been really committed to the group. I feel like you have one foot in and one foot out, and I don't feel like you have exposed yourself here.	Karen makes a series of attributions. She frames them as feelings.
Jane: I disagree. I feel that Mary has taken lots of risks in this group.	Jane makes a different attribution. She too frames it as a feeling.
Karen: Well, but you can't disagree with my feelings.	Karen evokes the unspoken rule to defend her view.
Jane: Okay, I realize that's how you feel. I'm saying that I feel differently.	Jane recognizes the rule and evokes it to defend her view.

What is Mary to do? Two sacred cows in her backyard,

eyeball to eyeball, and neither one willing to budge an inch. Both Karen and Jane couch their attributions as feelings, claim a right to them, and evoke a rule that makes them off limits for disagreement or exploration. By agreeing to disagree this way, Jane and Karen feel civilized and sensitive. After all, they are both abiding by the same rule to respect the rights of others to their feelings. But Mary doesn't know why one person sees her one way and the other another way. Implicit in Karen's view is an evaluation that Mary has been uncommitted and a prescription to change. If this is an accurate analysis, it is important for Mary to learn it. If it is not an accurate analysis, it is important for Karen to become aware of that because she may be misreading Mary's actions and not know it. But given the way that Karen and Jane regard their reactions, they will not be able to get at this question. Their reactions act as barriers beyond which others cannot move in order to discover what led to them, because to do so would risk evoking the maxim that this invalidates one's feelings: "How can you question how I feel? They're *my* feelings. I have a right to them and they're valid." Of course, individuals do have a right to their reactions, but the question is whether the inferences embedded in them are accurate descriptions of others and whether individuals have a right to impose them as if they were. In this instance we do not know whether Karen and Jane's reactions tell us more about them or about Mary, and we are stymied by this strategy from finding out. Since Mary cannot just disregard their feedback, she is left puzzled and with no means of resolving her puzzlement.

But expressing one's reactions does not have to yield this predicament. In fact, we regard the ability to express and explore one's reactions as essential to learning. Yet it is necessary to express them in ways that trigger rather than close off a process of inquiry. George illustrated this earlier when he described his reactions toward his client and asked that they be explored. He thus acted as if he saw his feelings as important clues that might suggest possible lines of inquiry into how he understood and experienced the situation before him.

2. Use fancy footwork, that is, switch to whatever view will defend your position and act as if you are not switching. This strategy is the Muhammed Ali of the action strategy set.

As an individual inquires into one view, the actor switches to another; the individual begins to dig in there, and yet a third position emerges, sometimes contradicting the first, and so on. To illustrate, we turn to an instance in which Paul expressed concern that the class was restricting itself to an overly cognitive approach and that it should be open to more intuitive approaches. Others said they would be glad to look at any approach that he thought would be helpful but that they needed an example. Paul agreed to provide one by role playing with a "client" in one of the cases, and he described the approach he would create as "helping her get in touch with her feelings, so she will reduce her fears of losing control."

When Paul role played, he used an easing-in strategy. He asked a series of questions designed to lead his client to the insight that she feared losing control. His client responded by curtly answering his questions but did not express any feelings or fears of losing control. Afterward his "client" said that at first she felt that he was withholding something but that after a while, she gradually came to think he was simply confused and could easily be intimidated. Both responses suggested that he would not be able to develop the trust necessary for his client to experience or express the feelings he believed she needed to acknowledge. Certainly no data existed to suggest that she had reduced her fears of losing control or had gotten more in touch with her feelings. We might therefore conclude that the approach he was experimenting with was negated in that it failed to bring about the outcomes he had intended. Yet when his client and others pointed this out, Paul defended his approach by arguing: "How do you know my approach didn't work? I didn't say it was going to work immediately. At this point, we do not have conclusive evidence that she is either more or less effective because of my approach. It might take two weeks, or it might take six months." When others then noted that this made his approach untestable, he argued that ultimately it is not clear that you can test this kind of approach, because you cannot design an experiment with human beings as you can with bowling balls, and you cannot control for all the variables that might have emerged six months later.

When his peers gave their reactions, Paul switched his

position. He no longer was an advocate of less restrictive, intuitive approaches; just the opposite, he now defended his position by calling on the most restrictive, cognitive approach to knowledge in existence: traditional experimental methods. He thus made his own approach untestable in the name of rigorous standards of testing, when it was the nonrigorous, intuitive form of knowing that he wished to defend.

What this case also illustrates is the oscillation possible between reflective and protective strategies. When Paul began his intervention, he publicly questioned the norms of the course and designed an experiment to test out an alternative approach. As we saw before, such strategies can open up new domains of inquiry; and, because of this, we have referred to them as reflective strategies. But once these initial actions were questioned and confronted, Paul drew on a second-order strategy of protection that decreased his vulnerability. He used the view he opposed to defend the one he favored, this former view made his approach untestable, and he acted as if this were not the case. Since he cannot receive the "conclusive evidence" he required, his view would remain airtight and his approach protected.

3. Cover up the cover-up. Earlier we described two first-order strategies that involved covering up one's reactions: withdrawing and keeping one's reactions private. Both are designed to minimize errors, and both result from a protective frame of errors, unrealistic aspiration levels, and a resulting fear of failure and humiliation. As the learning process unfolded and individuals reflected on their strategies, they began to realize that these strategies were themselves a kind of error, that is, the protective moves restricted their own and others' learning. For some this realization helped provide the impetus to change, and they began to make their reactions public. For others, however, it just compounded the problem. These strategies themselves were now experienced as an embarrassing error to be concealed. It is as if the participants reasoned: "At first I was afraid of appearing stupid so I said nothing. Now I certainly can't say that I said nothing for fear of appearing stupid. I'd just feel more stupid than if I had simply spoken up and said something stupid in the first place!" This suggests that gaining insight into with-

drawal as a kind of error may not be sufficient to alter such behavior. If the actor continues to consider errors taboo, this insight may only serve to generate deeper fears and the impetus
to cover up the cover-up. The dilemma is that this strategy
makes it virtually impossible to ever break out of this frame of
errors, because it precludes attempts to test whether in fact
errors might be regarded differently.

4. Seek and give protective support. A strategy similar to
the first-order one of saving face involves the seeking and giving
of support in a way that reinforces protective responses. With
face saving, we saw how individuals recruited others and were
easily recruited into following rules that precluded disagreements or critical feedback. By means of this strategy both quiet
and active participants cooperate in managing the dilemmas of
their uneven participation and the failure and guilt feelings that
they can trigger. But first recall the two dilemmas: Active participants feared being seen as competitive and unfair, yet did
not want to withdraw for fear of not learning; while quiet participants feared being seen as weak, yet did not want to say this
for fear of appearing even weaker. As we saw earlier, one way
quiet participants managed this dilemma was to privately reason: "I could participate if I wanted to, but who wants to sink
to their level—they're so competitive." Or: "If others weren't so
competitive and stopped cutting me off, I would say more."

When quieter participants then made their attributions
public, they expressed them in a way that made the following
claim: Others ought to make room for me, make sure I can participate, and anticipate when I need them to slow down without
my having to say so. Their more active counterparts, feeling
guilty because of their own participation and afraid of alienating their peers, were only too glad to cooperate. Many did not
need to be explicitly asked; their peers' strategy of withdrawal
was sufficient. They willingly jumped in and took control of
the process to ensure that their peers "got the chance" they
claimed was theirs. Some lobbied for structures that would
automatically give everyone a turn. Others closely monitored
the flow of conversation, making statements such as, "You
didn't get back to her question" and "Let's give X a chance to

speak." One person even began acting like a traffic cop, pointing silently to people who looked as though they were trying to
enter the conversation and giving them the okay to proceed.

That last approach, however, led the quiet participants to
become quite angry, since they saw this person's actions as con-
descending, patronizing, and controlling. It is as if they felt:
"Come on, we're not kids! Don't tell us when to come in!" The
verbal monitoring approach, in contrast, was usually wel-
comed. It was considered appropriately supportive and consid-
erate. So why the difference? One possibility is that the verbal
approach is more subtle than the other. The "traffic cop" approach includes a rather obvious insult along with the support it
gives. It communicates that the "cop" sees his peers as helpless,
and it makes no effort at mitigating the directives used to monitor the traffic of their actions. The verbal approach, however,
abides by rules of politeness that mitigate any implicit insult in
the directives and make them less noticeable (Garfinkel, 1967;
Brown and Levinson, 1978). But the purpose and implications
of the two approaches are the same. The persons using them intend to be supportive; both take control and responsibility for
creating the chances for participation; both therefore must assume that their peers are unable to do so; and neither helps
their peers to develop this ability on their own. Whether subtle
or direct, both monitoring moves thus serve to reinforce their
peers' dependence, need for protection, and fears of appearing
weak, creating conditions more conducive to a sense of failure
than of success. In fact, the paradox is that the more subtle approach may be just as problematic as the more direct one but
even more difficult to manage: How can you criticize or fault
someone for simply being supportive?

In this particular student culture it can be terribly hard
to do that. Counselors and consultants share an ideology of support that itself is almost impenetrable. Put most simply it goes
something like this:

- People feel vulnerable in the face of errors, and this vulnerability can trigger protective responses that hinder learning;
- therefore, in order to create conditions conducive to learning, we must create conditions of safety and trust;

- in order to create conditions of safety and trust, we should be "supportive";
- and in order to produce support, we should emphasize the positive, minimize criticism, and unilaterally see that the other's needs are met.

The problem with this ideology is that to question or criticize it is to violate it, since it requires uncritical acceptance. This is not to say that this ideology has no merit. In fact, our own research confirms three of the propositions embedded in it: People do feel vulnerable in the face of errors, these feelings can trigger protective responses, and conditions of safety and trust are conducive to learning. But our research has a different answer to the question of what creates conditions of safety and trust and what constitutes the kind of support that can produce them. Our theory and data suggest that notions of support that emphasize praise and minimize criticism can actually undermine trust. To illustrate this seeming contradiction by way of parody, imagine someone saying to a group: "I propose that the way to build trust and safety in this group is to withhold our negative reactions to each other and to act as if we were not withholding them, and to amplify our positive reactions to each other and to act as if we were not amplifying them."

Were someone actually to say this, the strategy would obviously backfire. The person explicitly communicates that the feedback will be distorted and that it therefore cannot be trusted. Of course, no one would ever come right out and state the rules of the game so explicitly. But such ideologies or notions can only be enacted if we all know the rules and know that we all know them. The effect is thus the same, even if the rules go unspoken: The feedback cannot be fully trusted. An experiment in Chapter Twelve examines data on participants' reactions toward this form of support, and there we consider an alternative form intended to produce trust without simultaneously producing mistrust.

To summarize, these second-order strategies are designed to make the dilemmas of the learning process more livable: Supportive moves make more active participants feel less guilty and make less active participants feel reassured that they are not seen as weak; the cover-up of the cover-up conceals the error of withholding; and both the feelings strategy and fancy mental footwork allow active participants to avert an examination of their errors. At the same time these strategies reinforce the very dilemmas that they are supposed to mitigate. Persons using them continue to act on, rather than test, the assumption that it is wrong to be wrong. They therefore do not create opportunities to make and reflect on mistakes and what it means to make them. As a result the aspirations of participants remain unrealistic and their fears of failure intense. In this way the strategies they call forth to make life livable end up making it unlivable.

Second-order reflective strategies involve examining one's actions and reactions so that one can map and work toward redesigning one's theory-in-use. Like their first-order counterparts, they are characterized by a sense of responsibility and initiative and a stance of vulnerability. What follows is a description of three such strategies: (1) publicly identify and inquire into dilemmas and apparent inconsistencies; (2) reflect on actions and redesign them; and (3) publicly examine one's own, as well as others', responsibility for actions and outcomes.

1. Publicly identify and inquire into dilemmas and apparent inconsistencies. By now it should be clear to the reader that learning requires participants to be active and to make their reactions public. These reactions are the raw material of the learning process and without them the process shuts down. But when participants do become active and make their reasoning public, their actions are then confronted, their reasoning is probed, and their errors are examined. Often they understand these responses as inconsistencies; it is as if they thought: "Gee, you told me to speak up, so I did. But when I did, you said I was wrong, so I shut up. Now you tell me I'm wrong to be quiet. What's a person to do?" It was this kind of reasoning that constituted the dilemmas discussed earlier in which individuals felt damned if they spoke up and damned if they remained silent. To deal with this dilemma, some participants began to make it public and to identify the inconsistency they saw in it. Vince did this after oscillating briefly between participating and

withdrawing. Recall that earlier we described how Vince had confronted the interventionist and that as a result he and others discovered that they held a frame about persons in positions of power that led them to distort such persons' actions. After this, Vince withdrew a bit and began to privately examine his reactions toward the interventionist in an effort to correct the distortions.

But a few sessions later the interventionist confronted those who were withdrawing, stressing that they had to "try to make errors or confront me." This advice struck Vince as puzzling. He thought that he had done just what the interventionist was now suggesting that he do, only to be told that he was wrong. It was because of this, he explained, that he had decided that "rather than act on my reactions, I'd wait for more data." Now he was being told that this too was wrong. Vince had a choice here. He could have drawn on a more protective strategy and covered up these reactions, using this puzzle to justify his withdrawal. He could have thought, "He's so inconsistent. He says he wants to be confronted, but when you do confront him, he says you're wrong. I'm not going to risk confronting him." Instead, Vince publicly identified the inconsistency he saw and the dilemma he felt it generated, describing how he had understood the interventionist's two responses.

Because Vince made his dilemma public, the interventionist was able to help reframe the problem and how he expressed his views so that he might resume participating. To paraphrase, the interventionist first reformulated the purpose of participation: It is not to make sure you are right, but to create the opportunity for learning. He then went on to suggest a strategy that builds on this reformulation: Confront others in ways that evidence a readiness to learn. Such a reformulation implied both new actions and new criteria by which to evaluate them. With this reformulation, the logic underlying Vince's dilemma no longer holds.

2. Reflect on errors and redesign actions. Regardless of what strategies participants draw on, they will act in accord with the existing theory-in-use they wish to change. This dilemma can be transformed into an opportunity by using one's ac-

tions and defenses as material for reflection and one's reflection as the basis for redesigning. One way to do this is to bring a "button-pushing" case into the group, while another way is to interrupt incidents that spontaneously occur on-line. While the former has the advantage of providing some distance from a threatening issue, the latter allows easier access to individuals' reactions and often provides the most vivid and critical incidents in their learning. To illustrate each, we can turn to a session in which Carol brought a case to class that involved her interactions with a client, who happened to be the director of a political organization. Because the case included data on what they both actually said, it allowed the group to reflect on what strategies Carol used and the implications these held for her client and their interaction. As the group examined what she did, they began to build a diagnostic map of someone who had used a series of deflecting moves to avoid a direct confrontation over her errors and over a potentially explosive political issue. As they did so, Carol began to enact the same strategies on-line, deflecting criticisms of how she had deflected criticisms in the case. In order to better grasp and unfreeze her defenses, the group first described her actions and then turned to look at what conditions might have triggered them, probing her reactions in the present and during her interaction with her client to generate hunches. Such probes often took the form of asking Carol to reflect on what she thought might happen were she to move counter to her defenses; this allowed the group to get at the deeper logic behind such defenses. In the end the group was able to map what Carol would have to change if she wished to redesign her actions.

None of these moves requires Model II skills, but they are pivotal in developing them. The case allowed the group the time to slow down its reflections and gave Carol the opportunity to distance herself enough from her reactions, so that both could begin to map out the defensive strategies displayed in it. The on-line responses made the learning more compelling and vivid, as Carol found herself acting the same way in class and experiencing some of the same feelings as she had with her clients. At the same time, it also provided more immediate access to her reactions, while giving peers the chance to practice accessing such data and thinking on their feet with a tough client.

3. Publicly examine one's own, as well as others', responsibility for actions and outcomes. We have described already how attributions that are kept private often hold others or external factors responsible for one's own actions or outcomes, thereby distancing actors from their own causal responsibility. This strategy asks that actors examine their own responsibility, as well as that of others, and that they make such processes public. An example of this strategy can be found in how George reflected on his responses to the interventionist after the passivity experiment (Chapter Four). At the time of the experiment George had held the interventionist responsible for how he had acted, saying that he was "only doing what the interventionist had asked." But when George went back and listened to the tape, he came to realize how he had also "laid a trap" for himself by not being forthright earlier in the session. At the same time he took another look at the interventionist's actions; and pointed out that while the interventionist's inferences were probably true, his actions had not given him as much of an opportunity to explore them as he thought necessary for his own learning.

Consequences for the Learning Context (Column 7). So far we have described two orientations distinguished on the basis of their capacity to sustain processes of experimentation and reflection on action. In the beginning most participants assume a protective orientation toward learning. They frame the process in ways that evoke experiences of anxiety and failure, that cue strategies that impede processes of reflection, and that generate immobilizing binds. As the map illustrates, these processes are self-reinforcing and eventually create a culture of protectionism (column 7). Protective strategies become the norms for interactions. The notions about support that we have just described and the protective role for learner and teacher become the predominant ideologies. And the emotional experience of the group members becomes one of walking on eggshells for fear of distressing one another. Under these conditions, reflection on action remains mostly private, and it is limited to avoiding those actions that would violate the prevailing norms, ideologies, and defenses.

As long as this culture and the processes that maintain it go uninterrupted, the learning that participants seek will be significantly limited. Their theories-in-use will remain intact and new theories-in-use out of reach. But as we will show in subsequent chapters, over time participants begin to move incrementally toward a more reflective orientation as a result of experiments designed by the interventionist to help them see the limits of their learning. Increasingly, they come to regard their errors as puzzles; and, faced with dilemmas, they are more apt to admit to them and to inquire into the inconsistencies that might account for them. At the same time, they make their own reasoning and actions the object of inquiry, so that they might discover the constraints and dilemmas that they might have inadvertently created for themselves.

As more participants in the seminar adopted this orientation toward learning, the culture of the group slowly began to change. Strategies more conducive to reflection and experimentation started to become the norm, supplanting those of protectionism. New ideologies arose and these themselves became the object of inquiry. Participant experiments emerged with greater spontaneity and were experienced with excitement and curiosity. And processes of reflection began to dig deeper into participants' theories-in-use and into the process of learning new ones. Gradually most participants began to evidence hybrid theories-in-use that combined features of both existing and new theories. Skills of reflection became more sophisticated, and participants managed the learning process on their own with greater competence. As a result they developed a deeper awareness of their theories-in-use, started to try out new ones, and acquired the competencies in reflection and experimentation necessary for continuing to learn on their own.

Invisible Responses

What is described in the action map goes on all the time, and it is found everywhere—at home, in schools, and at the work place. Yet as ubiquitous as these responses are, they are invisible. They comprise the deep structure of our social actions, and this structure itself has mechanisms built into it that keep us unaware. As the map illustrates, individuals act in ways that keep them blind to the consequences of their own actions and acutely aware of others'. They focus on the constraints others pose but not on those they pose for themselves. And they interact in accord with a tacit contract that states, "If you agree to overlook my inconsistencies, I will agree to overlook yours." As a result, they do not realize to what extent the actions they use yield consequences that they would consider unacceptable were they aware of them. Or in other words, they do not know that they are stuck in dilemmas of their own design. As one participant described it as she became increasingly aware (Higgins, 1985): "I was startled by the learning bind [described in the map]: 'If I'm quiet and withdrawn, others might see me as weak and dependent.' It had never occurred to me that others might see me as weak and dependent, even though I *was* dependent on others to ensure my learning. I didn't like that thought at all."

Individuals like this one start out unaware of their binds and the ways in which such binds limit their learning. As a first step, they must therefore come to *see* that they are "stuck" and responsible for it.

To help them do so, the interventionist designs opportunities for participants to hurry up and get stuck, so they can reflect on this "stuckness" and what leads to it. By drawing on the rules of action science, he enables participants to see what had once remained hidden: how they act, the logic informing this action, and the consequences these actions yield. In so doing these rules act as a kind of electron microscope that brings into focus the deep structure underneath action. At first, participants resist such examination, striving to hold the interventionist responsible for what they see. As the participant already quoted went on to reflect, "[Initially] I held the interventionist responsible for my not learning. I thought he's not doing his job. He's not giving me the answer. . . . It didn't occur to me that some of the responsibility for ensuring that I learned might be mine."

As the interventionist continues to design experiments

and to initiate reflection on them, participants increasingly see what the participant quoted here called "the potential outcomes of my current learning behaviors and none of them produced what I wanted." She was thus "propelled," as she put it, "toward taking a blind leap and deciding to give it a try." What this process of discovery and experimentation looks like is what the remainder of the book takes up.

10

Promoting Reflection
and Experimentation

At different times throughout the learning process participants refer to themselves as "being stuck." But what does it mean to be "stuck"? From the participants' perspective, it means that they cannot find a move from their repertoire of skills that yields acceptable consequences. They can go no further, and they are aware that they can go no further. But from our perspective individuals get stuck like this all the time, only they have fascinating ways of camouflaging it. To see through this camouflage, the interventionist creates a context in which participants can get stuck, reflect on their "stuckness," and not hold others responsible for it. Through an iterative process of experimentation, participants act, fail, get stuck, and try to get unstuck, while simultaneously reflecting on these attempts with their peers. Such a process of reflective experimentation reveals what would otherwise remain hidden, and it enables participants to try out new moves that might take them beyond the dilemmas that they discover.

This chapter considers three means by which the interventionist sets this context. The first is by establishing norms

319

that allow students to get stuck and to see their stuckness, while still keeping the inquiry moving. The second is by taking a stance toward participants' experience that enables them to express and reflect on it so they might begin to reconstruct it. And a third is through teaching concepts that can be used to understand and redesign the actions that get participants stuck.

Establishing Norms for Inquiry

From the outset of the learning process, the interventionist undertakes to enact the rules of action science as norms for inquiry (see Chapter Eight). But in doing so, he faces a problem. As the previous chapter illustrated, participants do not yet know how to enact these rules. Action science rules ask individuals to retrieve and make public their inferences, while participants' rules lead them to jump to abstract conclusions and to lose sight of the steps that brought them there. Other rules require that participants design valid tests, when their own rules tell them to conduct private tests that create self-sealing processes. And still other rules ask that participants inquire into their errors, when their own rules tell them to cover up those errors. If norms materialize out of ongoing activities, as Homans (1950) suggests, then left on their own participants will probably establish the norms of protectionism described in the map, not the norms of reflective experimentation characteristic of action science. This means that initially the interventionist must assume much of the responsibility for establishing these latter norms.

In doing so, he must take into account the ways in which norms are internalized and adopted in action. As a form of social control, norms might be adopted either as internalized moral prescriptions or as external constraints (Ross, 1910; Sumner, [1904], 1982; Durkheim, [1953], 1982; Mead, [1934], 1982; and Piaget, [1951], 1982). While the former results in what Durkheim calls "society living in us," the latter leads to what Piaget calls an annunciatory conception of truth: "The mind stops affirming what it likes to affirm and falls in with the opinion of those around it," and truth comes to mean whatever view conforms with the spoken word of superiors ([1951], 1982, p. 101). According to Piaget, the form in which norms are adopted depends on the nature of the relationship that produces them. In this view norms are "collective products," and whether or not they are internalized depends on the nature of this relationship or "collectivity." Relations of constraint and unilateral control contribute to an external code of moral conduct that results in the conformist notion of truth. Alternatively, relations of cooperation and mutual control contribute to an "interiorization of rules" that comes from public criticism and leads to the making of truth judgments independently of superiors. This latter process results in the free and open inquiry that philosophers since Peirce have regarded as the basis of valid knowledge in a community of scientists and that action scientists wish to enact in communities of practice (see Chapter Two).

As this distinction suggests, the interventionist strives to establish norms through a process of critical reflection akin to Piaget's notion of public criticism. Otherwise, participants would be obliged to accept the interventionist's view of reality, and this obligation would undercut the very norms he wishes to establish. The difficulty is that their process is not one that participants can initiate or sustain on their own. At the start they may hesitate to confront the interventionist and shy away from questioning the norms he holds. The interventionist must therefore initiate this process of public criticism without unilaterally imposing its norms. To do so he at once advocates and enacts these norms, while inviting inquiry into them and his actions. To illustrate, we will give a sample of excerpts from the opening session of the spring seminar, with the first excerpt laying the basis for further inquiry:

Interventionist: I sure would like not to be the person who is managing a lot of the interactions, and I realize that has to come partially by my being alert to when I'm overmanaging and by you helping me

Encourages participants to share responsibility for managing the learning process.

Invites participants to confront him when they think he is making errors.

to be alert when I'm over-managing, and I really plead and welcome that. On the other hand, I'll also feel free to make inputs and check out with you whether the inputs are helpful or not. I've got to find some balance. If you find I'm intervening at the wrong time or it's too long or not enough, I need some help.

States that he will intervene when he thinks that he can help. Says that he will inquire to see if his interventions are helpful.

Once again invites confrontation of errors.

There will be errors made and I really plead with you not to be bashful about, let's say, confronting me if you see something that isn't making sense, or "slowing down," or "why are we doing this?"

Communicates that errors are not to be feared.

Encourages confrontation of his own errors, describing what they might say.

The interventionist recognizes that on the one hand he might make errors in managing the process but that on the other hand participants might be "bashful" about pointing this out. Under these conditions, criticism is apt to be one sided, and the interventionist's dominance will be maintained. He therefore opens the seminar by stating that errors will be made, that he might make some of those errors himself, and that he will need the help of participants in order to learn. By anticipating errors and stating a willingness to learn, he encourages participants to move beyond their "bashfulness" so that they might mutually control the process. At the same time, he recognizes his own responsibility for "being alert" to when he is overmanaging, noting that he will check to see if his inputs are useful. Thus right from the start, he describes and encourages the kind of mutual responsibility and public criticism that can lay the basis for freely choosing and internalizing norms. But the interventionist also submits the norms themselves to critique:

Interventionist: I'm interested in insight that facilitates competence. So when you think of trying to help someone and you're trying to provide insight, I'm asking you to think of connecting that somehow with what are the implications of this insight for that human being's increasing his or her competence? To help a person see that they are angry would by this theory not be enough. I realize that there are other theories that say that that indeed is the right thing to do, and if that is what you believe let's experiment with that. Let's try it out. I want to be confrontable on all possible issues.

Advocates the norm "focus on competence."

Recognizes that competing norms exist and invites participants to voice them.

Encourages public tests that might disconfirm the view that insight should be connected to competence, thereby opening up to inquiry the norms of the process.

In this excerpt the interventionist did not shy away from taking an explicit normative stance. He explicitly stated his interests and criteria in putting forth the view that insight was not sufficient and that the focus of participants ought to be on competence. Yet he also recognized that competing theories hold different criteria, so he asked that his own position be challenged and other views considered. In this way he directs the inquiry into values and norms as well as strategies: he advocates a norm, invites others to do the same, and suggests they submit their competing values to experimentation and reflection. Of course, from the participants' vantage point the litmus test comes when they take the interventionist up on what he

espouses and begin to confront him. Ordinarily they do so in
the first session, suggesting that they take these invitations seriously. The excerpt given next shows how the interventionist responded to one such confrontation by Vince, who criticized
him for "stopping" Carol from finishing her intervention:

Interventionist: That's helpful, because my view was that
[I was elaborating on her
comment, not changing the
topic].

Welcomes confrontation
("that's helpful") and advocates his own view by making
his reasoning explicit (in passage not included here).

He then went on to describe the reasoning that led him to
intervene as he did:

Interventionist: I am acting
in ways that take up what
are generic problems in interventions: length, how do you
know when you're helping,
what is the nature of inference. I would hope that what
I'm doing now I could eventually decrease. If the group
would prefer I decrease it
early, that wouldn't be a
problem. But I thought I interrupted her in the sense of
adding, not taking away. What
was it that led you to say it
was taking it away from her?

Makes explicit what he understands himself to be doing.

Continues to encourage the
group to share responsibility
for managing his involvement.

Advocates his own view and
encourages inquiry into it by
asking for data and reasoning
that might disconfirm his
view.

From an action science perspective it is not sufficient to
encourage confrontation. Once confronted, the interventionist
must remain open. As we saw under the rules of action science
(Chapter Eight), this does not mean backing down but rather
stating one's view so that it can be disconfirmed and critiqued,
while inviting others to do the same. Here, the interventionist

followed this rule in a sequence of steps. He first affirmed the initial confrontation. He said he found it helpful *"because"* it departs from his own view, thereby encouraging continued disagreement. He then made explicit the reasoning that informed his participation in the group. He described the role that he had defined for himself (that of taking up the generic problems in interventions), and he expressed a desire to eventually redefine and reduce this role, as well as a willingness to do so earlier if the group preferred. At the same time, he also put forth his own view of this particular instance while inquiring into Vince's. The interventionist thought that he was "adding" to Carol's intervention, leading him to ask Vince what led him to the inference that he was "taking away" from her.

In this sequence the interventionist thus inquired both into his actions and into the role he defined for himself. The reader might recall Schön's (1983) description of the town planner who constructed a role that generated a perplexing dilemma (Chapter Seven). The planner's role was contingent on its being kept private, and it resulted in his unawareness of the binds that it generated for himself and others. In contrast, the interventionist uses a confrontation of his actions to make public his role and to test whether it might be creating constraints of which he is unaware.

In this way the interventionist acts consistently with the norms he advocates, making them public and inviting participants to critique both the norms and the way he enacts them. This allows participants to choose whether the norms make sense and whether to adopt them or to discard them on the basis of informed criticism. Like Piaget, we have found that those who choose to adopt norms under these conditions internalize them, but at first only as standards by which to evaluate themselves and the interventionist. While such internalization is necessary for establishing norms, it is not sufficient since participants do not yet have the skills that enable them to consistently produce the norms. In this sense we might think of these norms as goals that individuals strive to meet but that remain outside "the boundary of their ability."

Such a perspective raises another aspect of norms that

comes into play when individuals attempt to establish them. As a kind of goal, "a norm can be a mark to shoot for only if it is not too far away from what can be achieved in everyday life. If it gets impossibly remote, . . . it will be abandoned in favor of some more nearly attainable norm" (Homans, 1950, p. 126). According to this description, norms act like the aspiration levels described by Lewin (see Chapter Nine). As long as an aspiration level is challenging yet within reach, an individual will stay at a task; if the individual repeatedly falls short, however, he will experience a sense of failure, lower his sights, and eventually abandon the task altogether. This relationship between norms and aspiration levels thus suggests a dilemma. If the interventionist expects participants to adhere to norms outside "the boundary of their ability," he may create a sense of failure that will lead participants to withdraw from the learning process. Yet if he does not ask them to adhere to them, they will conduct business as usual and enact norms of protectionism.

One way to manage this dilemma is to "scaffold" participants as they try to reach norms that they cannot yet reach on their own. In doing this, the interventionist helps participants to act in ways that can keep the inquiry moving despite their becoming stuck. To illustrate, we turn to a session in which the interventionist used the norms to help the group move through several iterations of problem framing and experimentation. It began with a group member discovering a problem in one of the cases they were discussing. Specifically, they found that one of the clients was no longer following the consultant's point, and this discovery raised the generic problem of how to ensure communication with clients. Or, as the group first framed it: How to make sure that a client is following you.

What then unfolded was a series of impromptu experiments that began when one participant, Pierce, came in and suggested the following solution to the problem: Check with the client to see whether he understands. This approach sounded plausible enough; but, in accord with the norm of public testing, it was regarded as a hypothesis to be tested, and the interventionist helped Pierce to take his suggestion through the testing process. To do so, he began by asking Pierce what he might actually say to the client, and Pierce then role played the intervention: "Mr. Smith, are you following my presentation?" At this point the interventionist elicited the group's reactions, uncovering some counterintuitive results. His peers said that they would be embarrassed to say no and that they wouldn't want to look like "dummies." So what at first appeared to be an obvious solution began to look as though it were part of the problem. Yet if Pierce had not been asked to test his approach, the group might have prematurely thought the problem solved.

Out of this first experiment a new and more complex formulation of the problem emerged. As one participant put it: How do you make sure a client is following you without making him feel stupid? And along with that formulation came a new hypothesis for solving the problem: Help the client to ask questions without feeling dumb. Compared to the first suggestion of "check with your client," this new one specified the outcomes it wished to avoid; that is, those the previous intervention had created. At this level of abstraction the new intervention also sounded promising. The question, however, was whether it could produce the desired result without creating undesired results. In this case the participant sought to find out by role playing his invention and saying to the "client," "This stuff is very difficult to understand in the beginning. I'm sure you're going to have problems. Please stop me when you're not following." The responses were mixed. Some of the initial responses were favorable but vague ones such as "good" and "I like that." But then another participant spontaneously took the point of view of a client, role playing the reaction: "Why are you using language I'm not going to be able to understand?"

This last response raised the issue of who should be responsible for ensuring communication. So far the group members' formulations of the problem had focused primarily on the client's responsibility to let them know when they had fallen short of this intention. No one had focused on the consultant's responsibility for presenting his views in a way that is most apt to communicate them. When their suggestions for doing this were tested, a gap in their framing of the problem was discovered, in this case one that revealed a situation characteristic of redesigning a theory-in-use. So many rules and norms must be taken into account that it is easy to misapply them or to let one fall out of sight while satisfying another. In effect, the consultant here was trying to establish norms with his own client to ensure communication: Share responsibility (tell me when you're not following) and affirm that it is okay to make mistakes (this stuff is very difficult to understand). But as he applied these norms, he put more responsibility on the client than he took. It is as though he sees the client as more responsible for managing the material than he. For this reason, the consultant's sharing of responsibility is lopsided and his efforts at making it easy to ask questions problematic. His client might feel that it is okay to ask questions but resent having to do so because of the consultant's opaqueness. The consultant might not consider his client stupid for asking questions, but the client might consider the consultant incompetent for putting him in that position.

After the last participant role played the indignant client, a flurry of activity broke loose, and several people simultaneously jockeyed for the floor, ready to try out an approach that might now avoid these outcomes. But the lopsidedness of what was being asked of the client and of the consultant had not yet been explored, so the new attempts failed to solve the problem of disproportionate responsibility. So a third participant role played, "I'll do my best to present it in a way that you can understand it in simplified terms; but if something comes up that you don't understand, feel free to ask." As the interventionist said of this new attempt, its very "niceness" might compound the problem. The client might think, "She says she's going to try her best and use simple terms, so how can I possibly tell her that she's failed or that I don't understand." A second response came in the form of a role play of a possible client reaction: "The problem with high technology people is they present material so that you can't understand it. If it's so confusing, I have my doubts about it." And yet a third possibility is that the client could feel that he must be really stupid if he does not even understand "simplified terms," making it unlikely that he would "feel free to ask."

As a result of these experiments, participants began to see that they were stuck. The only way they could encourage questions was by emphasizing either their shortcomings or their good intentions. Either way, their clients might inadvertently be discouraged from raising questions or confronting them. Once participants recognized this, one person reframed their responsibility by suggesting that "they should think through how to present it, so they're not using technical overkill," but no one was sure how to go about this. At this point the interventionist suggested a proposition that built on this reframing: Communicate ideas so that they can be easily recognized by a client, while at the same time heightening their impetus to confront and inquire into the ideas. To illustrate this, he cited the initial unfreezing process they had all experienced. He recounted how he had provided data on their own actions and then drawn from them a short chain of inference, leading to a puzzle that had triggered confrontation and inquiry into his ideas. This new formulation of the problem and how to solve it made sense to participants. They retrieved their own reactions to this process and affirmed that it had evoked the impetus to challenge and inquire.

The impromptu experiments just discussed began with the discovery of a particular problem. The ensuing inquiry then followed a course that took it through three different problem frames and experiments, each one generating new problems and leading to new experiments in action. As this process ran its course, participants encountered a gap between their ideas and the consequences their actions yielded once these ideas were produced. By helping participants to follow the norms, the interventionist was able to help them see their stuckness, while simultaneously keeping the inquiry into it moving.

Let us consider for a moment the implications of what we have discussed so far. On the one hand, individuals have an ongoing opportunity to confront and inquire into the norms of the seminar, and most become committed to learning how to enact them. On the other hand, they start out unable to produce these norms on their own, so they have to depend on the instructor's help in following them. The process of experimentation that follows is characteristic of the process in which they will continue to be engaged. Participants put forth their ideas, and with the interventionist's help they test them out in action. As their peers report their reactions and reflect on them, they begin to see that their experiments produce unintended results. They keep trying to bridge the gap between theory and action, and they keep falling short. Early on in the process this sparks a mounting sense of failure, as participants recognize that they cannot hold the interventionist or others responsible for these results, since the interventionist has continually probed for his own and others' impact on them. As a result, participants start to look inward to their own responsibility, and they discover that they are creating their own stuckness. Gradually their sense of failure increases, often leaving them feeling anxious, frustrated, and helpless. As one participant put it, they can come to feel: "We're all just spinning our wheels. Does anybody else feel like there's static electricity in this room?"

As these experiences accumulate in the early phase of learning, the participants' willingness to make themselves vulnerable becomes harder and harder to sustain. Frustrated, they enact defenses that deflect attention away from their stuckness. They start to press, "So what's the correct answer?" "Show us the right way to do it." These kinds of requests carry multiple meanings. One is that participants are now aware of a gap but may see it as relatively easy to close (if they could just get the right answer). Another is a wish to avoid a process of reflection on the gaps uncovered in their theories-in-use. And yet a third is a desire to know that there's an alternative—that there is in fact some way to get the spinning wheels engaged again.

Taken together, these three meanings make a simple request complex. Certainly an interventionist should illustrate an alternative for the participants. But if the interventionist gives the equivalent of answers as soon as participants discover that they are stuck, he may create the kind of hope that will eventually produce a sense of despair. He could communicate that what comes easily to him can be easily replicated, when we have found that this is not the case. When participants try to circumvent reflection or limit redesign to strategies alone, we have discovered that they end up using the "right" technical moves as gimmicks. That is, they enact strategies that continue to satisfy the same theories-in-use, thereby leading to the same outcomes. So they might now illustrate inferences but do so in order to nail someone; they might inquire but in ways that are experienced as lawyering, and so forth. Before long, participants begin to realize that they are still stuck, and their despair and anxiety return only to run deeper. In terms of the action map in the previous chapter, the interventionist could end up reinforcing unrealistic levels of aspiration, heightening rather than reducing experiences of failure.

Early on the interventionist prefers not to emphasize "right answers" but instead to use the dissonance generated by failure and inconsistency to direct attention to what leads to them. The question to stress in this early phase is not so much "How should participants act differently" as "What are they doing, what leads them to act as they do, what prevents them from acting differently, and what are the skills they need to answer these questions on their own?" But if participants deflect attention away from such questions, it will be difficult for them to sustain and withstand the process of reflection necessary to answer them. Such deflection suggests, as do their other defenses, that they may wish to avoid looking at their theories-in-use and the inconsistencies they produce. The dissonance generated by these inconsistencies may become so great that it pushes them from a mode of attentiveness to one of protection. The interventionist must therefore help participants continue to make themselves vulnerable in the face of repeated failure and stuckness.

Encouraging Reflective Experimentation

The interventionist takes a stance toward participants' experience that encourages them to express, reflect on, and begin to reframe it. In part he does this by making himself vulnerable in the optimal sense of the word, consistently communicating to participants, "This is my view. I think it's right but I might be wrong, so let's take a look at it." By communicating this willingness to learn, the interventionist nurtures a willingness to tell. At the same time he recognizes that this involves risks, so he actively inquires into participants' reactions and invites confrontation of his own views while seeking to reduce the threats involved for participants.

One way he does this is by taking seriously what is expressed. Because reactions that range from anxiety to anger to excitement are often expressed, he anticipates them and is not thrown by them. Yet since the particulars of each participant's experience will vary, anticipating a range of reactions never takes the place of knowing what participants are experiencing in a particular instance. Therefore the interventionist at once affirms the expression of feelings while simultaneously inquiring into them by saying things such as, "That's important. Let's take a look at that." Or: "That's something I had been unaware of. Do others feel similarly?" Such responses encourage the expression of difficulties by communicating that much can be learned from what participants are experiencing.

Once expressed, participants' reactions can simultaneously fuel a process of inquiry and present new obstacles to it. When one participant exclaimed, "I find this really frustrating, and I'd rather leave if it's going to continue because I feel like I'm having a nervous breakdown," she drew attention to her experience of what was happening, yet she held others hostage to it: Others had better act in accord with her view or else. So she simultaneously made possible and warded off the help that might have reduced her frustration. In expressing her experience, she provided a start; but given the way she framed it, she stopped others from inquiring into it. The material she presented—so essential to a process of inquiry and learning—was put forth as an obstacle to it.

This poses the interventionist with a dual and apparently conflictual task. He must encourage the continued expression of her experience of the situation, while at the same time calling into question the way she frames it. These requirements generate a necessary tension. On the one hand, calling into question how she has framed the situation may create additional upset and only lead her to draw back and conceal her reactions.

Yet on the other hand, if her view is a priori accepted, she may simply withdraw and leave the group, while others may pull away from her.

To sustain the expression of such reactions as well as a process of inquiry into them, the interventionist adopts a stance toward participants' experience that takes account of how they frame what they see, while not taking it for granted. To illustrate, we turn to three instances in which the interventionist responds to participants as they express their reactions and try to help one another. He responds in this first excerpt to a participant's fears of being wrong:

Participant: [I'm scared] because I don't want to be wrong. I don't want to be stuck, and I don't want to be onstage.	Expresses her fears.
Interventionist: Okay, that's important. I don't want to skip over that point, because I can fully understand those feelings: Nobody wants to be wrong.	Takes seriously what is expressed. Expresses understanding. Communicates that her feelings are universal.
At the same time, if we're going to be a group that is helpful to our learning, it is important that we feel free to make errors.	Offers another view that implies an unintended consequence of hers: Being wrong may be the right thing to do. Provides a choice ("if we're going to . . .").
What I'd like help with is: Are there things I do that make it harder for people to say things that might be wrong?	Inquires into obstacles that might make his view unreachable; begins by focusing on his own responsibility.

In a second instance the interventionist pointed out the unintended effect of a participant's advice by saying, "I believe you were trying to be supportive; paradoxically, it may have had the opposite effect." And in a third instance he responded to the participant who said she felt everyone was spinning their wheels by saying that he could empathize with her feelings of being stuck and yet had a different view. From his perspective what was happening was productive; people were defending their views in ways that facilitated learning, and they were discovering their theories-in-use for the first time.

In each of these instances the interventionist empathizes with the participants' experience by taking into account what it is they are feeling or intending. Yet as he does so, he frames the situation before them from the vantage point of his perspective and theory. Some readers may not think this constitutes empathy, since it involves looking at another's perspective from one's own. But in our view this approach involves a caring kind of distancing. The interventionist does not just accept the participants' experience but reframes the situation before them so that it might be experienced differently. More precisely, he frames the situation in a way that will sustain the process of inquiry at hand. In the first excerpt the interventionist focused on the participant's not wanting to be wrong. As he did so, he recognized the experience as universal, yet he reframed the making of mistakes, stressing that they may be the right things to make. Similarly, he pointed out that supportive moves may undermine one's peers, and spinning wheels may mean that important discoveries are occurring. Such reframing moves provide participants with a paradoxical lens through which to view their experience. The interventionist does not say, "You think it's wrong to make errors but *really* it's okay." Instead he communicates: "It is possible to not want to be wrong, when making mistakes may be the right thing to do; it is possible to intend good effects while bringing about negative ones; and it is possible for spinning wheels to indicate an important advance and for repeated failures to lead to success." In short he recognizes their experience while reframing the situation in a way that enables them to better withstand the risks of reflection and experimentation.

This form of empathy takes participants' experience into account, while not taking it for granted. For this kind of empathy to be expressed and experienced as genuine, we believe that three requirements must be met. First, the interventionist must be able to accurately and usefully comprehend the participants' experience (Rogers, 1951; Schafer, 1959, 1983). He must therefore have some model or representation of the participants' experience in his head that will be useful to them. The model in the previous chapter (Figure 8) on how participants engage in the learning process is one such model:

• It is what Schafer (1983) calls "one step ahead" of participants' awareness, and it can therefore help participants to see their experience more clearly and usefully, so that they can begin to move into new domains.

• It is accurate and able to roughly anticipate a range of reactions, so the interventionist can predict and more readily manage expressions of difficulty, pain, and resistance.

• It frames participants' actions and reactions as unintended, but meaningful and necessary, expressions of the conditions they face and of the theories-in-use under reflection, thereby making their expression safe enough, reducing the potential for polarization between interventionist and participant, and sustaining "goodwill" toward participants and "good work" with them (see Schafer, 1983).

While such models make useful sense of participants' experience and enable the interventionist to anticipate participant responses, they are nonetheless models, and as such they might be wrong and they are surely incomplete. Because of this the interventionist must collaborate with participants to discover where these models are wrong or incomplete. Such collaboration itself requires that the interventionist take a stance of vulnerability that involves jointly controlling the process of inquiry —both the generation of data and the making of inferences—so that the models can continually be modified and made more complete.

A second requirement is that the interventionist have a position of his own that can sustain inquiry. We believe that this position should be one that can frame errors, difficulties, and resistances in a way that will allow interventionist and participants alike to explore these phenomena without triggering protective responses that will lead participants to withdraw. Three propositions that contribute to conditions conducive to vulnerability and risk taking are:

- Participants will all make mistakes.
- The consequences their actions yield are necessary, but unintended.
- Errors are puzzles to be engaged.

The first proposition stems from the finding that participants' theories-in-use are widely held and testifies to how successfully individuals have adapted to the world through a shared process of socialization. This proposition tends to make the discovery of one's own theory-in-use less threatening. As one participant expressed it: "If this theory is right, everybody is going to make mistakes, so we are all in the same boat." The second proposition holds that the negative outcomes of an individual's actions are necessary but unintended consequences of a theory-in-use. This proposition allows the interventionist to focus on the negative effects of actions, while simultaneously empathizing with an actor's good intentions. It makes possible the earlier empathic response of "I believe you were trying to be supportive; paradoxically, it may have had the opposite effect." The third proposition goes a step further. Not only are mistakes acceptable, they are the necessary raw material of learning and without them the process of inquiry into theories-in-use would grind to a halt. It is this third proposition that enables the interventionist to remain credible while saying, "Making mistakes may be the right thing to do." But to work, such a paradoxical move must come from the interventionist's own belief that errors, difficulties, and resistances are sources for reflection, the fuel that can keep a process of inquiry moving as long as participants are willing to take a look at them. Without such a proposition, we would predict that an interventionist could not sustain the right technical moves over time in the face of participants' defenses. At some point the interventionist would likely be experienced as inconsistent, insincere, or both. But when this proposition is used correctly, participants are most apt to respond as one did: "There is a strange paradox. . . . we are learning that we are ineffective. That's what makes people defensive—being told 'you are wrong.' The paradox is that there is something in this work that makes people willing to listen." And we would add: willing to continue to express and reflect on what it is they are experiencing. What we have tried to do here is explicate a little further what this something is.

So far we have taken a look at how the interventionist draws on norms that aid reflective experimentation by enabling individuals to act in ways that can sustain it. We have seen how he empathizes with their experience of this process while reframing their understanding of it, so that they can better withstand its risks. But what we have discussed so far is not sufficient to enable individuals to reflect on and redesign their actions. That requires in addition some way of making sense of what it is they are doing and of designing alternatives. A third component of the learning context therefore is cognitive, and it involves the teaching of concepts that can be used to understand and redesign actions.

Understanding and Redesigning Actions

Participants seek to redesign their actions from the start of the learning process, as soon as they discover that they have not been effective in consulting to clients. When easing-in doesn't work, they try being more forthright, or they try different ways of easing-in, or they oscillate between easing-in and being forthright. The unfreezing process really takes hold when participants discover that they are unable to redesign their strategies effectively. In our language, the problem is not the particular strategies they use, but the Model I theory-in-use that informs their design of particular strategies. It is the discovery that they are unable to correct their errors that leads participants to feel vulnerable, out of control, and hopeless.

For example, during the first round of role playing in one group, the participants recognized that their actions were ineffective. When they tried again, they repeated the same errors. At the beginning of role playing, they were confident that they could design more effective interventions. But as the role playing continued, they began to feel frustrated by their repetition of the same errors and by their inability even to understand what was wrong. One said, "I still don't have any more insight than I felt I walked in here with." Another said that she had tried to figure out how to help but realized that she "couldn't bring anything fresh into it." A third participant added that he couldn't think of an approach different from those that others had tried. He continued: "I find myself kind of floundering at this point, trying to figure out where the problems are, what went wrong. I don't know how anybody else feels, but I need some feedback before I'd even want to experiment at this point."

These reactions are not surprising. Left to their own devices, participants would be unable to redesign the Model I predispositions that lead to repetitive failures. Rather than continue to feel frustrated and hopeless, they might decide that it is impossible to produce Model II action and thereby justify their withdrawal; or they might decide that some Model I strategies are as good as could be expected, and not focus on their counterproductive features. In other words, the defenses that enable people to remain unaware of their theories-in-use in the Model I world would reassert themselves.

The task of the interventionist is to help participants begin to genuinely redesign their theories-in-use. In approaching this task, he can take a cue from the participant's comment that he could not understand "what went wrong." Human beings programmed with Model I theory-in-use will be blind to the features of interaction on which they must focus if redesign is to be successful. An initial step is to provide concepts that enable participants to recognize patterns of which they have been unaware. As they become better able to diagnose their errors, they will begin to feel less out of control. They will gain some satisfaction from their developing ability to recognize their failures. At the same time, if the patterns taught are closely related to designs for Model II action, participants will be laying a foundation for redesigning their actions and developing their expertise.

The use of concepts, we learn from cognitive psychology, is at the heart of expertise. Individuals who are experts in some activity have learned a particular vocabulary of patterns relevant to that activity, they know the implications for action of those patterns, and they have heuristics that guide their designing. For example, studies of chess players have been conducted to determine what cognitive strategies differentiate experts from novices (Simon, 1969; Glass, Holyoak, and Santa, 1979). When experts and novices are shown actual chess positions for a few seconds, the experts can later recall virtually the entire board whereas the novices cannot. But if experts and novices are shown random chess positions (that is, those that do not arise from actual play), there is no difference in their recall. It appears that experts have a large vocabulary of patterns that they encode as meaningful "chunks." Becoming an expert chess player is in part a matter of learning this vocabulary of patterns.

Expert play is also a matter of making the right moves. This means that chess experts have a network of knowledge about the implications of the various patterns. Some of this knowledge is in the form of heuristics such as "control the middle of the board." The expert understands a chess position as an interrelated set of meaningful patterns with implications for subsequent moves, and uses a set of heuristics to choose which of the possible moves deserves consideration. For example, Neisser tells the story of "Capablanca, the former world [chess] champion, [who] was once asked . . . how many moves he typically examined in a difficult position. He said, 'One, but it is the right one' " (Goleman, 1983, p. 56).

The participants in our seminars are already experts in designing action in everyday life. The difficulty is that their expertise is patterned after Model I. Their vocabularies of patterns of social interaction, the implications they attribute to those patterns, and the heuristics that guide their designing combine to inhibit double-loop learning. Moreover, they are not aware of these consequences while they are producing them. In this section we thus describe some of the conceptual tools that we use to help participants to unfreeze the Model I psychological set, as well as to design and implement Model II actions. Not only do these tools, once learned, help them to gain expertise, they may also be used to help others to do the same.

Concepts for Learning and Acting

Concepts in action science theories, we have suggested, are designed to serve the dual function of (1) describing and understanding reality and (2) enabling individuals to take action. The tools that we use in our seminars are designed to help individuals understand their behavior as well as to change it, should they wish to do so. For example, in using the X and Y case format we ask individuals to write scenarios (actual dialogue) in the right-hand column, and any thoughts and feelings that they do not communicate for whatever reasons in the left-hand column. They are not asked to specify the reasons.

This request derives from several key concepts in the action science approach. First, an individual's theory-in-use can be inferred only from behavioral data such as conversations. Conversations are the result of systematic causal reasoning that is informed by the actor's theory-in-use. In the action science approach, conversations are not viewed as anecdotal data but as systematic productions that provide a means of understanding the causality that actors believe exists in a context, as well as the causality that they use as a basis of action. Second, individuals automatically censor the important ideas and feelings upon which they construct their causal pictures if they believe that communicating these ideas and feelings will upset other individuals and hence make them responsible for causing defensiveness in others. These judgments, as we have seen, are made automatically and tacitly, and individuals tend to be unaware that they are producing them. The left-hand column therefore provides a window onto the self-censoring process, and that process in turn provides a window onto what individuals believe will threaten themselves or others.

Once individuals understand the conceptual basis for these two columns, they may use it to facilitate learning. For example, if they are uncertain what an individual is feeling or thinking because they suspect that he is censoring his feelings and thoughts, then they can use this approach: "May I ask, what is on the left-hand side of your column?" The question encourages disclosure of the self-censoring process without identifying it as self-censoring. This provides a way to distance adequately or to create what we call a "screen" upon which an individual may disclose information that he would otherwise be reluctant to reveal or would unknowingly distort.

There are six concepts that participants have found helpful. First is the ladder of inference, a concept that sets forth how the human mind reasons when trying to understand, design, and execute action. Second is the concept of prototype or exemplar, which focuses on the fact that some concepts are useful in organizing experience in ways that allow it to be generalized. Third is the puzzle intervention, a concept about how to initiate the processes of self-examination and change of behavior. Fourth is the theory-in-use proposition, a concept that focuses on ways to define in generalizable propositions the rules that individuals use when acting. Fifth is meaning-invention-production-evaluation, a concept about the nature of the learning process that makes it possible to slow it down in order to examine it more carefully. Sixth is the concept of hybrids, which helps to remind participants that early learning produces hybrid conversations that contain Model I and Model II features.

It is our experience that these concepts cannot be taught simultaneously, even though once they have been learned well, several may be used together. Thus individuals may make inferences about the meaning of some conversations by retrieving prototypes. They may then design an intervention to bring out an inconsistency, which means creating a puzzle intervention. In designing the intervention, they may retrieve a rule that they use to produce the intervention.

We strive to decompose the learning problem into one or two of the concepts at a time even though, as will be seen, any given episode may have more concepts embedded in it. As learning progresses, it becomes possible for the players to examine and use several concepts with ease.

The Ladder of Inference. An underlying assumption of the action science approach is that individuals use reasoning processes whenever they strive to diagnose and act. It is our hypothesis that these processes are generalizable in terms of steps that the human mind must go through if understanding or action is to be effective. The ladder of inference is a concept that describes what those processes may be (see Chapters Two and Eight). The first rung of the ladder of inference is directly observable data—for example, a sentence uttered by someone. The second rung is the cultural meaning of that utterance, that is, the meaning that would be understood by anyone who was a member of the relevant language community. The third and higher rungs are the meanings imposed on the cultural meaning by particular actors.

Once students learn the ladder of inference, they can use it to discover the kinds of inferences they are making, the connections or lack thereof between inferences, the data on which they are based, and the conclusions they lead to. It can be used to highlight patterns in the way individuals reason and act and can also be used to design an alternative set of patterns.

For example, during an early episode in the seminar, one participant made the following attempt to produce a Model II intervention:

Actual Dialogue	*Comments*
Sandra: When Len said, "How do you know [that Ann felt defensive]?" I can't remember what you [Beth] said.	Begins by trying to recollect the directly observable data: what Beth said that is the basis for the intervention Sandra wants to make.
Beth: I said that I was trying my best to invite her to have a joint conversation about this problem, but she just wouldn't open up. She kept saying, "No, there's no problem."	Beth repeats the data.

Actual Dialogue	Comments
Sandra: So, when you said, "It seems like it might be time to think about whether your roles—whether both counseling and being a client is kind of becoming a problem," you thought you were inviting her to respond to you.	Cites a sentence from the case.
	States the meaning that she understands Beth to attribute to her behavior in the case. (Hence, tests meaning.)
Beth: That's right.	

The actor (Sandra) used the ladder of inference in several ways. First, she remembered that she should begin her reasoning processes with the directly observable data. Since she could not recall them, she asked Beth to repeat what Beth had said. Sandra then took a sentence and inferred the meaning that she understood Beth to attribute to her case, thereby testing that meaning. Sandra could go on to impose her own meaning by drawing on features of her theory-in-use. This could lead her to design whatever action she wishes, presumably another way of dealing with the problem.

The ladder of inference is also a strategy for action. When it is followed, individuals collect directly observable data, connect inferences with the data, make the inferences explicit, and finally test them. This map of how the mind may work becomes a map of how the actor's mind should work when trying to be of help to others.

We will give a second example to show how the ladder of inference can help in the design of a more fully formed Model II intervention. This example, like the previous one, is from the discussion of a case in which Beth, a supervisor, is trying to help Ann, a counselor. Participants had been intervening with Beth, and the instructor was illustrating a Model II design for intervening with one of the participants:

Actual Dialogue	Comments
Instructor: Joan, when you said, "So do you think that	States data (rung one).

circumstance right there could have put a block into your effective handling," I infer that what you were telling Beth is, "Beth, your inconsistency led you to be ineffective." Is that a fair understanding?

Joan: Yes.

Instructor: Yet I also notice that you have put your intervention in question form, such that if Beth answers correctly she will state the evaluation that you are implying. Does that make sense to you?

Joan: Yes.

Instructor: Okay. That's a strategy that we call easing-in. Easing-in is when you ask questions such that if the other person answers correctly, they'll figure out what you're not saying. The difficulty with easing-in is that the recipient is likely to recognize the strategy, hence knows you are making a negative evaluation, and that you are not stating it forthrightly for fear he will become defensive. So the recipient can experience you as unilaterally controlling and may infer he has good reason to become defensive.

What are your reactions?

States inferred cultural meaning (rung two); asks for confirmation or disconfirmation.

States another set of inferred meanings.

Asks for confirmation or disconfirmation.

States theoretical meaning (easing-in) based on previous meanings.

Identifies negative consequences predicted by theory.

Encourages inquiry.

To summarize, the instructor produced an intervention in three steps that began with the directly observable data, and he stated his inferences step by step up the ladder of inference, testing the client's reactions at each step. He chose to test inferences that led to the idea of easing-in, and he also stated the negative consequences predicted by his theory.

Prototypes. Patterns in social interaction are not precisely defined. Their boundaries are often fuzzy. Fuzziness, however, is characteristic of ordinary language. Most concepts in ordinary language identify a class whose elements vary about a prototype. For example, a robin is a prototypical bird; a penguin is not. Observers will readily agree that some objects are tables (those with flat, rectangular surfaces and four legs), but may disagree whether a recycled cable spool merits the label (Glass, Holyoak, and Santa, 1979, pp. 337-353).

It appears that human beings process and store information in terms of prototypes. For example, several experiments have shown that when subjects study a set of drawings that vary about a prototype and then are shown another set of drawings and asked to identify those that are familiar, they recognize the prototype as familiar despite the fact that they had not seen it before (Glass, Holyoak, and Santa, 1979). People learn more quickly to identify objects as members of a category when they have had experience with a prototypical member of the category. They can more rapidly classify as members of a category those objects that closely resemble the prototype.

We suppose that similar considerations apply to social cognition. People identify a particular situation as one or another kind of situation and design action accordingly. The recognition process may be one of comparing the particular situation with prototypes stored in memory that express central tendencies of various kinds of situations (Forgas, 1982). Teaching people to recognize patterns of interaction of which they have been unaware would thus seem to be facilitated by presenting them with relatively prototypical exemplars. Indeed, all the examples used in this section of the book are intended to be prototypical.

The idea of prototypes is relevant not only in learning to recognize kinds of situations but also in learning to produce new action strategies. We can explain how this is so by returning to our notion of the ladder of inference as a concept to aid action. The ladder of inference may suggest that an actor ask for illustrations, test a meaning, or explain the consequences of not illustrating attributions. Whichever strategy the actor chooses as appropriate must be tailored to fit the unique details of the particular situation.

During an episode a participant said to the instructor, "I thought you mowed over her point." The ladder of inference may help participants to recognize "mowed over" as an attribution at a high level of inference and to think of asking for the directly observable data on which the attribution was based. Indeed, we have a rule for designing a Model II intervention for this situation: If an attribution is unillustrated, ask for the directly observable data. But what is it that the actor should actually say? This rule, like all rules, is quite abstract. Designing a concrete sentence that enacts the rule is a far from trivial problem.

We suppose that an important way that students learn to produce sentences that are consistent with Model II rules is by retrieving sentences that the interventionist has uttered. But there are a very large number of sentences that might enact a given rule. We may think of these sentences as varying around a prototype. For example, a prototypical sentence to enact the rule stated in the preceding paragraph might be, "What have I said or done that you saw as mowing over her point?" Students may remember this sentence and modify it to fit the particular details of a given situation in which they recognize that an unillustrated attribution has been made.

These ideas offer a way of understanding how interventionists become competent. Interventions may be organized around prototypical patterns of interaction that the interventionist recognizes in what clients say. Action is based on maps and prototypes that the interventionist has learned and seeks to pass on to clients so that they too may act in Model II ways. Later we will see how the rules and prototypes that students have learned may conflict or may be used inappropriately, and how inquiry into these errors and conflicts illuminates the reasoning that underlies competent performances.

The episode that follows shows how prototypes may arise during class interaction. The episode occurred while participants were role playing an interaction between Marilyn, the director of a counseling organization, and a member of her staff. After listening to the role playing for several minutes, one participant said:

Doug: Could I cut in? I feel you're both painting yourselves into a corner. Marilyn, I wonder if we could just talk about what happens in terms of painting into corners, and just discuss it and maybe come up with a way that that wouldn't happen.

Interventionist: If I could just point to "just discuss it," "maybe we could come up with a way," is the equivalent of "if you could just be in touch with" [*laughter*]. Do you agree? What is it you want her to do?

Doug: I want, in some way, to get across to her that I'm not going to confront her in a way that's going to push her psychological button, and make her get defensive.

Marilyn: Show me [*laughter*].

Interventionist: Is there anything you saw that was going on in this room that you can use to build your intervention? Seems to me—is this a correct attribution?—you were watching and you said, "Oh, oh, they're both getting defensive."

Doug: That's what I saw.

Interventionist: You interrupted and said, "You're both painting yourselves into a corner." Now, can you reflect on what was the theory behind that intervention?

Doug: It seemed to me that neither one of you was listening to what the other had to say. You were making arguments to support your own theories.

Interventionist: How about if you said, "Both of you were carefully listening to what each of you was saying, and carefully selecting the part you wanted"? Instead of saying "neither of you"—because I think they were really listening [*laughter*]. And they were listening to pick apart—

Doug: Yeah, I like that.

Tom: Write that one down!

The interventionist's suggestion is what we call a *reframing* move. Doug's framing of the problem was, "Neither one of you [was] listening." The interventionist's reframing was, "Both of you [were] carefully listening, . . . and carefully selecting." This formulation of the problem has several advantages over Doug's. First, it is more accurate. Second, it credits both parties with intentions to act responsibly. Third, it offers a means of getting at what is causing difficulty: the ways in which each person is selecting what to respond to.

It would seem that the essence of this reframing is seeing the simultaneous but contradictory intentions that people may hold. Marilyn and the staff member might simultaneously be listening to what the other was saying and seeking to show that his or her own view was correct. Each might be concerned about his or her own vulnerability and about the impact on the other person of any errors that might be made. Vernacular psychology may be oversimplified in assuming that people hold only one intention at a time, leading observers to attribute "not listening" or "not acting responsibly" when they see incompetent behavior. The interventionist's framing is based on a more complex picture of human beings. It is a useful complexity both because it can be stated publicly without causing more defensiveness and because it focuses more sharply on what is causing difficulty.

Notice that participants immediately recognize the interventionist's suggestion as a good one. Tom's comment—"Write that one down!"—suggests that participants see the words as a potential prototype to be stored for future use. The intervention is vivid, it calls to mind the web of reasoning associated with the reframing issues we have just discussed, and it is generalizable. The particular problem to which it refers, that of individuals who may appear not to be listening, is itself quite common; and it exemplifies the reframing of other kinds of problematic situations as well. It may suggest a useful means of reframing in situations in which someone is attributing "not helping," "not acting responsibly," "not caring," or other nasty motives.

There is another feature of the episode that may be generalizable. Participants were trying very hard to design effective interventions and were finding themselves repeatedly getting stuck. The interventionist then helped them to make public their reasoning, and was able to build on their reasoning to design an intervention that participants recognized as superior. The emotional involvement of participants, their building frustration followed by an "Ah, ha!" when they saw how their problem might be solved, increases the likelihood that the intervention will become prototypical for them.

Puzzle Intervention. A puzzle intervention is a way of pointing out a possible inconsistency in an actor's reasoning, espoused theory, theory-in-use, and behavior. The value of the puzzle intervention is predicated on the social psychological notion that individuals abhor inconsistency. If clients experience inconsistency, they feel jolted. They may defend themselves and/or try to redesign their behavior. The intervention makes vivid the features it confronts. It helps unfreeze automatic behavior and interrupt unawareness. The intervention risks, of course, evoking inhibiting defenses. However, it can be designed in ways to reduce this risk.

A classic form of the puzzle intervention appears in our opening exercise, the X-Y case. The interventionist asks clients to evaluate Y's performance and infers a microcausal theory: If someone behaves as Y behaved, then the other person will feel misunderstood and prejudged, and little learning will occur. Clients readily agree that this is their view. The interventionist then identifies the puzzle: If clients revealed to Y the words in their diagnosis, they would be enacting the very causal theory they criticize Y for enacting with X. To tell Y he is blunt and insensitive is itself blunt and insensitive.

This example illustrates three features important to the competent use of the puzzle intervention:

1. *Begin* by illustrating and testing one or two inferences that clients can easily confirm (for example, "There is a micro-

causal theory embedded in your diagnosis, which is: If someone behaves as Y behaved, then the recipient will feel misunderstood and prejudged, and little learning will occur.")

2. *Use* a short chain of inference from the directly observable
    data to whatever it is you are inferring.

3. *Show* how this illustrates that the client is acting in ways
    that the client himself finds unacceptable.

The third step is usually followed by encouraging inquiry,
either into the interventionist's reasoning or into the client's
reasoning. For example, the interventionist might say, "What
would lead you to design your action in a way that you yourself
criticize?"

Here is an example of a puzzle intervention from our
seminars:

Interventionist: When you say, "I guess I'm confused in that you're sort of alluding to a problem that you think exists, and you're citing evidence that it exists, but you don't want to say to her that it in fact exists," I infer the	Cites the directly observable data.
meanings that "you were withholding" and that "you acted inconsistently."	States cultural meanings.
These are negative evaluations and negative attributions.	States theoretical meanings.
Rather than state them explicitly, you cite the data that should lead the other to infer [what is in your head].	Identifies the participant's strategy.
But is that not the very thing that you are criticizing the other for doing? You are alluding to a problem that you think exists and citing evi-	States that this is the very strategy that the participant criticizes Beth for using (uses participant's words to establish puzzle).

dence that it exists, but not
saying to Beth that it in fact
exists.

    Am I communicating?   Encourages inquiry.

    Since the puzzle intervention is high risk, it is also neces-
sary that the interventionist be competent to follow up consistently with Model II theory-in-use. For example, if the intervention evokes what appear to be inhibiting defenses, the interventionist should look first to his personal causal responsibility
("I'm sorry if I've upset you; what did I say that distressed
you?"). It may be that the intervention was not produced consistently with the norms of Model II.

    Theory-in-Use Proposition. Recall that we conceive of
theories-in-use as systems of propositions. We provide a very
general model of participants' theory-in-use, Model I. We ask
participants to reflect on their own theories-in-use to specify in
more detail the patterns that are characteristic of their designs
for action. But it is not possible to completely specify a theory-
in-use because such theories are enormously complex. We recommend that participants seek to identify propositions in their
own theories-in-use.

    To illustrate the features of a theory-in-use proposition,
let us consider the theory-in-use characterization of easing in:
Ask questions such that, if the other answers correctly, he will
discover what you are hiding. This is a characterization of an action strategy, one of three elements in the schematic representation of a theory of action:

    Governing ⟶ Action ⟶ Consequences
    values   strategies

    The theory-in-use definition of easing-in leaves tacit the
governing values and consequences associated with the strategy.
These could easily be specified. The intended consequences are
to get the other to see what the actor sees and to avoid creating
defensiveness. The governing values are to define the goal unilaterally and seek to achieve it, to win (in the sense of getting
the other to see), and to minimize the generation of negative

emotions. We could also specify unintended consequences such as the generation of defensiveness.

In addition to strategies, consequences, and values, a fourth element that is frequently important is the contextual cue. A contextual cue is a feature of the situation that triggers a particular action strategy. After all, no one eases in all the time. Rather, it is when the actor is making a negative evaluation of another, and attributing that the other would get defensive if he were to state the evaluation forthrightly, that he is likely to ease in.

The customary form of a theory-in-use proposition is:

If (contextual cue), then (action strategy).

For example, one student identified the following two interventions as characteristic of a strategy she frequently used:

1. "Y, I was afraid that you'd ask me what I thought of your interview with X."
2. "Z, I find I do this all the time—asking a question designed to elicit a particular answer. Perhaps that's what you're doing in this case."

After several hours of reflection and with help from the instructor, she developed the following theory-in-use proposition: "If I am about to deprecate someone, I first deprecate myself." Notice that this proposition includes a contextual cue ("If I am about to deprecate someone") and an action strategy ("I first deprecate myself"). The associated consequences and governing values remain tacit. They could be specified, and indeed would be quite similar to those associated with easing-in. In fact, the "deprecate self" strategy itself appears to be a kind of easing-in.

In the early stages of learning we encourage students to specify consequences and governing values, because we want them to develop skills in doing so. But we leave the consequences and values tacit in most cases because brevity helps to make the theory-in-use propositions more retrievable. Indeed, since the point of identifying theory-in-use propositions is to help actors become aware of patterns so that they can begin to change them, it is quite important that the propositions be memorable. They should be short, dramatic, vivid. The repetition of the word *deprecate,* a word that is itself quite unusual, probably increases the retrievability and hence utility of the proposition.

Another set of criteria for good theory-in-use propositions has to do with the requirement that they be general enough to apply to a significant class of actions. It would be of no value to identify propositions that applied to a single strategy that an actor might use once a year. Neither would it be of value to identify propositions that were so abstract that they might apply to almost anything.

A third set of criteria is related to helping the actor interrupt unawareness of features that the theory of action approach identifies as important. Thus the propositions we design often have a form such as, "When (cue), do (action) and act as if not doing (action)." This highlights the camouflage and self-censorship that are characteristic of so many strategies in a Model I world and to which actors often remain blind. Stated another way, we use Model I as a template to help us identify key features of theory-in-use propositions. As a result, theory-in-use propositions typically characterize strategies in terms that the actor would not use. The strategies are recognizable but formulated in a way that highlights how they are inconsistent with the actor's espoused theory. The theory-in-use characterization of easing-in is an example. The actor who was unfamiliar with the theory of action would typically describe the strategy as "helping the client explore" or "helping him come around to seeing the problem." The theory-in-use characterization is thus often surprising to the actor, a feature that probably increases its memorability.

To propose a theory-in-use proposition, whether attributed to oneself or to someone else, is to propose a hypothesis. It is a way of explaining an actor's behavior by postulating a causal mechanism, a mental program that informs the design of action. It is also a prediction that when similar circumstances recur (that is, the contextual cue that triggers the proposition), the actor will behave as stated in the proposition. When we work with a client's case, we may propose theory-in-use propositions that we infer from the case data. We encourage the client to test the validity of the proposition by seeing if it is confirmed in the client's future behavior.

Once a client has tested the validity of a hypothesis that he acts according to a given theory-in-use proposition, he may decide that this is something he wishes to change. This can be done by designing a corrective proposition and experimenting with interventions that enact the corrective proposition. For example, a client with the "deprecate self" proposition might design the corrective, "When I am about to deprecate someone, state the data on which my evaluation is based and encourage inquiry." This is an invention that the client must learn iteratively to produce.

Meaning-Invention-Production-Evaluation Model of Learning. Another concept that we have found especially helpful for participants to use in redesigning their actions is based on the process of learning described earlier as discovery-invention-production-evaluation. We use this concept to help slow down the actions that usually occur in redesigning action. In this exercise the participants first write down the meanings they infer from a target sentence. Second, they write down an invention or strategy for dealing with the meanings they have identified. Third, they write the actual words they would say to the client to produce their invention. This format leads participants to deliberately consider inferential steps that would normally occur in milliseconds. It also reduces the inhibiting effects of participants' competitiveness and fear of failure, because they are experimenting privately on a piece of paper and can then choose whether to reveal what they have written.

In the following example, Joyce is apparently intending to reproduce the intervention modeled by the instructor (as described earlier in this chapter). Such mimicry is not a trivial exercise. The differences between what Joyce says and what the instructor modeled point to skills that participants have still to develop.

The target sentence is Joan's statement, "So do you think that perhaps that circumstance right there could have put a block into your effective handling of her perceived problem?"

Meanings: Joan is easing in. Rather than giving a negative evaluation, she's asking a question and trying to make Beth come to the conclusion.

Identifies meanings at levels three and four of the ladder of inference ("negative evaluation," "easing-in"). Skips level two, the cultural meaning.

Invention: State the data [what Joan said]; give my inference; and question her on her feelings about that inference. If she agrees, go on to explain the negative effects of easing-in.

The invention is consistent with heuristics for Model II: state data, give inference, test, state consequences. However, does not propose encouraging inquiry after stating consequences.

Production: "Joan, when you asked the question 'So do you think that perhaps . . .' it seemed like what you were doing was easing in, by asking a question rather than stating how Beth was being ineffective in her approach. What do you think about that?

Begins with the data.

Jumps to inference at level four (easing-in).

Encourages inquiry.

"But easing-in has consequences that would create defensiveness. For instance, it makes a person become suspicious that you're holding back information."

States negative consequences, but does not make explicit reasoning to explain consequences. Does not encourage inquiry.

The reader may wish to compare Joyce's production with that modeled by the instructor. The differences are noted in the right-hand column. Joyce did not proceed step by step up the ladder of inference, beginning with the data and cultural meanings. If the client did not already know about easing-in, Joyce might have some difficulty. We might speculate that she left out these intermediate steps because they seemed obvious. The recipient, however, might not see the chain of inferences by which a particular sentence was identified as easing-in. Another explanation for Joyce's not stating the intermediate steps is that she lacks the skills to do so.

However, Joyce did follow several rules for Model II action. She stated the data, made her inference, asked for reactions, and described a negative consequence. In producing this intervention, Joyce tried out what she had understood the instructor to be modeling, and she received confirmation that indeed these were important features of Model II action. Hence she experienced some success in redesign. She also learned where her understanding was incomplete and what she could do to produce a better intervention another time.

This episode illustrates several features that are characteristic of the process of learning to redesign strategies. First, with the help of the meaning-invention-production exercise, a participant slowed down her reasoning, and was able to design an intervention that was significantly different from those she produced when she was acting at normal speed. Second, in designing her intervention, she drew on the concept of the ladder of inference, and she used as a prototype something that she had heard the instructor say. Third, she experienced both success and failure; that is, her intervention was a hybrid.

Hybrids. As we have pointed out, students often have difficulty in producing Model II interventions because they have an unrealistically high level of aspiration. This same unrealistic level of aspiration may act to prevent them from recognizing the progress that they may be making. They may, for example, conceive of progress as a matter of producing meanings that have only Model II features. This makes it unlikely that they will recognize progress as occurring when they are producing a mixture of Model I and II features.

We use the concept of hybrid to help students identify the progress that is being made when their interventions contain combinations of Model I and II. Using this concept permits them to examine a protocol of their behavior and to see where progress is being made and where further work may be necessary.

Recognizing the value of hybrids also helps students to be more accepting of some mismatches in an intervention. Moreover, there may be some interventions that are effective only if they contain both Model I and Model II features.

We will describe three examples of hybrids. Let us begin with an episode in which Linda attempted to design an intervention with Beth (in the case described earlier). Beth had hesitated to suggest to Ann that a problem existed because she did not wish to upset Ann. Linda wanted to show that the unintended consequence was to create defensiveness in Ann.

Linda: That you neither confirmed nor disconfirmed the existence of the problem may be the part that elicited Ann's defensiveness. It sounded manipulative and probing, with a predetermined conclusion. I inferred you had a hidden agenda.	Unilateral advocacy; negative evaluation ("you caused Ann's defensiveness"); no inquiry. Unillustrated attributions.

As indicated by the comments in the right-hand column, Linda's production is vintage Model I. What is interesting is that Linda thought that she was following the rules for Model II. She saw herself as publicly testing her inferences. While she did state her attributions and evaluations forthrightly, she did nothing to encourage inquiry. And even if she had asked, "What are your reactions?" she would not have created conditions for public testing because she did not illustrate her attributions or make the steps in her reasoning explicit.

But the fact that Linda stated her views forthrightly represents progress. Her accustomed strategy would be to think that Beth was manipulative, probing, and so forth and to carefully avoid saying this to Beth. In other words, Linda's accustomed strategy would be to ease in. We may understand her view that she was "publicly testing" by noting that, were she to withhold her views, the other person would have no opportunity to disconfirm them. By stating them forthrightly, she at least gives the other person an opportunity to respond.

Linda's forthrightness is not Model II; and indeed her intervention might well create more inhibiting defenses than would her accustomed strategy of easing-in. In the present context, however, her forthrightness is a step forward because it gets her reasoning into the open. It is very difficult to help people redesign their reasoning if they continue to hide what that reasoning is. In this case, for example, Linda's forthrightness created an opportunity for others to help her see the gaps in her reasoning of which she was unaware. After Linda stated her production, the instructor asked other participants for their reactions. Their replies indicated that several were beginning to be able to identify Model I features of interaction. For example, one suggested that Linda should have stopped after her first sentence and asked Beth if she agreed. Hence, that participant noticed that Linda did not encourage inquiry. Another participant added that Linda had given no data in her first sentence, so it was an unillustrated attribution. He recommended that Linda say to Beth, "When you said, 'I'm not saying there is a problem. I'm just saying we haven't talked about this stuff for a long time,' you neither confirmed nor disconfirmed . . ." Hence, he was suggesting that Linda cite data and cultural meanings. A third participant continued by pointing out that the second half of Linda's intervention consisted of unillustrated attributions at a very high level of inference.

It appears, therefore, that Linda's production provided an opportunity for others in the class to experience success in identifying Model I features in what she had said. Linda, however, felt frustrated at her failure:

Linda: It seems like it requires so much dialogue just to say something [*laughter*].   Expresses frustration.

Instructor: I can empathize with that [*more laughter*].

Empathizes.

Linda: With the culture we live in, and our listening and hearing skills—I don't know. I feel frustrated about it, about the utility of it. It takes so much to say.

Expresses more frustration.

Questions practicality of Model II.

Instructor: Okay, I can appreciate that. Particularly when you're trying to learn, and you're struggling with your normal way of operating, and then trying to follow all these rules, it is going to take you a long time.

Empathizes.

Confirms that it takes time, but frames that as a feature of early stages of learning.

My experience is that when you get good at it, it doesn't take any longer. And in fact it takes less time. Because if you said to Beth, "What you did sounded manipulative and probing," I think you would be creating some defensiveness in Beth, because those are unillustrated attributions. And that would lead to a fair amount of noise in the interaction, which would take time.

Proposes that, when one becomes skillful, Model II will take less time to apply than Model I.
Illustrates time-consuming features of Linda's Model I intervention.

Linda expresses frustration and questions whether Model II is useful. The instructor empathizes with her frustration and confirms that it will be time consuming to design Model II action at first. But he reframes this problem as one that characterizes the early stages of all learning rather than one that characterizes Model II in general. And he substantiates this reframing by pointing out how Linda's Model I intervention could also become quite time consuming.

The instructor also attempts to moderate the unrealistic aspiration level of participants. If their goal is to produce competent Model II interventions in real time, it is certain that they will fail. If participants appreciate the difficulty of interrupting their Model I theories-in-use and consciously designing Model II interventions, however, they will have more patience with their need to design and redesign. A more realistic level of aspiration will help participants to feel less frustration.

The instructor also helped participants to see the positive features of their redesign experiments. It is necessary both to confirm the negative features, so that participants can develop their diagnostic skills, and to identify any progress that has been made:

Instructor: You saw yourself as testing your attributions. And you were stating them, so it's possible for the person to at least know what you're saying. But they are not illustrated, so it's hard to test; and you don't encourage the other person to disagree with you.	Confirms features that Linda saw as public testing.

Identifies features that inhibit genuine testing. |
| I think you're being forthright here. I think that is a step ahead. Because it helps us get it on the table and take a look at the reasoning. | Identifies forthrightness as a positive interim step. |

The second case describes an episode in which the consultant was working on the troubled relationship between Marilyn, the director of a counseling organization, and members of the staff. After a warm-up period in which seminar participants gave their impressions of the case, George began to intervene with the consultant:

George: I made an evaluation that I'd like to share: that your interventions would have been more effective had the group ended with Marilyn making some more clear declaration of what her intentions were.

State evaluation openly.

Does not give criteria of effectiveness.

She's very ambivalent, and she's threatened to leave [cites data]. And she's just been presented with what I'd think would be some very threatening information [cites data]. I can imagine on the basis of that, that she'd have lots of reasons to not want to come back.

Cites data for inference that Marilyn might not return.

So I wonder: Do you think it would have been helpful had she declared herself in some way about her intentions?

Inquires, but has not made explicit the reasoning behind belief that getting a declaration would be helpful.

And if you do, I have a suggestion. . . . I would ask, "Would you be willing to come to the next meeting?"

Suggests alternative, in directly observable language.

George's intervention is a hybrid, with both Model I and Model II features. Consider first the features that could lead George to believe he had designed a Model II intervention. He stated his evaluation openly rather than withhold it. He cited data for his inference that Marilyn might not return, so he both illustrated and made some of his reasoning explicit. He inquired whether the case writer agreed with his evaluation, so he may have seen himself as combining advocacy and inquiry. And he offered an alternative for what the case writer might say, so he focused on increasing competence. However, George did not make explicit the reasoning that led him to believe that the approach he advocated would be helpful. Hence, he gave the recipient no basis for evaluating the validity of his view. He both advocated and inquired, but he did not state the view he advocated in a way that would make his inquiry likely to generate valid information. Rather, his advocacy and inquiry are at the level of, "I believe X would be good; do you?"

In the third case, another hybrid intervention shows a deepening understanding and increasing use of Model II skills. The episode occurred during the first session of the spring semester after the interventionist had asked participants to give their views of a case that had been written by a participant. One participant, Larry, made a long intervention in which he set forth several unillustrated attributions about the case writer and then went on to make attributions about the people in the case. He was interrupted by another participant, Carol, who said:

> I want to go back to—you said a lot—but the very first thing you said was that [the case writer] was demeaning. I don't know how helpful that was, because you haven't given her any data about what she said or where that's coming from, and then you proceeded on to a lot of things, but I just wanted to stop at that first thing.

Two features of Carol's intervention are important. First, it was the first intervention in which a participant intervened with another participant whom she thought was making errors. This is important from the point of view of establishing a norm of confronting and inquiring into errors. Second, Carol's intervention shows that she was able to recognize that Larry had made an unillustrated attribution and that this would reduce Larry's effectiveness. It also shows that in intervening with Larry, she had the skill to give some directly observable data herself ("you said [the case writer] was demeaning"). Tom added:

When Larry was talking, I was having certain
reactions. First, he's making lots of mistakes, lots
of attributions. Perhaps he's going on too long.
And I myself didn't know how to deal with his
making mistakes. I didn't know how to intervene.
When Carol did it, I felt there was a beginning.

The participants appear to be struggling with competing
impulses. On the one hand, they know, at an espoused level,
that they should publicly inquire into error. And they have evidence, both from the interventionist's statements at the beginning of the seminar and from their own experience in the fall
semester, that confronting error will be positively evaluated by
the instructor. On the other hand, at a deeper level, they have
the automatic reactions stamped in by years of socialization in
a Model I world. These reactions tell them that confronting
error is dangerous, either because they might make errors themselves or because the recipient might react negatively.

Later in the same session, Larry said that he would like
to make an intervention with Tom, who had just questioned
what he had thought was an error on the part of the interventionist. Larry said, "The thing I noticed about your exchange
with [the interventionist] is that there was no discussion of
feelings. And what I'd like to know is, What are your feelings?"
Tom replied that he disagreed that feelings had not been part
of the exchange, and explained how he had been feeling. Then
other participants intervened with Larry:

What was said	Our comments
Paul: You said you were going to try an intervention, and you asked about his feelings. How was that going to help him to check out how he was feeling?	Cites what it was Larry had said; asks Larry to publicly reflect on his reasoning. Focuses on impact of Larry's intervention on client's (Tom's) competence.
Larry: [I thought the exchange did not focus on feel-	

ings.] By not focusing on feelings, which seemed to be the heart of the matter, it was avoiding the heart of the matter.

Doug: What data do you have that feelings were at the heart of the matter?

Asks Larry to illustrate his attribution.

Larry: It's an attribution.

Doug: Based on what?

Same.

Larry: It's based on my impression [*laughter*]. That's not okay?

Robin: Not in this class.

Laughter suggests norm that attributions should not be justified simply as "impressions" or "feelings."

Larry: I thought there was unexpressed anger.

Jim: What stopped you from saying you thought so?

Asks Larry to publicly reflect on his reasoning.
Focuses on self-censorship.

Larry: I guess between those two choices, I'd ask somebody what was going on with them rather than attribute anger to them. I felt if I put it that way, it would make it easier to express the anger. I'd rather let him express it.

Mary: But unless you ask him to disconfirm your attribution that he was angry, he's left in a bind, and can't

Identifies unintended negative consequences of Larry's strategy. Focuses on self-sealing quality.

do anything about your assumption that he's with-
holding feelings. You might
keep that assumption unless
he's able to disconfirm it.

As our comments indicate, participants appear to have
drawn on several Model II ideas in their interventions with
Larry. We could expect this episode to reinforce several norms
favorable to learning, including those that ask us to:

• confront and inquire into errors;
• reflect publicly on reasoning behind interventions;
• focus on impact on client competence;
• illustrate attributions with directly observable data;
• inquire into self-censorship;
• identify unintended negative consequences; and
• focus on self-sealing features of interaction.

These are heuristics for designing Model II interventions.
Episodes such as the one described here help establish them as
norms for group interaction, in the sense that participants begin to have reason to believe that members of the group will
approve of interventions designed in accordance with these
heuristics. If we are correct that such actions contribute to
learning and if participants are indeed increasingly able to design such actions, then participants will be able to take more
responsibility for managing the learning environment.

But there are features of the interventions with Larry
that indicate some limits to the skills of participants. For example, although they inquire into Larry's reasoning and advocate their own views, they do not encourage Larry to challenge
their views. They tell Larry, in effect, "You should have told
Tom that you thought he had unexpressed anger." They do not
add, "What do you see as less effective in the more forthright
approach?" Larry might feel that he is being told how he should
behave, and not that the group's standards of competent behavior are open to inquiry and test.

A key early step toward learning is for each individual to map the depth and width of his or her Model I action-space. The concepts discussed here facilitate that process of self-inquiry and mapping. For example, some individuals come to recognize the pervasiveness of the easing-in concept. They see how they use it to understand the actions of others, to design their actions, and to monitor their effectiveness. Easing-in becomes a prototype, which means it draws their attention to control tendencies of action strategies that cause them to be less effective than they intend. It also enables them to recognize the same tendencies in the strategies other individuals use in everyday life. The fact that this is a common way to act permits individuals to create a screen (why do so many of us use easing-in?) in order to eventually examine their own theory-in-use.

The discover-invent-produce-evaluate cycle provides actors with a way to slow down what is happening in order to study it more systematically. The ability to take hold of complexity by slowing down the action helps to reduce failure and individuals' fear that they may not be in control when trying to produce Model II actions.

The concept of hybrid provides a way for individuals to set realistic levels of aspiration and simultaneously to identify progress as it occurs. This, in turn, reduces the probability of experiencing failure and increases the probability of feeling successful.

These concepts, once learned, provide actors with several kinds of help. They help actors to understand or enact reality, they help them to design their actions, and they provide rules for producing action, as well as rules for monitoring the effectiveness of action. Herein lies an illustration of a key feature of action science: The concepts of action science contain within them the power to facilitate understanding, design, and action.

Not surprisingly, these concepts were developed in seminars in which we were trying to help individuals learn a new theory-in-use. Looking back on the discussions that produced each concept, we can see that the instigating factor was trying to make sense of what was happening *in such a way that we could help the participants.* We underline the last part of the sentence to emphasize that we were never happy with a concept that explained what was going on unless it had the power to help individuals redesign and implement new actions. In all our discussions we kept asking how a given concept could be used in the service of diagnosis and action. Again, not surprisingly, these requirements defined the meaning of understanding to include action. When someone asks us, When do you know when you know something, our answer is, When we can produce whatever it is we are talking about.

11

Expanding
and Deepening
the Learning

Learning new actions and new theories-in-use can be understood as a process of unlearning one set of rules and learning another. In previous chapters we have identified several rules for Model II action such as, "If an attribution is unillustrated, ask for the directly observable data." Producing such rules in ways that lead to good results in actual situations is difficult. As our discussion of hybrids indicated, participants may enact certain Model II rules only to discover that they have violated others. One reason for this difficulty is that human beings can pay attention to only a few things at a time. When an individual deliberately focuses on a Model II rule, other aspects of the situation may be managed by overlearned, highly skilled Model I behavior. A more interesting difficulty arises when using one rule appears to be inconsistent with using another. The conflicting demands may be temporary, existing primarily because individuals have not yet learned when to use what rule and how to produce each one. As we shall see, the conflicting demands can also be structural in that there are some inherent choices and trade-offs that must be made when using Model II rules.

This chapter deals with the important learning opportunities that arise when rules conflict or when interventions that seem consistent with a previously learned rule turn out to be wrong. As might be expected, such occurrences are frequent. The rules that participants learn are highly simplified, in the sense that they do not state all the conditions that govern their use. This is necessary, because the explicit statement of even a few of the relevant conditions would be immobilizing to the student. The way in which students discover these conditions is by inquiring into conflict among rules. Such inquiry can unearth the deeper reasoning that informs competence. It is through reflection on times when rules are misapplied or when individuals have not learned as yet how to apply several rules simultaneously that higher levels of expertise can be developed.

"Let's Think Forward"

The following episode occurred while participants were role playing an interaction between Marilyn, the director of a counseling organization, and a member of her staff. The staff member stated that Marilyn made herself unconfrontable. Marilyn replied that she acts as she does because of the way the staff members act toward her. When asked to illustrate what Marilyn has done that is problematic, the staff member mentioned an incident and said Marilyn had acted "in a way that I felt was extremely directive." After a few minutes of this, the interventionist stepped in:

Interventionist: Another way of dealing with this is, instead of saying "remember this and this." Another way would be [for the staff member to say], "I think I've done enough here that's been counterproductive and unhelpful to you, Marilyn, that what I'd like to do is not to try to think backward but to think forward and see if I can spot a situation in this session or the next one. How would you feel about that?"

Marilyn: I would welcome that.

Some of the participants objected to the interventionist's suggestions:

Paul: I feel some discomfort with that. Sounds like you're doing therapy, and like it gets people off the hook, but doesn't get into—everybody's going to be better next time, everybody's hoping, but there are theories-in-use there.

Carol: Were you trying to give Marilyn the sense that there was someone on her side? Or what was it that you were attempting to do with your intervention?

Interventionist: I started on the assumption it is true that she's damned if she does and damned if she doesn't; he's damned if he does and damned if he doesn't. We could sit here all night on that issue, because historically she's given them lousy data, and he [the staff member] has given her lousy data. Then when he made comments like, "I feel you came on strong," that is one of those statements that is [high on the ladder of inference], and it doesn't help her. . . . I think the theory is, Assist whomever is being given data that is not very helpful.

The interventionist went on to explain that he evaluates interaction by the standards of his theory of helpful communication and that he points out violations of those standards by any participant. This may lead him to appear to be "on the side of" one participant for several minutes and later to be "on the side of" another participant. It is important to identify the errors of each participant, lest the interventionist give the impression of being biased. People accustomed to a Model I world will be alert to cues that the interventionist is committed to helping one side or the other win. Hence, when there are several equally good interventions that might be made, a rule of thumb is to choose one that is critical of whoever has more recently been assisted. If the interventionist has recently been critical of the subordinates, then, other things being equal, he chooses an intervention that is critical of the superior, and vice versa.

Implementing such a strategy requires that the interventionist be able to empathize with each participant. One of the difficulties of members of the seminar was that they found it easy to empathize with the subordinates and difficult to empathize with Marilyn. Most of the discussion had been focused on Marilyn's errors; hence Carol's question, "Were you trying to give Marilyn the sense that there was someone on her side?"

The interventionist then returned to Paul's comment, and asked what he meant by "off the hook."

Paul: Your intervention has simply decreased the win-lose dynamics. They reached a position where they appeared very eager not to lose.

Interventionist: Okay. My view of it was, my intervention generated a commitment of responsibility on their part to look for the next one. I wouldn't call it off the hook, in the following sense: I think something will generate in an hour or so. What I didn't want to do was to go back to the previous histories, because both of them had made errors. [Here the interventionist illustrated some errors that each had made, and said that each could point to those sentences to support the view that the other was wrong.] And then we're caught in a circular position.

Notice that participants' questions are based on their view that what the interventionist has suggested is not consistent with what they understand to be Model II approaches. For example, Model II does not encourage face saving or the smoothing over of conflict, which are possible meanings of "off the hook." Similarly, supporting one side or the other does not seem consistent with the Model II value of generating valid information. The challenges by participants provide an opportunity for the interventionist to reflect on his reasoning, thereby connecting his intervention with Marilyn to the governing variables of Model II and to relevant features of the situation.

Another participant asked a question that focused more sharply on the conflict between the rules that had been guiding participants' behavior and what the interventionist had done:

Mary: Question I have: If the consultant is observing over time, and then it comes time to produce something. We have been learning that it's helpful to give DOD [directly observable data], and we have to go to the past for that. So I think that's why a lot of us were involved in this self-sealing process you were looking at, because we wanted to give DOD. So I'm thinking, "I thought we were supposed to use specific incidents." And I'm confused to hear that now we will rely on the future.

Interventionist: That's good. Paul, do you want to respond?

Paul: What was helpful to me was your comment about generating commitment. I put emphasis on generating valid information, and the other two issues, free choice and internal commitment, those are important too.

This episode illustrates, first, how the rules that guide learning can also get in the way of learning. Participants have learned that when someone makes an attribution, such as, "You act in ways that are unconfrontable," they should ask, "What has she said or done?" But in this case, asking for illustrations leads them to reinforce the escalating win-lose patterns in which Marilyn and her staff are caught.

Second, the episode illustrates how inquiry into conflicting rules creates opportunities for making explicit the reasoning that underlies the competent use of different rules. In this case, the interventionist was able to identify the relevant features of the situation that indicated it would be better to look to the future rather than ask for illustrations from the past.

Third, the episode illustrates how people may focus on different aspects of the web of reasoning that underlies competence. For example, Paul focused on the importance of free choice and internal commitment, as well as of valid information. An episode such as the one we have partially illustrated here is so rich in meanings that students cannot focus on all of them. Rather, what they focus on is a function of the learning path they are on. It is by participating in many learning episodes of this kind that students slowly build their understanding of the complex web of reasoning that underlies competence.

Case Team Membership and Clients with Power

In this section, we will describe how we attempt to expand and deepen learning by introducing students to the use of case teams and by exposing them to cases that are about the problems of actual clients, and that contain individuals in positions of power. It is our experience that these factors have an important impact on the quality of intervention that the students produce.

In becoming members of a case team that must work together, students begin to experience the problem of producing their own effective groups. And, by introducing real cases with client requirements, we expand the factors to which they must attend beyond the problem of learning to produce Model II skills on problems of their own choosing. By introducing cases with clients who have significant power in large organizations (public or private), we create conditions that activate the participants' biases and fears regarding power.

The faculty asked participants to study an edited transcript of a meeting of a case team at a consulting firm. The text of this case, and analyses of it, have been published elsewhere (Argyris, 1982, pp. 121-142). Briefly, the vice-president in charge of the team had asked the five members to meet with him to reflect on their effectiveness as a team and on the service provided to clients. He was interested in learning why a team of two competent consultants and three experienced managers, all of whom had successfully completed a similar project in another part of the client organization, had not produced the high-quality work expected by the firm and the client.

The vice-president opened the meeting by stating that he would talk last because he did not want to bias what others said. He encouraged everyone to be candid and promised that he would be candid. As each member gave his views, it became clear that everyone had sensed early in the project that the team was in trouble. The members said that it had not been clear who was in charge, because the vice-president had had to reduce his involvement in the case. Each member has concentrated on his own part of the project; and partly because everyone was under heavy time pressure, no one raised his concerns about how the team was working. Near the end of the project, the vice-president and one of the managers realized that the team's report was inadequate, and they rewrote it themselves. After discussing these and other features of the case, the team members agreed that the major problem had been the presence of "too many chiefs and not enough Indians."

The faculty asked participants to imagine that they were the consultants to this case team. They were to meet with the vice-president, role played by the senior instructor, with the task of helping the client to build a more effective case team. The vice-president wished to be cooperative. He also believed it important to apply rigorous, tough tests to the ideas his consultants suggested in order to decide whether to introduce them into his already pressured life, as well as into the lives of his colleagues.

The faculty asked participants to work in groups of four or five people. Three sessions were spent on this case, and each of four teams role played with the vice-president. Each team also met several times to plan its intervention. We begin with the first team's consultation to the vice-president:

Doug: Our consulting team felt that there was evidence that your team as a whole agreed that the project was somewhat ineffective.

Vice-president [*role played by faculty member*]: Yes, I think that's fair, although I think I was the leader in seeing that. And some of them went along. But certainly at our meeting, I think there was a consensus that the project was not as effective as it could have been, given the high-priced consultants we had.

Doug: Would you agree that the main purpose of the meeting was to explore the ineffectiveness of the project?

Vice-president: Oh, I think that was a very important purpose. Yes. And another purpose, of course, is what can we do about it. Which is why I'm really looking forward to what you have to say about it.

Doug began by asking the vice-president if he agreed with what appeared to be rather obvious inferences. It is not clear why Doug began with these questions. As the interventionist-as-vice-president said later, "I felt as if you wanted to document a position, that you didn't want to tell me what it was until you could document it."

Doug: Well, we as a team felt that one of the major difficulties we saw was that throughout the meeting, people could not easily test things that they brought up within the meeting.

Vice-president: I'm not sure I understand. What does that mean, test?

Doug: Well, we felt that you, as the vice-president, put yourself in a position, by making an opening statement that you were not going to bias what others said, and then in the conclusion summarized the case, and that by operating in that manner you left yourself least available for testing.

Vice-president: I can see how you might say that, but I don't think you really understand this team, and my relationship with the team. They're a pretty strong lot; and it's indeed because they're strong that I said to them at the beginning, "Look, I'd rather have you folks start off, and I'll wind up." So, I doubt that—if they didn't test, I don't think that has much to do with their not testing it.

Doug: Well, I guess our point was that by summarizing the case at the end, one of the things is that you as the vice-president never publicly tested any of the ideas that you felt about the project itself.

Vice-president: No, they stated their views, and I stated mine. I don't see how that prevented them from testing something that occurred before my summary.

Doug said that a major problem was that the group could not test their views; and when the vice-president asked him to explain, Doug started talking about what he thought the vice-president did that was wrong. So it appears that Doug believes that the vice-president was the problem, but he does not say so until he is pushed to explain. This indicates that Doug is easing-in, and this approach may lead the vice-president to mistrust him. The interventionist later said that, as the vice-president, he tried to hide his feelings and be cooperative but that he felt angry: "Here I'm taking all these initiatives, and the first thing they tell me is that I'm at fault."

Doug was acting as spokesman for a team, but the other

members of the team later said that Doug had not role played the intervention that they had helped design. One team member, Ralph, said that their idea had been to work with the vice-president to help him see how he had contributed to a case team learning process that was single loop rather than double loop. Another team member, George, then read the opening sentence of the intervention that had been agreed on by the team. It began, "Would you agree that the main purpose of the meeting was to explore why the case team was ineffective?" The interventionist pointed out that this was very similar to the way Doug had begun and that it too appeared to be an attempt to ease in to build a case. He asked George to recall the reasoning that lay behind that question, and George replied:

> It was our reasoning, that the way we were starting out was to just lay out our reasoning about the case. Okay, what do we have in common? One, these folks think they didn't do well, right? So let's check that out. Two, we the consultants think their meeting was ineffective, insofar as even trying to explore why they had been ineffective previously. So, let's make sure that was their purpose, check that out. Then, I think the meeting itself was ineffective in achieving its goal. I see some similarities between the ineffectiveness of the meeting and the ineffectiveness of the team on the case. I want to give some examples to support that conclusion, and then see if you agree.

George's account indicates that the team members were conscientiously trying to follow Model II guidelines in designing their intervention. They intended to make their reasoning explicit and to test each step in their reasoning process with their client. Despite their good intentions, however, the intervention came out as Model I. Indeed, the second step of George's reasoning illustrates what may be an automatic tendency to "build a case": Since he thought the meeting was ineffective, he decided to first check if the vice-president agreed about the meeting's purpose. If so, George could do on to say that the meeting had been ineffective in achieving that purpose. Hence, he was building a case while protecting himself by not revealing the point of the question until the vice-president publicly committed himself.

The interventionist role played another way of designing the intervention, which was to state the three attributions that the team was making and to be prepared to go on to the next part if the vice-president agreed. George found that suggestion helpful:

> That's good. I think that resolves a problem we struggled with, which is: There are two conflicting principles. One is to lay out as much as you can in advance, so that you don't give the v.p. the feeling that he's being led into a trap. The other is to give evidence for anything that you say, so you don't feel that attributions that are unsubstantiated are being leveled at you. And those are often in conflict. What you've done is give a sense of where you're going in a way that's clear that the data will follow, if he doesn't agree [with your attributions].

This is another example of what we earlier discussed as conflict among rules. In this case, George and others on his team explicitly recognize the conflict between being open with intentions that are at higher levels of inference and testing reasoning step by step, starting at lower levels of inference. The interventionist can produce designs that resolve the conflict; and, by reflecting on the differences between what he has done and what they have done, participants will gain a deeper understanding of Model II reasoning. Notice that George infers a new principle from the interventionist's design, "Give a sense of where you're going in a way that's clear that the data will follow, if he doesn't agree." The intervention thus functions as a prototype.

George's ability to publicly reflect on dilemmas of design

is itself a sign of learning. Such episodes occurred with increasing frequency in the seminar. For example, Tom identified another problem that indicates how a Model II rule such as "illustrate with directly observable data" can be used in the service of win-lose dynamics:

> What I find a tendency to happen is that to make your argument powerful you accrue tons of data that you can bang over the head of the person that you're talking to. And if they agree with you, you're holding this data and you have nothing to do with it. In other words, data [are] important, but you want to look beyond the data to what are the implications of the data for how you can help the client. And the other important thing is if that person disconfirms what you say, instead of throwing another piece of data at them, to listen to the disconfirmation.

We have discussed the reasoning that lay behind the first part of Doug's intervention. In the second part, Doug said that the vice-president had erred in saying that he would speak last. This too was based on a team design, and by looking at the reasoning informing that design we can gain insight into the participants' tendency to frame the situation as one in which the vice-president is the culprit.

George: [We had planned to focus on] the effect that the v.p. had on the meeting by saying at the outset that he didn't want to bias people's views, so he was going to hold his until last. [We felt] it was an important clue to the v.p.'s understanding of his own role in the group. Namely, that if he feels that expressing his views is going to bias other people, that implies that he feels he has a preeminent position in the group. And by alluding to that at the beginning, he is essentially asserting himself as preeminent by giving his own views special status.

Interventionist: Well, my reaction [as vice-president] is something like this: I am preeminent. I am the vice-president. I'm paid more than they are, and I'm an irresponsible person if I don't accept the preeminence.

George: The connection we were going to make with the rest of the case was that, what the v.p. did in his conduct of the meeting was hold off sharing his views until the very end. In the case, he withholds a variety of information (for example, his doubts about the competence of team members, and his perception that members are coming to him to complain about each other, but no one is taking responsibility for the case as a whole). He himself doesn't model the behavior that he's wanting them to do. So we see this parallel in the meeting, where by holding back and not testing his own views, he's doing in effect what he did in his leadership or nonleadership of the team, by not pointing to problems when he saw them, and so forth. That was the logic.

One of the interesting features of George's logic is that it is clearly built on prototypes that participants have learned in earlier seminars. For example, the X-Y case turns on the puzzle that participants do to Y what they criticize Y for doing to X. Interventions intended to unfreeze this kind of behavior often take the form, "You are doing the very thing you criticize." Such interventions serve to disconfirm the client's assumption that he has acted competently, and often lead clients to feel more personally responsible for the problem. This would seem to be the model behind George's observation that the vice-president "himself doesn't model the behavior that he's wanting them to do."

As the interventionist points out, there is a gap in George's criticism that the vice-president asserts himself as preeminent: In fact, the vice-president is preeminent and would be irresponsible to deny it. Other members of George's team tried to deal with this objection by role playing:

Paul: You want to hold the team responsible, right?

Vice-president: I want to hold them and myself responsible.

Paul: But, in the case and the meeting, in both of those situations what you did was rush in and fix the case, or rush in and tell them what was really wrong. And as long as you keep doing that, they aren't being held responsible.

Vice-president: And what might I have done? [*silence*]

Doug: You might have presented your ideas of the case, as the v.p., and asked the consultants if they indeed agreed with how you viewed the case. That's really what I was trying to get you to see [earlier].

Vice-president: But didn't you see here in the case, lots of data that they are willing to salute the chief? And I'm the biggest chief. So, I wanted to give the best possible deal that we would get openness and candidness. And so I owned up to the chief problem, and I said, "The chief's going to go last." Now, I think you're telling me that accents the very fact that I'm chief. I'm saying yes, but I'm in a Catch-22. You told me the consequences, which I buy. I haven't heard how do I get out of this Catch-22.

Notice that Paul produces another version of the puzzle model: You want to hold them responsible, but you act in ways that do not hold them responsible. There is an important degree of truth to this diagnosis, as it gets at how the vice-president contributes to the problem. But there are two difficulties with this view. First, it suggests that the vice-president is a culprit rather than someone caught in a cycle; and second, it does not suggest what he might do differently to untangle himself from this cycle. Paul has no suggestion to offer.

Doug has a suggestion, but it is an old one: that the vice-president begin by giving his views and asking for reactions. This suggestion appears to be based on the early heuristic, "Combine advocacy with inquiry." But it ignores the very real problem that led the vice-president to act as he did: If he goes first, he may bias what others say. Neither Doug nor the others seem to have understood or empathized with the problem that the vice-president faces.

The interventionist has guided the process of searching for a better design by role playing the vice-president to identify the dilemma or "Catch-22" in which he finds himself. Another team member picked up on this clue:

Ralph: I now hear you saying that you can sort of share our view that you're in a Catch-22. And I guess I'm hearing you say you want to get out of it.

Vice-president: Well, first of all, I want to be clear that I didn't think that that was your view. I thought your view was that I was wrong. And that no one saw me in a Catch-22. You only saw one part of it.

Ralph: Okay.

Interventionist: I just want to identify that, because that's part of that syndrome of, I think, how many of you automatically exhibit a blindness toward people with power. Now, let's go back [to the role playing].

Ralph: I can see your Catch-22. I think it would be very useful, for both you and the team, for you to acknowledge the Catch-22 that you experience to them. And perhaps begin this kind of discussion with that. And get it right out there.

Vice-president: And what might I say?

Ralph: I think you've said it very well today already, that "the way I experienced the work we did on the case was this Catch-22 situation; and I'm concerned that if I start the meeting this way it will have that effect, and if I start it that way, it will have this effect. And it's a dilemma that I experience."

Several participants found this discussion helpful in conceptualizing their learning. For example, Tom noted:

> A key point in this is the question of empathy toward your client. In particular, if the v.p. is your client, then you really have to empathize toward him. I know in my own development in this, that I went from a period of hostility, down to the period of, I can say, "I know it's not your

fault, it's a systemic thing." But I still can't get up
the empathy yet to really begin to look in terms of
Catch-22s, and what is that person facing. That's
sort of helpful; in listening to the word *Catch-22,*
it's been giving me a direction to think in.

Notice that the interventionist did not try to help participants get to this point by urging them to be empathic. Rather, he helped them to look at what they were doing by role
playing, reflecting on their reasoning, and role playing again. As
participants became more competent at understanding and dealing with the vice-president's situation, they also began to feel
more empathic with him. At the same time, they began to feel
more clear and secure and hence less threatened by the vice-
president.

Notice also that the shift to focusing on dilemmas can be
understood as another illustration of learning by discovering in-
adequacies in interventions based on earlier learning. For example, the team's strategy was based on its diagnosis that the vice-
president was acting in ways that reinforced the very behavior
he wanted to change, and this diagnosis was based on the model
of the X-Y puzzle: participants do to Y the very things they
criticize Y for doing to X. Through several iterations of role
playing and reflection, participants learned that this diagnosis,
though accurate as far as it went, was radically incomplete.
What they had missed were the features of the situation that the
vice-president had to manage and that had led him to act as he
had. Their new orientation did not eliminate the inconsistencies
they had discovered with the help of the puzzle model, but
added to them by allowing the participants to see the inconsistencies as one part of the dilemmas faced by the vice-president.

Along with this expansion of their vision, participants
came to appreciate the importance of empathizing with their
clients and also to appreciate their predisposition not to empathize with people in positions of power. The reflection papers
that participants wrote following this case also show that they
connected these issues of empathy and blame with their own
experiences in earlier seminars. They recalled that they had felt

defensive about being told they were incompetent, and in some cases their feelings of failure and guilt had impeded their willingness to experiment and to learn. They remembered that the interventionist had helped them to manage these feelings by pointing out that, while they were responsible for their actions, they were not responsible for the theory-in-use that they had learned through socialization and that led to these kinds of actions. He had also pointed out that the injustice and counterproductive consequences they created, although following necessarily from their actions, were not intended by them. In short, they began to apply to their work with their client (the vice-president) some of their new skills for managing the learning environment by recalling the importance of such intervention skills when they were in the position of the client. They were learning to combine a focus on the client's personal responsibility for error with deeper understanding of and empathy for the client's situation. This enabled them to help the client manage the feelings of failure and vulnerability that come with unfreezing.

Such learning does not come easily, nor does it happen all at once. As the following section will illustrate, the next teams to role play with the vice-president were able to build to some degree on the experience of the first team, but many of the same errors reappeared in a new guise.

The Second Team Consults to the Vice-President. One of the criticisms participants had made of the first team's approach was that it did not help the vice-president to understand what had led to the case team's inability to monitor itself. It was suggested that the vice-president be helped to see how the theories-in-use of the members of his team, including the theory-in-use of the vice-president himself, created difficulties. This was the approach chosen by the second team to role play.

Fred began the role playing by giving the vice-president a sheet of paper with a diagnosis of the espoused theory and theory-in-use of both the vice-president and the members of his team. According to the diagnosis, the espoused theory of the vice-president was to be straightforward, to work cooperatively with people, and to approach them when their work was not good enough, whereas his theory-in-use led him to fail to confront his group with evidence of the members' competitiveness and backstabbing and to cover up the group's error by rewriting the final report. The vice-president said that he thought "backstabbing" was too strong a word and that he was not sure that he was "covering up." He did, however, agree with the bulk of the diagnosis. Fred's team diagnosed the case team's theory-in-use as leading each member to work by himself and to refuse to raise problems with the team as a whole. Consequences of these theories-in-use included competitiveness, lack of interaction, and uncorrected errors. The vice-president said that the diagnosis made good sense to him and asked what was next. At this point Fred got into difficulty.

Fred: What we'd like to discuss next, if we're on common ground, is to look at possible solutions. As you see, we view the problem as something that happened interdependently, and we'd like the solution to take a similar shape. So that there is a sharing of responsibility for what happens. We also feel that the solution should incorporate a means of the group's monitoring each others' work. . . . Basically what we're interested in doing is to have you sit down with the group, and develop a new theory-in-use with the group. And do it jointly.

Vice-president: I like that idea. What do you have in mind?

Fred: Okay. I think one of the ways you could approach, and we can discuss this, this is a—there may be various different ways of getting at the same kind of thing. One of the ways that we see is that you could sit down with the group, present a similar kind of diagnosis, and then begin to discuss with them how they might explore ways of becoming self-monitoring, self-correcting, beginning to confront each others' errors, focus on the whole task, and so on. In other words, a meeting somewhat similar to what we're doing right now. With a great deal of openness and inquiry about each point.

Fred is careful to emphasize that responsibility for the problem is shared, a precaution that may be the result of his observing the first team's error in blaming the vice-president for being the culprit. But the most notable feature of Fred's suggestion is that it is highly vague. He proposes that the vice-president "begin to discuss with them how they might explore" solving the problems. But if Fred's diagnosis of the vice-president's theory-in-use is correct, then the vice-president would conduct such a discussion according to a theory-in-use that inhibits solving these problems.

While most clients would recognize that Fred is being vague, fewer would realize that he is giving advice that violates his own diagnosis. The interventionist saw this inconsistency as salient and chose to play the vice-president as recognizing it:

Vice-president: Well, if I understand this diagnosis, you're asking me to do something that it says I shouldn't be able to do.

Fred: Well, this involves a process of making an intervention of your own.

Vice-president: What do you have in mind?

Fred: Thinking through ways of your being able to present this to the group, in a way that would avoid most of the things you do in your theory-in-use.

Vice-president: Yeah, that I understand. And would you give me some examples? That's why I hired you people.

Fred: Okay. Before you have the meeting, we can have a role play, as a matter of fact, where you can work out some of the things and we can give you feedback. But some of the things that you could do is, for example—What do you think would be some of the problems you would have if you went in, knowing your theory-in-use, and presented your diagnosis to the group? What do you think some of those issues would be for you?

Fred continues to give vague answers. When he is finally pressed to give an example, he shifts in midsentence to a kind of client-centered strategy: "What do you think some of those issues would be for you?"

Fred's client-centered approach puts responsibility on the client to come up with the ideas about how to proceed. When participants gave their reactions to Fred's role play, some said that they thought he knew just what he wanted the vice-president to do but was masking his view with an inquiry-oriented, easing-in approach. Others thought that Fred simply didn't have a suggestion to offer and was covering up.

There may be validity to both interpretations. Fred may not have anything to suggest beyond his proposal that the vice-president present the diagnosis and "begin to explore" solutions with his team. Fred's unawareness that his own diagnosis indicates that the vice-president can't do this effectively suggests that he hasn't thought it through very carefully. At the same time, Fred may hold an espoused theory of consulting that says he need not think through what the vice-president could do. He may believe that, once he helps the client to have the right insights, appropriate action strategies will naturally follow. He may also believe that the client should be the source of these ideas and that he should put responsibility for generating them on the client. These espoused theories could serve to cover up, even to Fred himself, that he is covering up his incompetence by being vague and asking questions, because they provide rationalizations for these strategies.

Another team member, Kathy, then proceeded to role play a more forthright strategy. Building on the first team's experience, she suggested that the vice-president tell the team some of his dilemmas. She advised the vice-president to tell the team members how he would suggest resolving the dilemmas. For example, he might tell them that they should confront each other rather than coming to him with complaints about each other. The quality of Kathy's suggestions was mixed. She did not formulate the dilemmas well, and her advice that the vice-president say, "Don't come to me, talk to each other," might actually decrease the discussability of team problems, because it would do nothing to increase members' competence in discussing issues among themselves. Nonetheless, Kathy's approach was an improvement in that she was not engaged in a cover-up that might generate client mistrust. She put her ideas on the table where others could react to them and design improvements on them.

Following Kathy's role playing, Fred reflected on the reasoning behind his nondirective approach:

> I have a very strong feeling, which I'm looking at right now, it's a value that I have, that telling somebody what to do will eventually get into manipulation and build dependence. And I tend to see dependence as unconditionally negative. And it's very hard for me to, when I come up against that point, I bounce back.

This led to a discussion of the conditions under which dependence can promote growth. For example, Kathy's approach was to suggest a series of actions that the vice-president was capable of performing (state dilemmas, ask for people's suggestions) and that would help him and his team to learn. Hence, she was offering a kind of dependence that included ways of growing out of dependence. Equally important, this more forthright approach gives the client a choice whether to accept the suggestions or to raise objections. If the consultant offers ideas and identifies the consequences of those ideas, as well as the consequences of the ideas proposed by the client, then the client can make an informed choice, thereby reducing his dependence.

Paradoxically, Fred's nondirective approach actually involves more manipulation and dependence than does the forthright approach. Assuming for the moment that Fred was not simply covering up incompetence, then his questioning strategy was a way of getting the vice-president to discover what to do for himself, so that the vice-president would be internally committed to the ideas. But this puts Fred in the position of hiding what he thinks the vice-president might usefully do. The vice-president is likely to feel that he has to figure out what Fred is hiding, which makes it harder to reject Fred's ideas and puts him in a highly dependent position. Also, Fred is not saying that this is his strategy and so he is engaged in a kind of manipulation.

Replicating the Case Team's Problems. Not only were Fred's and Kathy's differences not resolved in their team meeting before the role playing, but the team also chose Fred to present what turned out to be the less effective of the two approaches. Despite the discussion of dilemmas the previous week, the team did not ask Fred to include these ideas in his intervention. What led the team to make these choices?

We will introduce our discussion of team process problems by discussing the role playing of a third team member. Jim intervened when Fred got in trouble with his questioning strategy and before Kathy had described her approach. The relevant conversation was:

Vice-president: And what advice do you have for me to do on that? I still—what is it that you think I should do?

Jim: Well, I think you, also, had information that the group was in trouble, and you didn't surface the problems with the group.

Vice-president: Yeah. That's true. And?

Jim: And I'm wondering what the reason was.

Vice-president: We're busy, swamped; the last thing in the world I want to do is spend a lot of time on this process stuff. It could pull them apart.

Jim: I don't understand why it would pull them apart.

Vice-president: Well, if I start confronting them on some of the issues, then they confront each other, my big fear is that the group will fly off in different directions. Especially if your analysis is correct.

Jim does not see the dilemma the vice-president was in because he does not see the validity of the vice-president's fear that confronting team process issues will be counterproductive. As we noted earlier, Jim and Fred's own diagnosis indicates that this is a likely result. Members of the case team, including the vice-president, act according to theories-in-use that inhibit the productive discussion of these issues.

There is another reason why it is remarkable that Jim does not see what is valid in the vice-president's fear: Fred and Jim's team itself had the very problem that the vice-president fears. This became evident in the discussion following the role playing, when the interventionist said that as the vice-president he had felt that he could pull apart the team that was consulting with him. Team members explained that there had been a deep disagreement over how to role play. Fred had wanted to begin with the theory-in-use diagnosis and use his more client-centered approach. Kathy did not want to use that diagnosis; she wanted to forthrightly tell the vice-president what to do, which was to state his dilemmas, ask other team members to state theirs, and then to discuss how to resolve them. Fred's and Kathy's disagreements were not resolved, but not because they were not discussed. Indeed, one team member said, "I felt that the meeting we had was 99.9 percent pushing your disagreements, and less on concentrating on interventions." It appeared that Fred and Kathy had become increasingly polarized, and other members of the team felt like helpless bystanders to their disagreement. This led Paula, the team member quoted earlier, to say:

> See, this is the problem I have with surfacing things. I'm wondering whether surfacing actually leads to some sort of resolution, or what happens after that? We could be great at surfacing, nobody's inhibited. But then what? How do you ever get a case team that's unified?

This was precisely the fear that the vice-president had about confronting process problems in his team and that Jim could not see validity to. When members of a team have only Model I theories-in-use, bringing disagreements to the surface can lead to win-lose dynamics and increasing polarization, and such a consequence was embedded in the very diagnosis that the team made of the vice-president's case.

The way in which the team reached the decision to go with Fred's approach is also instructive. After the meeting that ended with Fred and Kathy still far apart, the team did not meet again until an hour before the seminar. To the surprise of Jim and Paula, Fred and Kathy appeared to have reached agreement that Fred would begin. While Jim and Paula were puzzled, they did not ask how the agreement had come about because they feared reopening the conflict just before the team was supposed to role play. When Fred and then Jim got in trouble in the role playing, Kathy did not intervene, because she thought that proposing another approach would make the team look disorganized to the vice-president.

Kathy explained that she and Fred had talked after their team meeting and that Fred had told her, "I think [the interventionist] would chew you up, with the method you have proposed." Kathy continued, "And my mind clicked, and I thought, 'He will chew *you* up.' And I'm not really sure if I wanted to let you put your neck on the line, and let him chew." All this, of course, remained undiscussed until after the role playing. Kathy acted as if she agreed with Fred's going with his approach. Other members of the team thought that she didn't really agree and that she was going to let Fred begin, then step in with her own approach; but they didn't say anything. The team went before the vice-president with their pretense of unity, with the results that we have seen.

The reader will notice that participants were making many mistakes, despite having gone through the learning experiences described in the previous chapters. This illustrates something that is characteristic of the learning process: Participants go through many iterations of unfreezing, reflecting, redesigning, discovering new errors, and unfreezing again. Indeed, movement to new stages of learning typically begins with discoveries of ways one continues to act in accordance with Model I theory-in-use.

It was not only the second team that replicated many of the problems that had troubled the vice-president's case team. For example, the process by which the first team had chosen Doug to be its spokesman had similar features. Doug had advocated a different approach from the one that the team chose, but he also very much wanted to be a spokesman. Other members feared Doug was not committed to the team's design, but went along with Doug's speaking for the team. For his part, Doug didn't think much of the team's design, but what he said was that he would present it faithfully. After the session discussed in the previous section in which Doug role played with the vice-president, the team met to discuss its process problems. It discovered that members had been holding many negative evaluations of each other's level of commitment and of the design they had produced but that these had not been discussed.

The reflection papers written by participants reveal that they saw their replication of the case team's process problems as highly significant. Several participants reflected on the ways in which they had contributed to these problems. For example, Ralph, a member of the first group, wrote:

> Midway into the second meeting of our group, I found myself trapped in a corrective proposition I had formulated for myself (especially *vis à vis* the class) some weeks earlier. This corrective proposition was:

> When thinking the process or direction of the class or meeting is not productive or effective, reflect on why you think this and then surface your reasoning and invite inquiry only when you have an alternative to offer.

> I began finding myself immobilized since, although I experienced our case team as often ineffective and our process counterproductive, I had effectively precluded myself from acting because I found I could not come up with better alternatives or interventions which I thought would be useful or effective. In a meeting after our team intervention, I surfaced this dilemma and got some feedback leading to the following corrective proposition to the corrective proposition above:

> When thinking the process or direction of the class or meeting is not productive or effective,

reflect on why you think this, surface your reasoning and intervene with either a positive alternative
or an admission of your lack of one and invite help
or inquiry.

Notice that the learning process Ralph describes again illustrates the iterative, dialectical features we have discussed earlier: He discovered an error in his theory-in-use and went on to
develop a corrective proposition. When he then acted in accordance with this new proposition, he discovered that it, too,
led to errors, and he revised it. The process was dialectical in the
sense that he first sought to correct the error of throwing responsibility on others by thinking out loud before coming up
with an alternative, and then discovered that he was withholding negative evaluations. This is an aspect of a key dilemma experienced by participants: On the one hand they are striving to
craft interventions that are clear and competent, while on the
other hand they are supposed to be forthright, to experiment,
and to be willing to make errors.

Participants saw their team process problems as directly
relevant to their conduct in the seminar. They had had difficulty in creating self-monitoring teams because of the same
theory-in-use propositions that had led them to act in the seminar in ways that inhibited their ability to create a self-monitoring learning environment. Two participants wrote that they
thought the process problems showed that it was not enough to
be proactive in advocating one's views; it was equally important
to be proactive in listening to the views of others, clarifying the
various views expressed, and inquiring into differences among
them. A third participant expressed the same idea by writing
that collaboration "involves considering the other person's reactions to be as important in the communication process as the
expression of one's own ideas."

These do not seem like new ideas, especially for a group
of people who have been employed as psychological counselors.
But they represent new learning in the sense that participants
were digging deeper into their tacit Model I theories-in-use.
They had always espoused openness, empathy, and active lis-

tening, but they were now learning that their inquiries often masked unilateral advocacy. Once they began to make their advocacy forthright rather than covert, they saw that it was indeed important to inquire and empathize. In short, they were learning to make their theories-in-use more congruent with their espoused theories.

The case team exercise appeared to help participants to deepen their learning on three fronts. First, they became increasingly able to step outside of win-lose frames and to empathize with the dilemmas people face, even when those people are in positions of power. Second, they became increasingly aware of the gap between insight and action, and began to reduce their cover-up of their inability to bridge this gap. Third, they became increasingly aware of their responsibility for group process problems and began to develop skills to monitor their group process. In these ways participants were unfreezing and beginning to redesign the very features of their behavior that require an interventionist to manage the learning environment. They were beginning to reach a level of competence at which the learning process could be self-sustaining. They began to be as much a part of the solution as they were a part of the problem.

12

Developing
New Frames of Reference

At some point participants in an action science seminar will be on their own. They must be able to design their own experiments, to step back with others to reflect on what they see, and to sustain a process of inquiry into the surprises and puzzles that they discover. The impediments to these processes are not unique to action science; they often affect more traditional research as well. As Campbell and Stanley (1963) describe it: "For the usual highly motivated researcher the nonconfirmation of a cherished hypothesis is actually painful. . . . the experimenter is subject to laws of learning which lead him to associate this pain with . . . the experimental process itself, more vividly and directly than the 'true' source of frustration, that is, the inadequate theory. [Since] our science is one in which there are available more wrong responses than correct ones, we may anticipate that most experiments will be disappointing. We must somehow inoculate young experimenters against this effect" (Campbell and Stanley, 1963, p. 3).

Campbell and Stanley go on to recommend that, as experimenters, we ought to lower our sights, that is, increase our

394

time perspective, stop expecting clear-cut outcomes to resolve opposing theories, expect mixed results, and so on. All in all, we ought to "expand our students' vow of poverty to include . . . poverty of experimental results" (p. 2). Our work has tried to explicate the "somehow" of inoculation against a protective stance toward failed experiments. In some sense this work might be considered a kind of lowering of sights because it nurtures the expectation of mixed results, the recognition of ambiguity and paradox, the anticipation of failed hypotheses, even of cherished ones, and so forth. But from our perspective these phenomena are also what should make the experience of science a rich one. The surprise of a failed hypothesis might be either pleasant or disturbing depending on how one regards it. The puzzles presented by mixed results can be the most engaging. Einstein, for example, spent the latter part of his life delving into and trying to reconcile the inconsistencies between quantum physics and Newtonian physics.

What is it about the way we regard our practice as researchers that blinds us to these possibilities? Certainly, there are structural and professional constraints that have contributed to these responses. The professional norm has become "advance through proving your hunches." But within these constraints we have choices. We might dismiss the unexpected failure or herald it as a counterintuitive result worthy of further pursuit. We might grow angry and impatient with conflicting theories and despair of ever achieving a consistent paradigm. Or, we might see such conflicts as clues to the nature of our social world and thus regard them as questions to pursue instead of battlegrounds on which to stake out and protect our own territory. We believe that such a stance toward experimentation is possible and necessary for all research, not just for action science.

If this is so, the best inoculation may lie in the development of a reflective orientation toward experimentation. But how are we to achieve this? So far, we have seen that the interventionist takes this stance when participants experiment. Once on their own, participants must be able to assume this stance themselves, yet the previous chapter revealed some limits in their ability to do so. What follows in this chapter is a sequence of three frame experiments designed to stimulate a process of reframing what it means and takes to experiment in the face of failure, ambiguity, and conflicting results. Each one uncovers the inferential and emotional reactions that comprise how participants regard experimentation and the outcomes it yields. Each one is set into motion by making the obvious seem curious. And each experiment builds on the one before it, as it stimulates new actions that in turn reveal new paradoxes. We tell the story of these experiments in the sequence in which they unfold. They are intended to describe how the action scientist and participants experiment and reflect in action in a way that allows participants to renegotiate or reframe what it means to engage in reflective experimentation.

Withdrawing: Designing One's Own Injustice

Early in the second semester of the seminar the interventionist noticed a pattern of interactions that suggested participants were retreating from the risks of experimentation. One incident in particular stood out since it revealed a paradox. A participant who had been particularly active in discussing a consulting case also took the first opportunity to generate an alternative and experiment with it. But before doing so, he checked to see if others wished to go first. He waited before volunteering and then explicitly asked if anyone else would like to start. After being met by silence, he waited yet another moment, looked around the group, and then began to role play an alternative. The interventionist was puzzled. With participants aware of the limited amount of time left, what would lead them not to use their "fair share" of air time?

The interventionist initiated the first experiment in order to pursue this question, and he did so by making salient to participants what was puzzling to him about their actions, so that they might together inquire into what might account for them. In the language of the group, the experiment came to be known as the passivity experiment (see Chapter Four), and we saw a segment from it earlier in our case study on experimentation. In this section we return to it as an example of an experiment in frame breaking.

Phase One: Generating A Sense of Dissonance. The pattern that so engaged the interventionist's attention was taken for granted by participants. The responses that composed it were enacted automatically, and the group members assumed that others, not themselves, were responsible for their lack of participation. The interventionist thus initiated the experiment by framing their actions in a way that would make paradoxical what they regarded as obvious:

Interventionist: Okay, another one of my experiments. What I'd like to do is start by making two attributions about this class which I'd like to test out, if I may.

The interventionist says he is about to make attributions that require testing.

One, since our time is scarce, there is an issue of justice. Most of you believe you should not take more air time than however you measure your fair share. Is there anyone who'd disagree with that attribution?

And another one was that Paul, when he began, had the equivalent of what many of you might have felt was a fair share, regardless of whether you agreed with the way he began or not.

The interventionist makes and tests two attributions about the group's beliefs: First, the group believes air time is an issue of justice; the group also believes you should not take more than your fair share. Second, one participant, Paul, had already taken his fair share.

The class members confirmed the inferences, and one person said that he thought Paul had taken more than his fair share. The interventionist continued:

Interventionist: I then said, "Who would like to go first?" Utter silence. [Paul] looked at me; I looked at him. I

He then cites data from the last class in which persons let Paul go first.

looked around three or four
times. Paul looked around.
He finally took over.

I want to know: How
come? What's the dynamic
here that says the guy who's
already had enough air time
is now asked to even use
more?

He inquires into why the person who has already taken
his share of time, by their own
assessment, is asked to take
more.

During this first phase the interventionist made a series of
low-level inferences that, once confirmed, yielded a puzzle. Participants held as equally true conclusions that were psychologically inconsistent and that made them appear to be designing
their own injustice. On the one hand, they believed that air time
was an issue of justice and that Paul had already taken his fair
share of it, if not more. Yet on the other hand, they acted as if
they believed that Paul ought to take more time. Faced with
two such contradictory beliefs, individuals ordinarily experience
a sense of discomfort that they then try to reduce either by re-
sorting to fancy footwork or by holding others responsible for
their beliefs (see Chapter Nine). Similarly, Festinger and Carlsmith (1959) found that to reduce such dissonance, individuals
will bring in a third view to try to convince themselves that the
first two were untrue. Milgram (1974) discovered that people
who violate their values will blame external factors or those in authority. And Latané and Darley's work (1970) on the innocent
bystander showed how individuals will tend to think others are
more responsible for acting consistently with their values than
they themselves are.

The interventionist thus designed his intervention in a
way that made it less likely that others could be held responsible for participants' contradictory actions. He started out by
publicly testing his inferences about their beliefs, giving participants control over the meanings imposed on their actions. This
at once allowed them to reach agreement on what occurred and
made it harder for them to later assert that such meanings were
no longer true without creating further inconsistencies. He

based these inferences on data that they were responsible for generating. The data were not the result of a hoax that brings to light the errors of participants after it has been revealed. Unlike subjects in many psychological experiments, participants here did not have to contend with the added embarrassment of being set up, falling for the ruse, unknowingly exposing their inconsistencies, and having to make themselves look credible to the very person who just set them up. Their actions were a result of their own design, not the experimenter's. Consequently, they were more apt to pay attention to what *they* did in trying to account for the contradiction, and an inquiry into their actions was thus set into motion.

This first phase was directed at creating an optimal kind of dissonance, one that would spark an inquiry that would be minimally self-protective. The act of withdrawing was interrupted by helping participants to see how they were violating their own notion of fairness. At the same time, this interruption occurred in a context in which the participants created the data and confirmed the inferences that ignited their sense of dissonance and sparked the incentive to figure out what had led to their inconsistencies in the first place. This kind of dissonance can serve as a catalyst to jar participants into taking account of their actions.

Phase Two: Generating A Rich Description. As a result of the first phase, the interventionist opened up a process of reflection on withdrawal. But there was still no assurance that the group would end up with a full description of the conditions that triggered it. Such a description requires that participant and interventionist together reconstruct how participants understood and experienced the situation in which they withdrew: what they saw happening (the data they selected), how they understood what happened (the inferences they drew from these data about themselves and others), how they felt about the situation as they understood it (the emotional experience), and what actions they took and felt unable to take. Yet these are often not the kind of data put forth when individuals account for their actions (Nisbett and Wilson, 1977; Scott and Lyman, 1968). Instead, as the quotations that follow illustrate,

participants often capture their experience in highly inferential
categories, calling on plausible theories and metaphors to explain what occurred:

Actual Statements	*Comments*
I felt taken aback [by something the interventionist did].	Describes his reactions in metaphorical terms; does not say what it is he is actually feeling.
I feel on the spot, like I'm breaking ice.	
[After I listened to the tape], I felt I should say something smart or the interventionist [would] attack me.	Makes an inference about the interventionist; does not report the data that led to the inference.
I feel I'm hiding out and easing in like I did at the beginning of last semester.	Makes an inference about himself; does not report the data that led to the inference.
I'm waiting for someone to make a mistake to see what the interventionist will do.	Makes an inference about himself; does not report the data that led to the inference.
I felt my intervention had to be perfect; and I had no model of perfect.	Reports an inference he made at the time, but not what data led to it.
I have a sense of impending embarrassment.	Reports a feeling at the time.
I don't want to appear stupid.	Reports a feeling at the time that is based on an inference (she will appear stupid if she makes a mistake).

For the most part these are inferential accounts couched
as feelings, but they run the gamut from metaphors to causal
attributions about oneself and others to the occasional expression of affect. Without doubt all these data are crucial. They en-

able participants to make sense of their experience, and they can act as clues to direct our inquiry into how participants constructed a situation in which they withdrew. But by themselves they are not sufficient. The metaphors are so rich in meaning that we can easily take from them any number of unintended meanings: Does "on the spot" mean "anxious about errors," "resentful of unwarranted scrutiny," or both? Similarly, the attributions about self and others leave us stumped as to what led to them and whether or not they are accurate: Is the interventionist attacking the actor, is the actor magnifying the interventionist's actions, or is it a little of both? These accounts all raise such questions, and such questions are crucial to a process of inquiry into action. Different answers would hold significantly different implications for future moves: Should the interventionist change his actions, should the participants alter the way they make and hold inferences, or should both interventionist and participants do something else altogether.

As it stands, the group members do not have enough to go on to take the next step. They need to develop an additional set of data. They need to reconstruct what happened and how they thought and felt about it so they can figure out how to push beyond the responses that get in the way of learning. This means that the interventionist must mine the accounts quoted earlier for such data and begin to organize them in a way that will produce movement toward a more reflective orientation. Such a process begins in this phase with the probing of accounts for illustrations that will provide rich or "thick" descriptions of the situation and participants' experience of it. The interventionist thus asked one participant—"What was it in the tape that led you to see me as attacking?"—to inquire into his responsibility and to generate data to test the claim that his actions had constituted an attack. Similarly, he probed metaphors for their reference points, asking the participant who spoke of being "taken aback" what it was he was thinking and feeling at the time.

Once these data started to emerge, the interventionist sought to discover to what extent participants' inferences and experiences were shared. He thus asked not only what it meant to be on the spot but if others felt the same way and, if so, what it meant to them. When the interventionist discovered that a participant felt humiliated by his actions, he checked to see if he had had the same impact on others. Such queries served both to clarify meanings and to uncover differences and similarities that might otherwise have gone unnoticed. Once generated, these data allowed the interventionist to build from the individual to the group level, developing a collage that represented the group's collective experience. And as he took these steps, he tested with the participants to see if the connections and patterns he was developing were the right ones. This process of collage building was thus a public and collaborative one, with the interventionist reflecting out loud as he went along and participants filling in the gaps of his understanding.

To keep this process moving without triggering protective responses, the interventionist continued to assume the stance of vulnerability described previously. He consistently communicated a readiness to own up to his responsibility for what occurred by continually inquiring into his impact and acknowledging his errors. In one instance a participant confronted him for making a sexist remark. After hearing the data, the interventionist agreed, "Right on. It was sexist and I apologize for it, because I think you're dead right." These responses also increased trust, as participants came to see that the interventionist was not simply trying to nail participants with their own distortions. Instead, he communicated that he might be the one who needed to change if the group was to move forward. Unlike the protective notions of trust and safety described in the map (Figure 8 in Chapter Nine), the interventionist creates trust and safety not by minimizing the negative and emphasizing the positive but by evidencing a commitment to accuracy and learning.

Phase Three: Generating Frame Conflict. Once a collage was developed, the line of inquiry into participants' accounts gradually shifted, and new queries emerged as the group took a deeper cut into how participants constructed and experienced the situation before them. The first hint of this appeared when the interventionist began to organize the material generated in the previous phase into new puzzles. He made such a shift when he inquired into a participant's fears of appearing stupid by asking the question: "I don't know how easy it is for you to answer this. Does Paul appear stupid to you? [Several no's.] He made loads of errors. What is it that leads you to believe you'll appear stupid?" This inquiry not only elicited new data, it suggested a new inconsistency. It is inconsistent when one uses two different standards for evaluation, and it is puzzling when one does so at a disadvantage to oneself. Yet by their own definition this is what the participants were doing. And notice: This inconsistency was discovered in the course of their attempts to resolve a prior inconsistency. They were trying to explain that they had violated their own notion of fairness because of their fears of appearing stupid; but rather than resolving the first inconsistency, this explanation itself ends up being equally inconsistent and equally disadvantageous to participants. They consider themselves, but not others, stupid for making errors. Thus their efforts to achieve consistency fail as they end up creating new inconsistencies, and doubts begin to emerge about how well they are making sense of the world around them.

To describe this process more fully, let us turn to an interaction between the interventionist and Lee, the participant we described earlier as leaving it up to others to create the conditions that she believed she needed for learning (see Chapter Nine). There we saw that she withdrew; she privately blamed others for this withdrawal; and when she finally expressed what she was experiencing, she used this description as a lever to get others to conform to her views. An important logic characterizes this reasoning and action, a logic that we argued earlier is embedded in the framing of one's role as a recipient rather than as an agent of the learning process. Lee did not see, and she consistently did not act as if she saw, herself as mutually responsible for designing the learning that occurred. Similarly, she and others acted as if errors were taboo. They recoiled from the risks of experimentation, feared making or pointing out errors, and experienced errors as embarrassing or humiliating. These responses also contain a certain logic—the logic embedded in the frame that it is wrong to be wrong and that makes a sense of success contingent on not making mistakes. The most striking feature of these frames is that they lead individuals to consistently act in ways that they themselves consider illogical and inconsistent with their conscious intentions and beliefs. In this instance such logic led the members of the group to withdraw, even though they thereby violated their own beliefs and designed their own injustice.

In an interaction with Lee the interventionist brought this logic to the surface, so that the simultaneous "illogic" in it might be seen. The process began when Lee said that she had felt humiliated by the interventionist when he had confronted her on an error and that she feared that she herself had humiliated one of her peers, Melinda. After Melinda said that she had not felt humiliated, Lee recounted the reactions that she had had previously to both the interventionist and Melinda. It was at this point that the interventionist made two strategic probes that allowed him to build on the data about humiliation provided by Lee and Melinda and to formulate for the first time the problem of how participants construct and experience the learning situation before them:

Lee: There were repeated instances of your defending Melinda. It was at that point I felt, "Again he's defending her, and he's not really hearing what I'm saying."

Lee made repeated inferences that upset her: In her view the interventionist was treating her unfairly. But she kept these views and feelings private at the time.

Interventionist: And is there anything that prevented you from saying that?

The interventionist probes for obstacles to making such reactions public.

Lee: No, I thought after that, that it wouldn't be correct.

Lee thought it wrong to express these reactions but does not say what leads her to think so.

Interventionist: Might it be humiliating to the receiver?

The interventionist tests a hypothesis.

Lee: Yes.

Lee confirms.

In this excerpt we have another instance of an actor inadvertently colluding with others in designing a situation that she considers unfair to herself. In this instance Lee believed the interventionist was acting unfairly, yet she said nothing and by default contributed to the unfairness she saw. The interventionist had a choice point here. He might have intervened as he had in the previous phase, eliciting data to test her inferences and perhaps asking, "Can you say what I did that struck you as defending Melinda and not hearing you?" But instead he shifted the inquiry, probing for an additional kind of data: data on what stops participants from acting in ways that would ensure that they were treated fairly and that would allow them to learn. With this new focus, he went on to offer a hypothesis based on data about Lee's feelings of humiliation over her own errors and her fears of humiliating others. He posited that Lee held a set of propositions about humiliation that led her not to say what was on her mind because she anticipated humiliating herself or others. Once she confirmed this, he was able to organize these data into a pattern that suggested the following formulation:

Interventionist: So I have a problem: Those of you who feel easily humiliated also design your interventions so they do not humiliate someone else. But what you consider humiliation may not be even a pinprick to the receiver.	The interventionist begins by organizing the data elicited so far: People who are easily humiliated assume others will feel the same and sometimes they are wrong: Melinda didn't feel humiliated.
[So] we're both in an interesting bind: I can't make an error or a quasi error without humiliating. And Lee can't tell me what she feels without fearing humiliating me.	Then he builds on these data by identifying a bind: If he makes an error, he will humiliate. But he cannot learn this because others fear they will humiliate him by pointing out this error.
[And finally:] I don't know how to create Model II	And he builds on this to point out the implications

conditions, if the behavior on the peoples' part is . . . to withdraw.	for the learning context: If people withdraw, he cannot create conditions conducive to learning.

Combining new data with those from the previous phase, the interventionist reformulated and mapped out the problem of withdrawal. He began with conditions hypothesized to trigger withdrawal: People experience humiliation, predict others will experience the same, assume this to be true, and design their actions to avoid humiliating themselves or others. Notice that we now have data for the constellation of affect (humiliation), inference making (make predictions about others and assume them to be true), and intention (avoid humiliating self and others) that the interventionist originally sought because his model of participants regarded this constellation as crucial to understanding action. Next he connected this constellation to their tendency to withdraw and to blame others. Lee believes he made the error of humiliating her, yet she does not tell him so and instead withdraws. And finally he tied these actions to a series of consequences for the two of them and the learning process: Her actions put them in a bind, they assume people are humiliated who may not be, they prevent the interventionist from learning of his errors, and they thus end up undermining the conditions necessary for learning. Diagrammatically we might map these causal relationships as shown in Figure 9.

These data suggest the frame about what it means and takes to learn that we saw in the previous map of participants (Chapter Nine). It was through these processes of reflective experimentation that we began to generate the data and insights that eventually were organized into the more comprehensive map of their experience. From the vantage point of participants' frames, learning means making or exposing errors that are humiliating (it is wrong to be wrong), and it requires leaving the process up to others to avoid such humiliation (one's role is that of recipient of learning). By unearthing the structure of this logic-in-action and by pointing out its consequences, the interventionist started to unfreeze the participants' frames, saying

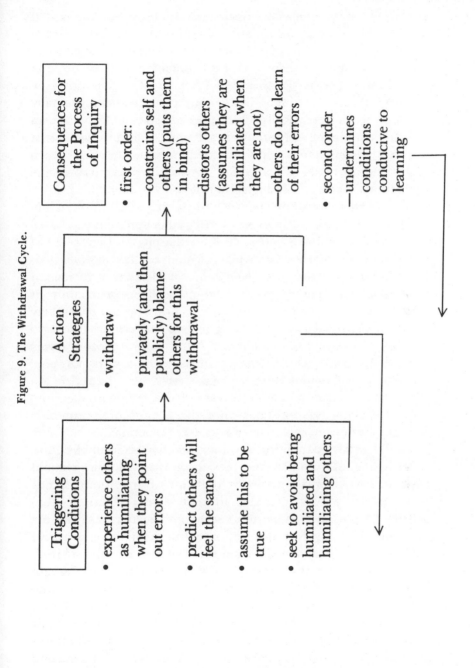

Figure 9. The Withdrawal Cycle.

Triggering Conditions

• experience others as humiliating when they point out errors

• predict others will feel the same

• assume this to be true

• seek to avoid being humiliated and humiliating others

Action Strategies

• withdraw

• privately (and then publicly) blame others for this withdrawal

Consequences for the Process of Inquiry

• first order:
  —constrains self and others (puts them in bind)
  —distorts others (assumes they are humiliated when they are not)
  —others do not learn of their errors

• second order
  —undermines conditions conducive to learning

in effect: "Your frames are backfiring, leading you to undercut the very beliefs, conditions, and values that brought you here in the first place." He identified factors they had overlooked (people may not be humiliated) and introduced new elements that their frames had not anticipated (they create their own constraints), thereby casting doubt on the usefulness and accuracy of these frames (see Kelly, 1955, on constructs). Such moves are the equivalent of critiquing a theory. The interventionist revealed inconsistencies and uncovered anomalies for which their theories could not account, in essence disconfirming the predictions that ought to logically follow from them.

All this was quite puzzling to participants and certainly unexpected. Since the interventionist's reformulation was based on data brought forth to resolve an earlier puzzle, their sense of dissonance was heightened instead of reduced. The interventionist then built on this unresolved sense of dissonance to suggest an alternative: "You've got to try to make errors or to confront me." It may sound odd to the reader to hear the injunction "try to make errors" when for so long most of us have tried so hard to avoid them or to cover them up. But in this context errors are the material that sustain a process of inquiry into action. Without a willingness both to make errors and to reflect on them, this process cannot go forward. So from the interventionist's perspective, the mistakes that the actions of participants brought forth were essential for success at learning.

When an existing frame is loosened by this kind of doubt, a reframing of mistakes becomes more plausible but remains suspect. Participants may doubt their own frames but continue to shrink away from testing an alternative one. As Kelly (1955) put it: "A person hesitates to experiment because he dreads the outcome. He may fear that the conclusion of the experiment will place him in an ambiguous position where he will no longer be able to predict and control. He does not want to be caught with his construct down" (p. 14). In essence, testing the interventionist's suggestion would require them to break out of their roles as recipients and out of their frame that it is wrong to be wrong. While this was making increasingly good sense to participants, they remained stymied. How were they to make the leap from a frame that no longer offers firm ground to another they cannot quite envision nor be certain exists? One participant expressed it this way: "I took this class because of its emphasis on not protecting and on reflecting the real world. And I've never been in an environment in which I'm being pushed in those places I'm not courageous! And the question for me is: If we're here, how do we get to out there? And how do we create this as a place, so we can keep pushing each other to go beyond where we've gone." This is the kind of question that comes out of phase three, and it was toward answering it that participants and interventionist turned next.

To summarize Phase Three, we might note that the interventionist began by shifting the direction of inquiry. He built on data already elicited and probed for new data that might now be used to bring about change. Informed by his model of participants (Figure 8 in Chapter Nine), he organized these data into a reformulation of their withdrawal that explained the withdrawal, helped to make them aware of the logic in it, and pointed out unanticipated results, thereby revealing new inconsistencies in their actions and in the premises upon which those actions were based. In this way the frames of participants were brought to the surface and cast in doubt, and participants began to reconsider them. The interventionist then posed an alternative that required them to break out of their existing frames, something they were now in a better position to do but at a loss how to do.

Phase Four: Working Through Dilemmas. At this point participants' efforts to diminish their sense of dissonance had failed, and they were growing increasingly doubtful of the way they were framing the learning process. Yet at the same time they remained hesitant and doubtful about the next step to make. The presence—and expression—of such doubts indicates a qualitative shift in participants' perspective and the emergence of a new phase in the experiment. These doubts suggest readiness, rather than resistance, to think through how they might actually negotiate such a reframing process and the obstacles to such a process. Or put differently, such doubts express the best kind of resistance, one that in effect says to an interventionist: "Don't forget. I may be questioning my own logic, but I'm not so sure about yours either. So before I try your logic, I'm going to hold you to explaining it, exploring it, and submitting it to the same scrutiny we've just submitted mine."

The interventionist regards this stance as a step forward and as an opportunity for collaboration, not as resistance aimed at undermining him or the process. The interventionist thus helped to initiate an iterative process that involved identifying doubts and dilemmas, designing ways out, eliciting new doubts and new dilemmas, designing new ways out, and so on. Each iteration incrementally served to test an alternative frame and moved participants toward a reframing of the learning process. To describe this last phase, we follow the interventionist and participants through two iterations of this process, and we start with his response to the participant who earlier expressed concern over how to move beyond where they were:

Interventionist [referring back to an earlier description]: That's the part I was unaware of. It sounds to me like you and Roy were saying something like this:

When I get into this situation, I get into a quick, automatic internal dialogue: "Oh, my God, am I going to do it? Is it going to be bad? My God, that would be terrible."

You're right. I'd get squeamish too; that kind of dialogue would immobilize me.

One thing we can do is if any of you feel that dialogue, how about raising your hand, getting in and just talking

The interventionist empathizes with and takes seriously their doubts: He communicates that he now understands that there are obstacles to enacting his advice: They dread errors so much that they become immobilized.

He poses an alternative that will allow the participants to make a move in the face of their feelings.

about how you're feeling and
not talking about the answer.

As we have seen earlier, the interventionist responds to
dilemmas by taking them seriously while not taking them for
granted. He learned from and empathized with the internal dialogue of participants, while pointing out that it had left them
immobilized. In this instance, he also went on to suggest a way
out of this dilemma by saying that they might make the dialogue itself public. This suggestion serves to lower their aspiration levels, because it implies that interim steps such as surfacing one's reactions are important. If enacted, such steps would
put them closer to the goal of a more reflective frame. Their internal dialogue might be full of protective reasoning, but they
would be in a better position to explore and move beyond this
reasoning once it was made public.

But from the participants' perspective, this suggestion itself posed a new dilemma. Participants conceal their internal
dialogues, because they anticipate that revealing them will result
in negative consequences. The interventionist is in effect asking
that they act as if they believe positive consequences might follow, when they believe otherwise. Not surprisingly, participants
were skeptical. In one person's mind she had already seen such a
test. When people had done what the interventionist suggested,
they were confronted and told that they had gone on too long
and that they were thus in some sense wrong. For this participant a new dilemma emerged. The interventionist was saying,
"Jump in, think out loud." Yet when people did this, they were
confronted and told that they were wrong. This raises an important issue. On the one hand, the interventionist does not want
to communicate that participants will not make errors or be
wrong. In fact, if the experiment succeeds, they will probably
make plenty of mistakes, and he and others will point out and
reflect on those errors. On the other hand, this does not mean
that people are wrong for making these mistakes or that they
should stop making them. But because of the conflicting frames
that participants and interventionist bring to this experience,

suggesting alternatives becomes problematic, with participants anticipating one set of results and the interventionist another. Participants reason: "If I am confronted, it will not only mean that I'm wrong but that I'm wrong for being wrong. Since I know I will make mistakes if I jump in and think out loud, the outcome of such advice can only be negative." The interventionist tries to counter such logic by suggesting a way to move past it:

Interventionist: Let's experiment with all sorts of different ways to design our intervention, including if it suddenly occurs and it's really boiling, that you say to the class, "I want a few minutes; it's going to be long."

But it would be okay for it to be long. It's when the class talks in a lengthy, circular manner and acts as if the manner isn't lengthy and circular [that is a problem].

The interventionist encourages experimenting with different ways to intervene.

He suggests that one experiment might include owning up to what you are doing as you intervene.

He communicates that making errors is okay, it is covering them up that is problematic.

In this excerpt, the interventionist reframes the problem: It is not the mistakes of length or circularity but the fact that people act as if these errors are not being made. This offered a heuristic for participating that is highly conducive to learning: Acknowledge what it is you are doing rather than cover it up.

Alternatively, the interventionist might reframe the way participants understand the results of their new attempts to break out of their withdrawal. From the participant's perspective, confrontation of their new actions suggests that their experimentation has failed and that such attempts ought to be abandoned. From the interventionist's perspective, however, such confrontation suggests that new learning can occur and that their attempts ought to continue. To convey this new view of the risks of experimentation, the interventionist might confirm that experiments will reveal errors and that these will be identified in the course of reflection. But he might then add that this means that their experimentation is fruitful: It is yielding important results that should further their own and others' learning. Seen in this light, their experimentation becomes a success, even when it reveals the failure of new actions.

This process continued through a series of iterations, each participant probing the interventionist's frame to see whether or not it merited a test and identifying data that he or she thought disconfirmed it. In each instance participants were saying something like: "We did what you suggest and we did not like the results. So your framing doesn't work." Hence, the overarching dilemma of being caught between two frames that seem equally dubious. To help resolve this dilemma, the interventionist reframed the meaning of these results and the participants' solutions for contending with them. In addition, he suggested methods that they might use to break out of each dilemma they raised: Get in and just talk about how you are feeling; acknowledge what it is you are doing and do not cover it up; and reflect on your reactions publicly here, not privately at home. Each of these methods might move them closer to more learning-oriented frames and actions. Throughout, the interventionist reiterated in his own stance of vulnerability and his encouragement of theirs that it is not only okay to make errors, it is a necessary prerequisite for learning.

Results. During that session and in subsequent weeks participants began to increasingly test out these steps. They confronted the norms of the course, posed alternatives to the interventionist's alternatives, confronted each other and the interventionist more frequently, and began to produce the actions represented on the reflection-oriented end of the continuum depicted in the learning map (Figure 8 in Chapter Nine). This led more and more participants to make mistakes publicly, providing them with opportunities to explore mistakes and what it means to make them. Nevertheless, in the course of this experimentation, new obstacles emerged, as participants continued to respond to each other's errors in ways that either reinforced or triggered the more protective frames. But even these responses provided new opportunities to probe the protective reasoning bracketed by these frames. We turn to one such opportunity next, as the group reflected on their tendency to rescue their peers from having to scrutinize their errors.

Rescue Maneuvers: Undercutting One's Peers

As soon as participants began to jump in and talk, to acknowledge what they were doing, and to discuss their reactions openly, they participated more, made more errors public and saw and pointed out more errors in others. All in all, they came to generate an abundance of mistakes that sparked and fueled a process of reflection. Yet such a process is an incremental one of two steps forward and one step back. With their frames in flux, they at times responded automatically to others' errors in ways that triggered and reinforced the protective frames that they were trying to break out of.

The interventionist regarded such responses as further opportunities for frame breaking and reframing, but he now assumed a somewhat different role in relation to them. Earlier, because so many participants withdrew, he necessarily had to take a primary role in sustaining the process of inquiry, making most of the moves to probe, confront, empathize, and so on. By this point, however, the movement stimulated by the first experiment had led others to come in and increasingly take on this role so that the interventionist could now begin to move back from center stage, giving up the role of a primary actor and taking on the role of a collaborative director who helps others to enact roles and scripts unfamiliar to them. Out of this renegotiation of roles, a new public dialogue emerged with the interventionist and participant together critiquing and reflecting on the latter's performance and on the interventionist's periodic demonstrations of an alternative script.

As with any dialogue that takes place across competing frames or assumptions, this discourse between interventionist and participant was often conflictual, with different meanings being brought to bear on the same performance. Working through these conflicting meanings and the frames that informed them became the key to further learning and reframing.

The experiment that follows occurred at this transitional period in the learning process. It evolved spontaneously as the interventionist began to see the following pattern of interlocking scripts emerge: One participant, Carol, would make an error either on-line or in the case that she had brought to class; her peers would help her to see the error; she would then grow upset and communicate that she was either helpless or overly harsh on herself; others would pick up these cues and come in either to take over the process that was upsetting her or to minimize her errors; she would then make another error; someone would point it out and the sequence would recur. Earlier we described the double-edged nature of this kind of support (see Chapter Nine). It is well intentioned but undercuts others by usurping control over, and/or circumventing, the process of reflection on errors. It thus confirms the other's role as a helpless recipient and reinforces the frame that it's wrong to make mistakes. The interventionist therefore used this rescue sequence for further frame breaking, interrupting participants' unawareness of it and unfreezing the notion of support embedded in these moves. As he did so, he demonstrated an alternative sequence of supportive moves based on different expectancies, and he reframed what it means to make mistakes and to support those who find them upsetting.

Phase One: Interrupting a Rescue in Progress. The experiment started as the group consulted to Carol on a case involving a client who had just confronted her for misusing a politically sensitive term. In the case, the client stressed that Carol was not dumb and kept asking her why she had used the term, while Carol kept deflecting his questions and minimized the mistake by saying, "I just forgot" and "It's just a term in my head." Internally, however, she was becoming increasingly upset, recounting to the group that she had felt, "God, am I dumb! It's not just like I'm making an error; it's a huge hammer [slaps the table to illustrate the force of the hammer]!" Similarly, as Carol's peers tried to point out in class how her deflections might have heightened her client's mistrust, Carol began to find it increasingly hard to follow what they were saying, finally coming in to tell them that she was blanking out. Such responses to looking at one's errors—both in the case and in class—are consistent with what we have seen before. Under the stress of being asked to take a look at her errors, a participant may grow increasingly upset and, as here, even blank out. At the same time, we have evidence that a new frame is emerging, that is, Carol revealed her inner dialogue, indicating a new willingness on her part to experiment with being wrong.

But as soon as Carol becomes distressed by her errors, her peers rush in and act as if they read her responses as cues to rescue her. In class, when she said that she was blanking out, they were quick to ask whether they were going too fast, whether they were giving too much information, and so on. In the case, they advised her to tell her client, as she just had told them, how badly she felt about her mistakes. Both of these moves suggest that participants are learning to take more responsibility (they come in to help Carol) and to make reactions public (they advise her to tell her client what she feels). But her peers apply this learning in a way that is apt to reinforce Carol's distress and the helplessness she experiences in blanking out. By coming in and taking over the process in class, they enact a form of support and responsibility (1) that does not help her to work through but rather circumvents her responses, saying in effect, "We will alter what we do to avoid your feeling what you feel"; (2) that implies that she is in fact helpless; and (3) that thus encourages her to give up control in a way that can only feed back to reinforce her sense of helplessness. By advising her to express to her client what she had just expressed in class, they suggest a form of disclosure with a client that is apt to cue him to rescue her as they themselves just did. Once her client realizes that she is hitting herself with a hammer, as it were, he may back down from asking her to take a look at her mistakes for fear he would only escalate her self-punishment.

The interventionist watched these sequences unfold until Carol said that she was unable to follow their advice to express how she felt about her mistake, because she was "already on the ground trying to breathe." Reading this as yet a third cue for support, the interventionist used it to make a two-pronged intervention directed at both Carol and her peers:

Interventionist: Yes, and it's terribly important not to get seduced by your reactions ... because if I do, I'm hooked into your button-pushing defense.

The interventionist formulates her responses as defenses.

What was happening in the class in the beginning, when people empathized and said, "Are we doing this too fast?" "Is this kind of complicated?" and so on.

The interventionist describes the way participants empathized with Carol.

There's a validity: We were doing it too fast, we were cutting each other off. So it's not that we were picking on the wrong variables. But as I was listening to it, she could pick it up and say, "You're moving too fast."

He identifies that their responses simultaneously had validity and ignored her capacity to monitor the process

So, I felt the class was being supportive, but that's where they could get caught in the button-pushing defenses that people have.

He points out a paradox: Their form of support could hook into her defenses and thus undermine her learning.

In this excerpt the interventionist disrupts the participants' finely tuned rescue maneuvers. Everyone was tacitly agreeing to enact a series of rescuing moves on cue, when all of a sudden the interventionist comes in on the same cue yet enacts an entirely different script, one that focuses on, rather than circumvents, Carol's responses to her errors and one that formulates them as defenses that can "hook" others. As he does so, he implies some paradoxes: The participants' support may both undermine Carol and reduce their own ability to help, because it ignores her capacity to monitor the process and because their efforts to help get tangled up in her defenses. Thus the interventionist at once interrupts their unawareness of these factors and redirects their attention to Carol's reactions. Combined, these moves build on the interventionist's prior use of empathy in the service of growth (see Chapter Ten). In the earliest phases he took participants' reactions into account while not taking them for granted. Now, by asking that they pay attention to Carol's reactions, while not getting hooked by them, he suggests that participants ought to assume this same stance.

But as the interventionist himself points out, the participants are already hooked. They take a qualitatively different stance from the one he suggests—one that focuses, as Carol does, on those factors that might produce a sense of helplessness (the pace of the process) and one that ignores, as Carol also does, those factors that might eventually produce a sense of mastery or efficacy (Carol's responsibility for slowing down the pace of the process). Consistent with our discussion of empathy, the participants' moves express an accurate understanding of Carol's experience (they recognize those factors she sees), but the participants omit the same features of the scene as she does, thereby reinforcing a view of the situation that leaves her feeling helpless and distressed. The problem is that their understanding *is* her understanding. They take her reactions for granted and see no need to question them because they share them. Garfinkel (1967) describes a similar kind of shared understanding in drawing on Schutz: "The person assumes, assumes the other person assumes as well, and assumes that as he assumes it of the other person, the other person assumes it of him" (p. 50).

In this instance both Carol and her peers hold a set of interlocking assumptions about what is happening and how best to manage it. They share the same assumptions about what it means and takes to learn; they see the situation as she sees it (Carol's errors are distressing and she is helpless); and they thus act as they might wish and expect others to act were they in her shoes (they rescue the helpless recipient distressed by errors); and consequently they end up confirming her views and main-

taining the cyclical sequence. Ironically, however, such closeness can be an uncaring kind of closeness. It allows Carol's peers
to be taken in by her defenses, it causes them to add to her
helplessness, and it precludes the optimal distance necessary for
a "generative" form of empathy, one that might help her move
beyond her present stance (Schafer, 1959; also see Minuchin,
1974; and see Umbarger, 1983, on the dysfunctional features of
enmeshed relationships).

Yet no one intended any of this. The intention of the
participants was to support Carol's learning. The problem is that
they hold a notion of support that is predicated on the assumption that errors are wrong to make and that individuals are recipients, not agents, of their distress. Given this framing, it becomes supportive to rescue "victims" from their distress and
their mistakes. If a process of reframing is to continue, the interventionist must continue to draw attention to this reasoning
as he begins to do here. His actions disrupt the expected rescue
sequence, and his framing of the problem points to critical features in the scene that theirs ignored.

Phase Two: Enacting An Alternative Notion Of Support.
As long as frames are in flux, participants will get into these
kinds of difficulties as they try to help one another to learn.
One way the interventionist deals with such difficulties is by
making the kinds of unfreezing moves described earlier, that is,
by helping participants to become aware of factors that they
have systematically been ignoring. Another way is to enact an
alternative notion of support. This has two simultaneous effects. It models how to deal differently with participants' protective responses, and it further unfreezes these responses by
bringing to the surface features of the design behind their actions that are usually kept hidden. To illustrate, we give an
excerpt of how the interventionist responded to Carol's distress
over her errors when she said, "God, am I dumb! It's not just
like I'm making an error. It's a hammer!":

Interventionist: There's a curious paradox. The way the director hits you on the	The interventionist identifies a paradox: The director confronts her by saying that she

head is to say, "You're not so dumb." And you're saying, "Yes, I am." So you get the hammer in fascinating ways. That's something to identify, and let's get the data later.

Here's an example of a program in a person's head that keeps her unaware of her program. Because if you can keep saying—"It's me that's dumb, it's me that's dumb"—then there's a lot of things that you can blank out from hearing when people are saying things that are relevant to you.

So the automatic response of "Oh, I am so stupid" on the one hand, has some validity; but maybe it's a very sharp thing, your being stupid, and that's now in quotes. [But to look at it as sharp], then you'd have to take it seriously as something to look at: What is it that led you to be blind, not only to what you sent him but in how you discussed it in the case.

is not dumb, but she confronts herself by saying that she is dumb.

This paradox leads him to hypothesize that her response is a program designed to avoid hearing about her errors: When she responds this way, she blanks out.

He recognizes the validity of her feeling that she is stupid in that she did in fact make a mistake.

He makes explicit the implications of framing her responses as "sharp": You have to take seriously what led you to be blind.

In tracing the steps of this intervention, we can get at the logic that underlies it. First, a puzzling feature in the case catches the interventionist's attention. The client is saying that Carol is not dumb and is trying to look at what led to her mistake, whereas Carol is doing just the opposite, saying she is dumb and deflecting his attempts to understand her mistake. In light of this puzzle, the hammer that Carol describes begins to take on a new meaning: It now becomes a clue that she may be designing ways to protect herself from looking at her errors. So while he recognizes some validity to her reaction that she is "dumb" (she did make a mistake), he begins to see her recitations of "I'm so dumb" as an expression of the kind of anguish that may serve to block out those who wish to look at her mistakes. Had she regarded her error as sharp not stupid, she would have to look at the knowledge embedded in her actions. What this suggests, then, is that the interventionist reads Carol's reactions in a qualitatively different way than participants did. She is not helpless or in anguish so much as she is designing a way to protect herself. This is not to say that she experiences no anguish but that the hammer she uses may be both tougher and safer than her client's: tougher because she uses it to punish herself with "I'm so dumb," yet safer because she also uses it to deflect attempts at exploring her mistakes.

In framing Carol's response this way, the interventionist focused on different features in the situation from those selected by the participants. He first focused on the discrepancy in how Carol and her client reacted to her mistake, examining their reactions in light of their accuracy and of how they both dealt with her error. In so doing he saw some validity to her reaction, but he did not regard it as a necessary response to the situation before her. This then led him to see that the actor who considered herself dumb (Carol) in some sense did less about her mistake than her client who did not see her as dumb. This paradox led to the following hypothesis: Her moves to "hammer" herself may have been designed to protect her from becoming aware of what she tacitly knows about managing threatening situations. This hypothesis, arising from this particular puzzle and shaped by the interventionist's theory of protection, posited the view that Carol's responses were designed. If so, then Carol was neither dumb nor helpless, but clever and a master of deflection.

By picking out these features in the situation and framing them as he does, the interventionist constructs a fundamentally different scene in which to support Carol's learning. In this scene, the problem is that Carol is designing her own anguish and blindness. This is the critical part of the plot to focus on and to help her move beyond. Formulated this way, the prescription for Carol is not to express to her client how upset she is about her errors, possibly cuing him to draw back from them. Rather it is to look at what role such responses play in keeping her blind and helpless. This framing of the situation brings to the surface features of how Carol designs her learning that her peer's framing will keep submerged: her automatic responses to errors and failure. As a result, what was once outside of her awareness and control can gradually come more within it, because she and others can now regard such actions as blanking out and berating herself, not as cues to deflect or rescue her from her errors, but as cues to help her become aware of how she may inadvertently keep others from helping her to learn.

Phase Three: Generating Frame Conflicts. Frames are remarkably resilient. Conceptually, the interventionist's reconstruction of the scene they had just enacted made good sense to participants. They could recognize the description of their behavior and see its usefulness. But frame breaking and reframing constitute an iterative process that involves repeated experimentation in which participants must continually experience the failure of their own frames and be helped to design ways to test out new ones. In this phase, participants walked back onstage and resumed their roles as consultants to Carol, experimenting with new ways of helping her on the basis of what they had just learned. What follows is the emergence of an interesting hybrid. One participant, David, builds on prior learning by trying to help Carol deal with her reactions so that they will become less immobilizing. How he does so reveals new features in the participants' notion of support and provides an opportunity for further unfreezing. We enter as David gives Carol advice on how to manage her reactions:

David: And I have another rule you might follow: Don't assume you're at fault or incompetent.	David suggests a rule: Do not assume that you have made a mistake or that you are incompetent.

Interventionist: But the data are that she is at fault.

The interventionist points to data that illustrate that this rule does not apply here: She did make a mistake.

David: No, I don't buy that.

David asserts that he does not agree but does not say why.

Interventionist: Why not?

The interventionist inquires into his reasoning.

David: I don't buy it.

David continues to assert his view without saying what led to it.

Interventionist: Well, hold on a minute: What do you do with a woman who blanks out? Do you consider that competent?

The interventionist confronts David: He points out actions in class that he sees as incompetent, and he asks David if he sees them as competent.

David: No, I'm talking about what preceded her button getting pushed.

David cites a different situation (the case).

Interventionist: This fellow [Vince] wasn't angry at her; he didn't yell and scream at her.

The interventionist follows his redirection, pointing to data in that situation.

David: But he suggested that she was in error.

David suggests that Vince, not Carol, is responsible for her actions.

Interventionist: That's right. [*Recalls what Vince did.*] He was trying his best, he wasn't trying to be punishing in my view. Now, for you to say that isn't Carol's fault is a terrible undercut of her.

The interventionist confirms these data, but not the inference drawn from them that Carol did not make a mistake.

The interventionist then builds on this to reframe David's support as an undercut of Carol.

David's efforts to support Carol run into an unanticipated snag that illustrates how participants build on prior learning to construct and test out new rules. The rule David designed
here—"Don't assume you're at fault or incompetent"—both redirects their help toward Carol's reactions and poses an alternative to the rule "assume your inferences are facts." Both features suggest that David is trying to move beyond a theory-in-
use that avoids looking at automatic responses and that makes
untested assumptions. Yet if we look at two other features of his
rule, we see some limits to this forward movement. First, his
rule ignores that in this instance Carol did make a mistake;
hence, the rule is misapplied here, and this misapplication itself
suggests a continued discomfort with errors and an effort to circumvent them. Second, while no one should simply assume that
he is at fault, a rule that merely poses the opposite will undermine another rule that participants are also trying to learn: Focus on one's personal responsibility. Given this combination of
features, David's rule is a kind of hybrid that draws on his
knowledge of a new theory-in-use while staying close to the
parameters of his existing one. More precisely, it maintains the
features of a protective framing of what is means to make mistakes.

Recognizing this, the interventionist resumes his frame-
breaking moves. He points out data that suggest that David's
rule will not work, and he identifies consequences that indicate
it may actually backfire. As we have seen before, such moves
cast doubt on an actor's logic, leading him to question it. But
unlike his previous reaction, David responded by more actively
confronting and questioning the interventionist, further illustrating the participants' movement forward and enabling David
and the interventionist to negotiate and inquire into their conflicting frames and rules. What emerges from this process is a
dilemma, one that further reveals the causal reasoning that leads
participants to enact the kind of supportive moves they do. In
what follows David identifies this dilemma for the first time,
and the interventionist continues to point out new gaps in
David's reasoning:

David: I don't understand that. If you assume that you're incompetent, how are you going to enter any consulting relationship without going into Model I behavior and screwing up? You have to have confidence, don't you?

David begins to make his causal reasoning explicit: If you assume you're incompetent, this will lead you to act incompetently. Hence, you must have confidence. Implicit in his view is that confidence is contingent on not making errors.

Interventionist: When somebody gets empirical data of an error and gets a pattern of escalating error, that's the thing that leads to the incompetence.

The interventionist reframes what leads to incompetence: If you make an error and these errors escalate, this will lead you to act incompetently.

And later on the interventionist conceptualizes David's approach:

Interventionist: I think you are trying to be supportive, and say, "Gee, Carol, if you don't have that other feeling, if you think positive about yourself."

The interventionist cites David's good intentions. David is trying to be supportive.

And I'm suggesting that she'll think, "That's fine. I'd love to think positive about myself, but how the hell do I do it?" I don't know any way she can do it if she is producing those kinds of errors, to put it dramatically.

He points out some gaps in David's reasoning: Given that she has made these errors, it is not likely that she can follow his advice to feel good about herself.

David: Okay, I see what you're saying. I'm reinforcing her.

David begins to see that his actions may be reinforcing Carol.

Interventionist: Well, it's a kind of Madison Avenue approach. It says, "Think positive." And she ain't thinking positive. Her automatic response is to punish herself.

The interventionist describes David's approach as one that fails to take into account her automatic responses, even though it is directed at them.

David: Well, I do believe there is something to that [approach]. If you believe you're going to be incompetent, it seems to me the chances are much better you're going to set up a self-reinforcing cycle and have it become a self-fulfilling prophecy.

David identifies a dilemma in giving up his framing: If you believe you will make mistakes, you may create a self-fulfilling prophecy.

Once the interventionist points out some gaps in David's approach, David runs up against a dilemma. On the one hand, what the interventionist says makes sense: Carol did make an error, and he may be reinforcing her by ignoring that. But on the other hand, if he focuses on her errors as the interventionist suggests, he will diminish her confidence and may actually create further incompetence. Such a dilemma stems from the following causal reasoning: Focusing on errors will result in diminished confidence that in turn will result in greater incompetence. This reasoning is actually quite similar to our description of what happens when someone holds a protective framing of errors (see Chapter Nine, the map of the learning process). If individuals assume that it is wrong to make errors and then try to avoid them yet go ahead and make them anyway, they do experience a sense of failure and a loss of confidence, and this can lead them to act in ways that get them into further trouble. So from our point of view, David's causal knowledge has much descriptive validity. But the prescription that follows from it should neither be to avoid looking at errors nor to feel good about them. Rather it should be to learn how to use them for one's learning without becoming so discouraged or frightened by them that one cannot acknowledge them. Implicitly, David's prescription requires that we cover up errors in order to maintain a sense of confidence, and it consequently simplifies the problem of how to create competence. With his theory one does not have to figure out how to develop greater competence in the face of errors or disruptions in one's sense of confidence. But his theory lops off a significant part of the problem: It overlooks a necessary condition for competence, the ongoing detection and correction of error. Therefore at best his theory can only create a *sense* of competence, and at worst it will create a sense of competence that becomes increasingly detached from the actor's actual level of competence, even as the actor himself would judge it were he aware.

As the interventionist pointed out these gaps in David's reasoning, David began to see that his approach might not work. The more he saw this, the more he experienced what we have seen before: the dilemma of being caught between two logics that seem equally doubtful and equally true. He sees that he is reinforcing Carol's method of framing the problem, but he sees no way out of this. To move beyond this frame conflict, he needs an alternative way of supporting a peer, and it is toward offering such an alternative that the interventionist turned next.

Phase Four: Working Through Dilemmas. While Carol observed this process, she began to infer the presence of a tacit frame about errors in what David was saying. In reflecting on someone else's logic, she was able to see the limitations of such a framing, and she reformulated how she understood her own errors. They were no longer evidence that she was terrible; they only suggested that she had a less flexible range of responses in some situations than in others. The interventionist built on this reformulation to suggest another way of thinking about Carol's errors, one that might help David and others out of their dilemma:

Interventionist: Now, to me you're getting at what's an answer. What you just said is equivalent to the metaphor we've used for incompetence.

It's the equivalent of

The interventionist builds on what Carol is saying and connects it to a metaphor.

The metaphor is one that de-

Carol's being a pretty good tennis player and saying, "You know what pushes my button, it's the backhand. You know, there are lots of other things, but we're working on the backhand today."

scribes Carol as a tennis player with a troublesome swing.

It doesn't mean she's a lousy tennis player; we're saying she is identifying her backhand as something she wants to work on.

It does not describe her as a lousy player; rather it focuses on a skill that requires work.

The interventionist's metaphor is one that frames errors in the context of learning a skill; errors become something to work on. It emphasizes aspects of a player's performance instead of global assessments. It follows from this that efforts should be made to improve a player's performance, to provide ample opportunity for lessons and practice, and to reflect on the results of this practice. Similarly, it would be rare, even odd, for anyone to ascribe nasty motives to a tennis player for making a mistake or to attribute that she was consciously trying to miss a shot. Rather we assume that a player's errors are due to the limits of her abilities at that point in time. Such assumptions are quite different from those embedded in the prevailing, although tacit, metaphor implicit in how participants frame their learning. For them the underlying metaphor is error-as-crime, replete with victims, the policing of violations, and the meting out of punishments. Within this frame, the overarching rule becomes one of outlawing errors, and all violations must be covered up or prosecuted. It is this metaphor that underlies Carol's move to berate herself for making an error and David's move to look the other way. Within the context of their shared frame, David knows that Carol cannot act without guilt or anxiety in the face of her errors. But rather than question the frame, he assumes it too and in effect suggests that they ignore the offense rather than punish it, the only two options within such a frame.

By drawing on a metaphor to reframe here, the interventionist provides a way of reconstructing the process that is easily retrievable. The picture of a tennis player working on the notoriously difficult backhand is more vivid and easy to imagine than a series of abstract propositions about what it means and takes to learn. This new metaphor carries with it assumptions that not only can withstand reflection on action but require it. A tennis player in action cannot see what she is doing wrong but must rely on others to observe her form and help her to become aware of what is causing her errors. If retrieved, this metaphor should lead David and others to no longer define their supporting roles as those of prosecutors or acquitters of transgressors but instead to see themselves as cohorts or instructors who can help Carol to see what she cannot see alone. Thus, in the context of this metaphor, support can take on a very different form and can resolve the dilemma that arises when we focus on another's errors.

Getting Angry at Mistakes

Sometimes participants take a kind of hammer to others as well as to themselves. Angered by mistakes, they deal with them not by trying to rescue the person who has erred but by making any one of several distancing moves. Some may blame and punish others for the difficulties they themselves face; others may psychologically detach themselves from what they regard as a frustrating situation over which they have no control and for which they feel no responsibility; and still others may suppress their anger, acting as if they were calm while giving off cues that they are not. But regardless of the move, each one is initially prompted by anger at another's mistakes, and most often each one ends up signaling that those in error should run for cover or retaliate in kind.

Left unexplored, this anger at mistakes can counteract a process of frame breaking and reframing, because the moves it triggers affirm a protective response to learning. It makes sense to guard oneself from those who make themselves invulnerable and who cannot handle fallibility—either their own or others'.

Thus as participants continue to experiment with breaking out of their frames and risking failure, they may discover that their existing frames are valid; that is, their mistakes do in fact get treated as transgressions to be censured and punished. Since such anger is a frequent occurrence in the real world, participants must learn how to work through it themselves and how to help others do the same. Like other obstacles to reframing, anger at mistakes can thus be regarded as both a constraint on learning and as a chance for participants and interventionist to test out ways of exploring and moving beyond such constraints.

Getting angry at mistakes is a common yet puzzling reaction. If we think of mistakes in any learning process as necessary and by definition unintended, it is curious that individuals should act as if their peers' mistakes were punishable offenses, particularly when they themselves make the same kinds of mistakes. Yet this is a frequent occurrence. Participants diagnose Y as judgmental, closed, and controlling and often express deep feelings of resentment toward him for acting in these ways. And since participants assume such diagnoses to be true, they themselves act in ways that are judgmental, closed, and controlling—no matter how hard they try to act otherwise. We might think that the discovery that they act as Y does would be conducive to empathy. But actually this may involve a closeness that is too close for comfort, that breeds contempt, and that triggers moves to distance oneself from one's own fallibility, from that of the other actors, or from the situation that ends up exposing both.

The experiment that follows had the purpose of discovering ways to explore and to work through these reactions by helping participants to see in a new way the situation in question. It inquired into the most puzzling domain of the three experiments, leading the interventionist to take the role of what Schafer (1983) calls a seasoned co-explorer: someone who knows well the methods of exploration but not the territory to be mapped. Along with this, participants took increasing responsibility for initiating new lines of inquiry, for mapping the problem before them, and for designing ways to resolve it. In this way the relationship between interventionist and participants continued to be renegotiated and to move from a state of dependence on the part of participants toward greater collaboration, with the interventionist assuming less control and the participants more control over the process of inquiry.

Phase One: Interrupting a Chain Reaction. The experiment sprang from reactions that participants had to a series of interactions that occurred after the interventionist had to leave a particular session early. It was thus by accident that we discovered that even relatively late in the learning process, participants still required help in enacting the norms of the course and in taking a stance toward one another that was conducive to inquiry. Without the interventionist's help, participants soon became abstract, acted as if they understood those who confused them, and rehashed what had already been said and said more clearly. This continued until one participant, Paula, came in and threatened to leave if the process continued. In this experiment participants' reactions to their own and others' mistakes became the object of inquiry. What we will see is that once Paula's frustration was expressed, it set off a chain reaction of angry responses. To illustrate, we give an excerpt from the session at the point Paula broke in:

Paula: I'm finding this really frustrating. I don't find anything different in what anybody is saying, and I feel like we are wasting a lot of time, and I would rather just leave if it's going to continue because I feel like I'm having a nervous breakdown because everybody's saying the same thing.

Paula expresses frustration with a process that she considers a waste of time.

She communicates anxiety and an intention to leave if its source continues.

Ken: Well, I have a little trouble with what you just said. It's sort of: "You guys are doing something I don't like and if it continues, I'm going to leave."

Ken acts as if he is calm: He uses qualifiers to mitigate his reactions and what he heard. He states the meanings he heard but not what is problematic in them.

Paula: No. All I'm saying is [*pauses*] okay, in some sense—	Paula begins by resisting his meanings but then affirms them.
Ken: That's what I was hearing.	Ken defends his reaction by stating that what he said was only what he heard.
Paula: Because I felt like people were saying the same sort of thing. And when Frank said something and wanted feedback, it was like it was getting circular and circular and circular.	Paula reiterates what others did to cause her reaction.
Ken: Yes. You did illustrate it. The problem I was having was sort of "And I'm going to leave because I don't like the situation."	Ken recognizes the description but not the necessity of the consequence.
Mary: [*with impatience in her tone*] What's your problem then?	Mary demands that Ken state what the problem is.
Paula: Yeah, what's your problem, 'cause I'm feeling—	Paula comes in on this to make a similar demand.
Ken: The problem with that is that it sounds like—	Ken begins to explain.
Paula: I'm not saying that you shouldn't continue, it's just that I do not wish to continue with this, so I would like to leave.	Paula cuts him off to reiterate her position in a way that denies Ken's implied criticism that she was coercive.

This excerpt provides a short but representative sample of a longer chain of angry reactions that reverberated throughout the group. It begins with Paula, who frames the process as a waste of time, acts as if she sees no role for herself, and becomes anxious and frustrated, threatening to leave if those she holds responsible do not take away the source of her reactions. A recipient of this threat, Ken, then responds by playing back the meanings he heard Paula communicate, mitigating his reactions and implying that Paula has acted coercively but not saying this directly. After initially resisting, Paula concedes that Ken has correctly heard what she said, and Ken takes this as an opportunity to reiterate what he heard, while continuing only to imply the problem in it. At this point, another participant, Mary, also grows angry and demands that Ken come out with it, spurring Paula on to do the same. Finally, as Ken starts to describe the problem, Paula interrupts to defend herself against the criticism of herself that she has inferred all along by insisting that the group was quite free to do whatever it wanted to do.

As we confirmed the following week, a rich subtext lay beneath what was said, and it was accurately read by those involved. First, at the time of Paula's intervention Ken reported that he "reacted very strongly," saying that he had felt threatened, stranded, and unhelped. While he tried to conceal this at the time and to act as if he were calm, he nonetheless gave off cues that this was not the case. By mitigating his reactions, by only implying a critique, and by strategically reiterating what he heard without stating the problem in it, he communicated that he was trying to minimize some negative reaction, which itself suggested that there was a negative reaction to be minimized. Mary, who inferred this template accurately, read in what Ken said what he left unsaid: that he was upset and trying hard not to show it. This lack of authenticity then pushed Mary's button; she later described herself as being very angry at Ken for not being more straightforward. Curiously, she then did to Ken what he had done to Paula. She herself concealed her anger and only implied a criticism of him in her impatient demand to know what the problem was.

The interventionist's departure was a serendipitous event that revealed a significant barrier to achieving independence. Making mistakes is to be expected; but if participants are to learn from them, they must develop the capacity to discover and reflect on them in an ongoing way. The reactions to mistakes expressed here reveal an important impediment to developing this capacity. With this in mind, the interventionist-in-training, who had remained in the group but had not taken an active role in the discussion, decided to interrupt this chain reaction by evoking the responsibility of participants to be of help to one another:

Interventionist-in-training: If we were to look at you [Paula] as a consultant to this group, what was right about what you did is you surfaced a problem in the group, and you said, "We're going around in circles and I don't think we're getting anywhere." That makes good sense, and I think it's tacitly illustrated: We were going around in circles, and anyone here would immediately recognize that as being true.

The interventionist evokes the role of a consultant as a lens through which to consider what Paula did.

From this perspective, she identifies what Paula did that could have helped the group: Paula accurately identified a problem.

As a consultant to the group though, you also said, "How I am now going to deal with the problem is by leaving." What that does is it presents this group with a bind, because on the one hand, we don't want to create conditions that are going to—and I think this is how you communicated it—force you to leave the group. And on the other hand, we're not yet clear about what it is we can

At the same time, the interventionist also describes how Paula's solution to the problem creates a problem for the group: She puts the group in a bind.

do differently in order to change the conditions that make you want to leave.

Paula: I thought this was going to continue, and my attribution was that there were individuals interested in discussing the situation. I thought we were going to go on and discuss another role play [*pauses*]. Well, I mean, I could have suggested I'd rather do that.

At first Paula tries to legitimate her actions by citing the attributions she was making at the time.

She then stops herself and pauses, recognizing that she might have done something to alter the situation that was frustrating her.

The interventionist's response to Paula models an alternative way of intervening that helps to interrupt the chain reaction. It contains many of the same meanings that Ken's did. Like Ken, she recognizes the data Paula cited, and she identifies the problems of helplessness and coercion. But her response also contains other meanings that Ken's response did not. It affirms Paula's move to publicly identify a problem, while at the same time making explicit how her solution was not only unhelpful but actually rendered the group subject to her reactions. The very explicitness of the intervention itself omits some of the meanings in Ken's intervention that continued the chain reaction. There is no effort to mitigate the negative evaluations in the critique. It is therefore at once tougher in that it explicitly spells out the problems in what Paula did and less likely to perpetuate the defensiveness and anger in that it communicates that the interventionist is not distressed by what she described.

In the meantime, the interventionist asked participants to regard their interventions in a new light. Paula had taken the role of an innocent bystander, seeing no responsibility for what the group did; and, when she did intervene, it was not her intention to try to help the group, as she said later. The problem that Paula set out to solve was how to get out of a situation that she felt no responsibility for creating or altering. She therefore withdrew psychologically, and when this was no longer possible,

she threatened to withdraw physically. By reframing her role as
that of a consultant, the interventionist revealed that the way in
which Paula understood the problem was inadequate: It was not
sufficient in this group to make the diagnosis and run. As a result, Paula began to recognize and acknowledge that there were
moves she could have made that might have changed the situation. But what was left unanswered was this twofold question:
What got in the way of Paula's impetus to help in the first place,
and what got in the way of Ken's ability to help once he saw
Paula's mistake? It was this that most crippled their capacity
to learn on their own, and so it was toward answering this dual
question that the participants turned next.

Phase Two: Initiating An Exploratory Process. The following week the interventionist was back in class with copies
of a transcript from the previous session that provided participants with both the data and the distance necessary to reflect
on their actions. In reading the transcript, each participant was
now able to see his or her own actions as easily as the actions
of others, while no longer feeling as caught up in the emotional
impact of the moment. This alone, however, was no guarantee
that individuals would use the transcript as a means of probing
more deeply into what was going on. In fact, as participants began to reflect on the transcript, Paula interrupted by saying,
"Before everyone starts agreeing that that wasn't effective, I
don't disagree. So I don't want to spend time on how that was
ineffective, because I know it wasn't effective." Instead she said
that she wished to focus on "how I could have said it differently."

Paula thus frames the problem as "what might I have said
differently," as if the problem were a purely technical one. But
what this excludes is that, at the time, Paula was so distressed
by the group that she felt as if she were having a nervous breakdown. The interventionist thus redirected the group's attention
to a somewhat different problem:

Interventionist: My problem is—I'm attributing to you that you are feeling—what? Frustrated? Angry at them?

The interventionist redirects attention to what Paula was feeling at the time.

Paula: Not at the personal qualities of the people but at the content of the discussion.

She replies that she was angry at the discussion, not the people.

Interventionist: At what they were doing?

The interventionist reformulates this to mean that she was angry at what her peers were doing.

Paula: Yes.

Interventionist: Then I know of no magic, no way you can hide that. So if that's what you're feeling, that may be what you need to take a look at first.

Given this, the interventionist identifies a problem in offering alternatives: If you are feeling angry, that will get communicated.

If you're feeling, "Boy, they're screwing up," I hope there'll never be a way that you can cover that up.

Given this, it is here, not on alternatives, that we should focus.

The interventionist believes that their push toward alternatives might backfire if part of the problem—the part not fully reflected in the transcript—is not taken into account: what they were feeling at the time and what led them to feel as they did. The interventionist thus interrupted this premature push toward alternatives by framing the problem, not as what people said, but as what they were feeling and by redirecting their inquiry into these reactions as he does in the following dialogue:

Interventionist: But now you have to ask the question: How come I feel that? [Do] these duds around here [know] that they're making mistakes? Where does the anger about them come from?

In focusing on her reactions, the interventionist frames the question in a way that makes it sound shocking: What leads you to feel angry at persons who are unknowingly making mistakes?

Paula: I don't know if it's so much anger as frustration at

Paula minimizes the strength of her feeling and claims that, seeing that circularity was recognized, but it was still going on.

Interventionist: And let's assume that they need help right now. How can you be angry at a group that's helpless? Let me put it that way.

although her peers recognized the problem, they did nothing about it.

The interventionist builds on what Paula says and reformulates the question: What leads you to feel angry at a group that is helpless?

The interventionist makes shocking what Paula must assume in order to react as she does. He first asks a question that, once answered, leads Paula into the box of her own reasoning: "[Do] these duds around here [know] that they're making mistakes?" If she answers yes, she risks hurting her peers by agreeing that they are duds, and she risks violating a sense of logic by saying that mistakes can be made knowingly when by definition they cannot. Yet if she answers no, she will offend her own sense of fair play: It is difficult to legitimate getting angry at those who are unaware that they are making mistakes. Paula tries to squeak out of this box by rejecting the premises embedded in the question. She says that she was not angry but frustrated and that her peers may not have knowingly made a mistake but that they certainly knew they were going around in circles. Rather than ask Paula to illustrate her assertion, the interventionist accepts her new premises since they pave the way into the same box. If she was right and the participants did know that they were going around in circles, then they must really be helpless, because no group would knowingly travel in circles unless it was unable to stop.

Discovering such boxes is itself shocking. Reactions like Paula's make such eminent good sense to participants that they rarely give them a second thought. Since participants see themselves as innocent recipients of mistakes that should not have been made in the first place, anger logically follows. To break through this kind of reasoning, the interventionist must provide participants with the impetus to think twice about these reactions. As we have seen before, he does so by making unacceptable to them the logic they have used to make their reactions acceptable. As a result, participants stop assuming that what they feel is a necessary consequence of the situations they face and start considering what elements went into their feelings.

Phase Three: Generating a Rich Description. With a new problem set, the group dug into a different question: What was happening at the time people became angry? In our first experiment we asked the same question when we set out to describe participants' withdrawal. Then, however, it was primarily the interventionist who pushed this inquiry along, at one moment probing participants' accounts for what they were actually seeing, feeling, and thinking; at another moment checking to see to what extent what they were discovering was shared; and all along testing to see whether he was understanding what they were saying. Now the participants themselves took up this task, following their own hunches and opening up their own lines of inquiry. Out of this process came a description of three modes of responding to anger at others' mistakes:

• Blaming, punishing, and coercing others. During this phase as well as earlier, the group discovered that, at the time Paula became angry, she no longer felt herself to be a part of the group, she defined the problem of circularity as the group's problem, and she could not isolate what led to the circularity and did not know how to stop it. Moreover, when she intervened, she was not aware of trying to help the group and so she set out to solve the problems of dealing with her reactions and with those persons whom she held responsible for triggering them. She thus blamed the group for the circularity and its emotional impact on her ("I'm having a nervous breakdown because everybody's saying the same thing"), and she came up with a solution that combined punitive and coercive features ("I would rather just leave if it's going to continue").

• Suppressing one's anger. In probing Ken's account, the group came up with a variation on the same theme. When Paula intervened, Ken saw what she did as a threat that was unhelpful and that left the group stranded. He described himself as having a "very strong reaction" to what Paula did, but at the same time he said he didn't know how to express these reactions without provoking defensiveness in Paula. And so when he did intervene, he solved the twofold problem of dealing with Paula and his own reactions by devising a compromise: He suppressed his anger, mitigating his reactions and acting as if he were calm. Similarly, Mary admitted that she had seen Ken as insincere. She was unaware of his dilemma about how to express his reactions, and she grew angry at his insincerity, replicating what Ken did by suppressing what was going on inside her.

• Detaching oneself from the situation. A third response is like Paula's, yet it involves such a great degree of psychological withdrawal that it is itself sufficient for solving the problem, as they define it. This response was described by Karen, who said that she thought that her peers were behaving incompetently but that she had no alternative to suggest. As she described it, she was not angry, she "just tuned out." Yet as she did so, she whispered back and forth with Paula, saying "grhh," "this is so boring," and so on, while saying nothing to the group. Thus, like Paula, she no longer felt herself part of the group, she defined the problem as the group's problem as if she were not a member of it, and she felt unable to alter what she saw.

Phase Four: Mapping the Territory. Once developed, these descriptions suggest some common themes. First, everyone focused on others' mistakes but acted as if they were unaware of the others' binds or limitations. Second, everyone described himself or herself as stuck in binds or at the limits of his or her own abilities. Third, although their particular strategies varied, everyone felt intensely angry and consequently tried to distance themselves from the experience: Paula no longer felt any responsibility for what was happening, Karen and others psychologically removed themselves from the group, and still others distanced themselves from their anger by suppressing it.

At this point the interventionist himself was stumped, unable to understand what led to these reactions. He thus came in to describe the dilemma in which he found himself:

Interventionist: There's a curious thing. First of all, everything going on is so real and happens so often, but I

The interventionist frames the situation before him as one that is at once genuine and curious.

feel so helpless about understanding it in the way I want
to.

Let me tell you what I see:
Both of you felt strongly,
and yet you were feeling
strongly about somebody
else's incompetence.

He expresses that he feels
helpless to understand the
situation as well as he would
like to.

That's my dilemma. If
some other human being is
acting incompetently, what's
the connection to your getting upset?

He goes on to help the group
to help him by first describing what he has seen so far
and then describing what he
does not yet understand.

As this suggests, the interventionist is at the limits of his
own ability to understand the situation before him. While he
can recognize the validity of the group's descriptions, recount
what it is he sees, and describe where it is that he is stuck, he
cannot go from describing what he sees to explaining it. Or put
differently, he does not yet know how to take the step from
the fragments of descriptions generated so far to explanations
that can connect these fragments and account for them in a
way that can be used to move beyond them. So the interventionist faces a situation similar to that faced by the participants
earlier, one that puts him in a dilemma and at the limits of his
own competence. Yet the interventionist acts as if such a situation poses neither threat nor frustration. He is puzzled and says
so; he feels helpless and says so; he needs help and so he helps
the group to provide the help he needs.

Once he had done this, the participants took up the
task of helping to map the problem by generating a series of
hypotheses, each one stemming from their own reactions and
connectable to the descriptions already developed:

Vince: I know I felt threatened, and I felt angry. When
Paula said what she said, the
message to me was, "You're
incompetent." And when

Vince begins by describing
his anger; he then begins to
retrace what he believes triggered it or might account for
it: He heard her calling him

somebody tells me I'm incompetent, my first reaction is to get very defensive and upset. Therefore, I was not getting angry at Paula because of her incompetence; I was angry because of my incompetence.

George: I have one idea which is that the anger has two parts. One is that Ken, or in this case, me because I would've had the same reaction; I would have gotten angry, because I was feeling coerced. But I would've been angry, as opposed to just seeing it as somebody's attempt to coerce me, because in fact I fear I am coercible.

Nancy: I felt a little angry, because if somebody just leaves, I cannot confront them. I did not feel angry about the [group's errors], because I was responsible to stop [them]. But Paula, if she leaves, I have no way to catch her.

incompetent, and he must have implicitly agreed with her, thus becoming upset and defensive. Hence, he was angry not at her, but at his own incompetence.

George traces the anger to a dual source: First, he would have felt coerced. Second, he feared he was coercible. Hence, he was angry not at her but at his own ability to be coerced.

Nancy retraces her reaction. First, if somebody leaves, I can no longer deal with them. Second, this puts me in a helpless position. Hence, I get angry.

Earlier, participants had held others primarily responsible for their own reactions. They each attributed the cause of their anger to somebody else's mistakes, and they thought that such causality made good sense. But then what was once obvious began to look strange as the interventionist pointed out some gaps in their reactions; and the more they tried to make their reactions acceptable, the more they found themselves in a box of their own design that they could not accept. Under the impact of these results, participants discarded their original hypotheses and began to construct the hypotheses that emphasized their own responsibility. Although not yet tested, these new hypotheses were connectable to their previous descriptions and useful as a basis for designing ways to move forward. For instance, the next time they find themselves getting angry at others' mistakes, they might do what the interventionist did. Rather than hold others responsible for their reactions, they might describe what it is they are experiencing and the help they need to work through it.

This shift in responsibility was evident in their actions as well. In contrast to their behavior in the first two experiments, the participants here took most of the responsibility for developing a description and then generating a series of hypotheses that might be mapped diagrammatically as shown in Figure 10.

Although the group did not take the step of actually diagramming these results, the necessary components were available to do so. In the process of reflecting on their actions, the participants had developed a rich description of the constellation of inference making, intention, affect, and action that makes up any mapping of action. They thereby brought to the surface the design that underlay their actions, so that they could gain greater awareness of and control over those actions.

Phase Five: Working Through Automatic Reactions. The more clearly that participants saw their own responsibility for these reactions, the more they wished to change them. But how to do so was a difficult problem. As a client once asked with indignation: "How do you control an automatic reaction?" One participant came at the problem this way: "I think it's a constructive use of anger if you acknowledge the anger as an indicator of something that [should] lead you to be curious rather than leveling it as charge or laying it on the group."

To be enacted, however, advice like this may require the very thing that it is trying to produce: optimal distance from one's reactions. Or in other words, if a participant had the distance necessary to follow this advice, he probably would not need the advice in the first place. As Mary put it: "I don't know

Figure 10. Reacting to Others' Mistakes.

Intention	Defensive Framing	Defensive Affective Reaction	Distancing Strategies	Consequences
To be in control (to not be helpless or coercible)	See other in error	Anger	Blame others	Little impetus to help those making mistakes
To be competent (to not make errors)	See self in a bind	Frustration	Psychologically detach self from the situation	Impedes ability to help: seen as insincere or too distanced from reactions
	Aware of others' responsibility but not one's own for the situation (creating it or altering it)	A sense of helplessness	Suppress one's own anger	Little empathy for other
	Unaware of others' binds, dilemmas, or limitations			

how to distance myself. I mean, once I feel anger, it's very hard for me to distance myself to the point where it's almost hard to remember what people are saying." Yet the advice is valid. Individuals are apt to learn more if they regard their reactions as curious and worthy of inquiry rather than as evidence of someone else's transgressions. But the question left unanswered is how to achieve the necessary distance from one's automatic reactions.

One possibility was described by the interventionist: "Here we may do best to express [our angry reactions] and to look at them. But the question is, Why do you feel hostile in the first place? Let's express negative feelings and find out why we have them; and number two: What kind of stance can we take toward life that will reduce the probability that we will even have those feelings?" The advice is thus twofold: Express one's reactions as they occur and inquire into what leads to them. Whereas the former requires only the willingness to make one's reactions public, the latter asks that, once public, these reactions be probed. As such, the advice is designed to begin where participants begin, with an eye on eventually developing "a stance . . . toward life that will reduce the probability that we will even have those feelings." With this alternative in mind, participants could now design their own experiments, ones aimed at producing the advice and seeing what it yielded. As they did so, they developed expertise in dealing with difficult emotional reactions, while at the same time opening these reactions up to inquiry and thus increasing the possibility of learning. In so doing they moved up the continuum described in the map (Figure 8 in Chapter Nine) from a more protective to a more reflective orientation.

Conclusion

Right from the start, the interventionist creates a context that will allow participants to discover the outcomes that their actions yield. Experiment after experiment brings them face-to-face with surprises, as they discover puzzles where a sense of obviousness had prevailed, a sense of stuckness where they had thought themselves skillful, and a sense of failure where they had experienced success. Participants and interventionist take a different stance toward these experiences. The interventionist strives to keep puzzles alive, to help participants to hurry up and get stuck, and to create ongoing opportunities for failure, all the while encouraging and aiding them to reflect on their experience. From the interventionist's vantage point, creating and reflecting on these experiences are the essence of what it means and takes to negotiate the learning process. Participants take a different view. They strive to settle puzzles quickly, to get their spinning wheels on dry ground as fast as they can, and to avoid failure, shrinking back from looking at and reflecting on these experiences. From their vantage point, minimizing or avoiding these experiences is the essence of what it means and takes to negotiate the learning process. In actuality, the distinctions between interventionist and participants are less stark than we have just drawn them, but they should make salient an essential feature of the learning process: The interventionist and the participant frame this process in qualitatively different ways.

The frame experiments in this chapter display an iterative, cyclical effort at stimulating a process of frame breaking and reframing, so that participants might come to regard their roles and the situations before them in new ways. While there are differences among these experiments, they also have features in common that provide insight into how individuals can be helped to reframe experiences central to their sense of self. What follows is an abstracted sequence of steps that constitutes the structure embedded in the experimental process.

In early phases the process is initiated by the interventionist, who discerns recurrent patterns that yield predicaments that participants seem to be unaware of. By withdrawing, they end up designing their own injustice. By supporting their peers, as they define support, they end up undercutting their peers. And by getting angry at mistakes, they suggest a blindness to their own limitations and that of others. Such patterns attract and engage the interventionist's attention. They puzzle him. But the participants whose interactions generate these patterns take them for granted and fail to notice them. What is puzzling to the interventionist is thus obvious to the participant.

The interventionist strives to make compelling as a puzzle what is taken for granted. Data that participants ignore are brought to light: Carol did make an error so David's rule does not hold, the group did not knowingly or intentionally go in circles, so Paul's anger becomes curious, and so forth. These data reveal the inconsistencies that make the interactions puzzling.

The interventionist reveals these inconsistencies in a way that does not make him responsible for generating them: The data are the participants' data, and the inferences he draws from them are consensually agreed upon. Aware of and responsible for the paradox, participants thus experience an optimal sense of dissonance; this motivates them to inquire into their own actions in order to account for them and to reduce their sense of dissonance.

As they do so, participants offer explanations of their actions that attempt to reconcile what was inconsistent in them. They cite fears of appearing stupid or being attacked; they put forth theories of support; or they offer explanations in an attempt to justify their anger toward their peers.

The interventionist then mines these explanations for new data, trying to surface the logic embedded in the actions of participants. In so doing he takes a two-pronged approach. On the one hand, he helps to generate a rich description and group collage of how participants understood, felt, and acted or did not act. On the other hand, he organizes, reflects on, and inquires into these new data, constructing moves that reveal new gaps and new inconsistencies in the reasoning of participants. As a consequence, he keeps the inquiry into the puzzle alive and heightens the sense of dissonance still further.

The participants' efforts to make acceptable the unacceptable thus fall short. Slowly they begin to question the way in which they construct their social world, in terms of both how they see it and how they interact in it. Paula finds herself in a box of her own design; David discovers that his theory for creating competence would simultaneously create conditions of incompetence; and Lee sees that her theory of humiliation generates conditions for more failure and humiliation.

At this point participants recognize that their way of understanding and acting in the world requires reexamination and change. But they are stymied, unaware of an alternative or of how to enact it. Carol asks how she can learn to take a more courageous stance, David asks how one can examine errors without disrupting the other's confidence to the point of creating incompetence, and Mary asks how she can come to distance herself from her feelings when she can no longer even retrieve what is being said. As the client asked, "How do you control automatic reactions?" This is experienced as a contradiction and participants feel stuck. Their frames are inadequate but how are they to move beyond them?

As this stuckness reveals itself, the interventionist takes a stance toward the participants' experience that can keep the process of inquiry moving despite their being stuck. He encourages them to express what is difficult to express, and he empathizes with their experience while continuing to call into question how they are framing it.

At the same time, he poses alternatives and does so at three different levels. The first is at the level of strategy, and here he suggests interim moves that, if tried, might free the participants from the particular dilemma at hand and help them to break out of their frames: Jump in and talk, express your negative feelings, reflect publicly on your reactions. The second is at the level of frames, where he offers new ways of seeing a problem and suggests new questions to ask of it. For example, he reframes Vince's solution, saying the important thing is not to be right but to be willing to learn; he reframes the underlying metaphor used for thinking about errors; and so on. The third level is that of action; here, the interventionist enacts these understandings himself. His supportive moves toward Carol and the group display a different construction of the situation from the one they held. Thus, as he acts and reflects publicly on his actions, participants become more familiar with an unfamiliar way of framing the process.

But at some point participants must design their own frame experiments. They must test out the alternatives that are posed. Yet they feel caught between two frames, neither one of which they fully trust. To design such experiments thus requires acting in the face of doubt and taking risks.

To reduce these risks, participants scan for data that might help them to anticipate the results of fundamentally new moves. But this scanning process is conducted from the vantage point of existing frames, and the results they anticipate are therefore problematic: "He tells me to confront him; but when I do, I am told I am wrong." Apparent inconsistencies are discovered and brought to the surface, and opportunities arise for the interventionist to elaborate on the meanings he brings to these moves. The gaps that result from their conflicting frames thus begin to be filled in, and participants start to design tests of these alternatives.

At this point new actions emerge and new puzzles are revealed. Once again, the interventionist and, increasingly, the participants are drawn to them, and the cycle repeats itself, iteratively moving forward from a more protective orientation toward a more reflective one.

References

Anscombe, G. E. M. *Intention.* Oxford, England: Basil Black-well, 1957.

Apel, K.-O. "The a Priori of Communication and the Foundation of the Humanities." In F. Dallmayr and T. McCarthy (eds.), *Understanding and Social Inquiry.* Notre Dame, Ind.: University of Notre Dame Press, 1977.

Argyris, C. *Personality and Organization.* New York: Harper & Row, 1957.

Argyris, C. *Interpersonal Competence and Organizational Effectiveness.* Homewood, Ill.: Dorsey Press, 1962.

Argyris, C. *Integrating the Individual and the Organization.* New York: Wiley, 1964.

Argyris, C. *Intervention Theory and Method.* Reading, Mass.: Addison-Wesley, 1970.

Argyris, C. *Increasing Leadership Effectiveness.* New York: Wiley, 1976.

Argyris, C. "Reflecting on Laboratory Education from a Theory of Action Perspective." *Journal of Applied Behavioral Science,* 1979, *15* (3), 296–310.

Argyris, C. *Inner Contradictions of Rigorous Research.* New York: Academic Press, 1980.

Argyris, C. *Reasoning, Learning and Action: Individual and Organizational.* San Francisco: Jossey-Bass, 1982.

Argyris, C. *Strategy, Change, and Defensive Routines.* Boston: Pitman, 1985.

Argyris, C., and Schön, D. A. *Theory in Practice: Increasing Professional Effectiveness.* San Francisco: Jossey-Bass, 1974.

Argyris, C., and Schön, D. A. *Organizational Learning.* Reading, Mass.: Addison-Wesley, 1978.

Asch, S. E. *Social Psychology.* Englewood Cliffs, N.J.: Prentice-Hall, 1952.

Asplund, J. "On the Concept of Value Relevance." In J. Israel and H. Tajfel (eds.), *The Context of Social Psychology.* New York: Academic Press, 1972.

Au, H.-P., and Jordan, C. "Teaching Reading to Hawaiian Children: Finding a Culturally Appropriate Solution." In H. Trueba, G. Guthrie, and K. H. Au (eds.), *Culture and the Bilingual Classroom.* Rowley, Mass.: Newbury House, 1981.

Austin, J. L. *How To Do Things with Words.* Oxford, England: Oxford University Press, 1962.

Barker, R., Dembo, T., and Lewin, K. "Frustration and Regression." University of Iowa, *Studies in Child Welfare,* 1941, *1,* 1–43.

Barnard, C. *The Functions of the Executive.* 30th ed. Cambridge, Mass.: Harvard University Press, 1968.

Benne, K. D. "The Processes of Reeducation: An Assessment of Kurt Lewin's Views." In W. Bennis and others (eds.), *The Planning of Change.* (3rd ed.) New York: Holt, Rinehart and Winston, 1976.

Bennis, W., and others. *Interpersonal Dynamics.* (3rd ed.) Homewood, Ill.: Dorsey Press, 1973.

Bennis, W., and others (eds.). *The Planning of Change.* (3rd ed.) New York: Holt, Rinehart and Winston, 1976.

Berger, P. L., and Luckmann, T. *The Social Construction of Reality.* New York: Doubleday, Anchor Books, 1966.

Bernstein, R. J. *Praxis and Action.* Philadelphia: University of Pennsylvania Press, 1971.

Bernstein, R. J. *The Restructuring of Social and Political Theory.* Philadelphia: University of Pennsylvania Press, 1976.

Bernstein, R. J. *Beyond Objectivism and Relativism.* Philadelphia: University of Pennsylvania Press, 1983.

Bickman, L. "Some Distinctions Between Basic and Applied Approaches." In L. Bickman (ed.), *Applied Social Psychology Annual.* Beverly Hills: Sage, 1981.

Birdwhistell, R. *Kinesics and Context.* Philadelphia: Urban Press, 1970.

Blake, R., and Mouton, J. *The Managerial Grid.* Houston: Gulf, 1964.

Bowditch, J. L., and Buono, A. *Quality of Work Life Assessment.* Boston: Auburn House, 1982.

Bradford, L., Gibb, J., and Benne, K. (eds.). *T-Group Theory and Laboratory Method.* New York: Wiley, 1964.

Brown, P., and Levinson, S. "Universals in Language Usage." In E. N. Goody (ed.), *Questions and Politeness.* Cambridge, England: Cambridge University Press, 1978.

Burrell, G., and Morgan, G. *Sociological Paradigms and Organizational Analysis.* London: Heinemann Educational Books, 1979.

Campbell, D. T., and Stanley, J. C. *Experimental and Quasi-Experimental Design for Research.* Chicago: Rand McNally, 1963.

Caplan, N., and Nelson, S. D. "On Being Useful." *American Psychologist,* 1973, *28,* 199–211.

Carlston, D. "The Recall and Use of Traits and Events in Social Inference Process." *Journal of Experimental Psychology,* 1980, *16,* 303–328.

Cassell, J. "Does Risk-Benefit Analysis Apply to Moral Evaluation of Social Research?" In T. L. Beauchamp and others (eds.), *Ethical Issues in Social Science Research.* Baltimore, Md.: Johns Hopkins University Press, 1982.

Cazden, C. B. "Can Ethnographic Research Go Beyond the Status Quo?" *Anthropology and Education Quarterly,* 1983, *14,* 33–41.

Cicourel, A. *Cognitive Sociology.* New York: Free Press, 1974.

Coleman, J. S. *Policy Research in the Social Sciences.* Morristown, N.J.: General Learning Press, 1972.

Cook, T. D., and Campbell, D. T. *Quasi-Experimentation.* Boston: Houghton Mifflin, 1979.

Cyert, R., and March, J. *A Behavioral Theory of the Firm.* Englewood Cliffs, N.J.: Prentice-Hall, 1963.

Dallmayr, F., and McCarthy, T. (eds.). *Understanding and Social Inquiry.* Notre Dame, Ind.: University of Notre Dame Press, 1977.

Davidson, D. *Essays on Actions and Events.* Oxford, England: Oxford University Press, Clarendon Press, 1980.

Davis, R., Buchanan, B., and Shortliffe, E. "Production Rules as a Representation for a Knowledge-Based Consultation Program." *Artificial Intelligence,* 1977, *8,* 15–45.

Dewey, J. *The Quest for Certainty.* New York: Minton, Balch, 1929.

Dewey, J. *How We Think.* (Rev. ed.) Lexington, Mass.: Heath, 1933.

Diamond, M. "Limits to Growth: A Psychodynamic View of Argyris' Contribution to Organization Theory." Unpublished paper, University of Missouri, Columbia, 1983.

Douglas, J. *The Social Meanings of Suicide.* Princeton, N.J.: Princeton University Press, 1967.

Durkheim, E. "The Internalization of Social Control I." In L. A. Coser and B. Rosenberg (eds.), *Sociological Theory.* (5th ed.) New York: Macmillan, 1982. (Originally published 1953 in *Sociology and Philosophy.*)

Edgley, R. "Practical Reason." In J. Raz (ed.), *Practical Reasoning.* Oxford, England: Oxford University Press, 1978.

Efron, D. *Gesture and Environment.* New York: Teachers College Press, 1941.

Einhorn, H. J., and Hogarth, R. M. "Behavioral Decision Theory: Processes of Judgment and Choice." *Annual Review of Psychology,* 1981, *31,* 53–88.

Ericcson, K. A., and Simon, H. A. "Verbal Reports as Data." *Psychological Review,* 1980, *87,* 215–251.

Erickson, F. "Gatekeeping and the Melting Pot." *Harvard Educational Review,* 1975, *45* (1), 44–70.

Evan, W. M. *Organization Theory: Structures, Systems, and Environments.* New York: Wiley-Interscience, 1976.

Festinger, L. (ed.). *Retrospections on Social Psychology.* New York: Oxford University Press, 1980.

Festinger, L., and Carlsmith, J. M. "Cognitive Consequences of Forced Compliance." *Journal of Abnormal and Social Psychology,* 1959, *58,* 203–210.

Florio, S., and Walsh, M. "The Teacher as Colleague in Classroom Research." In H. Trueba, G. Guthrie, and K. H. Au (eds.), *Culture and the Bilingual Classroom.* Rowley, Mass.: Newbury House, 1981.

Forgas, J. P. "Episode Cognition: Internal Representations of Interaction Routines." In *Advances in Experimental Social Psychology.* Vol. 15. New York: Academic Press, 1982.

French, W. L., and Bell, C. H. *Organization Development.* Englewood Cliffs, N.J.: Prentice-Hall, 1973.

Friedrichs, R. W. *A Sociology of Sociology.* New York: Free Press, 1970.

Garfinkel, A. *Studies in Ethnomethodology.* Englewood Cliffs, N.J.: Prentice-Hall, 1967.

Geertz, C. *The Interpretation of Cultures.* New York: Basic Books, 1973.

Geertz, C. *Local Knowledge.* New York: Basic Books, 1983.

Gergen, K. *Toward Transformation in Social Knowledge.* New York: Springer-Verlag, 1982.

Geuss, R. *The Idea of a Critical Theory.* Cambridge, England: Cambridge University Press, 1981.

Glass, A. L., Holyoak, K. J., and Santa, J. L. *Cognition.* Reading, Mass.: Addison-Wesley, 1979.

Goffman, E. *The Presentation of Self in Everyday Life.* New York: Doubleday, Anchor Books, 1959.

Goffman, E. *Interaction Ritual.* Hawthorne, N.Y.: Aldine, 1967.

Goleman, D. "A Conversation with Ulric Neisser." *Psychology Today,* 1983, *17* (5), 54–62.

Gouldner, A. "Theoretical Requirements of the Applied Social Sciences." In W. Bennis, K. Benne, and R. Chin (eds.), *The Planning of Change.* New York: Holt, Rinehart and Winston, 1961.

Gronn, P. C. "Accomplishing the Doing of School Administration: Talk as the Work." Paper presented at the annual conference of the Australian Communication Association, Sydney, 1981.

Gronn, P. C. "Talk as the Work: The Accomplishment of School Administration." *Administrative Science Quarterly,* 1983, *23,* 1-21.

Habermas, J. *Knowledge and Human Interests.* Boston: Beacon Press, 1971.

Habermas, J. *Communication and the Evolution of Society.* Boston: Beacon Press, 1979.

Hackman, J. R. "Designing Work for Individuals and Group." In J. R. Hackman, E. E. Lawler, and L. W. Porter (eds.), *Perspectives on Behavior in Organizations.* New York: McGraw-Hill, 1983.

Hackman, J. R., and Lawler, E. E. "Employee Reactions to Job Characteristics." *Journal of Applied Psychology Monograph,* 1971, *55,* 259-286.

Hackman, J. R., and Oldham, G. R. "Development of the Job Diagnostic Survey." *Journal of Applied Psychology,* 1975, *60,* 159-170.

Hackman, J. R., and Oldham, G. R. "Motivation Through the Design of Work: Test of a Theory." *Organizational Behavior and Human Performance,* 1976, *16,* 250-279.

Hackman, J. R., and Oldham, G. R. *Work Redesign.* Reading, Mass.: Addison-Wesley, 1980.

Hackman, J. R., and Suttle, J. L. (eds.). *Improving Life at Work.* Santa Monica, Calif.: Goodyear, 1977.

Harmon, M. *Action Theory for Public Administration.* New York: Longman, 1981.

Harré, R., and Secord, P. F. *The Explanation of Social Behavior.* Oxford, England: Basil Blackwell, 1972.

Harvey, J. H., Harris, B., and Barnes, R. D. "Actor-Observer Differences in the Perception of Responsibility and Freedom." *Journal of Personality and Social Psychology,* 1975, *32,* 22-28.

Hayek, F. A. *Studies in Philosophy, Politics, and Economics.* New York: Simon & Schuster, 1967.

Heath, S. B. "Questioning at Home and at School: A Comparative Study." In G. Spindler (ed.), *Doing the Ethnography of Schooling.* New York: Holt, Rinehart and Winston, 1982.

Heath, S. B. *Ways with Words.* Cambridge, England: Cambridge University Press, 1983.

Heider, F. *The Psychology of Interpersonal Relations.* New York: Wiley, 1958.

Hempel, C. *Aspects of Scientific Explanation.* New York: Free Press, 1965a.

Hempel, C. "The Function of General Laws in History." In C. Hempel (ed.), *Aspects of Scientific Explanation.* New York: Free Press, 1965b.

Hempel, C. *Philosophy of Natural Science.* Englewood Cliffs, N.J.: Prentice-Hall, 1966.

Higgins, J. "A Self-Reflection." Unpublished manuscript, Harvard University, 1985.

Hirschhorn, L. "The Organization's Climate and Its Primary Task." Working paper, Wharton School, University of Pennsylvania, 1982.

Hollingworth, H. L., and Poffenberger, A. T. *Applied Psychology.* New York: Appleton-Century-Crofts, 1917.

Homans, G. C. *The Human Group.* New York: Harcourt Brace Jovanovich, 1950.

Hopkins, J. "Introduction: Philosophy and Psychoanalysis." In R. Wollheim and J. Hopkins (eds.), *Philosophical Essays on Freud.* Cambridge, England: Cambridge University Press, 1982.

Hoppe, F. "Success and Failure." In J. de Rivera (ed.), *Field Theory as Human Science.* New York: Gardner Press, 1976. (Originally published 1930).

Howard, R. J. *Three Faces of Hermeneutics.* Berkeley: University of California Press, 1982.

James, W. *The Principles of Psychology.* Vol. 2. New York: Dover, 1890.

Janis, I. L. *Victims of Groupthink.* Boston: Houghton Mifflin, 1972.

Jaques, E. *The Changing Culture of a Factory.* London: Tavistock, 1951.

Joiner, B. B. "Searching for Collaborative Inquiry: The Evolution of Action Research." Unpublished doctoral dissertation, Graduate School of Education, Harvard University, 1983.

Jones, E., and Nisbett, R. "The Actor and the Observer: Divergent Perceptions of the Causes of Behavior." In E. Jones and others (eds.), *Attribution: Perceiving the Causes of Behavior.* Morristown, N.J.: General Learning Press, 1972.

Jordan, C. "The Selection of Culturally Compatible Classroom Practice: Educational Perspectives." *Journal of Education,* 1981, *20* (1), 16–19.

Kahnemann, D., and Tversky, A. "Choices, Values, and Frames." *American Psychologist,* 1984, *39,* 341–350.

Keeley, M. "The Impartiality and Participant Interest Theories of Organizational Effectiveness." *Administrative Science Quarterly,* 1984, *29,* 1–25.

Kelley, H. *Attribution in Social Interaction.* Morristown, N.J.: General Learning Press, 1971.

Kelly, G. A. *A Theory of Personality.* New York: Norton, 1955.

Kleinfeld, J. "First Do No Harm: A Reply to Courtney Cazden." *Anthropological and Education Quarterly,* 1983, *14* (4), 282–287.

Kuhn, T. *The Structure of Scientific Revolutions.* Chicago: University of Chicago Press, 1962.

Kuhn, T. "Reflections on my Critics." In I. Lakatos and A. Musgrave (eds.), *Criticism and the Growth of Knowledge.* Cambridge, England: Cambridge University Press, 1970a.

Kuhn, T. *The Structure of Scientific Revolutions.* (2nd ed.) Chicago: University of Chicago Press, 1970b.

Labov, W., and Fanshel, D. *Therapeutic Discourse.* New York: Academic Press, 1977.

Lakatos, I. "Falsification and the Methodology of Scientific Research Programmes." In I. Lakatos and A. Musgrave (eds.), *Criticism and the Growth of Knowledge.* Cambridge, England: Cambridge University Press, 1970.

Lakatos, I., and Musgrave, A. (eds.). *Criticism and the Growth of Knowledge.* Cambridge, England: Cambridge University Press, 1970.

Landy, F. J. "An Opponent Process Theory of Job Satisfaction." *Journal of Applied Psychology,* 1978, *63* (5), 533–547.

Langer, E. "Rethinking the Role of Thought in Social Interaction." In J. H. Harvey and W. J. Ickes (eds.), *New Directions in Attribution Research.* Vol. 2. Hillsdale, N.J.: Erlbaum, 1976.

Latané, B., and Darley, J. *The Unresponsive Bystander: Why Doesn't He Help.* Englewood Cliffs, N.J.: Prentice-Hall, 1970.

Lawler, E. E., III, and others. *Doing Research That Is Useful for Theory and Practice.* San Francisco: Jossey-Bass, 1985.

Lewin, K. *The Conceptual Representation of the Measurement of Psychological Forces.* Durham, N.C.: Duke University Press, 1938.

Lewin, K. "Action Research and Minority Problems." In K. Lewin, *Resolving Social Conflicts.* (G. Lewin, ed.) New York: Harper & Row, 1948a.

Lewin, K. *Resolving Social Conflicts.* (G. Lewin, ed.) New York: Harper & Row, 1948b.

Lewin, K. "Cassirer's Philosophy of Science and Social Science." In P. A. Schlipp (ed.), *The Philosophy of Ernst Cassirer.* New York: Tudor, 1949.

Lewin, K. "Frontiers in Group Dynamics." In K. Lewin, *Field Theory in Social Science.* New York: Harper & Row, 1951.

Lewin, K. "Group Dynamics and Social Change." In A. Etzioni and E. Etzioni (eds.), *Social Change.* New York: Basic Books, 1964.

Lewin, K., and Grabbe, P. "Conduct, Knowledge, and Acceptance of New Values." In K. Lewin, *Resolving Social Conflicts.* (G. Lewin, ed.) New York: Harper & Row, 1948.

Lewin, K., Lippett, R., and White, R. K. "Patterns of Aggressive Behavior in Experimentally Created Social Climates." *Journal of Social Psychology,* 1939, *10,* 271–301.

Lewin, K., and others. "Levels of Aspiration." In J. M. V. Hunt (ed.), *Personality and the Behavior Disorders.* New York: Ronald Press, 1944.

Likert, R. *New Patterns of Management.* New York: McGraw-Hill, 1961.

Lindblom, C. E., and Cohen, D. K. *Usable Knowledge: Social Science and Social Problem Solving.* New Haven, Conn.: Yale University Press, 1979.

Lord, C. G., Ross, L., and Lepper, M. R. "Biased Assimilation and Attitude Polarization." *Journal of Personality and Social Psychology,* 1979, *37* (11), 2098-2109.

McDermott, R., Goldman, S., and Varenne, H. "When School Goes Home." *Teachers College Record,* in press.

McDermott, R., and Gospodinoff, H. "Social Contexts for Ethnic Borders and School Failure." In H. Trueba, G. Guthrie, and K. H. Au (eds.), *Culture and the Bilingual Classroom: Studies in Classroom Ethnography.* Rowley, Mass.: Newbury House, 1981.

McGregor, D. *The Human Side of Enterprise.* New York: McGraw-Hill, 1960.

Manicas, P., and Secord, P. "Implications for Psychology of the New Philosophy of Science." *American Psychologist,* April 1983, *38,* 399-413.

March, J., and Simon, H. *Organizations.* New York: Wiley, 1958.

Marrow, A. *The Practical Theorist.* New York: Basic Books, 1969.

Masterman, M. "The Nature of a Paradigm." In I. Lakatos and A. Musgrave (eds.), *Criticism and the Growth of Knowledge.* Cambridge, England: Cambridge University Press, 1970.

Mead, G. H. "The Internalization of Social Control II." In L. A. Coser and B. Rosenberg (eds.), *Sociological Theory.* (5th ed.) New York: Macmillan, 1982. (Originally published 1934.)

Merton, R. *On Theoretical Sociology.* New York: Free Press, 1967.

Michaels, S. "Sharing Time, Children's Narrative Styles, and Differential Access to Literacy." *Language in Society,* 1981, *10* (3), 423-442.

Milgram, S. *Obedience to Authority.* New York: Harper & Row, 1974.

Mills, C. W. *The Sociological Imagination.* Oxford, England: Oxford University Press, 1959.

Minuchin, S. *Families and Family Therapy.* Cambridge, Mass.: Harvard University Press, 1974.

Mohr, L. B. *Explaining Organizational Behavior: The Limits and Possibilities of Theory and Research.* San Francisco: Jossey-Bass, 1982.

Morgan, G. (ed.). *Beyond Method.* Beverly Hills, Calif.: Sage, 1983.

Mynatt, C., Doherty, M., and Tweney, R. "Consequences of Confirmation and Disconfirmation in a Simulated Research Environment." *Quarterly Journal of Experimental Psychology,* 1978, *30,* 395–406.

Nagel, E. *The Structure of Science.* Indianapolis: Hackett, 1979.

Nisbett, R., and Ross, L. *Human Inference: Strategies and Shortcomings of Social Judgment.* Englewood Cliffs, N.J.: Prentice-Hall, 1980.

Nisbett, R., and Wilson, T. "Telling More than We Can Know: Verbal Reports on Mental Processes." *Psychological Review,* 1977, *84,* 231–259.

Ogbu, J. "Cultural Discontinuities and Schooling." *Anthropology and Education Quarterly,* 1982, *13,* 269–274.

O'Keefe, D. "Ethnomethodology." *Journal for the Theory of Social Behavior,* 1979, *9* (2), 187–219.

Outhwaite, W. "Toward a Realist Perspective." In G. Morgan (ed.), *Beyond Method.* Beverly Hills, Calif.: Sage, 1983.

Pearce, W. B., and Cronen, V. E. *Communication, Action, and Meaning: The Creation of Social Realities.* New York: Praeger, 1980.

Peirce, C. S. "The Rules of Philosophy." In M. Konvitz and G. Kennedy (eds.), *The American Pragmatists.* New York: New American Library, 1960. (Originally published 1868.)

Peters, M., and Robinson, V. "The Origins and Status of Action Research." *Journal of Applied Behavioral Science,* 1984, *20* (2), 113–124.

Pfeffer, J. *Power in Organizations.* Marshfield, Mass.: Pitman, 1981.

Pfeffer, J. *Organizations and Organization Theory.* Marshfield, Mass.: Pitman, 1982.

Philips, S. *The Invisible Culture.* New York: Longman, 1983.

Piaget, J. "The Internalization of Social Control III." In L. A. Coser and B. Rosenberg (eds.), *Sociological Theory.* (5th ed.) New York: Macmillan, 1982. (Originally published 1951 in *The Moral Judgment of the Child.*)

Polanyi, M. *The Tacit Dimension.* New York: Doubleday, Anchor Books, 1967.

Popper, K. *The Logic of Scientific Discovery.* New York: Harper & Row, 1959.

Popper, K. *Conjectures and Refutations.* New York: Harper & Row, 1963.

Pressman, J., and Wildavsky, A. *Implementation.* Berkeley: University of California Press, 1973.

Putnam, H. *Meaning and the Moral Sciences.* Boston: Routledge & Kegan Paul, 1978.

Raz, J. (ed.). *Practical Reasoning.* Oxford, England: Oxford University Press, 1978.

Reich, J. W. "An Historical Analysis of the Field." In L. Bickman (ed.), *Applied Social Psychology Annual Review.* Beverly Hills, Calif.: Sage, 1981.

Ricoeur, P. "The Model of the Text: Meaningful Action Considered as a Text." In F. Dallmayr and T. McCarthy (eds.), *Understanding and Social Inquiry.* Notre Dame, Ind.: University of Notre Dame Press, 1977.

Rogers, C. R. *Client-Centered Therapy: Its Current Practice, Implications, and Theory.* Boston: Houghton Mifflin, 1951.

Rorty, R. *Philosophy and the Mirror of Nature.* Princeton, N.J.: Princeton University Press, 1979.

Ross, E. A. *Social Control.* New York: Macmillan, 1910.

Ryan, W. *Blaming the Victim.* New York: Random House, Vintage Books, 1976.

Ryle, G. *The Concept of Mind.* New York: Barnes & Noble, 1949.

Schafer, R. "Generative Empathy in the Treatment Situation." *Psychoanalytic Quarterly,* 1959, *28,* 347–373.

Schafer, R. *A New Language for Psychoanalysis.* New Haven, Conn.: Yale University Press, 1976.

Schafer, R. *Psychoanalytic Attitude.* New York: Basic Books, 1983.

Scheffler, I. *The Anatomy of Inquiry.* Indianapolis: Hackett, 1981.

Scheffler, I. *Science and Subjectivity.* (2nd ed.) Indianapolis: Hackett, 1982.

Schein, E. "Personal Change Through Interpersonal Relationships." In W. G. Bennis and others (eds.), *Essays in Interpersonal Dynamics.* Homewood, Ill.: Dorsey Press, 1979.

Scholte, B. "Toward a Reflexive and Critical Anthropology." In D. Hymes (ed.), *Reinventing Anthropology.* New York: Random House, Vintage Books, 1974.

Schön, D. A. "Generative Metaphor." In A. Ortony (ed.), *Metaphor and Thought.* Cambridge, England: Cambridge University Press, 1979.

Schön, D. A. *The Reflective Practitioner.* New York: Basic Books, 1983.

Schön, D. A., Drake, W. D., and Miller, R. I. "Social Experimentation as Reflection in Action: Community-Level Nutrition Intervention Revisited." *Knowledge: Creation, Diffusion, Utilization,* 1984, *6* (1), 5–36.

Schutz, A. *Collected Papers.* (M. Natanson, ed.) Vol. 1. The Hague: Nijhoff, 1962.

Schutz, A. *The Phenomenology of the Social World.* Evanston, Ill.: Northwestern University Press, 1967.

Scollon, R., and Scollon, S. "Narrative, Literacy, and Face in Interethnic Communication." In *Advances in Discourse Processes.* Vol. 7. Norwood, N.J.: Ablex, 1981.

Scott, M. B., and Lyman, S. M. "Accounts." *American Sociological Review,* 1968, *33,* 46–62.

Searle, J. *Speech Acts.* Cambridge, England: Cambridge University Press, 1969.

Simon, H. *The Sciences of the Artificial.* Cambridge, Mass.: MIT Press, 1969.

Sloat, K. "Characteristics of Effective Instruction: Educational Perspectives." *Journal of Education,* 1981a, *20* (1), 10–12.

Sloat, K. "Issues in Teacher Training." *Journal of Education,* 1981b, *20* (1), 38–41.

Smith, D., and Argyris, C. "Transitional Dilemmas: An Organizational Map." 1983.

Spindler, G. (ed.). *Doing the Ethnography of Schooling.* New York: Holt, Rinehart and Winston, 1982.

Spradley, J. *Participant Observation.* New York: Holt, Rinehart and Winston, 1980.

Sullivan, H. S. *The Interpersonal Theory of Psychiatry.* New York: Norton, 1953.

Sumner, W. G. "The Mores." In L. A. Coser and B. Rosenberg (eds.), *Sociological Theory.* (5th ed.) New York: Macmillan, 1982. (Originally published 1904.)

Susman, G. "Action Research: A Sociotechnical Systems Perspective." In G. Morgan (ed.), *Beyond Method.* Beverly Hills, Calif.: Sage, 1983.

Taylor, C. *The Explanation of Behaviour.* London: Routledge & Kegan Paul, 1964.

Taylor, C. "Interpretation and the Sciences of Man." In F. Dallmayr and T. McCarthy (eds.), *Understanding and Social Inquiry.* Notre Dame, Ind.: University of Notre Dame Press, 1977.

Tolman, E. C. "Principles of Purposive Behavior." In S. Koch (ed.), *Psychology: A Study of a Science.* Vol. 2. New York: McGraw-Hill, 1959.

Trist, E. "The Sociotechnical Perspective." In A. Van de Ven and W. F. Joyce (eds.), *Perspectives on Organization Design and Behavior.* New York: Wiley, 1981.

Tversky, A., and Kahnemann, D. "Availability." *Cognitive Psychology,* 1973, *5,* 207–232.

Umbarger, C. C. *Structural Family Therapy.* New York: Grune & Stratton, 1983.

Van de Ven, A., and Ferry, D. L. *Measuring and Assessing Organizations.* New York: Wiley-Interscience, 1980.

Van Maanen, J. "The Self, the Situation, and the Rules of Interpersonal Relations." In W. G. Bennis and others (eds.), *Essays in Interpersonal Dynamics.* Homewood, Ill.: Dorsey Press, 1979.

von Wright, G. H. *Explanation and Understanding.* Ithaca, N.Y.: Cornell University Press, 1971.

Watson-Gegeo, K., and Boggs, S. "From Verbal Play to Talk Story: The Roles of Routines in Speech Events Among Hawaiian Children." In S. Ervin-Tripp and C. Mitchell-Kernan (eds.), *Child Discourse.* New York: Academic Press, 1977.

Watzlawick, P., Beavin, J. H., and Jackson, D. D. *Pragmatics of Human Communication.* New York: Norton, 1967.

Watzlawick, P., Weakland, J., and Fisch, R. *Change*. New York: Norton, 1974.

White, R. W. "Motivation Reconsidered: The Concept of Competence." *Psychological Review*, 1959, *66*, 297-333.

Wiggins, D. "Deliberation and Practical Reason." In J. Raz (ed.), *Practical Reasoning*. Oxford, England: Oxford University Press, 1978.

Zimbardo, P. G. "The Human Choice: Individuation, Reason, and Order Versus Deindividuation, Impulse, and Chaos." In W. J. Arnold and D. Levine (eds.), *Nebraska Symposium on Maturation*. Vol. 17. Lincoln: University of Nebraska, 1969.

Zuniga, R. B. "The Experimenting Society and Social Reform." *American Psychologist*, 1975, *30*, 99-115.

Index

392; critical theory and possibility of, 74; leads to single- or double-loop learning, 86, 87; motivation to correct, 172; motivation to discover, 66; productive confrontation of, 370-371, 383; reasoning that produces, 61-62, 89, 96; and recognition of competent performance, 25, 50; and scientific progress, 13, 16, 32. *See also* Distancing; Emotional reactions; Norms, action science; Protective strategies; Reflective strategies

Espoused theory: definition of, 81-82; as distinguished from theories-in-use, 81-82, 243, 245; inaccuracies in, 68; inconsistencies with theory-in-use, 89-92, 98, 102, 184, 186, 349, 392-393; may reinforce unawareness, 156, 353, 386; policies as, 150; questionnaires focus on, 147; questions that elicit, 243; variance in, 88

Exemplar, 282-283, 341, 345. *See also* Prototype

Experimentation, action science: action as, 6-7, 40, 51, 63-67; action experiments as a form of, 118, 240-241; control in, 239-241, 321-325; criteria for assessing, 133, 135-136, 300; frame experiments as a form of, 396, 445-449; impromptu experiments initiated by participants as a form of, 298-300, 326-329; purposes of, 118, 133-134, 135, 396, 430, 446; reflective, 273, 319, 329-330, 396; roleplaying as, 67-68, 326-329. *See also* Frame experiments; Passivity experiment; Public testing; Rules of action science

Experimentation, normal science: generalizability of laboratory experiments, 111; laboratory rules for, 110-115; limits of, 107, 111-117, 197-198, 206-207; preci-

sion, 42; role of values in, 113-114; simplicity in, 111-112; unilateral control in, 42, 112-113; view of, 16. *See also* Basic researchers

Expertise, 49, 338, 339-340, 369. *See also* Competence; Prototype; Skill

Explanation. *See* Causal explanation; Covering-law model; Pragmatic explanation

F

Face-saving, 61, 89, 97, 294-295

Falsifiability: in action science, 66-67, 225, 232-233; mainstream conception of, 15-16, 32-33; obstacles to in action, 65-66, 96. *See also* Experimentation; Public testing

Family systems theory, 87-88, 419

Fancy footwork, 130, 306-308

Fanshel, D., 26, 50, 57, 458

Ferry, D. L., 139, 464

Festinger, L., 7, 398, 455

Fisch, R., 87-88, 465

Fit, 140-143, 146, 147, 153. *See also* Assessment models; Cultural match

Florio, S., 177, 455

Forgas, J. P., 345, 455

Frame experiments: conflicting frames of interventionist and participant during, 411-413, 414-415, 421-422, 424-426, 446, 449; dilemmas raised by, 409-410, 424-427, 448; emotional impact of, 398-399, 408; evidence of learning in, 413-414, 416, 424, 439-440, 441-442, 443; frame-breaking in, 407-408, 447-448; generating dissonance in, 398-399, 408, 438-439; generating frame-conflict in, 402-409, 422-427; generating a rich description in, 399-402, 406, 439-440, 447; identifying inconsistencies in, 398-399, 402-403,